Selected Speeches

f

Selected Speeches from American History

edited by Robert T. Oliver and Eugene E. White
The Pennsylvania State University

ALLYN AND BACON, INC.
BOSTON, 1966

Library of Congress Catalog Card No. 66-24248

Printed in the United States of America

Contents

Selected Speeches
from American History

Introduction

THIS anthology has been designed to help students achieve the purposes of the beginning course in speech. A study of the speeches and exercises in this volume will help students improve the various insights and skills which will make their own speaking more effective. This study will also enable students to understand better and appreciate more fully how public speaking has shaped and developed the ideas, ideals, and institutions of our nation.

The approach used in this anthology is roughly similar to that of a laboratory manual in the social sciences. Each speech represents a case study in persuasion. Each is distinctive in either the rhetorical problems confronted or the rhetorical procedures applied, or both. Some were influential in the making of crucial national decisions. Some were significant statements of factors that had to be considered before decisions could be formulated. Some presented broadly based attitudes and convictions. Some sought to sustain important human and spiritual values, or to convince hostile auditors, or to energize despondent followers, or to awaken self-seekers to a new consciousness of their community responsibilities. All speeches in this collection were consequential. All helped shape the American mind and spirit. All illuminate the principles of effective speech, and all dramatize the central role that speech has played from the earliest days in the ongoing process of making democracy work.

As a means of orienting the student to the case studies, the text of each speech is preceded by a brief foreword introducing the speaker and focusing the speech against the historical backdrop. In all instances, the full speech is presented, thereby affording students a better opportunity to evaluate the speaker's utilization of the available means of persuasion. Appending each speech is a series of questions which are intended to stimulate thought, provoke class discussion, and suggest avenues for further study.

In presenting the various case studies, our intent has been unobtrusively to direct the student's attention over a wide range of rhetorical processes, stretching from relatively simple matters of organization and development to the most complicated matters of persuasion and style. It is hoped that this inductive process will strikingly reinforce the deductive generalizations advanced in the course textbook and in the classroom lecture-discussions. In this collection, students will learn how outstanding speakers in our history have successfully answered the rhetorical needs of their subject, the needs of the speaking situation, and the needs of their immediate audience—and possibly the needs of a wider secondary reading audience.

Some of the exercises accompanying the individual speeches involve rudimentary rhetorical concerns and can be readily worked out by the typical student after a careful reading of the speech text. Other exercises are somewhat more difficult and may require a searching reexamination of both the editors' introduction to the speech and the speech text itself. Still other exercises are designed primarily to stretch the minds of interested students. For these "mind stretchers," there are no readily secured or absolute answers. Although collateral reading may help provide tentative answers, the student is brought to the realization that despite the marvelous advances in computer science, depth interviewing, and so on, speechmaking still remains an art and not a science. The present state of our knowledge concerning the predictabilities of human nature and the relationships between stimulus and response is woefully inadequate to permit the feeding of a set of rhetorical assessments into a computer and, after a few seconds of electronic legerdemain, the receiving from the machine of a speech text that solves all the perplexing and mysterious equations of a communicative act.

From the study of the speeches in this anthology students will learn much concerning our American civilization. From their study of these speakers in the process of dealing concurrently with the complexity of issues and with the recipient potentialities of their listeners, they will find the encouragement, as well as the ways and means, to improve their own skills in speaking.

As general study guides for students who are concerned with how to improve their own speaking and also with how to understand better the role of public address in a democratic society, the following patterns of inquiry are suggested:

Guide for Study of Individual Speeches

I. What was the nature of the speech?
   A. What was its theme or subject matter?
   B. What were its general and specific purposes?
   C. Was its tone argumentative, conciliatory, sarcastic, hortatory, appealing, or explanatory?
   D. Was its style plain, lively, or elevated?

II. How was it adapted to its audience and to the occasion?
   A. Were there internal evidences of adaptation?
   B. From a review of the historical circumstances, what factors apparently influenced the speaker in his selection of lines of argument and proof?
   C. Did the speech challenge or support views held by the audience?
   D. Did the speech incorporate developmental material especially adapted to the audience?

III. What was the organizational pattern of the speech?
   A. What did the introduction seek to accomplish—and how?
   B. Was the theme developed deductively or inductively?
   C. Did the speaker use internal summaries, restatements of the theme, and transitions?
   D. What did the conclusion seek to accomplish—and how?

IV. What was the intellectual quality of the speech?
   A. Would the speech serve as a valuable reference source for its subject matter? Was it factually sound? How analytically did it examine its subject? Were its proofs dependable?
   B. How objective was the speaker concerning his subject? Was he fair-minded and well balanced in his interpretations? What was his attitude toward opposing views? Did he invite rational consideration of his subject or did he seek an uncritical emotional response?
   C. Judging from this speech, how would you evaluate the quality of the speaker's mind? What did the speech indicate concerning his range of knowledge, his sensitivity to

moral values, his concern for people, his discriminative judgment?

V. What evidence did you find concerning effects of the speech?
  A. Did the speaker himself, in letters or in subsequent public or private comments, indicate satisfaction or disappointment with the results he thought he obtained through his speech?
  B. What did you find concerning reactions of the immediate audience? Of the secondary audience? Of posterity?
  C. Was there objective evidence of specific results directly attributable to the speech? Could the results properly be attributed to other causes?
  D. Did the speech have significant indirect effects—such as favorable or harmful effects upon the speaker's later career?

Guide for Study of Individual Speakers

I. Place the orator intellectually.
  A. What were his principal themes, subjects, philosophy, beliefs?
  B. What were his intellectual sources or antecedents?
  C. How do you evaluate his intellectual contribution?
  D. To what extent was he influential in shaping the beliefs of the general public? Of the American civilization? Of a particular group of followers?

II. Place the orator stylistically.
  A. Considered as a written composition, how good was his speech? Does it deserve to be read as literature? Is it interesting? Would you characterize it as "timely" or as "timeless"?
  B. Was his style plain or elevated? Formal and ornate or conversational and colloquial? Clear, formal, and vivid, or involved, qualified, and complicated? Personal and particular, or generalized? Compressed or amplified?
  C. Was his structure clear and sequential? Logical? Definitive? Indirect?
  D. To what extent and by what means did he adapt his language to his audience?

III. Place the orator historically.
  A. What influence did he seek to exert in the formation of basic policies?
  B. Was he an initiator of policies or a supporter of the policies of others—perhaps as a memorializer of past glories or an apologist for an outworn status quo?

C. Did he deal with issues that were fundamental, national, ephemeral, or local?
D. Did he advocate centralized powers? Diffused governmental powers?
E. Did he support entrenched wealth and power? Was he a spokesman for the disenfranchised, the poor, the underprivileged?

IV. Place the orator in terms of his popular appeal.
A. Did he aim his influence at broad or particularized audiences?
B. Was he listened to appreciatively, enthusiastically, thoughtfully?
C. Was his chief influence immediate and transient, or delayed and lasting, or both immediate and long-term?
D. What were his characteristics of delivery—including voice, posture, diction, gestures, and platform bearing?
E. How would you estimate and evaluate his ethos?

V. Place the orator in relation to others.
A. With what other orators would you associate him in relation to his ideas, style, historic importance, and effectiveness?
B. What contributions did he make to speech theory or practice?
C. Did he speak primarily for himself or as a spokesman for a group?

George Whitefield

"Abraham's Offering Up His Son Isaac,"
preached many times in Colonial America

For thirty-four years, from 1736 to 1770, the English evangelist George Whitefield (1714–1770) followed the Biblical dictum: "Go ye into all the world, and preach the gospel to every creature." Traveling by horseback, by schooner, and even by rowboat, he sought converts in England, Scotland, Wales, Ireland, Bermuda, Gibraltar, and—during seven extended visits—Colonial America. The out-of-doors was often his chapel; and a mound, tree-stump, hogshead, or horse's back served frequently as his pulpit. In his itinerant wanderings, Whitefield sometimes exhorted more than forty hours a week and, according to his own estimate, he eventually delivered eighteen thousand sermons to some ten million auditors. William Warren Sweet has called him "the greatest evangelist of his time and perhaps of all time"; Curtis Nettels has described him as the most powerful revivalist of his age; and Edward Cheyney has characterized him as "the greatest popular preacher England ever had." Along with John and Charles Wesley, Whitefield stimulated the great Methodist revival in England during the early 1740's and thereafter. Of perhaps even greater significance, he was the principal actuator of the tremendously significant religious revival in America, 1739–1745, called the Great Awakening.

Although the causes of the Great Awakening have not yet been adequately explained, this profile is accepted by many specialists. During the last half of the 17th century and the early decades of the

18th century, traditional patterns of thinking and behaving were gradually yielding to the new spirit of a new era. In the Western World, orthodoxy and religious piety were losing much of their control over men's minds. Society was being reshaped into new contours, characterized to some extent by liberalism and skepticism, formalism in worship, and materialism. In parts of Colonial America both the clergy and numbers of the people were keenly disturbed by the declining authority and appeal of the church, and by the increasing democratization in social customs and in church and civil government. To our modern view, such changes in society were the normal side-effects of expanding commerce, increasing population, improving technology, and of the new dimensions of understanding provided by thinkers like Newton, Locke, Boyle, Gassendi, Huygens, Puffendorf, and Descartes. To many colonists, however, the breakdown of old values was disquieting. They recognized that changes were occurring; but they did not understand the causation and they feared the consequences. Somehow, so their thinking ran, they had failed their God: their changes in attitude were a vitiation of the faith of their fathers. Partly as a result of the public sense of need for a reawakening, a series of small revivals was stirred into life in Massachusetts by Solomon Stoddard between 1679 and 1718, several "harvests" occurred in New Jersey during the 1720's, and in 1734 and 1735 a tumultuous revival took place in Northampton, Massachusetts, under the exhortations of Jonathan Edwards. These revivals were not widespread nor of long duration. Nevertheless, as passionate rejections of the "free and liberal spirit," they probably helped prepare the colonists for the wildfire of religious fervor which swept much of America between 1739 and 1745.

Early in 1737 reports began to appear frequently in the colonial newspapers describing the twenty-three-year-old Whitefield's phenomenally successful evangelism in England. Upon his arrival in Philadelphia, November 2, 1739, after a lengthy crossing from England, Whitefield found the colonists eager to receive him. During the ensuing fifteen months, so Ola Winslow writes, "his personal triumph was unparalleled in American pulpit history. . . . He held the center of all stages and was crowned with more laurels than any alien who had yet set foot on American soil. As he made his triumphant progress from village to village, he was received as no less than an 'angel of God.' . . . His glory mounted higher and higher, until those who followed him lost all sense of rational discrimination. The story of his amazing pilgrimage . . . reads like fictionalized biography of the age of the Crusades, not solid history of eighteenth century America."

Although it is clear that conditions in the colonies were ripe for an outburst of religious zeal, it is also true that Whitefield was sensationally successful in gathering the harvest. Almost constantly itinerating, he delivered over five hundred sermons, as well as several hundred exhortations to small groups in private homes. He journeyed over five thousand miles by horseback and by schooner, and made five separate visits to Philadelphia, three to New York City, two to Boston, and six to Charleston. Unlike the logical, formalized sermons customarily delivered at that time, Whitefield's extempore, dramatic sermons brought a new experience in religion to the masses. Contemporaries, including Mrs. Jonathan Edwards and Alexander Garden, referred to the "charming music of his tongue" and described his speech as a "lovely song." Josiah Smith asked the rhetorical questions: "How awfully, with what *thunder* and sound did he discharge the artillery of Heaven upon us? And yet, how could he soften and melt, even a *soldier of Christ*, with the love and mercy of God?" Even Benjamin Franklin testified to Whitefield's eloquence: "Every accent, every emphasis, every modulation of voice, was so perfectly well turn'd and plac'd, that, without being interested in the subject, one could not help being pleas'd with the discourse; a pleasure of much the same kind with that receiv'd from an excellent piece of music."

In February of 1741, as the *Minerva* pushed her way slowly through the cold Atlantic waters toward England, the Reverend George Whitefield labored in his cabin, recording the context of "Abraham Offering Up His Son Isaac" and of other sermons he had preached during the Great Awakening. There must have been a touch of triumph in his manner as he wrote out the words which had thrilled thousands of eager seekers. He had kept faith with the Biblical injunction: he had come to the New World and had preached the gospel to every creature who would listen, in the streets and fields, in private homes and churches, in the market places and on the wharfs. Perhaps not again for generations would the spoken eloquence of one man so deeply affect the lives of so many.

The text of this speech comes from *Memoirs of Rev. George Whitefield*, 1834, edited by John Gillies.

Abraham's Offering Up His Son Isaac

And he said, Lay not thine hand upon the lad, neither do thou any thing unto him; for now I know that thou fearest God, seeing thou hast not withheld thy son, thine only son from me. Genesis xxii. 12.

The great apostle Paul, in one of his epistles, informs us, that "whatsoever was written aforetime, was written for our learning, that we through patience and comfort of the holy scripture might have hope." And as without faith it is impossible to please God, or to be accepted in Jesus, the Son of his love; we may be assured, that whatever instances of a more than common faith are recorded in the book of God, they were more immediately designed by the Holy Spirit for our learning and imitation, upon whom the ends of the world are come. For this reason, the author of the epistle to the Hebrews, in the eleventh chapter, mentions a noble catalogue of Old Testament saints and martyrs, "who subdued kingdoms, wrought righteousness, stopped the mouths of lions, &c. and are gone before us to inherit the promises." A sufficient confutation, I think, of their error, who lightly esteem the Old Testament saints, and would not have them mentioned to Christians, as persons whose faith and patience we are called upon more immediately to follow. If this was true, the apostle would never have produced such a cloud of witnesses out of the Old Testament, to excite the Christians of the first, and consequently purest age of the church, to continue steadfast and immovable in the possession of their faith. Amidst this catalogue of saints, methinks, the patriarch Abraham shines the brightest, and differs from the others, as one star differeth from another star in glory; for he shone with such distinguished luster, that he was called the *friend of God*, the *father of the faithful*; and those who believe on Christ, are said to be sons and daughters of, and to be blessed with, faithful Abraham. Many trials of his faith did God send this great and good man, after he had commanded him to get out from his country, and from his kindred, unto a land which he should show him; but the last was the most severe of all, I mean, that of offering up his only son. This, by the divine assistance, I propose to make the subject of your present meditation, and, by way of conclusion, to draw some practical inferences, as God shall enable me, from this instructive story.

The sacred penman begins the narrative thus; verse 1. "And it came to pass, after these things, God did tempt Abraham." "After these things," that is, after he had underwent many severe trials before, after he was old, full of days, and might flatter himself perhaps that the troubles and toils of life were now finished; "after these things, God did tempt Abraham." Christians, you know not what trials you may meet with before you die: notwithstanding you may have suffered, and been tried much already, yet, it may be, a greater measure is still behind, which you are to fill up. "Be not high-minded, but fear." Our last trials, in all probability, will be the greatest: and we can never say our warfare is accomplished, or our trials finished, till we bow down our heads, and give up the ghost. "And it came to pass, after these things, that God did tempt Abraham."

"God did tempt Abraham." But can the scripture contradict itself? Does not the apostle James tell us, that God tempts no man; and God does tempt no man to evil, or on purpose to draw him into sin; for, when a man is thus tempted, he is drawn away of his own heart's lust, and enticed. But in another sense, God may be said to tempt, I mean, to try his servants; and in this sense we are to understand that passage of Matthew, where we are told, that "Jesus was led up by the Spirit (the good Spirit) into the wilderness, to be tempted of the devil." And our Lord, in that excellent form of prayer which he has been pleased to give us, does not require us to pray that we may not absolutely be led into temptation, but delivered from the evil of it; whence we may plainly infer, that God sees it fit sometimes to lead us into temptation, that is, to bring us into such circumstances as will try our faith, and other Christian graces. In this sense we are to understand the expression before us, "God did tempt or try Abraham."

How God was pleased to reveal his will at this time to his faithful servant, whether by the Shechinah, or divine appearance, or by a small still voice, as he spoke to Elijah, or by a whisper, like that of the Spirit to Philip, when he commanded him to join himself to the Eunuch's chariot, we are not told, nor is it material to inquire. It is enough that we are informed, God said unto him, Abraham; and that Abraham knew that it was the voice of God: for "he said, behold, here I am." O what a holy familiarity (if I may so speak) is there between God and those holy souls that are united to him by faith in Christ Jesus! God says, Abraham; and Abraham said, (it should seem without the least surprise,) "Behold, here I am." Being reconciled to God by the death and obedience of Christ, which he rejoiced in, and saw by faith afar off; he did not, like guilty Adam, seek the trees of the garden to hide himself from, but takes pleasure in conversing with God, and talketh with him, as a man talketh with his friend. O that Christless sinners knew what it is to have fellowship with the Father and the Son! They would envy the happiness of saints, and count it all joy to be termed enthusiasts and fools for Christ's sake.

But what does God say unto Abraham; ver. 2. "Take now thy son, thine only son Isaac, whom thou lovest, and get thee into the land of Moriah, and offer him there for a burnt-offering upon one of the mountains which I shall tell thee of."

Every word deserves our particular observation. Whatever he was to do, he must do it now, immediately, without conferring with flesh and blood. But what must he do? *Take now thy son.* Had God said, take now a firstling, or choicest lamb or beast of thy flock, and offer it up for a burnt-offering, it would not have appeared so ghastly: but for God to say, "Take now thy son, and offer him up for a burnt-offering," one would have imagined, was enough to stagger the strongest faith. But this is not all: It must not only be a son, but *thine only son Isaac, whom thou lovest.* If it must be a son, and not a beast, that must be offered, why will not Ishmael do, the son of the bond-woman? No, it must be his *only son,* the heir of all, his Isaac, by interpretation *laughter,* the son of his old age, in whom his soul delighted; *whom thou lovest,* says God, in whose life his own was wrapped up: And this son, this only son, this Isaac, the son of his love, must be taken now, even now without delay, and be offered up by his own father, for a burnt-offering, upon one of the mountains of the which God would tell him.

Well might the apostle, speaking of this man of God, say, that *against hope he believed in hope, and, being strong in faith, gave glory to God:* For, had he not been blessed with faith which man never before had, he must have refused to comply with this severe command. For how many arguments might nature suggest to prove that such a command could never come from God, or to excuse himself from obeying it? "What! (might the good man have said) butcher my child! it is contrary to the very law of nature: Much more to butcher my dear son Isaac, in whose seed God himself has assured me, that all the families of the earth shall be blessed. But supposing I could give up my own affections, and be willing to part with him, though I love him so dearly, yet, if I murder him, what will become of God's promise? Besides I am now like a city built upon a hill; I shine as a light in the world, in the midst of a crooked and perverse generation: How then shall I cause God's name to be blasphemed, how shall I become a by-word among the heathen, if they hear that I have committed a crime which they abhor! But, above all, what will Sarah my wife say? How can I ever return to her again, after I have imbued my hands in my dear child's blood? O that God would pardon me in this thing, or take my life in the place of my son's!" Thus, I say, Abraham might have argued, and that too seemingly with great reason, against complying with the divine command. But, as before by faith he considered not the deadness of Sarah's womb, when she was past age, but believed on him, who said, "Sarah thy wife shall bear thee a son indeed"; so now being convinced that the same God spoke to, and commanded him to offer up that son, and knowing that God was able to raise him from the dead, without delay he obeys the heavenly call.

O that unbelievers would learn of faithful Abraham, and believe whatever is revealed from God, though they cannot fully comprehend it! Abraham knew God commanded him to offer up his son, and therefore believed, notwithstanding carnal reasoning might suggest many objections. We have sufficient testimony, that God has spoken to us by his Son; why should we not also believe, though many things in the New Testament are above our reason? For, where reason ends faith begins. And, however infidels may style themselves reasoners, of all men they are the most unreasonable: For is it not contrary to all reason, to measure an infinite by a finite understanding, or think to find out the mysteries of godliness to perfection?

But to return to the patriarch Abraham: We observed before what plausible objections he might have made; but he answered not a single word: No, without replying against his Maker, we are told, ver. 3. that "Abraham rose up early in the morning, and saddled his ass, and took two of his young men with him, and Isaac his son, and clave the wood for the burnt-offering, and rose up and went unto the the place of which God had told him."

From this verse we may gather that God spoke to Abraham in a dream, or vision of the night: For it is said, he *rose up early*. Perhaps it was near the fourth watch of the night, just before break of day, when God said, *Take now thy son;* and Abraham rises up early to do so; as I doubt not but he used to rise early to offer up his morning sacrifice of praise and thanksgiving. It is often remarked of people in the Old Testament, that they rose early in the morning; and particularly of our Lord in the New, that he rose a great while before day to pray. The morning befriends devotion: and if people cannot use so much self-denial as to rise early to pray, I know not how they will be able to die at a stake (if called to it) for Jesus Christ.

The humility, as well as piety of the patriarch, is observable: He saddled his own ass (great men should be humble;) and to show his sincerity, though he took two of his young men with him, and Isaac his son, yet he keeps his design as a secret from them all: Nay, he does not so much as tell Sarah his wife: For he knew not but she might be a snare unto him in this affair; and, as Rebecca afterwards, on another occasion, advised Jacob to flee, so Sarah also might persuade Isaac to hide himself; or the young men, had they known of it, might have forced him away, as in after ages the soldiers rescued Jonathan out of the hands of Saul. But Abraham sought no such evasion, and therefore, like an Israelite indeed, in whom there was no guile, he himself resolutely "clave the wood for the burnt-offering, rose up and went unto the place of which God had told him." In the second verse, God commanded him to offer up his son upon one of the mountains which he would tell him of. He commanded him to offer his son up, but would not then directly tell him the place where: This was to keep him dependent and watching unto prayer: For there's nothing like being kept waiting upon God; and, if we do, assuredly God will reveal himself unto us yet further in his own time. Let us practice what we know, follow providence so far as we can see already; and what we know not, what we see not as yet, let us only be found in the way of duty, and the Lord will reveal even that unto us. Abraham knew not directly where he was to offer up his son; but he rises up and sets forward, and behold now God shows him; and he went to the place of which God had told him. Let us go and do likewise.

Ver. 4. Then on the third day, Abraham lifted up his eyes, and saw the place afar off.

So that the place, of which God had told him, was no less than three days journey distant from the place where God first appeared to him, and commanded him to take his son. Was not this to try his faith, and to let him see what he did, was not merely from a sudden pang of devotion, but a matter of choice and deliberation? But who can tell what the aged patriarch felt during these three days? Strong as he was in faith, I am persuaded his bowels often yearned over his dear son Isaac. Methinks I see the good old man walking with his dear child in his hand, and now and then looking upon him, loving him, and then turning aside to weep. And perhaps, sometimes he stays a little behind to pour out his heart before God; for he had no mortal to tell his case to. Then, methinks, I see him join his son and servants again, and talking to them of the things pertaining to the kingdom of God, as they walked by the way. At length, on the third day, he lifted up his eyes and saw the place afar off. And, to show that he was yet sincerely resolved to do whatsoever the Lord required of him, he even now will not discover his design to his servants, but said, ver. 5. to his young men, (as we should say to our worldly thoughts when about to tread the courts of the Lord's house) "abide you here with the ass; and I and the lad will go up yonder and worship, and come again to you." This was a sufficient reason for their staying behind; and, it being their master's custom to go frequently to worship, they could have no suspicion of what he was going about. And Abraham's saying, that he and the lad would come again, I am apt to think he believed God would raise him from the dead, if so be he permitted him to offer his child up for a burnt offering. However that be, he is yet resolved to obey God to the uttermost; and therefore,

Ver. 6. "Abraham took the wood of the burnt-offering, and laid it upon Isaac his son; and he took the fire in his hand, and a knife, and they went both of them together." Little did Isaac think that he was to be offered on that very wood which he was carrying upon his shoulders; and therefore, ver. 7, Isaac innocently, and with a holy freedom (for good men should not keep their children at too great a distance) spake unto Abraham his father, and said, My father; and he (with equal affection and holy condescension) said, Here am I, my son. And to show how careful Abraham had been (as all Christian parents ought to be) to instruct his Isaac how to sacrifice to God, like a youth trained up in the way wherein he should go; Isaac said, Behold the fire and the wood; but where is the lamb for a burnt offering? How beautiful is early piety! How amiable, to hear young people ask questions about sacrificing to God in an acceptable way! Isaac knew very well that a lamb was wanting, and that a lamb was necessary for a proper sacrifice: Behold the fire and the wood; but where is the lamb for a burnt-offering? Young men and maidens, learn of him.

Hitherto, it is plain, Isaac knew nothing of his father's design: but I believe, by what his father said in answer to his question, that now was the time Abraham revealed it unto him.

Ver. 8. "And Abraham said, my son, God will provide himself a lamb for a burnt-offering." Some think that Abraham by faith saw the Lord Jesus afar off, and here spake prophetically of that Lamb of God already slain in decree, and hereafter to be actually offered up for sinners. This was a lamb of God's providing indeed (we dared not have thought of it) to satisfy his own justice, and to render him just in justifying the ungodly. What is all our fire and wood, the best preparation and performances we can make or present, unless God had provided himself this Lamb for a burnt offering? He could not away with them. The words will well bear this interpretation. But, whatever Abraham might intend, I cannot but think he here made an application, and acquainted his son with God's dealing with his soul; and at length, with tears in his eyes, and the utmost affection in his heart, cried out, "Thou art to be the lamb, my son; God has commanded me to provide thee for a burnt-offering, and to offer thee upon the mountain which we are now ascending." And, as it appears from a subsequent verse, Isaac, convinced that it was the divine will, made no resistance at all: for it is said, "they went both of them together"; and again, ver. 9, when we are told that Abraham bound Isaac, we do not hear of his complaining, or endeavoring to escape, which he might have done, being (as some think) near thirty years of age, and it is plain, was capable of carrying wood enough for a burnt-offering. But he was partaker of the like precious faith with his aged father, and therefore is as willing to be offered, as Abraham is to offer him; and so they went both of them together.

Ver. 9. At length "they came to the place of which God had told Abraham. He built an altar there and laid the wood in order, and bound Isaac his son, and laid him on the altar upon the wood."

And here let us pause a while, and by faith take a view of the place where the father has laid him. I doubt not but the blessed angels hovered round the altar and sang, Glory be to God in the highest, for giving such faith to man. Come, all ye tender hearted parents, who know what it is to look over a dying child: Fancy that you saw the altar erected before you, and the wood laid in order, and the beloved Isaac bound upon it: Fancy that you saw the aged parent standing by weeping. (For, why may we not suppose that Abraham wept, since Jesus himself wept at the grave of Lazarus?) O what pious endearing expressions passed now alternately between the father and the son! Josephus records a pathetic speech made by each, whether genuine I know not; but methinks I see the tears trickle down the patriarch Abraham's cheeks; and, out of the abundance of the heart, he cries, Adieu, adieu, my son; the Lord gave thee to me, and the Lord calls thee away; blessed be the name of the Lord; adieu, my Isaac, my only son, whom I love as my own soul; adieu, adieu. I see Isaac at the same time meekly resigning himself into his heavenly Father's hands, and praying to the most High to strengthen his earthly parent to strike the stroke. But why do I attempt to describe what either son or father felt? It is impossible; we may indeed form some faint idea of, but shall never fully comprehend it, till we come and sit down with them in the kingdom of heaven, and hear them tell the pleasing story over again. Hasten, O Lord, that blessed time! O let thy kingdom come!

And now, ver. 10. The fatal blow is going to be given. "And Abraham stretched forth his hand, and took the knife to slay his son." But do you not think he intended to turn away his head, when he gave the blow? Nay, why may we not suppose he sometimes drew his hand in, after it was stretched out, willing to take another last farewell of his beloved Isaac, and desirous to defer it a little, though resolved at last to strike home? Be that as it will, his arm is now stretched out, the knife is in his hand, and he is about to put it to his dear son's throat.

But sing, O heavens! and rejoice, O earth! Man's extremity is God's opportunity: for behold, just as the knife, in all probability, was near his throat, ver. 11. "the angel of the Lord, (or rather, the Lord of angels, Jesus Christ, the angel of the everlasting covenant,) called unto him, (probably in a very audible manner,) from heaven, and said, Abraham, Abraham. (The word is doubled, to engage his attention; and perhaps the suddenness of the call made him draw back his hand, just as he was going to strike his son.) And Abraham said, Here am I."

And he said, ver. 12. "Lay not thine hand upon the lad, neither do thou any thing unto him: for now know I that thou fearest God, seeing thou hast not withheld thy son, thine only son from me."

Here then it was that Abraham received his son Isaac from the dead in a figure. He was in effect offered upon the altar, and God looked upon him as offered and given unto him. Now it was that Abraham's faith, being tried, was found more precious than gold purified seven times in the fire. Now as a reward of grace, though not of debt, for this signal act of obedience, by an oath, God gives and confirms the promise, "that in his seed all the nations of the earth should be blessed," ver. 17, 18. With what comfort may we suppose the good old man and his son went down from the mount, and returned unto the young men! With what joy we imagine he went home, and related all that had passed to Sarah! And above all, with what triumph is he exulting now in the paradise of God, and adoring rich, free, distinguishing, electing, everlasting love, which alone made him to differ from the rest of mankind, and rendered him worthy of that title which he will have so long as the sun and the moon endure: "The father of the faithful!"

But let us now draw our eyes from the creature, and do what Abraham, if he was present, would direct to; I mean, fix them on the Creator, God blessed for evermore.

I see your hearts affected, I see your eyes weep, (and indeed, who can refrain weeping at the relation of such a story?) But, behold, I show you a mystery hid under the sacrifice of Abraham's only son, which, unless your hearts are hardened, must cause you to weep tears of love, and that plentifully too. I would willingly hope you even prevent me here, and are ready to say, "it is the love of God, in giving Jesus Christ to die for our sins. Yes, that is it." And yet perhaps you find your hearts at the mentioning of this, not so much affected. Let this convince you, that we are fallen creatures, and that we do not love God or Christ as we ought to do: if you admire Abraham offering up his Isaac, how much more ought you to extol, magnify, and adore the love of God, who so loved the world, as to give his only begotton Son, Christ Jesus our Lord, "that whosoever believeth on him should not perish, but have everlasting life?" May we not well cry out, Now know we, O Lord, that thou hast loved us, since thou hast not withheld thy Son, thine only son from us? Abraham was God's creature, (and God was Abraham's friend) and therefore under the highest obligation to surrender up his Isaac. But O stupendous love! Whilst we were his enemies, God sent forth his Son, made of a woman, made under the law, that he might become a curse for us. O the freeness, as well as the infinity, of the love of God our Father! It is unsearchable: I am lost in contemplating it; it is past finding out. Think, O believers, think of the love of God, in giving Jesus Christ to be a propitiation for our sins. And when you hear how Abraham built an altar, and laid the wood in order, and bound Isaac his son, and laid him on the altar upon the wood; think how your heavenly Father bound Jesus Christ his only Son, and offered him upon the altar of his justice, and laid upon him the iniquities of us all. When you read of Abraham's stretching forth his hand to slay his son, think, O think, how God actually suffered his Son to be slain, that we might live for evermore. Do you read of Isaac carrying the wood upon his shoulders, upon which he was to be offered? Let this lead you to Mount Calvary, (this very mount of Moriah where Isaac was offered, as some think,) and take a view of the antitype Jesus Christ, that Son of God, bearing and ready to sink under the weight of that cross on which he was to hang for us. Do you admire Isaac so freely consenting to die, though a creature, and therefore obliged to go when God called? O do not forget to admire infinitely more the dear Lord Jesus, that promised seed, who willingly said, "Lo, I come," though under no obligation so to do, "to do thy will," to obey and die for men, O God! Did you weep just now, when I bid you fancy that you saw the altar, and the wood laid in order, and Isaac laid bound on the altar? Look up by faith, behold the blessed Jesus, our all-glorious Immanuel, not bound, but nailed on an accursed tree: see how he hangs crowned with thorns, and had in derision of all that are round about him: see how the thorns pierce him, and how the blood in purple streams trickles down his sacred temples! Hark! how the God of nature groans! See how he bows his head, and at length humanity gives up the ghost! Isaac is saved, but Jesus, the God of Isaac dies; a ram is offered up in Isaac's room, but Jesus has no substitute; Jesus must bleed, Jesus must die: God the Father provided this Lamb for himself from all eternity. He must be offered in time, or man must be damned for evermore. And now where are all your tears? Shall I say, refrain your voice from weeping? No, rather let me exhort you to look to him whom you have pierced, and mourn, as a woman mourneth for her first born: for we have been the betrayers, we have been the murderers of this Lord of glory; and shall we not bewail those sins, which brought the blessed Jesus to the accursed tree? Having so much done, so much suffered for us, so much forgiven, shall we not love much? O! let us love him with all our hearts, and minds, and strength, and glorify him in our souls and bodies; for they are his. Which leads me to a second inference I shall draw from the foregoing discourse.

From hence we may learn the nature of true justifying faith. Whoever understands and preaches the truth as it is in Jesus, must acknowledge, that salvation is God's free gift, and that we are saved, not by any or all the works of righteousness which we have done or can do:

no; we can neither wholly nor in part justify ourselves in the sight of God. The Lord Jesus Christ is our righteousness; and if we are accepted with God, it must be only in and through the personal righteousness, the active and passive obedience of Jesus Christ his beloved Son. This righteousness must be imputed, or counted over to us, and applied by faith to our hearts, or else we can in no wise be justified in God's sight: and that very moment when a sinner is enabled to lay hold on Christ's righteousness by faith, he is freely justified from all his sins, and shall never enter into condemnation, notwithstanding he was a fire brand of hell before. Thus it was that Abraham was justified before he did any good work: he was enabled to believe on the Lord Christ; it was accounted to him for righteousness; that is, Christ's righteousness was made over to him, and so accounted his. This, this is gospel; this is the only way of finding acceptance with God: good works have nothing to do with our justification in his sight. We are justified by faith alone, as saith the article of our church; agreeable to which the apostle Paul says, "By grace ye are saved, through faith; and that not of yourselves; it is the gift of God." Notwithstanding good works have their proper place: they justify our faith, though not our persons; they follow it, and evidence our justification in the sight of men. Hence it is that the apostle James asks, was not Abraham justified by works, (alluding, no doubt, to the story on which we have been discoursing,) that is, did he not prove he was in a justified state, because his faith was productive of good works? This declarative justification in the sight of men, is what is directly to be understood in the words of the text: "Now know I," says God, "that thou fearest me, since thou hast not withheld thy son, thine only son from me." Not but that God knew it before; but this is spoken in condescension to our weak capacities, and plainly shows, that his offering up his son was accepted with God, as an evidence of the sincerity of his faith, and for this, was left on record to future ages. Hence then you may learn, whether you are blessed with, and are sons and daughters of faithful Abraham. You say you believe; you talk of free grace, and free justification: you do well; the devils also believe and tremble. But has the faith which you pretend to, influenced your hearts, renewed your souls, and, like Abraham's, worked by love? Are your affections, like his, set on things above? Are you heavenly minded, and like him, do you confess yourselves strangers and pilgrims on the earth. In short, has your faith enabled you to overcome the world, and strengthened you to give up your Isaacs, your laughter, your most beloved lusts, friends, pleasures, and profits for God? If so, take the comfort of it; for justly may you say, "We know assuredly, that we do fear and love God, or rather are loved of him." But if you are only talking believers, have only a faith of the head, and never felt the power of it in your hearts, however you may bolster yourselves up, and say, "we have Abraham for our father, or Christ is our Savior;" unless you get a faith of the heart, a faith working by love, you shall never sit with Abraham, Isaac, Jacob, or Jesus Christ in the kingdom of heaven.

But I must draw one more inference, and with that I shall conclude.

Learn, O saints! from what has been said, to sit loose to all your worldly comforts; and stand ready prepared to part with every thing, when God shall require it at your hand. Some of you perhaps may have friends, who are to you as your own souls, and others may have children, in whose lives your own lives are bound up: all I believe have their Isaacs, their particular delights of some kind or other. Labor, for Christ's sake, labor, ye sons and daughters of Abraham, to resign them, daily in affection to God, that, when he shall require you really to sacrifice them, you may not confer with flesh and blood, any more than the blessed patriarch now before us. And as for you that have been in any measure tried like unto him, let his example encourage and comfort you. Remember, Abraham your father was tried so before you: think, O think, of the happiness he now enjoys, and how he is incessantly thanking God for tempting and trying him when here below. Look up often by the eye of faith, and see him sitting with his dearly beloved Isaac in the world of spirits. Remember, it will be but a little while, and you shall sit with them also, and tell one another what God has done for your souls. There I hope to sit with you, and hear this story of his offering up his son from his own mouth, and to praise the Lamb that sitteth upon the throne, for what he hath done for all our souls, for ever and ever.

Exercises

1. After reading this speech, are you inclined to believe, or disbelieve, the testimony of contemporaries who lauded the sermon's emotional impact upon hearers? If you are inclined to discount the effectiveness of the speech, reread the introduction supplied by the editors and try to project yourself into the role of a colonist listening to the evangelist. The richer your imagination and the better informed you are concerning the colonists' modes of thinking, the amount of recreation available to them, and the styles of preaching which were conventional to the times, the better able you should be to re-create the speaking situation. If silent reading of the sermon fails to bring the words to life, read several extended passages aloud, or ask a classmate to read them to you. If you still feel unsatisfied that this sermon could have evoked the alleged responses, refer to the editors' introduction concerning the way in which the copy of the sermon was prepared. What causal relationship might exist between

the method of Whitefield's composition and your evaluation of the sermon?

2. What seems to be Whitefield's purpose in this sermon? How would you characterize the basic tone: Hortatory? Explanatory? Argumentative? Etc.?

3. Would Whitefield's beginning have been more effective if, departing from traditional practice, he had referred to the circumstances of the meeting, or to the historical significance of the locale, or to his appreciation of the warmth of the listeners' greeting, etc.? Why or why not? How does Whitefield set the stage for the main portion of his sermon?

4. What aspects of the style of this speech particularly impress you for their "rhetorical quality" or their probable effectiveness? Would this speech be considered good literature? Is the style personal? Colloquial? Direct? Involved? Clear? How suitable is Whitefield's use of rhetorical questions? Exclamations? Dialogue? Narration of hypothetical situations? Reference to the tears being shed by some listeners? What "factors of interest" [such as suspense, familiarity, and imagery] does Whitefield use? How does he employ them? Describe his use of the dramatic element.

5. How effective do you believe this speech would be if delivered to a modern audience? What values does it possess which tend to give it enduring and "universal" appeal? What types of persons today would be more apt to respond favorably to this speech? Less favorably? Unfavorably?

6. What type of thought sequence is used in the Body of the sermon: Time? Topical? Cause and effect? Problem and solution? Other? Outline the speech, indicating both major and secondary divisions. How would you characterize the organization of the Body: Loose? Simple? Abstruse? Climactic? Complicated? Clear? Etc.?

7. What does Whitefield attempt to accomplish in the Conclusion? How does he tie together the basic lines of thought and relate them to the theme? Does he seem to have an "action step"? How does he personalize his appeal?

8. Defend or attack the following assertion: "In this speech Whitefield employs few scraps of rationalism. He resorts almost exclusively to vehement assertions documented by a fictional dramatic narration and buttressed by maudlin hortations."

9. If Whitefield believed that each person is predestined either to be "saved" or to be condemned to hell, how do you account for his seeming to hold open the doors of salvation to everyone?

10. Can this be considered a "hell fire and damnation" sermon? Does Whitefield place greater stress on fear or on love? On thinking or feeling? On negative or positive attitudes? How does he attempt to transfer the love for one's own children to the love for God? How does he make faith seem attractive? How does he try to make salvation by faith seem more reasonable than salvation by "works"?

11. Compare the style and tone of this speech with that of "The Man with the Muck-Rake," a speech which is considered by some to be political evangelism.

Patrick Henry

"Liberty or Death," delivered to the Virginia Provincial Convention, March 23, 1775, in St. John's Church, Richmond, Virginia

ALTHOUGH George Washington, Thomas Jefferson, and John Marshall attained greater national prominence, in Virginia no man's fame or influence exceeded that of Patrick Henry (1736–1799). His position as the outstanding leader of the Revolution in Virginia was recognized by both admirers and detractors. George Mason, a close collaborator, whose writings provided the basis for the first ten amendments to the United States Constitution, characterized Henry as "the first man upon this continent, as well in abilities as public virtues." If Henry had "lived in Rome about the time of the first Punic War, when the Roman people had arrived at their meridian glory, and their virtue not tarnished," said Mason, his "talents must have put him at the head of that glorious commonwealth." Thomas Jefferson, one of Henry's most astringent critics, recognized him as "the greatest orator that ever lived." According to Jefferson, Henry's "consummate knowledge of the human heart" in conjunction with "his eloquence enabled him to attain a degree of popularity with the people at large never perhaps equalled." The people responded to his bold leadership and electric eloquence by electing him to every office he sought: to the state legislature in 1765, and thereafter whenever he chose to return; to the First and Second Continental Congresses; to the governor's office, in 1776 as the first governor of the state, and in subsequent years to that office four more times.

Henry's "torrents of sublime eloquence" first won him regional attention as a fledgling lawyer in the Parson's Case, 1763, in which he defended Virginia's right to veto unjust laws of the King. He won fame throughout the Colonies for his speaking in the Virginia House of Burgesses, especially for his defense of a series of resolutions concerning the Stamp Tax, 1765. John Adams and other leaders of the Continental Congresses acknowledged his preeminence as an orator who preached a stirring new faith—Americanism. "The distinctions between Virginians, Pennsylvanians, New Yorkers, and New Englanders, are no more," he told the First Congress. "I am not a Virginian, but an American."

Long obscured by myth, Henry's profile has emerged in recent investigations with reasonably clear delineation. Henry, the man, was greater than Henry, the legend. No shambling backwoods yokel, Henry came from a substantial middle-class family. His father at one time owned joint title to more than sixty thousand acres of land and, being one of the very few college-trained men in the area, he served as tutor to Patrick, affording him an academic education considerably superior to that of Washington. No bucolic idler, Henry became an ambitious, hard-driving, astute lawyer and dominant political leader. No uncouth bumpkin, Henry possessed the customary cultural values of the middle-class gentry. No demagogue, he was genial, gay, generous to opponents, and highly respected by all levels of society. No more hungry for fame and fortune than were other prominent contemporaries, he worked hard in achieving position and wealth. No single-speech orator, his unparalleled effectiveness on the hustings, in jury trials, in congresses, and in committees made him a major force throughout the entire Revolutionary and Constitution-making era.

On March 23, 1775, Henry sat in the St. John's Church in Richmond, listening to the debate among his fellow delegates to the Virginia Provincial Convention. The resolutions before the Convention were Henry's. He had proposed means to organize the militia and put the colony in a posture of defense. When he gained the floor, he delivered one of the most famous speeches in history. Unfortunately, no pen took down the words. More than forty years later, William Wirt—nationally known lawyer, speaker, and author—reconstructed the language of the speech as best he could from the accounts of witnesses. Published in Wirt's *The Life and Character of Patrick Henry*, 1817, the speech received instant acclaim from a nation experiencing a new consciousness of national strength and purpose, resulting from the War of 1812. The sustained, brilliant, and somewhat contrived language of the printed speech probably reflects the style of Wirt, but it is also suggestive of the slashing eloquence and courageous spirit of a patriot in the process of making history.

The text stems from William Wirt, *Life and Character of Patrick Henry*, Philadelphia: Henry T. Coates and Co., 1817.

LIBERTY OR DEATH

Mr. President: No man thinks more highly than I do of the patriotism, as well as abilities, of the very worthy gentlemen who have just addressed the House. But different men often see the same subjects in different lights; and, therefore, I hope that it will not be thought disrespectful to those gentlemen, if, entertaining as I do, opinions of a character very opposite to theirs, I shall speak forth my sentiments freely and without reserve. This is no time for ceremony. The question before the House is one of awful moment to this country. For my own part I consider it as nothing less than a question of freedom or slavery; and in proportion to the magnitude of the subject ought to be the freedom of the debate. It is only in this way that we can hope to arrive at truth, and fulfill the great responsibility which we hold to God and our country. Should I keep back my opinions at such a time, through fear of giving offense, I should consider myself as guilty of treason toward my country, and of an act of disloyalty toward the majesty of heaven, which I revere above all earthly kings.

Mr. President, it is natural to man to indulge in the illusions of hope. We are apt to shut our eyes against a painful truth, and listen to the song of that siren, till she transforms us into beasts. Is this the part of wise men, engaged in a great and arduous struggle for liberty? Are we disposed to be of the number of those who, having eyes, see not, and having ears, hear not, the things which so nearly concern their temporal salvation? For my part, whatever anguish of spirit it may cost, I am willing to know the whole truth; to know the worst and to provide for it.

I have but one lamp by which my feet are guided; and that is the lamp of experience. I know of no way of judging of the future but by the past. And judging by the past, I wish to know what there has been in the conduct of the British ministry for the last ten years to justify those hopes with which gentlemen have been pleased to solace themselves and the House? Is it that insidious smile with which our petition has been lately received? Trust it not, sir; it will prove a snare to your feet. Suffer not yourselves to be betrayed with a kiss. Ask yourselves how this gracious reception of our petition comports with these warlike preparations which cover our waters and darken our land. Are fleets and armies necessary to a work of love and reconciliation? Have we shown ourselves so unwilling to be reconciled, that force must be called in to win back our love? Let us not deceive ourselves, sir. These are the implements of war and subjugation; the last arguments to which kings resort. I ask gentlemen, sir, what means this martial array, if its purpose be not to force us to submission? Can gentlemen assign any other possible motives for it? Has Great Britain any enemy, in this quarter of the world, to call for all this accumulation of navies and armies? No, sir, she has none. They are meant for us; they can be meant for no other. They are sent over to bind and rivet upon us those chains which the British ministry have been so long forging. And what have we to oppose to them? Shall we try argument? Sir, we have been trying that for the last ten years. Have we anything new to offer on the subject? Nothing. We have held the subject up in every light of which it is capable; but it has been all in vain. Shall we resort to entreaty and humble supplication? What terms shall we find which have not been already exhausted? Let us not, I beseech you, sir, deceive ourselves longer. Sir, we have done everything that could be done to avert the storm which is now coming on. We have petitioned; we have remonstrated; we have supplicated; we have prostrated ourselves before the tyrannical hands of the ministry and parliament. Our petitions have been slighted; our remonstrances have produced additional violence and insult; our supplications have been disregarded; and we have been spurned, with contempt, from the foot of the throne. In vain, after these things, may we indulge the fond hope of peace and reconciliation. There is no longer any room for hope. If we wish to be free—if we mean to preserve inviolate those inestimable privileges for which we have been so long contending—if we mean not basely to abandon the noble struggle in which we have been so long engaged, and which we have pledged ourselves never to abandon until the glorious object of our contest shall be obtained, we must fight! I repeat it, sir, we must fight! An appeal to arms and to the God of Hosts is all that is left us!

They tell us, sir, that we are weak; unable to cope with so formidable an adversary. But when shall we be stronger? Will it be the next week, or the next year? Will it be when we are totally disarmed, and when a British guard shall be stationed in every house? Shall we gather strength by irresolution and inaction? Shall we acquire the means of effectual resistance by lying supinely on our backs, and hugging the delusive phantom of hope, until our enemies shall have bound us hand and foot? Sir, we are not weak, if we make a proper use of the means which the God of nature hath placed in our power. Three millions of people, armed in the holy cause of liberty, and in such a country as that which we possess, are invincible by any force which our enemy can send against us. Besides, sir, we shall not fight our battles alone. There is a just God who presides over the destinies of nations; and who will raise friends to fight our battles for us. The battle, sir, is not to the strong alone; it is to the vigilant, the active, the brave. Besides, sir, we have no election. If we were base enough to desire it, it is now too late to retire from the contest. There is no retreat but in submission and slavery! Our chains are forged! Their clanking may be heard on the plains of Boston! The war is inevitable—and let it come! I repeat it, sir, let it come!

It is in vain, sir, to extenuate the matter. Gentlemen may cry peace, peace—but there is no peace. The war is actually begun! The next gale that sweeps from the North will bring to our ears the clash of resounding arms! Our brethren are already in the field! Why stand we here idle? What is it that gentlemen wish? What would they have? Is life so dear, or peace so sweet, as to be purchased at the price of chains and slavery? Forbid it, Almighty God! I know not what course others may take; but as for me, give me liberty, or give me death!

Exercises

1. In the introduction to this speech, how does Henry attempt to conciliate the opposition? What rhetorical strength does he achieve by weaving together elements of conciliation, personal proof, and significance of the topic?
2. What proposition is Henry recommending? Does he spell it out clearly and in specific detail? In what ways may the expression of Henry's proposition be related to the manner in which the speech has been reported?
3. Outline this speech. Does the speech seem to follow a pattern of Problem-Solution or one of Need for Change-Policy Recommendation? Is the basic organization a natural one for a speech advocating a proposition of policy?
4. How comprehensive is Henry's review of the previous relationships between England and the Colonies? How objective? In what ways does Henry's historical sketch prepare the listeners for his recommendations?
5. In your estimation, how effective is Henry's indirect reference to Judas' betrayal of Christ?
6. Identify three figures of speech used by Henry. Explain why these would be especially striking for the auditors.
7. How does Henry stimulate fear for the consequences, if his proposals are not accepted? How does he attempt to harness these fears, once they are aroused?

8. How does Henry attempt to make persuasive his contention that there is no alternative to accepting his recommendations?

9. What prognostication does he make? How accurate was he? Is this prediction of the future a strong or a weak persuasive strategy?

10. Why do you suppose Thomas Jefferson said that Henry was "rotten hearted," interested only in fame and money, and "all tongue, without either head or heart"? At what period in the relationship between the two men did Jefferson make these observations? Do Jefferson's words indict the Sage of Monticello as much or more than they do the orator from Red Hill? What do you think might have motivated Jefferson's negative judgments? What was Henry's expressed attitude toward Jefferson? If there is a difference between the stated attitudes of the two men toward each other, how do you account for the difference?

11. How famous was Henry's speech prior to the publication of Wirt's volume in 1817? To what extent did the climate of the early 19th century affect the popular reception of Wirt's book?

12. Compare the style and organization of Henry's "Liberty or Death" speech with that of his speeches during the Virginia Ratification Convention, as reported by shorthand transcription in Jonathan Elliot's *Debates in the Several State Conventions on the Adoption of the Federal Constitution.*

Thomas Jefferson

First Inaugural Address, given March 4, 1801

THOMAS Jefferson (1743–1826) rarely made speeches. Disliking what he called the "morbid rage of debate," and lacking the voice and temperament of a parliamentary advocate, he left speechmaking to the Richard Henry Lees and the Patrick Henrys. As John Adams wrote, "During the whole time I sat with him in Congress, I never heard him utter three sentences together. . . . Mr. Jefferson could stand no competition with him [Richard Henry Lee] or anyone else in elocution and public debate." In spite of his being a "silent member," Jefferson was nevertheless a prominent, and sometimes a foremost, member of the Virginia House of Burgesses, 1769–1775, of each special assembly and convention of that colony, 1769–1775, and of the Continental Congress, 1775–1776. He achieved leadership partly through his speaking effectiveness in committees and in small informal groups. John Adams recognized that "not even Sam Adams" was more "prompt, frank, explicit and decisive upon committees and in conversation."

In addition to his facility in speaking to small groups, Jefferson's rise to national leadership depended partly upon family connections (his well-to-do father had married into one of the most prestigious colonial families, the Randolphs) and upon his industry and scholarship, which he demonstrated as a student at William and Mary, law student in George Wythe's office, and successful barrister. Possibly of greatest importance to his career, however, was his skill in writing. Largely because of his widely circulated *A Summary View of the*

Rights of America he became a foremost leader of the Revolution and was selected to draft the Declaration of Independence. He employed with great effectiveness his skill in writing and speaking to small groups during his service as governor of Virginia, 1779–1781, minister to France, 1784–1789, Secretary of State under Washington, 1789–1794, Vice-President, 1797–1801, and President, 1801–1809.

On March 4, 1801, Jefferson eschewed the pomp of previous inaugurations. For his own inauguration Adams had purchased a new carriage and liveries for his footman and coachman, had strapped a sword to his side, and had carried a cockaded hat beneath an arm. With studied purposefulness, Jefferson walked from his boarding-house to the capitol at the head of a boistrous crowd, including a company of infantry and one of artillery. As he climbed the steps to take the oath of office in the Senate chamber, the discharge of cannons sent hearty accolades racing through the unfinished capitol. Despite the festive temper of the crowd, however, there were compelling reasons why Jefferson should have felt apprehensive. Retiring President Adams had abruptly left town before the ceremonies. Jefferson's cousin and long-term political enemy, Chief Justice John Marshall was to administer the oath. Of vastly greater importance, the country was uneasy and talk of rebellion was being heard.

In the election of 1800 a revolution had taken place, and American political history had taken a new turning. Never has "party feeling in America been more dangerously impassioned" than immediately preceding that election. Although neither Jefferson nor Adams had given speeches or issued statements during the campaign, their followers had engaged in scurrilous propaganda, making and believing ridiculous charges. Furthermore, Jefferson assumed the Presidency with no clear majority. His party had won because it had "manipulated more astutely the method of choosing electors in Virginia and Pennsylvania, and had had the advantage of Aaron Burr's skillful ward-heeling in New York City in the election of the New York legislature in May 1800," or so Samuel F. Bemis later believed. "A change of 250 votes in New York City" in the vote for the legislature "would have made Adams President . . . in the Federal election of November." The narrowness of the Republican victory had been disturbing enough to the country, but the tie vote between Jefferson and Burr had provoked further agitation. When the electoral votes had been counted on February 11, the Republican candidates for President and Vice-President had received the same total, throwing the election into the House of Representatives. With the Federalists voting for Burr, the House cast thirty-five ballots before Jefferson secured a majority. During the balloting, which included one all-night session, wild rumors had disturbed the public peace: Virginia militia were about to march on the capital; an army was being recruited and armed in Philadelphia to take over the federal government; Adams was plotting to make Burr the President.

When an old order passes, as in this case the Federalist Party, and a new order of dominant new life emerges, as the Republican Party, the resulting disruption in familiar patterns of living and thinking tends to produce fear and abrasive apprehension. As Jefferson opened his manuscript and prepared to read his Inaugural Address, he was aware of the rhetorical needs of the occasion and, perhaps, conscious of his deficiencies as a speaker. His speech, noble in sentiment and phrased in language which was felicitous though more oratorical than the Declaration of Independence, was to become one of the two or three most memorable Inaugurals. His purposes were persuasively stated: to tranquilize partisan emotions, to woo those who could be reached, and to set forth in sanguine terms his unlimited faith in the American people and in the national destiny. The text is from *Inaugural Addresses of the Presidents of the United States,* Washington, D.C.; U.S. Government Printing Office, 1961.

FIRST INAUGURAL ADDRESS

Friends and Fellow-Citizens: Called upon to undertake the duties of the first executive office of our country, I avail myself of the presence of that portion of my fellow-citizens which is here assembled to express my grateful thanks for the favor with which they have been pleased to look toward me, to declare a sincere consciousness that the task is above my talents, and that I approach it with those anxious and awful presentiments which the greatness of the charge and the weakness of my powers so justly inspire. A rising nation, spread over a wide and fruitful land, traversing all the seas with the rich productions of their industry, engaged in commerce with nations who feel power and forget right, advancing rapidly to destinies beyond the reach of mortal eye—when I contemplate these transcendent objects, and see the honor, the happiness, and the hopes of this beloved country committed to the issue, and the auspices of this day, I shrink from the contemplation, and humble myself before the magnitude of the undertaking. Utterly, indeed, should I despair did not the presence of many whom I here see remind me that in the other high authorities provided by our Constitution I shall find resources of wisdom, of virtue, and of zeal on which to rely under all difficulties. To you, then, gentlemen, who are charged with the sovereign functions of legislation, and to those associated with you, I look with encouragement for that guidance and support which may enable us to steer with safety the vessel in which we are all embarked amidst the conflicting elements of a troubled world.

During the contest of opinion through which we have passed the animation of discussions and of exertions has sometimes worn an aspect which might impose on strangers unused to think freely and to speak and to write what they think; but this being now decided by the voice of the nation, announced according to the rules of the Constitution, all will, of course, arrange themselves under the will of the law, and unite in common efforts for the common good. All, too, will bear in mind this sacred principle, that though the will of the majority is in all cases to prevail, that will to be rightful must be reasonable; that the minority possesses their equal rights, which equal law must protect, and to violate would be oppression. Let us, then, fellow-citizens, unite with one heart and one mind. Let us restore to social intercourse that harmony and affection without which liberty and even life itself are but dreary things. And let us reflect that, having banished from our land that religious intolerance under which mankind so long bled and suffered, we have yet gained little if we countenance a political intolerance as despotic, as wicked, and capable of as bitter and bloody persecutions. During the throes and convulsions of the ancient world, during the agonizing spasms of infuriated man, seeking through blood and slaughter his long-lost liberty, it was not wonderful that the agitation of the billows should reach even this distant and peaceful shore; that this should be more felt and feared by some and less by others, and should divide opinions as to measures of safety. But every difference of opinion is not a difference of principle. We have called by different names brethren of the same principle. We are all Republicans, we are all Federalists. If there be any among us who would wish to dissolve this Union or to change its republican form, let them stand undisturbed as monuments of the safety with which error of opinion may be tolerated where reason is left free to combat it. I know, indeed, that some honest men fear that a republican government can not be strong, that this Government is not strong enough; but would the honest patriot, in the full tide of successful experiment, abandon a government which has so far kept us free and firm on the theoretic and visionary fear that this Government, the world's best hope, may be possibility want energy to preserve itself? I trust not. I believe this, on the contrary, the strongest Government on earth. I believe it the only one where every man, at the call of the law, would fly to the standard of the law, and would meet invasions of the public order as his own personal concern. Sometimes it is said that man can not be trusted with the government of himself. Can he, then, be trusted with the government of others? Or have we found angels in the forms of kings to govern him? Let history answer this question.

Let us, then, with courage and confidence pursue our own Federal and Republican principles, our attachment to union and representative government. Kindly separated by nature and a wide ocean from the exterminating havoc of one quarter of the globe; too high-minded to endure the degradations of the others; possessing a chosen country, with room enough for our descendants to the thousandth and thousandth generation; entertaining a due sense of our equal right to the use of our own faculties, to the acquisitions of our own industry, to honor and confidence from our fellow-citizens, resulting not from birth, but from our actions and their sense of them; enlightened by a benign religion, professed, indeed, and practiced in various forms, yet all of them inculcating honesty, truth, temperance, gratitude, and the love of man; acknowledging and adoring an overruling Providence, which by all its dispensations proves that it delights in the happiness of man here and his greater happiness hereafter—with all these blessings, what more is necessary to make us a happy and a prosperous people? Still one thing more, fellow-citizens—a wise and frugal Government, which shall restrain men from injuring one another, shall leave them otherwise free to regulate their own pursuits of industry and improvement, and shall not take from the mouth of labor the bread it has earned. This is the sum of good government, and this is necessary to close the circle of our felicities.

About to enter, fellow-citizens, on the exercise of duties which comprehend everything dear and valuable to you, it is proper you should understand what I deem the essential principles of our Government, and consequently those which ought to shape its Administration. I will compress them within the narrowest compass they will bear, stating the general principle, but not all its limitations. Equal and exact justice to all men, of whatever state or persuasion, religious or political; peace, commerce, and honest friendship with all nations, entangling alliances with none; the support of the State governments in all their rights, as the most competent administrations for our domestic concerns and the surest bulwarks against antirepublican tendencies; the preservation of the General Government in its whole constitutional vigor, as the sheet anchor of our peace at home and safety abroad; a jealous care of the right of election by the people—a mild and safe corrective of abuses which are lopped by the sword of revolution where peaceable remedies are unprovided; absolute acquiescence in the decisions of the majority, the vital principle of republics, from which is no appeal but to force, the vital principle and immediate parent of despotism; a well-disciplined militia, our best reliance in peace and for the first moments of war, till regulars may relieve them; the supremacy of the civil over the military authority; economy in the public expense, that labor may be lightly burthened; the honest payment of our debts and sacred preservation of the public faith; encouragement of agriculture, and of commerce as its handmaid; the diffusion of information and arraignment of all abuses at the bar of the public reason; freedom of religion; freedom of the press, and freedom of person under the protection of the habeas corpus, and trial by juries impartially selected. These principles form the bright constellation which has gone before us and guided our steps through an age of revolution and reformation. The wisdom of our sages and blood of our heroes have been devoted to their attainment. They should be the creed of our political faith, the text of civic instruction, the touchstone by which to try the services of those we trust; and should we wander from them in moments of error or of alarm, let us hasten to retrace our steps and to regain the road which alone leads to peace, liberty, and safety.

I repair, then, fellow-citizens, to the post you have assigned me. With experience enough in subordinate offices to have seen the difficulties of this the greatest of all, I have learnt to expect that it will rarely fall to the lot of imperfect man to retire from this station with the reputation and the favor which bring him into it. Without pretentions to that high confidence you reposed in our first and greatest revolutionary character, whose preeminent services had entitled him to the first place in his country's love and destined for him the fairest page in the volume of faithful history, I ask so much confidence only as may give firmness and effect to the legal administration of your affairs. I shall often go wrong through defect of judgment. When right, I shall often be thought wrong by those whose positions will not command a view of the whole ground. I ask your indulgence for my own errors, which will never be intentional, and your support against the errors of others, who may condemn what they would not if seen in all its parts. The approbation implied by your suffrage is a great consolation to me for the past, and my future solicitude will be to retain the good opinion of those who have bestowed it in advance, to conciliate that of others by doing them all the good in my power, and to be instrumental to the happiness and freedom of all.

Relying, then, on the patronage of your good will, I advance with obedience to the work, ready to retire from it whenever you become sensible how much better choice it is in your power to make. And may that Infinite Power which rules the destinies of the universe lead our councils to what is best, and give them a favorable issue for your peace and prosperity.

Exercises

1. In the Introduction, does Jefferson make effective references to the occasion? Is his use of personal proof well-suited to mollifying the opposition and to establishing him as a person of probity and sagacity? How does he employ compliments as a means of establishing rapport? Was the figure of speech involving the steering of a vessel better adapted to Jefferson's audience than it would be to a modern-day audience?

2. Was there hidden meaning in Jefferson's reference to religious intolerance? What was the nature of Jefferson's religious beliefs? What part did religion play in the campaign of 1800?

3. How do you suppose Jefferson's followers reacted to his attempt to placate the opposition, by saying "We are all Republicans—we are all Federalists"? Did this attitude spell trouble for Jefferson as regards the dispensation of Presidential patronage? Does every President face the problem of soliciting the support of opponents without alienating his own followers? Was Jefferson's problem in this regard especially difficult? To what extent did the Republican Party begin to suffer schisms? If such a tendency existed, could the origin be traced to the Inaugural Address?

5. In you opinion, how accurate is Samuel Eliot Morison's statement: "Jefferson's first inaugural address was eighteenth-century idealism rubbed through the sieve of practical politics"? Give reasons for your views.

6. Read the speech orally. Is it easy for you to read it effectively? Is the style better adapted for written or oral communication? Select a paragraph and break it into vocal phrases. Does this improve its oral readability? Try rewriting the paragraph to make it sound more conversational. In terms of the times, the occasion, and the speaker, would your version have been more or less effective than that of Jefferson? Why?

7. Compare the style of this speech with that of John F. Kennedy's Inaugural, presented later in this volume. What similarities do you find? What differences? In your study, consider the following: sentence length, complexity, and variety; word length; colloquialism or directness of language; clarity of expression; rhythm; hortative qualities; specificity; interestingness; use of imagery and figurative language.

8. Did Jefferson's promise to conduct a "wise and frugal government" have special implications for his audience?

9. Jefferson's statement of "the essential principles of our government" is frequently referred to as "eloquent." Do you find it to consist of a long series of similar items with little variety in manner of presentation? If a speaker were to present such a list to you, how would you respond as an analytical listener? In your imagination, try to picturize yourself at the capitol listening to Jefferson. In that situation, how would you perhaps have responded to the above-cited passage?

10. What persuasive purpose did Jefferson seek to achieve by praising George Washington? Why did he not refer to him by name? Since Jefferson had sharp reservations concerning Washington, did this reference violate his personal beliefs?

11. As a result of your background reading, estimate the effectiveness of the Inaugural in establishing a more favorable climate for Jefferson's administration.

Daniel Webster 

"Reception at Madison," delivered in Madison, Indiana, June 1, 1837

AT the time of this speech, Daniel Webster (1782–1852) was at the height of his fame as a statesman and as an orator. As a lawyer he was renowned for his speeches in the Dartmouth College case (1818) and in the White-Knapp murder trial (1830). His debates with Robert Y. Hayne (1830) and John C. Calhoun (particularly in 1833) in the United States Senate had established his reputation as a defender of the Constitution. His commemorative addresses at Plymouth (1820) and at the Bunker Hill Monument (1825), followed by his eulogy of John Adams and Thomas Jefferson (1826), established his reputation as an orator skilled in depicting the glories of American history. His speech on the Greek Revolution, delivered in the House of Representatives (1824), had demonstrated his interest in international affairs. And his numerous campaign addresses had spelled out his conservative political philosophy. Webster arrived in Indiana as indubitably a great man; and the people who gathered to hear him were no doubt honored by his coming to them.

The Hoosiers already had a long and notable history. The area had been penetrated by increasing numbers of French fur traders during the second half of the 17th century, and, following the French and Indian War, had become a part of the British territory soon to be called the Old Northwest. In 1778, George Rogers Clark took possession for the United States. Heavy Indian fighting continued in the region until the defeat of the great Shawnee chief Tecumseh, by William Henry Harrison, at the Battle of Tippecanoe, in 1811. Settlement proceeded rapidly, aided by the congressional decision to build a canal from Lake Erie to the Ohio River. The year before Webster's arrival, the state legislature provided for an elaborate program of internal improvements, consisting largely of canals and railways. The population was increasing steadily, work was plentiful, and the citizens were prospering and hopeful for continuing growth. The importance of the state nationally was enhanced in 1836, when William Henry Harrison was a Whig candidate for the presidency. Although he was defeated by Martin Van Buren, he won enough votes to encourage his renomination in 1840, at which time he was elected. The listeners that gathered to hear Webster must have been conscious not only of his own prominence but also of the growing greatness of their state.

The arrangements for the speech had been carefully and elaborately planned. Webster arrived on the steamboat *Ben Franklin*, which drew up to the wharf amidst a salute of cannon-fire "echoing from hill and glen." Accompanied by Governor Hendricks he was escorted into an "elegant barouche," and was followed to the town square by a parade of prominent citizens from Cincinnati, from Louisville, and from various parts of Indiana. The speaker's platform was decorated with shrubbery and wreaths of flowers, huge portraits of Washington and Lafayette, and with a banner inscribed with a phrase from Webster's speech in reply to Hayne, "Liberty and Union, now and forever, one and inseparable." Every care had been taken to emphasize the importance of the occasion.

The hour-long speech which Webster delivered is perhaps representative of the ideal he described for public speaking—that the style should resemble "elevated conversation." Webster customarily devoted considerable care to revising his speech texts for publication, and he may also have improved the wording of this one before it was printed. As it stands, it exhibits the qualities for which Webster was most noted: clarity of exposition, a style that was simple yet exalted, and a capacity to discuss specific issues in the context of broad historical developments.

Webster's customary manner of speaking was dignified and impressive. He spoke slowly, possibly less than one hundred words a minute. He used few gestures, yet projected the impression of great vitality and intensity of feeling. He felt himself to be a great man, and his audiences agreed with his estimation. How he appeared to his listeners was reported (on another occasion) by Oliver Dyer, who wrote that Webster was "godlike in appearance and in power. . . . The head, the face, the whole appearance of Webster was kingly, majestic, godlike. And when one heard him speak, he found that Webster's voice was just exactly the kind of voice such a man ought to have. It was deep, resonant, mellow, sweet, with a thunder roll in it which, when let out to its full power, was awe inspiring." An Englishman echoed what many felt when he wrote: "No man could be as great as Daniel Webster looked." This was the Webster who stood on the arbored platform in the town square of Madison, surrounded by all the panoply of public approbation, and gave his analysis of the state of the nation in 1837.

The text of the speech is taken from *The Writings and Speeches of Daniel Webster*, National Edition, 1903, Vol. II.

RECEPTION AT MADISON

If, fellow-critizens, I can make myself heard by this numerous assembly, speaking, as I do, in the open air, I will return to you my heartfelt thanks for the kindness you have shown me. I come among you a stranger. On the day before yesterday I placed my foot, for the first time, on the soil of the great and growing State of Indiana. Although I have lived on terms of great intimacy and friendship with several Western gentlemen, members of Congress, among whom is your estimable townsman near me, (Governor Hendricks,) I have never before had an opportunity of seeing and forming an acquaintance for myself with my fellow-citizens of this section of the Union. I travel for this purpose. I confess that I regard with astonishment the evidences of intelligence, enterprise, and refinement everywhere exhibited around me, when I think of the short time that has elapsed since the spot where I stand was a howling wilderness. Since I entered public life, this State was unknown as a political government. All the country west of the Alleghanies and northwest of the Ohio constituted but one Territory, entitled to a single delegate in the counsels of the nation, having the right to speak, but not to vote. Since then, the States of Ohio, Indiana, Illinois, Michigan, and the long strip of country known as the Territory of Wisconsin, have been carved out of it. Indiana, which numbers but twenty years since the commencement of her political existence, contains a population of six hundred thousand, equal to the population of Massachusetts, a State of two hundred years' duration. In age she is an infant; in strength and resources a giant. Her appearance indicates the full vigor of maturity, while, measured by her years, she is yet in the cradle.

Although I reside in a part of the country most remote from you, although I have seen you spring into existence and advance with rapid strides in the march of prosperity and power, until your population has equalled that of my own State, which you far surpass in fertility of soil and mildness of climate; yet these things have excited in me no feelings of dislike, or jealousy, or envy. On the contrary, I have witnessed them with pride and pleasure, when I saw in them the growth of a member of our common country; and with feelings warmer than pride, when I recollect that there are those among you who are bone of my bone and flesh of my flesh, who inherit my name and share my blood. When they came to me for my advice, before leaving their hearths and homes, I did not oppose their desires or suggest difficulties in their paths. I told them, "Go and join your destinies with those of the hardy pioneers of the West, share their hardships, and partake their fortunes; go, and God speed you; only carry with you your own good principles, and whether the sun rises on you, or sets on you, let it warm American hearts in your bosoms."

Though, as I observed, I live in a part of the country most remote from you, fellow-citizens, I have been no inattentive observer of your history and progress. I have heard of the reports made in your legislature, and the acts passed in pursuance thereof. I have traced on the map of your State the routes marked out for extensive turnpikes, railroads, and canals. I have read with pleasure the acts providing for their establishment and completion. I do not pretend to offer you my advice; it would perhaps be presumptuous; but you will permit me to say, that, as far as I have examined them, they are conceived in wisdom, and evince great political skill and foresight. You have commenced at the right point. To open the means of communication, by which man may, when he wishes, see the face of his friend, should be the first work of every government. We may theorize and speculate about it as we please,—we may understand all the metaphysics of politics; but if men are confined to the narrow spot they inhabit, because they have not the means of travelling when they please, they must go back to a state of barbarism. Social intercourse is the corner-stone of good government. The nation that provides no means for the improvement of its communications, has not taken the first step in civilization. Go on, then, as you have begun; prosecute your works with energy and perseverance; be not daunted by imaginary difficulties, be not deterred by exaggerated calculations of their cost. Go on; open your wilderness to the sun; turn up the soil; and in the wide-spread and highly-cultivated fields, the smiling villages, and the busy towns that will spring up from the bosom of the desert, you will reap a rich reward for your investment and industry.

Another of the paramount objects of government, to which I rejoice to see that you have turned your attention, is education. I speak not of college education, nor of academy education, though they are of great importance; I speak of free-school education, common-school education.

Among the luminaries in the sky of New England, the burning lights which throw intelligence and happiness on her people, the first and most brilliant is her system of common schools. I congratulate myself that my first speech on entering public life was in their behalf. Education, to accomplish the ends of good government, should be universally diffused. Open the doors of the school-house to all the children in the land. Let no man have the excuse of poverty for not educating his own offspring. Place the means of education within his reach, and if they remain in ignorance, be it his own reproach. If one object of the expenditure of your revenue be protection against crime, you could not devise a better or cheaper means of obtaining it. Other nations spend their money in providing means for its detection and punishment, but it is the principle of our government to provide for its never occurring. The one acts by *coercion*, the other by *prevention*. On the diffusion of education among the people rest the preservation and perpetuation of our free institutions. I apprehend no danger to our country from a foreign foe. The prospect of a war with any powerful nation is too remote to be a matter of calculation. Besides, there is no nation on earth powerful enough to accomplish our overthrow. Our destruction, should it come at all, will be from another quarter. From the inattention of the people to the concerns of their government, from their carelessness and negligence, I must confess that I do apprehend some danger. I fear that they may place too implicit a confidence in their public servants, and fail properly to scrutinize their conduct; that in this way they may be made the dupes of designing men, and become the instruments of their own undoing. Make them intelligent, and they will be vigilant; give them the means of detecting the wrong, and they will apply the remedy.

The gentleman who has just addressed me in such flattering, but unmerited terms, has been pleased to make kind mention of my devotion to the Constitution, and my humble efforts in its support. I claim no merit on that account. It results from my sense of its surpassing excellences, which must strike every man who attentively and impartially examines it. I regard it as the work of the purest patriots and wisest statesmen that ever existed, aided by the smiles of a benignant Providence; for when we regard it as a system of government growing out of the discordant opinions and conflicting interests of thirteen independent States, it almost appears a Divine interposition in our behalf. I have always, with the utmost zeal and the moderate abilities I possess, striven to prevent its infraction in the slightest particular. I believed, if that bond of union were broken, we should never again be a united people. Where, among all the political thinkers, the constitution-makers and the constitution-menders of the day, could we find a man to make us another? Who would even venture to propose a reunion? Where would be the starting-point, and what the plan? I do not expect miracles to follow each other. No plan could be proposed that would be adopted; the hand that destroys the Constitution rends our Union asunder for ever.

My friend has been pleased to remember, in his address, my humble support of the constitutional right of Congress to improve the navigation of our great internal rivers, and to construct roads through the different States. It is well known that few persons entertain stronger opinions on this subject than myself. Believing that the great object of the Union is to secure the general safety and promote the general welfare, and that the Constitution was designed to point out the means of accomplishing these ends, I have always been in favor of such measures as I deemed for the general benefit, under the restrictions and limitations prescribed by the Constitution itself. I supported them with my voice, and my vote, not because they were for the benefit of the West, but because they were for the benefit of the whole country. That they are local in their advantages, as well as in their construction, is an objection that has been and will be urged against every measure of the kind. In a country so widely extended as ours, so diversified in its interests and in the character of its people, it is impossible that the operation of any measure should affect all alike. Each has its own peculiar interest, whose advancement it seeks; we have the sea-coast, and you the noble river that flows at your feet. So it must ever be. Go to the smallest government in the world, the republic of San Marino, in Italy, possessing a territory of but ten miles square, and you will find its citizens, separated but by a few miles, having some interests which, on account of local situation, are separate and distinct. There is not on the face of the earth a plain, five miles in extent, whose inhabitants are all the same in their pursuits and pleasures. Some will live on a creek, others near a hill, which, when any measure is proposed for the general benefit, will give rise to jarring claims and opposing interests. In such cases, it has always appeared to me that the point to be examined was, whether the principle was general. If the principle were general, although the application might be partial, I cheerfully and zealously gave it my support. When an objection has been made to an appropriation for clearing the snags out of the Ohio River, I have answered it with the question, "Would you not vote for an appropriation to clear the Atlantic Ocean of snags, were the navigation of your coast thus obstructed? The people of the West contribute their portion of the revenue to fortify your sea-coast, and erect piers, and harbors, and light-houses, from which they derive a remote benefit, and why not contribute yours to improve the navigation of a river whose commerce enriches the whole country?"

It may be expected, fellow-citizens, that I should say something on a topic which agitates and distracts the public mind, I mean the deranged state of the currency, and the general stagnation of business. In giving my opinions on this topic, I wish it to be distinctly understood, that I force them on no man. I am an independent man, speaking to independent men. I think for myself; you, of course, enjoy and exercise the same right. I cheerfully concede to every one the liberty of differing with me in sentiment, readily granting that he has as good a chance of being right as myself, perhaps a better. But I have some respect for my character as a public man. The present state of things has grown out of a series of measures, to which I have been in uniform opposition. In speaking of their consequences, I am doing but justice to myself in showing them in justification of my conduct. I am performing a duty to my fellow-citizens, who have a right to know the opinions of every public man. The present state of things is unparalleled in the annals of our country. The general suspension of specie payments by the banks, beginning I know not where, and ending I know not where, but comprehending the whole country, has produced wide-spread ruin and confusion through the land. To you the scene is one as yet of apprehension; to us, of deep distress. You cannot understand, my fellow-citizens, nor can I decsribe it so as to enable you to understand, the embarrassment and suffering which are depressing the spirit and crushing the energies of the people of the sea-girt States of the East. You are agriculturists, you produce what you consume, and always have the means of living within your reach. We depend on others for their agricultural productions; we live by manufactures and commerce, of which credit is the lifeblood. The destruction of credit is the destruction of our means of living. The man who cannot fulfil his daily engagements, or with whom others fail to fulfil theirs, must suffer for his daily bread. And who are those who suffer? Not the rich, for they can generally take care of themselves. Capital is ingenious and farsighted, ready in resources and fertile in expedients to shelter itself from impending storms. Shut it out from one source of increase, and it will find other avenues of profitable investment. It is the industrious, working part of the community, men whose hands have grown hard by holding the plough and pulling the oar, men who depend on their daily labor and their daily pay, who, when the operations of trade and commerce are checked and palsied, have no prospect for themselves and their families but beggary and starvation,—it is these who suffer. All this has been attributed to causes as different as can be imagined; over-trading, over-buying, over-selling, over-speculating, over-production, terms which I acknowledge I do not very well understand. I am at a loss to conceive how a nation can become poor by over-production, producing more than she can sell or consume. I do not see where there has been over-trading, except in public lands; for when everything else was up to such an enormous price, and the public land tied down to one dollar and a quarter an acre, who would not have bought it if he could?

These causes could not have produced all those consequences which have occasioned such general lamentation. They must have proceeded from some other source. And I now request you, my fellow-citizens, to bear witness, that here, in this good city, on the banks of the Ohio, on the first day of June, 1837, beneath the bright sun that is shining upon us, I declare my conscientious conviction that they have proceeded from the measures of the general government in relation to the currency. I make this declaration in no spirit of enmity to its authors; I follow no man with rebukes or reproaches. To reprobate the past will not alleviate the evils of the present. It is the duty of every good citizen to contribute his strength, however feeble, to diminish the burden under which a people groans. To apply the remedy successfully, however, we must first ascertain the causes, character, and extent of the evil.

Let us go back, then, to its origin. Forty-eight years have elapsed since the adoption of our Constitution. For forty years of that time we had a national bank. Its establishment originated in the imperious obligation imposed on every government to furnish its people with a circulating medium for their commerce. No matter how rich the citizen may be in flocks and herds, in houses and lands, if his government does not furnish him a medium of exchange, commerce must be confined to the petty barter suggested by mutual wants and necessities, as they exist in savage life. The history of all commercial countries shows that the precious metals can constitute but a small part of this circulating medium. The extension of commerce creates a system of credit; the transmission of money from one part of the country to the other gives birth to the business of exchange. To keep the value of this medium and the rates of exchange equal and certain, was imperiously required by the necessities of the times when the bank was established. Under the old confederacy, each of the thirteen States established and regulated its own money, which passed for its full value within the State, and was useless the moment it crossed the State border. The little State of Rhode Island, for instance, (I hope no son of hers present will take offence at what I say,) so small that an Indiana man might almost cover her territory with his hand, was crowded with banks. A man might have been rich at Providence, but before he could travel to Boston, forty miles distant, he would starve for want of money to pay for his breakfast.

Had this state of things contunued, some of the provisions of the Constitution would have been of no force or virtue. Of what value to Congress would have been the right to levy taxes, imposts, and duties, and to regulate commerce among different States, and of what effect or consequence the prohibition on the different States of levying and collecting imposts, if each and every one of them had possessed the right of paying her taxes and duties in a currency of her own, which would not pass one hundred miles, perhaps, from the bank whence it was issued? The creation of a national bank presented the surest means of remedying these evils, and accomplishing one of the principal objects of the Constitution, the establishment and maintenance of a currency whose value would be uniform in every part of the country. During the forty years it existed, under the two charters, we had no general suspension of specie payments, as at present. We got along well with it, and I am one of those who are disposed to let *well* alone. I am content to travel along the good old turnpike on which I have journeyed before with comfort and expedition, without turning aside to try a new track. I must confess that I do not possess that soaring self-respect, that lofty confidence in my own political sagacity and foresight, which would induce me to set aside the experience of forty years, and risk the ruin of the country for the sake of an *experiment*. To this is all the distress of the country attributable. This has caused such powerful invasions of bank paper, like sudden and succeeding flights of birds of prey and passage, and the rapid disappearance of specie at its approach. You all know that bank-notes have been almost as plenty as the leaves of the forest in the summer. But of what value are they to the holder, if he is compelled to pay his debts in specie? And who can be expected to pay his debts in this way, when the government has withdrawn the specie from circulation?

You have not yet felt the evil in its full extent. It is mostly in prospect, and you are watching its approach. While you are endeavoring to guard against it, strive to prevent its future recurrence. As you would hunt down, with hound and horn, the wolf who is making nightly havoc of your flocks and herds, pursue and keep down those who would make havoc in your business and property by experiments on our currency.

Although the country has bowed beneath the pressure, I do not fear that it will be broken down and prostrated in the dust. Depress them as it may, the energy and industry of the people will enable them to rise again. We have for a long time carried a load of bad government on our shoulders, and we are still able to bear up under it. But I do not see that, for that reason, we should be willing and eager to carry it. I do not see why it should prevent us from wishing to lessen it as much as possible, if not to throw it off altogether, when we know that we can get along so much easier and faster without it. While we are exerting ourselves with renewed industry and economy to recover from its blighting effects, while we plough the land and plough the sea, let us hasten the return of things to their proper state, by such political measures as will best accomplish the desired end. Let us inform our public servants of our wishes, and pursue such a course as will compel them to obey us.

In conclusion, my fellow-citizens, I return you my thanks for the patience and attention with which you have listened to me, and pray the beneficent Giver of all good, that he may keep you under the shadow of his wing, and continue to bless you with peace and prosperity.

Exercises

1. Webster's persuasive task in this speech was difficult. He was seeking to gain support for his presidential ambitions while addressing an audience that had a candidate from its own state, William Henry Harrison. Webster's general campaign theme was that the party in power had caused a disastrous depression—the Panic of 1837—which indeed depressed the industries and commerce of the East but had not yet disturbed the prosperity of Indiana. He was known to be a spokesman for the propertied, industrial, and banking interests of New England; his listeners were mainly small landholders and farmers. He was famous as a celebrant of the glories of New England and, as he indicated in this speech, was relatively unfamiliar with the western frontier. To what extent, if any, did Webster attempt to contend with these road blocks to persuasion? How do you account for his failure to mention William Henry Harrison? Should he have done so?

2. In his comparison of Indiana with Massachusetts, cite passages which illustrate how he sought to compliment his hosts without detracting from the pride which he felt in Massachusetts. In your judgment, would he have been better advised to have avoided references to his own state?

3. By what means did Webster seek to identify himself with his listeners—even while admitting to them that this was his first visit to Indiana?

4. How did Webster seek to make vivid for his audience the issue of "deranged currency" and economic depression?

5. Note that this is, in a sense, two separate speeches—one on Indiana, the other on national economic problems. Why, in your opinion, did Webster decide to incorporate two such different topics into one address? How did he manage the transition from one topic to the other?

6. Since Indiana did not at that time have a system of free public education, was Webster wise in his comments on this subject? What was his apparent purpose in this passage?

7. Do you find elements in Webster's Introduction and Conclusion which justify the development of two separate themes in this

speech? Does he finally unify them to a degree that makes them one basic theme?

8. Cite passages in this speech which indicate Webster's mastery of oral style. Do you find passages which seem trite, or platitudinous? Are there passages which seem better suited to readers than to listeners? Explain.

9. Note ways in which this speech resembles present-day political campaign speeches. Do you find aspects of it which our contemporary politicians might imitate with advantage? Judging from this speech, how might Webster have improved his own political campaigning?

10. Cite passages from this speech which suggest Webster's basic conservatism. Could he have phrased these views in a manner more appealing to western settlers, while still maintaining his own convictions? How?

11. From your study of this speech, how would you characterize Webster's personality? Do you find evidence to justify the high regard in which he was held by many of his countrymen? Do you find factors in this speech which suggest possible reasons why he failed in his ambition to be elected President?

12. In comparing this speech with others in this volume, do you find evidence to indicate why Webster is generally considered to be one of America's greatest orators? Explain.

13. Does this speech illustrate the principle stated elsewhere by Webster as a guiding standard for public speakers: "It is a noble faculty of our nature which enables us to connect our thoughts, our sympathies and our happinesss with what is distant in place and time; and, looking before and after, to hold communion at once with our ancestors and our posterity." What other speakers included in this volume especially well illustrate this capacity?

Ralph Waldo Emerson

"The American Scholar," delivered to the Phi Beta Kappa Society, at Harvard, August 31, 1837

It was natural for Ralph Waldo Emerson (1803–1882) to attend Harvard College and the Harvard Divinity School. His New England ancestors had traditionally been clergymen, including Peter Buckeley, who helped found Concord, Massachusetts; his grandfather, who is said to have watched the battle of Concord from a window in his study only a slingshot distance from old North Bridge; and his father, who was minister of the First Church, Boston, before his untimely death in 1811. It was more than family tradition, however, that enticed Emerson into the pulpit, as minister of the Second Church of Boston, 1829. He had felt himself called because of his "passionate love for the strains of eloquence," and because of his spiritual ardour which pushed him to assist others toward lives of greater virtue and character. Much as other Unitarian ministers of this time and earlier had rebelled against the irrationality and determinism of Calvinism, Emerson soon found himself at increasing odds with the rationalism and traditional forms of Unitarianism. Resigning from his pastorate in 1832, he was free to seek a broader sphere of influence more congenial to his nature: the life of public lecturer and man of letters.

The wellspring of his fame and influence was a trilogy of personal manifestoes, produced in a three-year period. In 1836 he published *Nature*, a small book which expressed the essentials of a revolutionary philosophy which was to be his theme for nearly a half century of speaking and writing. During the next two years he attracted considerable attention and some notoriety by his "American

Scholar Address" and his "Divinity School Address," delivered to the graduating class at the Harvard Divinity School. About the time of the publication of *Nature,* Emerson began to attract around him a loosely knit group of young New England intellectuals, soon to be known as the "Transcendentalists." Greatly stimulated by fresh ideas which originated with German idealists and were spread by Carlyle, Coleridge, Wordsworth, and other English writers, Emerson and his fellow transcendentalists sought a deeper, more spiritual, more moving significance in life than could be found in the pragmatic values of a business-oriented society. He considered that the most meaningful truths could not be discovered, much less appreciated, by logic and factual experience. Such truths transcended common sense and reason and were discoverable only by the individual through a personal revelation, supplied by intuition or spiritual "hunches." To Emerson, the swiftly developing material prosperity of the country threatened man's spiritual and intellectual values. "Things are in the saddle," he cried, "and ride mankind." His emphasis was on the individual, upon the goodness and rightness—even Divineness—of human instincts, upon self-reliance, upon the emancipation of American thought from the domination of Europe, upon the immanence of God in the hearts of men, upon the sovereignty of ideas, upon the goodness of change, upon the power of man to shape the universe, and upon the creative sufficiency of man to draw the essence of meaning from the "facts of the consciousness" rather than from the "data of the senses." His orientation was the inward probing of Platonist idealism rather than the outward grounding in experience of Franklin materialism.

Although a substantial part of his income was derived from lecturing about the country during the span of three decades, and although he was a keen student and critic of oral eloquence, Emerson never developed the voice, bearing, or polish of the skilled platform speaker. He never acquired the ability to speak extemporaneously or to read from manuscript with the immediacy of communication which was characteristic of the more popular Henry Ward Beecher and Robert G. Ingersoll. Nevertheless, he had an engaging, quiet sincerity and power of character which, along with striking ideas and an aphoristic style, made him quite successful, especially with the intellectual classes.

In his essays and speeches his typical method of development was to cluster wise and vividly concrete sayings around a central theme, rather than to unravel a continuous pattern of argument. According to James Truslow Adams, Emerson's thinking was "a bit thin and puerile" because he "trusted too much to that spirit of spontaneity, of the 'spontaneous glance,' rather than to the harder process of scholarship and thinking through coherently." Perhaps, however, Emerson's significance as a man thinking and speaking lies in a direction unrecognized by Adams. Ralph Henry Gabriel suggests that Emerson impressed his mark upon the American spirit "because he preached a philosophy of individualism that not only seemed to set men free, but to provide them with dynamic, creative energy. He gave the doctrine of the free individual sharpness of definition, causing it to emerge, with the clarity of an etching, from the cloudy background of half-formulated ideas."

One of Emerson's most important efforts to "set men free" was his "American Scholar" address. In the midst of the panic of 1837, just after he had recorded in his diary that there were "loud cracks in the social edifice" and that "young men have no hope," he received an invitation to address the annual meeting of Harvard's chapter of Phi Beta Kappa. On July 29, he entered in his journal some preliminary thoughts for the speech, and on August 18 (just two weeks before the event) he recorded what he intended as his theme: "to arouse young men . . . to a worthier view of . . . the scholar's function. . . . To arouse the intellect; to keep it erect and sound; to keep admiration in the hearts of the people; to keep the eye upon its spiritual aims." Although only a few more than two hundred persons were in the small meetinghouse, Emerson's portrayal of the liberated intellect has been for generations of Americans an "intellectual Declaration of Independence."

The text of the speech is from *Complete Works of Ralph Waldo Emerson*, ed. Edward Waldo Emerson, New York: Wm. H. Wise, 1929, Vol. I, and has been reprinted by special permission of the present copyright holder, Houghton Mifflin Company.

THE AMERICAN SCHOLAR

Mr. President and Gentlemen: I greet you on the recommencement of our literary year. Our anniversary is one of hope, and, perhaps, not enough of labor. We do not meet for games of strength or skill, for the recitation of histories, tragedies, and odes, like the ancient Greeks; for parliaments of love and poesy, like the Troubadours; nor for the advancement of science, like our contemporaries in the British and European capitals. Thus far, our holiday has been simply a friendly sign of the survival of the love of letters amongst a people too busy to give to letters any more. As such it is precious as the sign of an indestructible instinct. Perhaps the time is already come when it ought to be, and will be, something else; when the sluggard intellect of this continent will look from under its iron lids and fill the postponed expectation of the world with something better than the exertions of mechanical skill. Our day of dependence, our long apprenticeship to the learning of other lands, draws to a close. The millions that around us are rushing into life, cannot always be fed on the sere remains of foreign harvests. Events, actions arise, that must be sung, that will sing themselves. Who can doubt that poetry will revive and lead in a new age, as the star in the constellation Harp, which now flames in our zenith, astronomers announce, shall one day be the pole-star for a thousand years?

In this hope I accept the topic which not only usage but the nature of our association seem to prescribe to this day,—the American Scholar. Year by year we come up hither to read one more chapter of his biography. Let us inquire what light new days and events have thrown on his character and his hopes.

It is one of those fables which out of an unknown antiquity convey an unlooked-for wisdom, that the gods, in the beginning, divided Man into men, that he might be more helpful to himself; just as the hand was divided into fingers, the better to answer its end.

The old fable covers a doctrine ever new and sublime; that there is One Man,—present to all particular men only partially, or through one faculty; and that you must take the whole society to find the whole man. Man is not a farmer, or a professor, or an engineer, but he is all. Man is priest, and scholar, and statesman, and producer, and soldier. In the *divided* or social state these functions are parcelled out to individuals, each of whom aims to do his stint of the joint work, whilst each other performs his. The fable implies that the individual, to possess himself, must sometimes return from his own labor to embrace all the other laborers. But, unfortunately, this original unit, this fountain of power, has been so distributed to multitudes, has been so minutely subdivided and peddled out, that it is spilled into drops, and cannot be gathered. The state of society is one in which the members have suffered amputation from the trunk, and strut about so many walking monsters,—a good finger, a neck, a stomach, an elbow, but never a man.

Man is thus metamorphosed into a thing, into many things. The planter, who is Man sent out into the field to gather food, is seldom cheered by any idea of the true dignity of his ministry. He sees his bushel and his cart, and nothing beyond, and sinks into the farmer, instead of

Man on the farm. The tradesman scarcely ever gives an ideal worth to his work, but is ridden by the routine of his craft, and the soul is subject to dollars. The priest becomes a form; the attorney a statute-book; the mechanic a machine; the sailor a rope of the ship.

In this distribution of functions the scholar is the delegated intellect. In the right state he is *Man Thinking*. In the degenerate state, when the victim of society, he tends to become a mere thinker, or still worse, the parrot of other men's thinking.

In this view of him, as Man Thinking, the theory of his office is contained. Him Nature solicits with all her placid, all her monitory pictures; him the past instructs; him the future invites. Is not indeed every man a student, and do not all things exist for the student's behoof? And, finally, is not the true scholar the only true master? But the old oracle said, "All things have two handles: beware of the wrong one." In life, too often, the scholar errs with mankind and forfeits his privilege. Let us see him in his school, and consider him in reference to the main influences he receives.

I. The first in time and the first in importance of the influences upon the mind is that of nature. Every day, the sun; and, after sunset, Night and her stars. Ever the winds blow; ever the grass grows. Every day, men and women, conversing–beholding and beholden. The scholar is he of all men whom this spectacle most engages. He must settle its value in his mind. What is nature to him? There is never a beginning, there is never an end, to the inexplicable continuity of this web of God, but always circular power returning into itself. Therein it resembles his own spirit, whose beginning, whose ending, he never can find,–so entire, so boundless. Far too as her splendors shine, system on system shooting like rays, upward, downward, without centre, without circumference,–in the mass and in the particle, Nature hastens to render account of herself to the mind. Classification begins. To the young mind every thing is individual, stands by itself. By and by, it finds how to join two things and see in them one nature; then three, then three thousand; and so, tyrannized over by its own unifying instinct, it goes on tying things together, diminishing anomalies, discovering roots running under ground whereby contrary and remote things cohere and flower out from one stem. It presently learns that since the dawn of history there has been a constant accumulation and classifying of facts. But what is classification but the perceiving that these objects are not chaotic, and are not foreign, but have a law which is also a law of the human mind? The astronomer discovers that geometry, a pure abstraction of the human mind, is the measure of planetary motion. The chemist finds proportions and intelligible method throughout matter; and science is nothing but the finding of analogy, identity, in the most remote parts. The ambitious soul sits down before each refractory fact; one after another reduces all strange constitutions, all new powers, to their class and their law, and goes on forever to animate the last fibre of organization, the outskirts of nature, by insight.

Thus to him, to this schoolboy under the bending dome of day, is suggested that he and it proceed from one root; one is leaf and one is flower; relation, sympathy, stirring in every vein. And what is that root? Is not that the soul of his soul? A thought too bold; a dream too wild. Yet when the spiritual light shall have revealed the law of more earthly natures,—when he has learned to worship the soul, and to see that the natural philosophy that now is, is only the first gropings of its gigantic hand, he shall look forward to an ever expanding knowledge as to a becoming creator. He shall see that nature is the opposite of the soul, answering to it part for part. One is seal and one is print. Its beauty is the beauty of his own mind. Its laws are the laws of his own mind. Nature then becomes to him the measure of his attainments. So much of nature as he is ignorant of, so much of his own mind does he not yet possess. And, in fine, the ancient precept, "Know thyself," and the modern precept, "Study nature," becomes at last one maxim.

II. The next great influence into the spirit of the scholar is the mind of the Past,—in whatever form, whether of literature, of art, of institutions, that mind is inscribed. Books are the best type of the influence of the past, and perhaps we shall get at the truth,—learn the amount of this influence more conveniently,—by considering their value alone.

The theory of books is noble. The scholar of the first age received into him the world around; brooded thereon; gave it the new arrangement of his own mind, and uttered it again. It came into him life; it went out from him truth. It came to him short-lived actions; it went out from him immortal thoughts. It came to him business; it went from him poetry. It was dead fact; now, it is quick thought. It can stand, and it can go. It now endures, it now flies, it now inspires. Precisely in proportion to the depth of mind from which it issued, so high does it soar, so long does it sing.

Or, I might say, it depends on how far the process had gone, of transmuting life into truth. In proportion to the completeness of the distillation, so will the purity and imperishableness of the product be. But none is quite perfect. As no air-pump can by any means make a perfect vacuum, so neither can any artist entirely exclude the conventional, the local, the perishable from his book, or write a book of pure thought, that shall be as efficient, in all respects, to a remote posterity, as to contemporaries, or rather to the second age. Each age, it is found, must write its own books; or rather, each generation for the next succeeding. The books of an older period will not fit this.

Yet hence arises a grave mischief. The sacredness which attaches to the act of creation, the act of thought, is transferred to the record. The poet chanting was felt to be a divine man: henceforth the chant is divine also. The writer was a just and wise spirit: henceforward it is settled the book is perfect; as love of the hero corrupts into worship of his statue. Instantly the book becomes noxious: the guide is a tyrant. The sluggish and perverted mind of the multitude, slow to open to the incursions of Reason, having once so opened, having once received this book, stands upon it, and makes an outcry if it is disparaged. Colleges are built on it. Books are written on it by thinkers, not by Man Thinking; by men of talent, that is, who start wrong, who set out from accepted dogmas, not from their own sight of principles. Meek young men grow up in libraries, believing it their duty to accept the views which Cicero, which Locke, which Bacon, have given; forgetful that Cicero, Locke, and Bacon were only young men in libraries when they wrote these books.

Hence, instead of Man Thinking, we have the bookworm. Hence the book-learned class, who value books, as such; not as related to nature and the human constitution, but as making a sort of Third Estate with the world and the soul. Hence the restorers of readings, the emendators, the bibliomaniacs of all degrees.

Books are the best of things, well used; abused, among the worst. What is the right use? What is the one end which all means go to effect? They are for nothing but to inspire. I had better never see a book than to be warped by its attraction clean out of my own orbit, and made a satellite instead of a system. The one thing in the world, of value, is the active soul. This every man is entitled to; this every man contains within him, although in almost all men obstructed and as yet unborn. The soul active sees absolute truth and utters truth, or creates. In this action it is genius; not the privilege of here and there a favorite, but the sound estate of every man. In its essence it is progressive. The book, the college, the school of art, the institution of any kind, stop with some past utterance of genius. This is good, say they,—let us hold by this. They pin me down. They look backward and not forward. But genius looks forward: the eyes of man are set in his forehead, not in his hindhead: man hopes: genius creates. Whatever talents may be, if the man create not, the pure efflux of the Deity is not his;—cinders and smoke there may be, but not yet flame. There are creative manners, there are creative actions, and creative words; manners, actions, words, that is, indicative of no custom or authority, but springing spontaneous from the mind's own sense of good and fair.

On the other part, instead of being its own seer, let it receive from another mind its truth, though it were in torrents of light, without periods of solitude, inquest, and self-recovery, and a fatal disservice is done. Genius is always sufficiently the enemy of genius by overinfluence. The literature of every nation bears me witness. The English dramatic poets have Shakespearized now for two hundred years.

Undoubtedly there is a right way of reading, so it be sternly subordinated. Man Thinking must not be subdued by his instruments. Books are for the scholar's idle times. When he can read God directly, the hour is too precious to be wasted in other men's transcripts of their readings. But when the intervals of darkness come, as come they must,—when the sun is hid and the stars withdraw their shining,—we repair to the lamps which were kindled by their ray, to guide our steps to the East again, where the dawn is. We hear, that we may speak. The Arabian proverb says, "A fig tree, looking on a fig tree, becometh fruitful."

It is remarkable, the character of the pleasure we derive from the best books. They impress us with the conviction that one nature wrote and the same reads. We read the verses of one of the great English poets, of Chaucer, of Marvell, of Dryden, with the most modern joy,—with a pleasure, I mean, which is in great part caused by the abstraction of all *time* from their verses. There is some awe mixed with the joy of our surprise, when this poet, who lived in some past world, two or three hundred years ago, says that which lies close to my own soul, that which I also had well-nigh thought and said. But for the evidence thence afforded to the philosphical doctrine of the identity of all minds, we should suppose some pre-established harmony, some foresight of souls that were to be, and some preparation of stores for their future wants, like the fact observed in insects, who lay up food before death for the young grub they shall never see.

I would not be hurried by any love of system, by any exaggeration of instincts, to underrate the Book. We all know, that as the human body can be nourished on any food, though it were boiled grass and the broth of shoes, so the human mind can be fed by any knowledge. And great and heroic men have existed who had almost no other information than by the printed page. I only would say that it needs a strong head to bear that diet. One must be an inventor to read well. As the proverb says, "He that would bring home the wealth of the Indies, must carry out the wealth of the Indies." There is then creative reading as well as creative writing. When the mind is braced by labor and invention, the page of whatever book we read becomes luminous with manifold allusion. Every sentence is doubly significant, and the sense of our author is as broad as the world. We then see, what is always true, that as the seer's hour of vision is short and rare among heavy days and months, so is its record, perchance, the least part of his volume. The discerning will read, in his Plato or Shakespeare, only that least part,—only the authentic utterances of the oracle;—all the rest he rejects, were it never so many times Plato's and Shakespeare's.

Of course there is a portion of reading quite indispensable to a wise man. History and exact science he must learn by laborious reading. Colleges, in like manner, have their indispensable office,—to teach elements. But they can only highly serve us when they aim not to drill, but to create; when they gather from far every ray of various genius to their hospitable halls, and by the concentrated fires, set the hearts of their youth on flame. Thought and knowledge are natures in which apparatus and pretension avail nothing. Gowns and pecuniary foundations, though of towns of gold, can never countervail the least sentence or syllable of wit. Forget this, and our American colleges will recede in their public importance, whilst they grow richer every year.

III. There goes in the world a notion that the scholar should be a recluse, a valetudinarian,—as unfit for any handiwork or public labor as a penknife for an axe. The so-called "practical men" sneer at speculative men, as if, because they speculate or *see*, they could do nothing. I have heard it said that the clergy,—who are always, more universally than any other class, the scholars of their day,—are addressed as women; that the rough, spontaneous conversation of men they do not hear, but only a mincing and diluted speech. They are often virtually disfranchised; and indeed there are advocates for their celibacy. As far as this is true of the studious classes, it is not just and wise. Action is with the scholar subordinate, but it is essential. Without it he is not yet man. Without it thought can never ripen into truth. Whilst the world hangs before the eye as a cloud of beauty, we cannot even see its beauty. Inaction is cowardice, but there can be no scholar without the heroic mind. The preamble of thought, the transition through which it passes from the unconscious to the conscious, is action. Only so much do I know, as I have lived. Instantly we know whose words are loaded with life, and whose not.

The world,—this shadow of the soul, or *other me*,—lies wide around. Its attractions are the keys which unlock my thoughts and make me acquainted with myself. I run eagerly into this resounding tumult. I grasp the hands of those next me, and take my place in the ring to suffer and to work, taught by an instinct that so shall the dumb abyss be vocal with speech. I pierce its order; I dissipate its fear; I dispose of it within the circuit of my expanding life. So much only of life as I know by experience, so much of the wilderness have I vanquished and planted, or so far have I extended my being, my dominion. I do not see how any man can afford, for the sake of his nerves and his nap, to spare any action in which he can partake. It is pearls and rubies to his discourse. Drudgery, calamity, exasperation, want, are instructors in eloquence and wisdom. The true scholar grudges every opportunity of action past by, as a loss of power. It is the raw material out of which the intellect moulds her splendid products. A strange process too, this by which experience is converted into thought, as a mulberry leaf is converted into satin. The manufacture goes forward at all hours.

The actions and events of our childhood and youth are now matters of calmest observation. They lie like fair pictures in the air. Not so with our recent actions,–with the business which we now have in hand. On this we are quite unable to speculate. Our affections as yet circulate through it. We no more feel or know it than we feel the feet, or the hand, or the brain of our body. The new deed is yet a part of life,– remains for a time immersed in our unconscious life. In some contemplative hour it detaches itself from the life like a ripe fruit, to become a thought of the mind. Instantly it is raised, transfigured; the corruptible has put on incorruption. Henceforth it is an object of beauty, however base its origin and neighborhood. Observe too the impossibility of antedating this act. In its grub state, it cannot fly, it cannot shine, it is a dull grub. But suddenly, without observation, the selfsame thing unfurls beautiful wings, and is an angel of wisdom. So is there no fact, no event, in our private history, which shall not, sooner or later, lose its adhesive, inert form, and astonish us by soaring from our body into the empyrean. Cradle and infancy, school and playground, the fear of boys, and dogs, and ferules, the love of little maids and berries, and many another fact that once filled the whole sky, are gone already; friend and relative, profession and party, town and country, nation and world, must also soar and sing.

Of course, he who has put forth his total strength in fit actions has the richest return of wisdom. I will not shut myself out of this globe of action, and transplant an oak into a flower-pot, there to hunger and pine; nor trust the revenue of some single faculty, and exhaust one vein of thought; much like those Savoyards, who, getting their livelihood by carving shepherds, shepherdesses, and smoking Dutchmen, for all Europe, went out one day to the mountain to find stock, and discovered that they had whittled up the last of their pine trees. Authors we have, in numbers, who have written out their vein, and who, moved by a commendable prudence, sail for Greece or Palestine, follow the trapper into the prairie, or ramble round Algiers, to replenish their merchantable stock.

If it were only for a vocabulary, the scholar would be covetous of action. Life is our dictionary. Years are well spent in country labors; in town; in the insight into trades and manufactures; in frank intercourse with many men and women; in science; in art; to the one end of mastering in all their facts a language by which to illustrate and embody our perceptions. I learn immediately from any speaker how much he has already lived, through the poverty or the splendor of his speech. Life lies behind us as the quarry from whence we get tiles and copestones for the masonry of today. This is the way to learn grammar. College and books only copy the language which the field and the work-yard made.

But the final value of action, like that of books, and better than books, is that it is a resource. That great principle of Undulation in nature, that shows itself in the inspiring and expiring of the breath; in desire and satiety; in the ebb and flow of the sea; in day and night; in heat and cold; and, as yet more deeply ingrained in every atom and every fluid, is known to us under the name of Polarity,—these "fits of easy transmission and reflection," as Newton called them, are the law of nature because they are the law of spirit.

The mind now thinks, now acts, and each fit reproduces the other. When the artist has exhausted his materials, when the fancy no longer paints, when thoughts are no longer apprehended and books are a weariness,—he has always the resource *to live.* Character is higher than intellect. Thinking is the function. Living is the functionary. The stream retreats to its source. A great soul will be strong to live, as well as strong to think. Does he lack organ or medium to impart his truths? He can still fall back on this elemental force of living them. This is a total act. Thinking is a partial act. Let the grandeur of justice shine in his affairs. Let the beauty of affection cheer his lowly roof. Those "far from fame," who dwell and act with him, will feel the force of his constitution in the doings and passages of the day better than it can be measured by any public and designed display. Time shall teach him that the scholar loses no hour which the man lives. Herein he unfolds the sacred germ of his instinct, screened from influence. What is lost in seemliness is gained in strength. Not out of those on whom systems of education have exhausted their culture, comes the helpful giant to destroy the old or to build the new, but out of unhandselled savage nature; out of terrible Druids and Berserkers come at last Alfred and Shakespeare.

I hear therefore with joy whatever is beginning to be said of the dignity and necessity of labor to every citizen. There is virtue yet in the hoe and the spade, for learned as well as for unlearned hands. And labor is everywhere welcome; always we are invited to work; only be this limitation observed, that a man shall not for the sake of wider activity sacrifice any opinion to the popular judgments and modes of action.

I have now spoken of the education of the scholar by nature, by books, and by action. It remains to say somewhat of his duties.

They are such as become Man Thinking. They may all be comprised in self-trust. The office of the scholar is to cheer, to raise, and to guide men by showing them facts amidst appearances. He plies the slow, unhonored, and unpaid task of observation. Flamsteed and Herschel, in their glazed observatories, may catalogue the stars with the praise of all men, and the results being splendid and useful, honor is sure. But he, in his private observatory, cataloguing obscure and nebulous stars of the human mind, which as yet no man has thought of as such,—watching days and months sometimes for a few facts; correcting still his old records;—must relinquish display and immediate fame. In the long period of his preparation he must betray often an ignorance and shiftlessness in popular arts, incurring the disdain of the able who shoulder him aside.

Long he must stammer in his speech; often forego the living for the dead. Worse yet, he must accept—how often!—poverty and solitude. For the ease and pleasure of treading the old road, accepting the fashions, the education, the religion of society, he takes the cross of making his own, and, of course, the self-accusation, the faint heart, the frequent uncertainty and loss of time, which are the nettles and tangling vines in the way of the self-relying and self-directed; and the state of virtual hostility in which he seems to stand to society, and especially to educated society. For all this loss and scorn, what offset? He is to find consolation in exercising the highest functions of human nature. He is one who raises himself from private considerations and breathes and lives on public and illustrious thoughts. He is the world's eye. He is the world's heart. He is to resist the vulgar prosperity that retrogrades ever to barbarism, by preserving and communicating heroic sentiments, noble biographies, melodious verse, and the conclusions of history. Whatsoever oracles the human heart, in all emergencies, in all solemn hours, has uttered as its commentary on the world of actions,—these he shall receive and impart. And whatsoever new verdict Reason from her inviolable seat pronounces on the passing men and events of today,—this he shall hear and promulgate.

These being his functions, it becomes him to feel all confidence in himself, and to defer never to the popular cry. He and he only knows the world. The world of any moment is the merest appearance. Some great decorum, some fetish of a government, some ephemeral trade, or war, or man, is cried up by half mankind and cried down by the other half, as if all depended on this particular up or down. The odds are that the whole question is not worth the poorest thought which the scholar has lost in listening to the controversy. Let him not quit his belief that a popgun is a popgun, though the ancient and honorable of the earth affirm it to be the crack of doom. In silence, in steadiness, in severe abstraction, let him hold by himself; add observation to observation, patient of neglect, patient of reproach, and bide his own time,—happy enough if he can satisfy himself alone that this day he has seen something truly. Success treads on every right step. For the instinct is sure, that prompts him to tell his brother what he thinks. He then learns that in going down into the secrets of his own mind he has descended into the secrets of all minds. He learns that he who has mastered any law in his private thoughts, is master to that extent of all men whose language he speaks, and of all into whose language his own can be translated. The poet, in utter solitude remembering his spontaneous thoughts and recording them, is found to have recorded that which men in crowded cities find true for them also. The orator distrusts at first the fitness of his frank confessions, his want of knowledge of the persons he addresses, until he finds that he is the complement of his hearers;—that they drink his words because he fulfils for them their own nature; the deeper he dives into his privatest, secretest presentment, to his wonder he finds that is the most acceptable, most public, and universally true. The people delight in it; the better part of every man feels. This is my music; this is myself.

In self-trust all the virtues are comprehended. Free should the scholar be,—free and brave. Free even to the definition of freedom, "without any hindrance that does not arise out of his own constitution." Brave; for fear is a thing which a scholar by his very function puts behind him. Fear always springs from ignorance. It is a shame to him if his tranquillity, amid dangerous times, arise from the presumption that like children and women his is a protected class; or if he seek a temporary peace by the diversion of his thoughts from politics or vexed questions, hiding his head like an ostrich in the flowering bushes, peeping into microscopes, and turning rhymes, as a boy whistles to keep his courage up. So is the danger a danger still; so is the fear worse. Manlike let him turn and face it. Let him look into its eye and search its nature, inspect its origin,—see the whelping of this lion,—which lies no great way back; he will then find in himself a perfect comprehension of its nature and extent; he will have made his hands meet on the other side, and can henceforth defy it and pass on superior. The world is his who can see through its pretension. What deafness, what stone-blind custom, what overgrown error you behold is there only by sufferance,—by your sufferance. See it to be a lie, and you have already dealt it its mortal blow.

Yes, we are the cowed,—we the trustless. It is a mischievous notion that we are come late into nature; that the world was finished a long time ago. As the world was plastic and fluid in the hands of God, so it is ever to so much of his attributes as we bring to it. To ignorance and sin, it is flint. They adapt themselves to it as they may; but in proportion as a man has any thing in him divine, the firmament flows before him and takes his signet and form. Not he is great who can alter matter, but he who can alter my state of mind. They are the kings of the world who give the color of their present thought to all nature and all art, and persuade men by the cheerful serenity of their carrying the matter, that this thing which they do is the apple which the ages have desired to pluck, now at last ripe, and inviting nations to the harvest. The great man makes the great thing. Wherever Macdonald sits, there is the head of the table. Linnæus makes botany the most alluring of studies, and wins it from the farmer and the herb-woman; Davy, chemistry; and Cuvier, fossils. The day is always his who works in it with serenity and great aims. The unstable estimates of men crowd to him whose mind is filled with a truth, as the heaped waves of the Atlantic follow the moon.

For this self-trust, the reason is deeper than can be fathomed,—darker than can be enlightened. I might not carry with me the feeling of my audience in stating my own belief. But I have already shown the ground of my hope, in adverting to the doctrine that man is one. I believe man has been wronged; he has wronged himself. He has almost lost the light that can lead him back to his prerogatives. Men are become of no account. Men in history, men in the world of to-day, are bugs, are spawn, and are called "the mass" and "the herd." In a century, in a millennium, one or two men; that is to say, one or two approximations to the right state of every man. All the rest behold in the hero or the poet their own green and crude being,—ripened; yes, and are content to be less, so *that* may attain to its full stature. What a testimony, full of grandeur, full of pity, is borne to the demands of his own nature, by the poor clansman, the poor partisan, who rejoices in the glory of his chief. The poor and the low find some amends to their immense moral capacity, for their acquiescence in a political and social inferiority. They are content to be brushed like flies from the path of a great person, so that justice shall be done by him to that common nature which it is the dearest desire of all to see enlarged and glorified. They sun themselves in the great man's light, and feel it to be their own element. They cast the dignity of man from their downtrod selves upon the shoulders of a hero, and will perish to add one drop of blood to make that great heart beat, those giant sinews combat and conquer. He lives for us, and we live in him.

Men, such as they are, very naturally seek money or power; and power because it is as good as money,—the "spoils," so called, "of office." And why not? for they aspire to the highest, and this, in their sleep-walking, they dream is highest. Wake them and they shall quit the false good and leap to the true, and leave governments to clerks and desks. This revolution is to be wrought by the gradual domestication of the idea of Culture. The main enterprise of the world for splendor, for extent, is the upbuilding of a man. Here are the materials strewn along the ground. The private life of one man shall be a more illustrious monarchy, more formidable to its enemy, more sweet and serene in its influence to its friend, than any kingdom in history. For a man, rightly viewed, comprehendeth the particular natures of all men. Each philosopher, each bard, each actor has only done for me, as by a delegate, what one day I can do for myself. The books which once we valued more than the apple of the eye, we have quite exhausted. What is that but saying that we have come up with the point of view which the universal mind took through the eyes of one scribe; we have been that man, and have passed on. First, one, then another, we drain all cisterns, and waxing greater by all these supplies, we crave a better and more abundant food. The man has never lived that can feed us ever. The human mind cannot be enshrined in a person who shall set a barrier on any one side to this unbounded, unboundable empire. It is one central fire, which, flaming now out of the lips of Etna, lightens the capes of Sicily, and now out of the throat of Vesuvius, illuminates the towers and vineyards of Naples. It is one light which beams out of a thousand stars. It is one soul which animates all men.

But I have dwelt perhaps tediously upon this abstraction of the Scholar. I ought not to delay longer to add what I have to say of nearer reference to the time and to this country.

Historically, there is thought to be a difference in the ideas which predominate over successive epochs, and there are data for marking the genius of the Classic, of the Romantic, and now of the Reflective or Philosophical age. With the views I have intimated of the oneness or the identity of the mind through all individuals, I do not much dwell on these differences. In fact, I believe each individual passes through all three. The boy is a Greek; the youth, romantic; the adult, reflective. I deny not, however, that a revolution in the leading idea may be distinctly enough traced.

Our age is bewailed as the age of Introversion. Must that needs be evil? We, it seems, are critical; we are embarrassed with second thoughts; we cannot enjoy any thing for hankering to know whereof the pleasure consists; we are lined with eyes; we see with our feet; the time is infected with Hamlet's unhappiness,—

"Sicklied o'er with the pale cast of thought."

It is so bad then? Sight is the last thing to be pitied. Would we be blind? Do we fear lest we should outsee nature and God, and drink truth dry? I look upon the discontent of the literary class as a mere announcement of the fact that they find themselves not in the state of mind of their fathers, and regret the coming state as untried; as a boy dreads the water before he has learned that he can swim. If there is any period one would desire to be born in, is it not the age of Revolution; when the old and the new stand side by side and admit of being compared; when the energies of all men are searched by fear and by hope; when the historic glories of the old can be compensated by the rich possibilities of the new era? This time, like all times, is a very good one, if we but know what to do with it.

I read with some joy of the auspicious signs of the coming days, as they glimmer already through poetry and art, through philosophy and science, through church and state.

One of these signs is the fact that the same movement which effected the elevation of what was called the lowest class in the state, assumed in literature a very marked and as benign an aspect. Instead of the sublime and beautiful, the near, the low, the common, was explored and poetized. That which had been negligently trodden under foot by those who were harnessing and provisioning themselves for long journeys into far countries, is suddenly found to be richer than all foreign parts. The literature of the poor, the feelings of the child, the philosophy of the street, the meaning of household life, are the topics of the time. It is a great stride. It is a sign—is it not?—of new vigor when the extremities are made active, when currents of warm life run into the hands and the feet. I ask not for the great, the remote, the romantic; what is doing in Italy or Arabia; what is Greek art, or Provençal minstrelsy; I embrace the common, I explore and sit at the feet of the familiar, the low. Give me insight into to-day, and you may have the antique and future worlds. What would we really know the meaning of? The meal in the firkin; the milk in the pan; the ballad in the street; the news of the boat; the glance of the eye; the form and the gait of the body:—show me the ultimate reason of these matters; show me the sublime presence of the highest spiritual cause lurking, as always it does lurk, in these suburbs and extremities of nature; let me see every trifle bristling with the polarity that ranges it instantly on an eternal law; and the shop, the plough, and the ledger referred to the like cause by which light undulates and poets sing;—and the world lies no longer a dull miscellany and lumber-room, but has form and order; there is no trifle, there is no puzzle, but one design unites and animates the farthest pinnacle and the lowest trench.

This idea has inspired the genius of Goldsmith, Burns, Cowper, and, in a newer time, of Goethe, Wordsworth, and Carlyle. This idea they have differently followed and with various success. In contrast with their writing, the style of Pope, of Johnson, of Gibbon, looks cold and pedantic. This writing is blood-warm. Man is surprised to find that things near are not less beautiful and wondrous than things remote. The near explains the far. The drop is a small ocean. A man is related to all nature. This perception of the worth of the vulgar is fruitful in discoveries. Goethe, in this very thing the most modern of the moderns, has shown us, as none ever did, the genius of the ancients.

There is one man of genius who has done much for this philosophy of life, whose literary value has never yet been rightly estimated;—I mean Emanuel Swedenborg. The most imaginative of men, yet writing with the precision of a mathematician, he endeavored to engraft a purely philosophical Ethics on the popular Christianity of his time. Such an attempt of course must have difficulty which no genius could surmount. But he saw and showed the connection between nature and the affections of the soul. He pierced the emblematic or spiritual character of the visible, audible, tangible world. Especially did his shade-loving muse hover over and interpret the lower parts of nature; he showed the mysterious bond that allies moral evil to the foul material forms, and has given in epical parables a theory of insanity, of beasts, of unclean and fearful things.

Another sign of our times, also marked by an analogous political movement, is the new importance given to the single person. Every thing that tends to insulate the individual,—to surround him with barriers of natural respect, so that each man shall feel the world is his, and man shall treat with man as a sovereign state with a sovereign state,—tends to true union as well as greatness. "I learned," said the melancholy Pestalozzi, "that no man in God's wide earth is either willing or able to help any other man." Help must come from the bosom alone. The scholar is that man who must take up into himself all the ability of the time, all the contributions of the past, all the hopes of the future. He must be an university of knowledges. If there be one lesson more than another which should pierce his ear, it is, The world is nothing, the man is all; in yourself is the law of all nature, and you know not yet how a globule of sap ascends; in yourself slumbers the whole of Reason; it is for you to know all; it is for you to dare all. Mr. President and Gentlemen, this confidence in the unsearched might of man belongs, by all motives, by all prophecy, by all preparation, to the American Scholar. We have listened too long to the courtly muses of Europe. The spirit of the American freeman is already suspected to be timid, imitative, tame. Public and private avarice make the air we breathe thick and fat. The scholar is decent, indolent, complaisant. See already the tragic consequence. The mind of this country, taught to aim at low objects, eats upon itself. There is no work for any but the decorous and the complaisant. Young men of the fairest promise, who begin life upon our shores, inflated by the mountain winds, shined upon by all the stars of God, find the earth below not in unison with these, but are hindered from action by the disgust which the principles on which business is managed inspire, and turn drudges, or die of disgust, some of them suicides. What is the remedy? They did not yet see, and thousands of young men as hopeful now crowding to the barriers for the career do not yet see, that if the single man plant himself indomitably on his instincts, and there abide, the huge world will come round to him. Patience,—patience; with the shades of all the good and great for company; and for solace the perspective of your own infinite life; and for work the study and the communication of principles, the making those instincts prevalent, the conversion of the world. Is it not the chief disgrace in the world, not to be an unit;—not to be reckoned one character;—not to yield that peculiar fruit which each man was created to bear, but to be reckoned in the gross, in the hundred, or the thousand, of the party, the section, to which we belong; and our opinion predicated geographically, as the north, or the south? Not so, brothers and friends—please God, ours shall not be so. We will walk on our own feet; we will work with our own hands; we will speak our own minds. The study of letters shall be no longer a name for pity, for doubt, and for sensual indulgence. The dread of man and the love of man shall be a wall of defence and a wreath of joy around all. A nation of men will for the first time exist, because each believes himself inspired by the Divine Soul which also inspires all men.

Exercises

1. Does the Introduction of this speech seem of optimum length? Inasmuch as it is somewhat longer than most of the speech Introductions in this volume, what especial purposes do you believe it is designed to serve? What attempt, if any, does Emerson make to secure favorable attention? Do his references to the occasion possess attention-getting qualities as well as clarification qualities? In addition to referring to the occasion, what other means does Emerson use to orient the listeners to the Body of his speech? If definitions are employed, how explicit are they? Does this degree of explicitness promote or detract from the speaker's objectives?

2. In what thematic ways does Emerson link the Conclusion with the Introduction? Does the Conclusion consist of an informal, detailed recapitulation of the various points presented in the Body? Is it primarily an extension of the last major point of the Body? Is it merely a reinforcement of the basic thrust of the speech? Is the emotional component more apparent in the Conclusion than elsewhere? Did Emerson call for specific action from his listeners? Or, was his appeal a generalized exhortation to become "involved"? Was the response he sought immediate actuation? Delayed? Sustained?

3. On the basis of your having read the speech, do you agree with Matthew Arnold's indictment that Emerson's style is desultory, lacking the "requisite wholeness of good tissue"? Now, outline carefully the entire speech, paying particular attention to the transitions. As a result of your attempt to structure the speech, do you find that your impressions have changed concerning the unity and coherence of the work?

4. Make a list of all the different forms of supporting materials and factors of interest you find represented in the speech. Which ones predominate? From your background reading, is this use of materials consistent with Emerson's rhetorical practices in his other works? Is it representative of the man himself?

5. How would you characterize Emerson's style and method of development? Is his use of language specific or general? Concrete, abstract, or a blend of both? Does he offer documentation? Does he prove his points by argumentation, or does he assume them by explanation? To what extent, if at all, does he use suggestion? Does he reason primarily from demonstrable fact or from alleged fact? Does this practice agree or disagree with his theory that a speaker must keep his feet ever upon a fact? Would you describe his primary mode of reasoning as inductive or deductive?

6. Are you familiar with the following words drawn from the speech: sere, Marvell, ferules, Savoyards, Davy, Cuvier, Etna, Swedenborg, Druids, Berserkers? Would these words probably have been familiar to the listeners?

7. How would you characterize Emerson's sentence structure and development? Do long or short sentences predominate? Is there a pleasing blending of long, medium-length, and short sentences? Can you find at least one example of the periodic and balanced construction and of the interrogative, exclamatory, and imperative sentence?

8. Make a list of twenty figures in the speech. Keeping in mind the audience to which the speech was directed, for each figure estimate its degree of directness and its straining for effect. Would you characterize Emerson's style generally as vivid and impressive? Explain your view.

9. Is the meaning of this sentence clear to you? "It is one of those fables which out of an unknown antiquity convey an unlooked-for wisdom, that the gods, in the beginning, divided Man into men, that he might be more helpful to himself; just as the hand was divided into fingers, the better to answer its end." Try rewriting it to improve its clarity. Does your draft impair the impact of Emerson's idea? In your opinion, did Emerson deliberately employ ambiguity to accomplish his rhetorical purposes? Explain. See if you can find in the speech a paragraph that weaves a spell rather than states with clarity.

10. In discussing the duties of the scholar, Emerson suggests that the orator can estimate the nature of an audience by realizing that he is "the complement of his hearers." To what extent is this advice true? False? What cautions should a speaker keep in mind if he accepts Emerson's view that the listener mirrors the speaker?

11. In what ways did Emerson in his own work-a-day life violate the injunctions in this speech?

12. To what extent is this speech a protest against the "Protestant ethic"? If this is a protest, how representative was it of national attitudes of the time? Of modern times? Which do you believe offers a fuller life, the spirit of Frankin or that of Emerson?

13. What is meant by the statement, "Emerson's *Essays*, though not in the tradition of Montaigne and Lamb, were rich in lofty thought and utterance"? Inasmuch as many of Emerson's individual essays were originally conceived as lectures for a listening audience, how much influence do you think that such an orientation might have exerted upon the style, organization, and development of the published *Essays?*

Henry Clay 

Speech in the United States Senate, on February 5, 1850, in support of the Compromise Bills which he had introduced

HENRY Clay (1777–1852) was variously known as "Harry of the West" and "The Great Pacificator," indicative of two outstanding facets of his political career. As a Senator from Kentucky, he fought for the development of roads, railways, and communication facilities that would aid in the growth of the West; and he was a principal leader of the compromise solutions worked out between the Southern and Northern sections in the debates on the admission of Missouri in 1820 and 1821, the "nullification" controversy between the federal government and South Carolina in 1833, and the compromises of 1850, temporarily tranquilizing the sectional quarrels accentuated by the Mexican War.

While the war with Mexico was continuing, Senator David Wilmot of Pennsylvania introduced into the Senate a "proviso" that would bar slavery from any territory taken from Mexico. Calhoun took direct issue: "The South like the North had fought to win the war; now the South must not be cheated of its share of the spoils." President James K. Polk noted in his diary that "The slavery question is assuming a fearful and most important aspect." Threats of secession by Southern fire-eaters became commonplace, and extremists in the North felt, too, that a division of the Union was the best available solution for the sectional differences.

Henry Clay, at the close of the Mexican War, was more than 70 years old, was in failing health, and was living in retirement in Lexington, Kentucky, disappointed from long years of failure to attain his dream of becoming President of the United States. Three times he had been nominated for that office, and twice had been refused the nomination in years when his party (the Whigs) was relatively assured of victory. When he observed the danger that the Union might break apart in acrimonious dispute over the policies to be applied to the Southwestern territories which were taken from Mexico, he permitted the Kentucky Legislature to elect him once again to the Senate of the United States. On the evening of January 21, 1850, he called upon Daniel Webster at the latter's home and requested that the Massachusetts senator join him in support of one more great effort to prevent civil war through compromise. Webster agreed—and brought down the opprobrium of his constituents upon his head by a speech on March 7, in which he supported the Fugitive Slave Law. Clay, weary and ill though he was, spoke more than 70 times during the months-long debate and held innumerable behind-the-scenes conferences trying to win support for his bills.

The status of Clay as a national leader was well stated by his colleague, Senator John C. Breckinridge, of Kentucky: "As a leader in a deliberative body, Mr. Clay had no equal in America. In him, intellect, person, eloquence, and courage united to form a character fit to command. He fired with his own enthusiasm, and controlled by his amazing will, individuals and masses. . . . In the assemblies of the people, at the bar, in the Senate—everywhere within the circle of his personal presence, he assumed and maintained a position of preëminence." It is also true, however, that by 1850 Clay's political influence had greatly lessened. There is merit in a private observation by Senator Stephen A. Douglas during the debates that "if Mr. Clay's name had not been associated with the bills they would have passed long ago. The Administration was jealous of him and hated him and some Democrats were weak enough to fear that the success of his bill would make him President." Clay spoke, then, on this occasion, under heavy handicaps.

The text of the speech is from *The Works of Henry Clay,* ed. Calvin Colton, New York: Putnam's, 1904, Vol. IX.

COMPROMISE SPEECH OF 1850

Mr. President, never on any former occasion have I risen under feelings of such painful solicitude. I have seen many periods of great anxiety, of peril, and of danger in this country, and I have never before risen to address any assemblage so oppressed, so appalled, and so anxious; and sir, I hope it will not be out of place to do here, what again and again I have done in my private chamber, to implore of Him who holds the destinies of nations and individuals in His hands, to bestow upon our country His blessing, to calm the violence and rage of party, to still passion, to allow reason once more to resume its empire. And may I not ask of Him too, sir, to bestow on his humble servant, now before him, the blessing of his smiles, and of strength and ability to perform the work which now lies before him? Sir, I have said that I have seen other anxious periods in the history of our country, and if I were to venture, Mr. President, to trace to their original source the cause of all our present dangers, difficulties, and distraction, I should ascribe it to the violence and intemperance of party spirit. To party spirit! Sir, in the progress of this session we have had the testimony of two senators here, who, however they may differ on other matters, concur in the existence of that cause in originating the unhappy differences which prevail throughout the country, on the subject of the institution of slavery.

Parties, in their endeavors to obtain, the one ascendancy over the other, catch at every passing or floating plank in order to add strength and power to each. We have been told by the two senators to whom I have referred, that each of the parties at the North, in its turn, has moved and endeavored to obtain the assistance of a small party called Abolitionists, in order that the scale in its favor might preponderate against that of its adversary. And all around us, every where, we see too many evidences of the existence of the spirit and intemperance of party. I might go to other legislative bodies than that which is assembled in Congress, and I might draw from them illustrations of the melancholy truth upon which I am dwelling, but I need not pass out of this Capitol itself. I say it, sir, with all deference and respect to that other portion of Congress assembled in the other wing of this Capitol; but what have we seen there? During this very session one whole week has been exhausted—I think about a week—in the vain endeavor to elect a doorkeeper of the House.

And, Mr. President, what was the question in this struggle to elect a doorkeeper? It was not as to the man or the qualities of the man, or who is best adapted to the situation. It was whether the doorkeeper entertained opinions upon certain national measures coincident with this or that side of the House. That was the sole question which prevented the election of a doorkeeper for about the period of a week. Sir, I make no reproaches—none, to either portion of that House; I state the fact; and I state the fact to draw from it the conclusion and to express the hope that there will be an endeavor to check this violence of party.

Sir, what vicissitudes do we not pass through in this short mortal career of ours? Eight years, or nearly eight years ago, I took my leave finally, and, as I supposed, forever from this body. At that time I did not conceive of the possibility of ever again returning to it. And if my private wishes and particular inclinations, and the desire during the short remnant of my days to remain in repose and quiet, could have prevailed, you would never have seen me occupying the seat which I now occupy upon this floor. The Legislature of the State to which I belong, unsolicited by me, chose to designate me for this station, and I have come here, sir, in obedience to a sense of stern duty, with no personal objects, no private views, now or hereafter, to gratify. I know, sir, the jealousies, the fears, the apprehensions which are engendered by the existence of that party spirit to which I have referred; but if there be in my hearing now, in or out of this Capitol, any one who hopes, in his race for honors and elevation, for higher honors and higher elevation than that which he now occupies, I beg him to believe that I, at least, will never jostle him in the pursuit of those honors or that elevation. I beg him to be perfectly persuaded that, if my wishes prevail, my name shall never be used in competition with his. I beg to assure him that when my service is terminated in this body, my mission, so far as respects the public affairs of this world and upon this earth, is closed, and closed, if my wishes prevail, forever.

But, sir, it is impossible for us to be blind to the facts which are daily transpiring before us. It is impossible for us not to perceive that party spirit and future elevation mix more or less in all our affairs, in all our deliberations. At a moment when the White House itself is in danger of conflagration, instead of all hands uniting to extinguish the flames, we are contending about who shall be its next occupant. When a dreadful crevasse has occurred, which threatens inundation and destruction to all around it, we are contending and disputing about the profits of an estate which is threatened with total submersion.

Mr. President, it is passion, passion—party, party, and intemperance—that is all I dread in the adjustment of the great questions which unhappily at this time divide our distracted country. Sir, at this moment we have in the legislative bodies of this Capitol and in the States, twenty old furnaces in full blast, emitting heat, and passion, and intemperance, and diffusing them throughout the whole extent of this broad land. Two months ago all was calm in comparison to the present moment. All now is uproar, confusion, and menace to the existence of the Union, and to the happiness and safety of this people. Sir, I implore senators, I entreat them, by all that they expect hereafter, and by all that is dear to them here below, to repress the ardor of these passions, to look to their country, to its interests, to listen to the voice of reason—not as it shall be attempted to be uttered by me, for I am not so presumptous as to indulge the hope that anything I may say will avert the effects which I have described, but to listen to their own reason, their own judgment, their own good sense, in determining upon what is best to be done for our country in the actual posture in which we find her. Sir, to this great object have my efforts been directed during the whole session.

I have cut myself off from all the usual enjoyments of social life, I have confined myself almost entirely, with very few exceptions, to my own chamber, and from the beginning of the session to the present time my thoughts have been anxiously directed to the object of finding some plan, of proposing some mode of accommodation, which would once more restore the blessings of concord, harmony and peace to this great country. I am not vain enough to suppose that I have been successful in the accomplishment of this object, but I have presented a scheme, and allow me to say to honorable senators that, if they find in that plan any thing that is defective, if they find in it any thing that is worthy of acceptance, but is susceptible of improvement by amendment, it seems to me that the true and patriotic course is not to denounce it, but to improve it—not to reject without examination any project of accommodation having for its object the restoration of harmony in this country, but to look at it to see if it be susceptible of elaboration or improvement, so as to accomplish the object which I indulge the hope is common to all and every one of us, to restore peace and quiet, and harmony and happiness to this country.

Sir, when I came to consider this subject, there were two or three general purposes which it seemed to me to be most desirable, if possible, to accomplish. The one was, to settle all the controverted questions arising out of the subject of slavery. It seemed to me to be doing very little, if we settled one question and left other distracting questions unadjusted, it seemed to me to be doing but little, if we stopped one leak only in the ship of State, and left other leaks capable of producing danger, if not destruction, to the vessel. I therefore turned my attention to every subject connected with the institution of slavery, and out of which controverted questions had sprung, to see if it were possible or practicable to accommodate and adjust the whole of them. Another principal object which attracted my attention was, to endeavor to form such a scheme of accommodation that neither of the two classes of States into which our country is so unhappily divided should make any sacrifice of any great principle. I believe, sir, the series of resolutions which I have had the honor to present to the Senate accomplishes that object.

Sir, another purpose which I had in view was this: I was aware of the difference of opinion prevailing between these two classes of States. I was aware that, while one portion of the Union was pushing matters, as it seemed to me, to the greatest extremity, another portion of the Union was pushing them to an opposite, perhaps not less dangerous extremity. It appeared to me, then, that if any arrangement, any satisfactory adjustment could be made of the controverted questions between the two classes of States, that adjustment, that arrangement, could only be successful and effectual by extracting from both parties some concessions —not of principle, not of principle at all, but of feeling, of opinion, in relation to matters in controversy between them. Sir, I believe the resolutions which I have prepared fulfill that object. I believe, sir, that you will find, upon that careful, rational, and attentive examination of them, which I think they deserve, that neither party in some of them make any concession at all; in others the concessions of forbearance are mutual; and in the third place, in reference to the slaveholding States, there are resolutions making concessions to them by the opposite class of States, without any compensation whatever being rendered by them to the non-slaveholding States. I think every one of these characteristics which I have assigned, and the measures which I proposed, is susceptible of clear and satisfactory demonstration by an attentive perusal and critical examination of the resolutions themselves. Let us take up the first resolution.

The first resolution, Mr. President, as you are aware, relates to California, and it declares that California, with suitable limits, ought to be admitted as a member of this Union, without the imposition of any restriction either to interdict or to introduce slavery within her limits. Well now, is there any concession in this resolution by either party to the other? I know that gentlemen who come from slaveholding States say the North gets all that it desires; but by whom does it get it? Does it get it by any action of Congress? If slavery be interdicted within the limits of California, has it been done by Congress—by this Government? No, sir. That interdiction is imposed by California herself. And has it not been the doctrine of all parties that when a State is about to be admitted into the Union, the State has a right to decide for itself whether it will or will not have slavery within its limits?

The great principle, sir, which was in contest upon the memorable occasion of the introduction of Missouri into the Union, was, whether it was competent or not competent for Congress to impose any restrictions which should exist after she became a member of the Union. We who were in favor of the admission of Missouri, contended that no such restriction should be imposed. We contended that, whenever she was once admitted into the Union, she had all the rights and privileges of any pre-existing State in the Union, and that among these rights and privileges was one to decide for herself whether slavery should or should not rest within her limits; that she had as much a right to decide upon the introduction of slavery or its abolition as New York had a right to decide upon the introduction or abolition of slavery; and that, although subsequently admitted, she stood among her peers, equally invested with all the privileges that any one of the original thirteen States had a right to enjoy.

Sir, I think that those who have been contending with so much earnestness and perseverance for the Wilmot proviso, ought to reflect that, even if they could carry their object and adopt the proviso, it ceases the moment any State or Territory to which it was applicable came to be admitted as a member of the Union. Why, sir, no one contends now, no one believes, that with regard to those North-western States to which the ordinance of 1787 applied—Ohio, Indiana, Illinois, and Michigan—no one can now believe but that any one of those States, if they thought proper to do it, have just as much right to introduce slavery within their borders, as Virginia has to maintain the existence of slavery within hers. Then, sir, if in the struggle for power and empire between the two classes of States a decision in California has taken place adverse to the wishes of the Southern States, it is a decision not made by the General Government.

It is a decision respecting which they can utter no complaint toward the General Government. It is a decision made by California herself; which California had unquestionably the right to make under the Constitution of the United States. There is, then, in the first resolution, according to the observation which I made some time ago, a case where neither party concedes; where the question of slavery, neither its introduction nor interdiction, is decided in reference to the action of this Government; and if it has been decided, it has been by a different body—by a different power—by California itself, which had a right to make the decision.

Mr. President, the next resolution in the series which I have offered I beg gentlemen candidly now to look at. I was aware, perfectly aware, of the perseverance with which the Wilmot proviso was insisted upon. I knew that every one of the free States in this Union, without exception, had by its Legislative body passed resolutions instructing their Senators and requesting their Representatives to get that restriction incorporated in any Territorial Government which might be established under the auspices of Congress. I knew how much, and I regretted how much, the free States had put their hearts upon the adoption of this measure. In the second resolution I call upon them to waive persisting in it. I ask them, for the sake of peace and in the spirit of mutual forbearance to other members of the Union, to give it up—to no longer insist upon it—to see, as they must see, if their eyes are open, the dangers which lie ahead, if they persevere in insisting upon it.

When I called upon them in this resolution to do this, was I not bound to offer, for a surrender of that favorite principle or measure of theirs, some compensation, not as an equivalent by any means, but some compensation in the spirit of mutual forbearance, which, animating one side, ought at the same time to actuate the other side? Well, sir, what is it that is offered them? It is a declaration of what I characterized, and must still characterize, with great deference to all those who entertain opposite opinions, as two truths, I will not say incontestible, but to me clear, and I think they ought to be regarded as indisputable truths. What are they? The first is, that by law slavery no longer exists in any part of the acquisitions made by us from the Republic of Mexico; and the other is, that in our opinion, according to the probabilities of the case, slavery never will be introduced into any portion of the territories so acquired from Mexico. Now, I have heard it said that this declaration of what I call these two truths is equivalent to the enactment of the Wilmot proviso.

I have heard this asserted, but is that the case? If the Wilmot proviso be adopted in Territorial Governments established over these countries acquired from Mexico, it would be a positive enactment, a prohibition, an interdiction as to the introduction of slavery within them; but with regard to these opinions I had hoped, and I shall still indulge the hope, that those who represent the free States will be inclined not to insist–indeed it would be extremely difficult to give to these declarations the form of positive enactment. I had hoped that they would be satisfied with the simple expression of the opinion of Congress, leaving it upon the basis of that opinion, without asking for what seems to me almost impracticable, if not impossible–for any subsequent enactment to be introduced into the bill by which Territorial Governments should be established.

And I can only say that the second resolution, even without the declaration of these two truths expressed, would be much more acceptable to me than with them–but I could not forget that I was proposing a scheme of arrangement and compromise, and I could not, therefore, depart from the duty which the preparation of such a scheme seems to me to impose, of offering, while we ask the surrender on one side of a favorite measure, of offering to the other side some compensation for that surrender or sacrifice. What are the truths, Mr. President? The first is, that by law slavery does not exist within the Territories ceded to us by the Republic of Mexico. It is a misfortune, sir, in the various weighty and important topics which are connected with the subject that I am now addressing you upon, that any one of the five or six furnishes a theme for a lengthened speech; and I am therefore reduced by the necessity, I think–at least in this stage of the discussion–of limiting myself rather to the expression of opinions, than going at any great length into the discussion of all these various topics.

With respect to the opinion that slavery does not exist in the Territories ceded to the United States by Mexico, I can only refer to the fact of the passage of the law by the Supreme Government of Mexico abolishing it, I think, in 1824; and to the subsequent passage of a law by the Legislative body of Mexico, I forget in what year, by which they proposed —what it is true they have never yet carried into full effect—compensation to the owners of slaves for the property of which they were stripped by the act of abolition. I can only refer to the acquiescence of Mexico in the abolition of slavery from the time of its extinction down to the time of the treaty by which we acquired these countries. But all Mexico, so far as I know, acquiesced in the non-existence of slavery. Gentlemen, I know, talk about the irregularity of the law by which that act was accomplished; but does it become us, a foreign power, to look into the mode by which an object has been accomplished by another foreign power, when she herself is satisfied with what she has done; and when, too, she is the exclusive judge whether an object which is local and municipal to herself, has been or has not been accomplished in conformity with her fundamental laws? Why, Mexico upon this subject showed to the last moment, her anxiety in the documents which were laid before the country upon the subject of the negotiation of this treaty, by Mr. Trist.

In the very act, in the very negotiation by which the treaty was concluded, ceding to us the countries in question, the diplomatic representatives of the Mexican Republic urged the abhorrence with which Mexico would view the introduction of slavery into any portion of the Territory which she was about to cede to the United States. The clause of prohibition was not inserted in consequence of the firm ground taken by Mr. Trist, and his declaration that it was an utter impossibility to mention the subject.

I take it then, sir—and availing myself of the benefit of the discussions which took place on a former occasion on this question, and which I think have left the whole country under the impression of the non-existence of slavery within the whole of the Territory in the ceded Territories—I take it for granted that what I have said, aided by the reflection of gentlemen, will satisfy them of that first truth, that slavery does not exist there by law, unless slavery was carried there the moment the treaty was ratified by the two parties, and under the operation of the Constitution of the United States. Now, really, I must say that upon the idea that *eo instanti* upon the consummation of the treaty, the Constitution of the United States spread itself over the acquired Territory, and carried along with it the institution of slavery, the proposition is so irreconcilable with any comprehension or reason that I possess, that I hardly know how to meet it.

Why, these United States consist of thirty States. In fifteen of them there was slavery, in fifteen of them slavery did not exist. Well, how can it be argued that the fifteen slave States, by the operation of the Constitution of the United States, carried into the ceded Territory their institution of slavery, any more than it can be argued on the other side that, by the operation of the same Constitution, the fifteen free States carried into the ceded territory the principle of freedom which they from policy have chosen to adopt within their limits? Why, sir, let me suppose a case. Let me imagine that Mexico had never abolished slavery there at all—let me suppose that it was existing in point of fact and in virtue of law, from the shores of the Pacific to those of the Gulf of Mexico, at the moment of the cession of these countries to us by the treaty in question.

With what patience would gentlemen coming from slaveholding States listen to any argument which should be urged by the free States, that notwithstanding the existence of slavery within those territories, the Constitution of the United States abolished it the movement it operated and took effect in the ceded territory? Well, is there not just as much ground to contend that, where a moiety of the States is free, and the other moiety is slaveholding, the principle of freedom which prevails in the one class shall operate as much as the principle of slavery which prevails in the other? Can you come, amid this conflict of interests, principles, and legislation which prevails in the two parts of the Union, to any other conclusion than that which I understand to be the conclusion of the public law of the world, of reason, and justice—that the *status of law*, as it existed at the moment of the conquest or the acquisition, remains until it is altered by the sovereign authority of the conquering or acquiring power? That is the great principle which you can scarcely turn over a page of the public law of the world without finding recognized, and every where established. The laws of Mexico, as they existed at the moment of the cession of the ceded Territories to this country, remained the laws until, and unless, they were altered by that new sovereign power which this people and these Territories come under, in consequence of the treaty of cession to the United States.

I think, then, Mr. President, that without trespassing further or exhausting the little stock of strength which I have, and for which I shall have abundant use in the progress of the argument, I may leave that part of the subject with two or three observations only upon the general power which I think appertains to this Government on the subject of slavery.

Sir, before I approach that subject, allow me to say that, in my humble judgment, the institution of slavery presents two questions totally distinct, and resting on entirely different grounds—slavery within the States, and slavery without the States. Congress, the General Government, has no power, under the Constitution of the United States, to touch slavery within the States, except in three specified particulars in that instrument; to adjust the subject of representation; to impose taxes when a system of direct taxation is made; and to perform the duty of surrendering, or causing to be delivered up, fugitive slaves that may escape from service which they owe in slave States, and take refuge in free States. And, sir, I am ready to say that if Congress were to attack, within the States, the institution of slavery, for the purpose of the overthrow or extinction of slavery, then, Mr. President, my voice would be for war; then would be made a case which would justify in the sight of God, and in the presence of the nations of the earth, resistance on the part of the slave States to such an unconstitutional and usurped attempt as would be made on the supposition which I have stated.

Then we should be acting in defense of our rights, our domicils, our property, our safety, our lives; and then, I think, would be furnished a case in which the slaveholding States would be justified by all considerations which pertain to the happiness and security of man, to employ every instrument which God or nature had placed in their hands, to resist such an attempt on the part of the free States. And then, if unfortunately civil war should break out, and we should present to the nations of the earth the spectacle of one portion of this Union endeavoring to subvert an institution in violation of the Constitution and the most sacred obligations which can bind men; we should present the spectacle in which we should have the sympathies, the good wishes, and the desire for our success of all men who love justice and truth. Far different, I fear, would be our case–if unhappily we should be plunged into civil war–if the two parts of this country should be placed in a position hostile toward each other, in order to carry slavery into the new Territories acquired from Mexico.

Mr. President, we have heard, all of us have read of the efforts of France to propagate–what, on the continent of Europe? Not slavery, sir; not slavery, but the rights of man; and we know the fate of her efforts in a work of that kind. But if the two portions of this Confederacy should unhappily be involved in civil war, in which the effort on the one side would be to restrain the introduction of slavery into new Territories, and on the other side to force its introduction there, what a spectacle should we present to the contemplation of astonished mankind! An effort not to propagate right, but I must say–though I trust it will be understood to be said with no desire to excite feeling–an effort to propagate wrong in the territories thus acquired from Mexico. It would be a war in which we should have no sympathy, no good wishes, and in which all mankind would be against us, and in which our own history itself would be against us; for, from the commencement of the Revolution down to the present time, we have constantly reproached our British ancestors for the introduction of slavery into this country; and allow me to say that, in my opinion, it is one of the best defenses which can be made to preserve the institution in this country, that it was forced upon us against the wishes of our ancestors, our own colonial ancestors, and by the cupidity of our British commercial ancestors.

The power then, Mr. President, in my opinion—and I will extend it to the introduction as well as the prohibition of slavery in the new territories—I think the power does exist in Congress, and I think there is that important distinction between slavery outside of the States and slavery inside of the States, that all outside is debatable, all inside of the States is undebatable. The Government has no right to touch the institution within the States; but whether she has, and to what extent she has the right or not to touch it outside of the States, is a question which is debatable, and upon which men may honestly and fairly differ, but which, decided however it may be decided, furnishes, in my judgment, no just occasion for breaking up this happy and glorious Union of ours.

Now, I am not going to take up that part of the subject which relates to the power of Congress to legislate either within this District—(I shall have occasion to make some observations upon that when I approach the resolution relating to the District)—either within this District or the Territories. But I must say, in a few words, that I think there are two sources of power, either of which is, in my judgment, sufficient to warrant the exercise of the power, if it was deemed proper to exercise it, either to introduce or to keep out slavery outside the States, within the territories.

Mr. President, I shall not take up time, of which already so much has been consumed, to show that, according to my sense of the Constitution of the United States, or rather according to the sense in which the clause has been interpreted for the last fifty years, the clause which confers on Congress the power to regulate the Territories and other property of the United States conveys the authority.

Mr. President, with my worthy friend from Michigan—and I use the term in the best and most emphatic sense, for I believe he and I have known each other longer than he and I have known any other senator in this hall—I can not concur, although I entertain the most profound respect for the opinions he has advanced upon the subject, adverse to my own; but I must say, when a point is settled by all the elementary writers of our country, by all the departments of our Government, legislative, executive, and judicial—when it has been so settled for a period of fifty years, and never was seriously disturbed until recently, that I think, if we are to regard any thing as fixed and settled under the administration of this Constitution of ours, it is a quesiton which has thus been invariably and uniformly settled in a particular way. Or are we to come to this conclusion that nothing, nothing on earth is settled under this Constitution, but that every thing is unsettled?

Mr. President, we have to recollect it is very possible–sir, it is quite likely–that when that Constitution was framed, the application of it to such Territories as Louisiana, Florida, California, and New Mexico was never within the contemplation of its framers. It will be recollected that when that Constitution was framed the whole country northwest of the river Ohio was unpeopled; and it will be recollected also, that the exercise and the assertion of the power to make governments for Territories in their infant state, are, in the nature of the power, temporary, and to terminate whenever they have acquired a population competent for self-government. Sixty thousand is the number fixed by the ordinance of 1787. Now, sir, recollect that when this Constitution was adopted, and that Territory was unpeopled, is it possible that Congress, to whom it had been ceded by the States for the common benefit of the ceding State and all other members of the Union–is it possible that Congress had no right whatever to declare what description of settlers should occupy the public lands?

Suppose they took up the opinion that the introduction of slavery would enhance the value of the land, and enable them to command for the public treasury a greater amount from that source of revenue than by the exclusion of slaves, would they not have had the right to say, in fixing the rules, regulations, or whatever you choose to call them, for the government of that Territory, that any one that chooses to bring slaves may bring them, if it will enhance the value of the property, in the clearing and cultivation of the soil, and add to the importance of the country? Or take the reverse:–Suppose Congress had thought that a greater amount of revenue would be derived from the waste lands beyond the Ohio river by the interdiction of slavery, would they not have had a right to interdict it? Why, sir, remember how these settlements were made, and what was their progress. They began with a few. I believe that about Marietta the first settlement was made.

It was a settlement of some two or three hundred persons from New England. Cincinnati, I believe, was the next point where a settlement was made. It was settled perhaps by a few persons from New Jersey, or some other state. Did those few settlers, the moment they arrived there, acquire sovereign rights? Had those few persons power to dispose of these territories? Had they even power to govern themselves–the handful of men who established themselves at Marietta or Cincinnati? No, sir, the contemplation of the Constitution no doubt was, that, inasmuch as this power was temporary, as it is applicable to unpeopled territory, and as that territory will become peopled gradually, insensibly, until it reaches a population which may entitle it to the benefit of self-government, in the mean time it is right and proper that Congress, who owns the soil, should regulate the settlement of the soil, and govern the settlers on the soil, until those settlers acquire number and capacity to govern themselves.

Sir, I will not further dwell upon this part of the subject; but I said there is another source of power equally satisfactory, equally conclusive in my mind, as that which relates to the territories, and that is the treaty-making power—the acquiring power. Now, I put it to gentlemen, is there not at this moment a power somewhere existing either to admit or exclude slavery from the ceded territory? Is it not an annihilated power? This is impossible. It is a subsisting, actual, existing power; and where does it exist? It existed, I presume no one will controvert, in Mexico prior to the cession of these territories. Mexico could have abolished slavery or introduced slavery either in California or New Mexico. That must be conceded. Who will controvert this position? Well, Mexico has parted from the territory and from the sovereignty over the territory; and to whom did she transfer it? She transferred the territory and the sovereignty of the territory to the Government of the United States.

The Government of the United States acquires in sovereignty and in territory over California and New Mexico, all, either in sovereignty or territory, that Mexico held in California or New Mexico, by the cession of those territories. Sir, dispute that who can. The power exists or it does not; no one will contend for its annihilation. It existed in Mexico. No one, I think, can deny that. Mexico alienates the sovereignty over the territory, and her alience is the government of the United States. The Government of the United States, then, possesses all power which Mexico possessed over the ceded territories, and the Government of the United States can do in reference to them—within, I admit, certain limits of the Constitution—whatever Mexico could have done. There are prohibitions upon the power of Congress within the Constitution, which prohibitions, I admit, must apply to Congress whenever she legislates, whether for the old States or for new territories; but, within those prohibitions, the powers of the United States over the ceded territories are co-extensive and equal to the powers of Mexico in the ceded territories, prior to the cession.

Sir, in regard to this treaty-making power, all who have any occasion to examine into its character and to the possible extent to which it may be carried, know that it is a power unlimited in its nature, except in so far as any limitation may be found in the Constitution of the United States; and upon this subject there is no limitation which prescribes the extent to which the powers should be exercised. I know, sir, it is argued that there is no grant of power in the Constitution, in specific terms, over the subject of slavery any where; and there is no grant in the Constitution to Congress specifically over the subject of a vast variety of matters upon which the powers of Congress may unquestionably operate. The major includes the minor. The general grant of power comprehends all the particulars and elements of which that power consists. The power of acquisition by treaty draws after it the power of government of the country acquired.

If there be a power to acquire, there must be, to use the language of the tribunal that sits below, a power to govern. I think, therefore, sir, without, at least for the present, dwelling further on this part of the subject, that to the two sources of authority in Congress to which I have referred, and especially to the last, may be traced the power of Congress to act in the territories in question; and, sir, I go to the extent, and I think it is a power in Congress equal to the introduction or exclusion of slavery. I admit the argument in both its forms; I admit if the argument be maintained that the power exists to exclude slavery, it necessarily follows that the power must exist, if Congress choose to exercise it, to tolerate or introduce slavery within the territories.

But, sir, I have been drawn off so far from the second resolution—not from the object of it, but from a particular view of it—that it has almost gone out of my recollection. The resolution asserts—

> That as slavery does not exist by law, and is not likely to be introduced into any of the territory acquired by the United States, from the Republic of Mexico, it is inexpedient for Congress to provide by law either for its introduction into or exclusion from any part of the said territory; and that appropriate territorial governments ought to be established by Congress in all of the said territory, not assigned as the boundaries of the proposed State of California, without the adoption of any restriction or condition on the subject of slavery.

The other truth which I respectfully and with great deference conceive to exist, and which is announced in this resolution is, that slavery is not likely to be introduced into any of these territories. Well, sir, is not that a fact? Is there a member who hears me that will not confirm the fact? What has occurred within the last three months? In California, more than in any other portion of the ceded territory, was it most probable, if slavery was adapted to the interest of the industrial pursuits of the inhabitants, that slavery would have been introduced. Yet, within the space of three or four months, California herself has declared, by a unanimous vote of her convention, against the introduction of slavery within her limits. And, as I remarked on a former occasion, this declaration was not confined to non-slaveholders.

There were persons from the slaveholding States who concurred in that declaration. Thus this fact which is asserted in the resolution is responded to by the act of California. Then, sir, if we come down to those mountain regions which are to be found in New Mexico, the nature of its soil and country, its barrenness, its unproductive character, every thing which relates to it, and every thing which we hear of it and about it, must necessarily lead to the conclusion which I have mentioned, that slavery is not likely to be introduced into them.—Well, sir, if it be true that by law slavery does not now exist in the ceded territories, and that it is not likely to be introduced into the ceded territories—if you, senators, agree to these truths, or a majority of you, as I am persuaded a large majority of you must agree to them—where is the objection or the difficulty to your announcing them to the whole world? Why should you hesitate or falter in the promulgation of incontestable truths? On the other hand, with regard to senators coming from the free States, allow me here to make, with reference to California, one or two observations.

When this feeling within the limits of your States was gotten up; when the Wilmot proviso was disseminated through them, and your people and yourselves attached themselves to that proviso, what was the state of facts? The state of facts at the time was, that you apprehended the introduction of slavery there. You did not know much—very few of us now know much—about those very territories. They were far distant from you. You were apprehensive that slavery might be introduced there. You wanted as a protection to introduce the interdiction called the Wilmot proviso. It was in this state of want of information that the whole North blazed up in behalf of this Wilmot proviso. It was under the apprehension that slavery might be introduced there that you left your constituents. For when you came from home, at the time you left your respective residences, you did not know the fact, which has only reached us since the commencement of the session of Congress, that a constitution has been unanimously adopted by the people of California, excluding slavery from their Territory.

Well, now, let me suppose that two years ago it had been known in the free states that such a constitution would be adopted; let me suppose that it had been believed that in no other portion of these ceded territories would slavery be introduced; let me suppose that upon this great subject of solicitude, Negro slavery, the people of the North had been perfectly satisfied that there was no danger; let me also suppose that they had foreseen the excitement, the danger, the irritation, the resolutions which have been adopted by Southern Legislatures, and the manifestations of opinion by the people of the slaveholding States—let me suppose that all this had been known at the North at the time when the agitation was first got up upon the subject of this Wilmot proviso—do you believe that it would have ever reached the height to which it has attained? Do any of you believe it? And if, prior to your departure from your respective homes, you had had an opportunity of conferring with your constituents upon this most leading and important fact—of the adoption of a constitution excluding slavery in California—do you not believe, senators and representatives coming from the free States, that if you had the advantage of that fact told in serious, calm, fire-side conversation with your constituents, they would not have told you to come here and to settle all these agitating questions without danger to this Union?

What do you want? What do you want who reside in the free States? You want that there shall be no slavery introduced into the territories acquired from Mexico. Well, have not you got it in California already, if admitted as a State? Have you not got it in New Mexico, in all human probability, also? What more do you want? You have got what is worth a thousand Wilmot provisos. You have got nature itself on your side. You have the fact itself on your side. You have the truth staring you in the face that no slavery is existing there. Well, if you are men; if you can rise from the mud and slough of party struggles and elevate yourselves to the height of patriots, what will you do? You will look at the fact as it exists. You will say, this fact was unknown to my people. You will say, they acted on one set of facts, we have got another set of facts here influencing us, and we will act as patriots, as responsible men, as lovers of unity and above all of this Union. We will act on the altered set of facts unknown to our constituents, and we will appeal to their justice, their honor, their magnanimity, to concur with us on this occasion, for establishing concord and harmony, and maintaining the existence of this glorious Union.

Well, Mr. President, I think, entertaining these views, that there was nothing extravagant in the hope in which I indulged when these resolutions were prepared and offered—nothing extravagant in the hope that the North might content itself even with striking out as unnecessary these two declarations. They are unnecessary for any purpose the free States have in view. At all events, if they should insist upon Congress expressing the opinions which are here asserted, they should limit their wishes to the simple assertion of them, without insisting on their being incorporated in any territorial Government which Congress may establish in the territories.

I pass on from the second resolution to the third and fourth, which relate to Texas; and allow me to say, Mr. President, that I approach the subject with a full knowledge of all its difficulties; and of all the questions connected with or growing out of this institution of slavery, which Congress is called upon to pass upon and decide, there are none so difficult and troublesome as those which relate to Texas, because, sir, Texas has a question of boundary to settle, and the question of slavery, or the feelings connected with it, run into the question of boundary. The North, perhaps, will be anxious to contract Texas within the narrowest possible limits, in order to exclude all beyond her to make it a free territory; the South, on the contrary, may be anxious to extend their limits to the source of the Rio Grande, for the purpose of creating an additional theater for slavery; and thus, to the question of the limits of Texas, and the settlement of her boundary, the slavery question, with all its troubles and difficulties, is added, meeting us at every step we take.

There is, sir, a third question, also, adding to the difficulty. By the resolution of annexation, slavery was interdicted in all north of 36° 30′; but of New Mexico, that portion of it which lies north or 36° 30′ embraces, I think, about one third of the whole of New Mexico east of the Rio Grande; so that you have free and slave territory mixed, boundary and slavery mixed together, and all these difficulties are to be encountered. And allow me to say, sir, that among the considerations which induced me to think it was necessary to settle all these questions, was the state of things that now exists in New Mexico, and the state of things to be apprehended both there and in other portions of the territories. Why, sir, at this moment—and I think I shall have the concurrence of the two senators from that State when I announce the fact—at this moment there is a feeling approximating to abhorrence on the part of the people of New Mexico at the idea of any union with Texas.

(Mr. Rusk. Only, sir, on the part of the office-seekers and army followers, who have settled there, and attempted to mislead the people.

Mr. Clay. Ah! sir, that may be, and I am afraid that New Mexico is not the only place where this class composes a majority of the whole population of the country. [Laughter.])

Now, sir, if the questions are not settled which relate to Texas, her boundaries, and so forth, and to the territory now claimed by Texas and disputed by New Mexico—the territories beyond New Mexico which are excluded from California—if these questions are not all settled, I think they will give rise to future confusion, disorder and anarchy there, and to agitation here. There will be, I have no doubt, a party still at the North crying out, if these questions are not settled this session, for the Wilmot proviso, or some other restriction upon them, and we shall absolutely do nothing, in my opinion, if we do not accommodate all these difficulties and provide against the recurrence of all these dangers.

Sir, with respect to the state of things in New Mexico, allow me to call the attention of the Senate to what I consider as the highest authority I could offer to them as to the state of things there existing. I mean the acts of their Convention, unless that Convention happens to have been composed altogether of office-seekers, office-holders, and so forth. Now, sir, I call your attention to what they say in depicting their own situation.

(Mr. Underwood, at Mr. Clay's request, read the following extract from instructions adopted by the Convention, appended to the journal of the Convention of the Territory of New Mexico, held at the city of Santa Fé, in September, 1849.

> We, the people of New Mexico, in Convention assembled, having elected a delegate to represent this Territory in the Congress of the United States, and to urge upon the Supreme Government a redress of our grievances, and the protection due to us as citizens of our common country, under the Constitution, instruct him as follows: That whereas, for the last three years we have suffered under the paralyzing effects of a government undefined and doubtful in its character, inefficient to protect the rights of the people, or to discharge the high and absolute duty of every Government, the enforcement and regular administration of its own laws, in consequence of which, industry and enterprise are paralyzed and discontent and confusion prevail throughout the land. The want of proper protection against the various barbarous tribes of Indians that surround us on every side has prevented the extension of settlements upon our valuable public domain, and rendered utterly futile every attempt to explore or develop the great resources of the territory.
>
> Surrounded by the Utahs, Comanches, and Apaches, on the North, East and South, by the Navajos on the West, with Jicarillas within our limits, and without any adequate protection against their hostile inroads, our flocks and herds are driven off by thousands, our fellow-citizens, men, women, and children, are murdered or carried into captivity. Many of our citizens, of all ages and races, are at this moment suffering all the horrors of barbarian bondage, and it is utterly out of our power to obtain their release from a condition to which death would be preferable. The wealth of our territory is being diminished. We have neither the means nor any adopted plan of Government for the education of the rising generation. In fine, with a government temporary, doubtful, uncertain, and inefficient in character and in operation, surrounded and despoiled by barbarous foes, ruin appears inevitably before us, unless speedy and effectual protection be extended to us by the Congress of the United States.)

There is a series of resolutions, Mr. President, which any gentleman may look at, if he chooses; but I think it is not worth while to take up the time of the Senate in reading them.

That is the condition, sir, of New Mexico. Well, I suspect that to go beyond it, to go beyond the Rio Grande to the territory which is not claimed by Texas, you will not find a much better state of things. In fact, sir, I can not for a moment reconcile it to my sense of duty to suffer

Congress to adjourn without an effort, at least, being made to extend the benefits, the blessings of government to those people who have recently been acquired by us.

Sir, with regard to that portion of New Mexico which lies east of the Rio Grande, undoubtedly, if it is conceded to Texas, while she has two parties, disliking each other as much as those office-holders and office-seekers alluded to by the senator from Texas, if they could possibly be drawn together and governed quietly, peaceably, and comfortably, there might be a remedy, so far as relates to the country east of the Rio Grande; but all beyond it—Deseret and the North of California—would be still open and liable to all the consequences of disunion, confusion and anarchy, without some stable government emanating from the authority of the nation of which they now compose a part, and with which they are but little acquainted. I think, therefore, that all these questions, difficult and troublesome as they may be, ought to be met—met in a spirit of candor and calmness, and decided upon as a matter of duty.

Now, these two resolutions which we have immediately under consideration propose a decision of these questions. I have said, sir, that there is scarcely a resolution in the series which I have offered that does not contain some mutual concession or evidence of mutual forbearance, where the concession was not altogether from the non-slaveholding to the slaveholding States.

Now, with respect to the resolution proposing a boundary for Texas, what is it? We know the difference of opinion which has existed in this country with respect to that boundary. We know that a very large portion of the people of the United States have supposed that the western limit of Texas was the Nueces, and that it did not extend to the Rio Grande. We know, by the resolution of annexation, that the question of what is the western limit and the northern limit of Texas was an open question—that it has been all along an open question. It was an open question when the boundary was run, in virtue of the Act of 1838, marking the boundary between the United States and Texas. Sir, at that time the boundary authorized by the Act of 1838 was a boundary commencing at the mouth of the Sabine and running up to its head, thence to Red River, thence westwardly with Red River to, I think, the hundredth degree of west longitude. Well, sir, that did not go so far as Texas now claims, and why? Because it was an open question. War was yet raging between Texas and Mexico, it was not foreseen exactly what might be her ultimate limits. But, sir, we will come to the question of what was done at the time of her annexation.

The whole resolution which relates to the question of boundary, from beginning to end, assumes an open boundary, an unascertained, unfixed boundary to Texas on the West. Sir, what is the first part of the resolution? It is that "Congress doth consent that the Territory properly included within and rightfully belonging to the Republic of Texas may be erected into a new State." Properly including–rightfully belonging to. The resolution specifies no boundary. It could specify none. It has specified no western or northern boundary for Texas. It has assumed in this state of uncertainty what we know in point of fact existed. But then the latter part of it: "Said State to be formed subject to the adjustment of all questions of boundary that may arise with other Governments, and the constitution thereof," &c. That is to say, she is annexed with her rightful and proper boundaries, without a specification of them; but inasmuch as it was known that these boundaries at the west and the north were unsettled, the Government of the United States retained to itself the power of settling with any foreign nation what the boundary should be.

Now, sir, it is impossible for me to go into the whole question and to argue it fully. I mean to express opinions or impressions, rather than to go into the entire argument. The western and northern limit of Texas being unsettled, and the Government of the United States having retained the power of settling it, I ask, suppose the power had been exercised, and that there had been no cession of territory by Mexico to the United States, but that the negotiations between the countries had been limited simply to the fixation of the western and northern limits of Texas, could it not have been done by the United States and Mexico conjointly? Will any one dispute it? Suppose there had been a treaty of limits of Texas concluded between Mexico and the United States, fixing the Nueces as the western limit of Texas, would not Texas have been bound by it? Why, by the express terms of the resolution she would have been bound by it; or if it had been the Colorado or the Rio Grande, or any other boundary, whatever western limit had been fixed by the joint action of the two powers, would have been binding and obligatory upon Texas by the express terms of the resolution by which she was admitted into the Union. Now, sir, Mexico and the United States conjointly, by treaty, might have fixed upon the western and northern limits of Texas, and if the United States have acquired by treaty all the subjects upon which the limits of Texas might have operated, have not the United States now the power solely and exclusively which Mexico and the United States conjointly possessed prior to the late treaty between the two countries? It seems to me, sir, that this conclusion and reasoning are perfectly irresistible. If Mexico and the United States could have fixed upon any western limit for Texas, and did not do it, and if the United States have acquired to themselves, or acquired by the treaty in question, all the territory upon which the western limit must have been fixed, when it was fixed, it seems to me that no one can resist the logical conclusion, that the United States now have themselves a power to do what the United States and Mexico conjointly could have done.

Sir, I admit it is a delicate power—an extremely delicate power. I admit that it ought to be exercised in a spirit of justice, liberality, and generosity toward this the youngest member of the great American family. But here the power is. Possibly, sir, upon that question—however I offer no positive opinion—possibly, if the United States were to fix it in a way unjust in the opinion of Texas, and contrary to her rights, she might bring the question before the Supreme Court of the United States, and have it there again investigated and decided. I say possibly, sir, because I am not one of that class of politicians who believe that every question is a competent and proper question for the Supreme Court of the United States. There are questions too large for any tribunal of that kind to try; great political questions, national territorial questions, which transcend their limits; for such questions their powers are utterly incompetent. Whether this be one of those questions or not, I shall not decide; but I will maintain that the United States are now invested solely and exclusively with that power which was common to both nations—to fix, ascertain, and settle the western and northern limits of Texas.

Sir, the other day my honorable friend who represents so well the State of Texas said that we had no more right to touch the limits of Texas than we had to touch the limits of Kentucky. I think that was the illustration he gave us—that a State is one and indivisible, and that the General Government has no right to sever it. I agree with him, sir, in that; where the limits are ascertained and certain, where they are undisputed and indisputable. The General Government has no right, nor has any other earthly power the right, to interfere with the limits of a State whose boundaries are thus fixed, thus ascertained, known, and recognized. The whole power, at least, to interfere with it is voluntary. The extreme case may be put—one which I trust in God may never happen in this nation—of a conquered nation, and of a constitution adapting itself to the state of subjugation or conquest to which it has been reduced; and giving up whole States, as well as parts of States, in order to save from the conquering arms of the invader what remains. I say such a power in case of extremity may exist. But I admit that, short of such extremity, voluntarily, the General Government has no right to separate a State—to take a portion of its territory from it, or to regard it otherwise than as integral, one and indivisible, and not to be affected by any legislation of ours. But, then, I assume what does not exist in the case of Texas, and these boundaries must be known, ascertained, and indisputable. With regard to Texas, all was open, all was unfixed; all is unfixed at this moment, with respect to her limits west and north of the Nueces.

But, sir, we gave fifteen millions of dollars for this territory that we bought, and God knows what a costly bargain to this now distracted country it has been! We gave fifteen millions of dollars for the territory ceded to us by Mexico. Can Texas justly, fairly, and honorably come into the Union and claim all that she asserted a right to, without paying any portion of the fifteen millions of dollars which constituted the consideration of the grant by the ceding nation to the United States? She proposes no such thing. She talks, indeed, about the United States having been her agent, her trustee. Why, sir, the United States was no more her agent or her trustee than she was the agent or trustee of the whole people of the United States. Texas involved herself in war—(I mean to make this no reproach—none—none—upon the past)—Texas brought herself into a state of war, and when she got into that war, it was not the war of Texas and Mexico, but it was the war of the whole thirty United States and Mexico; it was a war in which the Government of the United States, which created the hostilities, was as much the trustee and agent of the twenty-nine other States composing the Union as she was the trustee and agent of Texas. And, sir, with respect to all these circumstances—such, for example, as a treaty with a map annexed, as in the case of the recent treaty with Mexico; such as the opinion of individuals highly respected and eminent, like the lamented Mr. Polk, late President of the United States, whose opinion was that he had no right, as President of the United States, or in any character otherwise than as negotiating with Mexico—and in that the Senate would have to act in concurrence with him—that he had no right to fix the boundary; and as to the map attached to the treaty, it is sufficient to say that the treaty itself is silent from beginning to end on the subject of the fixation of the boundary of Texas. The annexation of the map to the treaty was a matter of no utility, for the treaty is not strengthened by it; it no more affirms the truth of any thing delineated upon the map in relation to Texas than it does any thing in relation to any other geographical subject that composed the map.

Mr. President, I have said that I think the power has been concentrated in the Government of the United States to fix upon the limits of the State of Texas. I have said also that this power ought to be exercised in a spirit of great liberality and justice; and I put it to you, sir, to say, in reference to this second resolution of mine, whether that liberality and justice have not been displayed in the resolution which I have proposed. In the resolution, what is proposed? To confine her to the Nueces? No, sir. To extend her boundary to the mouth of the Rio Grande, and thence up that river to the southern limit of New Mexico; and thence along that limit to the boundary between the United States and Spain, as marked under the treaty of 1819.

Why, sir, here is a vast country. I believe—although I have made no estimate about it—that it is not inferior in extent of land, of acres, of square miles, to what Texas east of the river Nueces, extending to the Sabine, had before. And who is there can say with truth and justice that there is no reciprocity, nor mutuality, no concession in this resolution, made to Texas, even in reference to the question of boundary alone? You give her a vast country, equal, I repeat, in extent nearly to what she indisputably possessed before; a country sufficiently large, with her consent, hereafter to carve out of it some two or three additional States when the condition of the population may render it expedient to make new States. Sir, is there not in this resolution concession, liberality, justice? But this is not all that we propose to do. The second resolution proposes to pay off a certain amount of the debt of Texas. A blank is left in the resolution, because I have not heretofore been able to ascertain the amount.

(Mr. Foote—Will the honorable Senator allow me to suggest that it may be agreeable to him to finish his remarks to-morrow? If such be the case, I will move that the Senate now go into Executive session.

Mr. Clay—I am obliged to the worthy Senator from Mississippi; I do not think it possible for me to conclude to-day, and I will yield with great pleasure if—

Mr. Foote—I now move—

Mr. Clay—If the Senator will permit to conclude what I have to say in relation to Texas, I will then cheerfully yield the floor for his motion.)

I was about to remark that, independently of this most liberal and generous boundary which is tendered to Texas, we propose to offer her in this second resolution a sum which the worthy Senator from Texas thinks will not be less than three millions of dollars—the exact amount neither he nor I can furnish, not having the materials at hand upon which to make a statement. Well, sir, you get this large boundary and three millions of your debt paid. I shall not repeat the argument which I urged upon a former occasion, as to the obligation of the United States to pay a portion of this debt, but was struck the other day, upon reading the treaty of limits, first between the United States and Mexico, and next the treaty of limits between the United States and Texas, to find, in the preamble of both of those treaties, a direct recognition of the principle from which I think springs our obligation to pay a portion of this debt, for the payment of which the revenue of Texas was pledged before her annexation. The principle asserted in the treaty of limits with Mexico is, that whereas by the treaty of 1819, between Spain and the United States, a limit was fixed between Mexico and the United States, Mexico comprising then a portion of the possessions of the Spanish Government, although Mexico was at the date of the treaty severed from the crown of Spain, yet she, as having been a part of the possessions of the crown of Spain when the treaty of 1819 was made, was bound by that treaty as much as if it had been made by herself instead of Spain—in other words, that the severance of no part of a common empire can exonerate either portion of that empire from the obligations contracted when the empire was entire and unsevered. And, sir, the same principle is asserted in the treaty of 1838, between Texas and the United States. The principle asserted is, that the treaty of 1828 between Mexico and the United States having been made when Texas was a part of Mexico, and that now Texas being dissevered from Mexico, she nevertheless remains bound by that treaty as much as if no such severance had taken place. In other words, the principle is this—that when an independent power creates an obligation or debt, no subsequent political misfortune, no subsequent severance of the territories of that power, can exonerate it from the obligation that was created while an integral and independent power; in other words, to bring it down and apply it to this specific case—that, Texas being an independent power, and having a right to make loans and to make pledges, having raised a loan and pledged specifically the revenues arising from the customs to the public creditor, the public creditor became invested with a right to that fund; and it is a right of which he could not be divested by any other act than one to which his own consent was given—it could be divested by no political change which Texas might think proper to make. In consequence of the absorption or merging of Texas into the United States, the creditor, being no party to the treaty which was formed, does not lose his right—he retains his right to demand the fulfillment of the pledge that was made upon this specific fund, just as if there had not been any annexation of Texas to the United States.

That was the foundation upon which I arrived at the conclusion expressed in the resolution—that the United States having appropriated to themselves the revenue arising from the imports, which revenue had been pledged to the creditor of Texas, the United States as an honorable and just power ought now to pay the debt for which those duties were solemnly pledged by a power independent in itself, and competent to make the pledge. Well, sir, I think that when you consider the large boundary which is assigned to Texas—and when you take into view the abhorrence, for I think I am warranted in using this expression—with which the people of New Mexico east of the Rio Grande will look upon any political connection with Texas—and when, in addition to this, you take into view the large grant of money that we propose to make, and our liberality in exonerating her from a portion of her public debt, equal to that grant—when we take all these circumstances into consideration, I think I have presented a case in regard to which I confess I shall be greatly surprised if the people of Texas themselves, when they come to deliberate upon these liberal offers, hesitate a moment to accede to them.

I have now got through with what I had to say in reference to this resolution, and if the Senator from Mississippi wishes it, I will give way for a motion for adjournment.

Exercises

1. What was the proposition Clay was supporting?

2. What were his principal arguments?

3. What different kinds of proof did he utilize?

4. How did he support his reasoning with analogies and comparisons? With appeal to historical antecedents? With logic? With appeal to generally accepted principles?

5. By what means did he seek to establish the view that his arguments and conclusions were already widely accepted?

6. How did he attempt to help his opponents rationalize a change of their position so that they might more easily agree with him?

7. Formulate the unstated syllogism underlying Clay's argument that the boundary of Texas might have been settled between the United States and Mexico prior to agreement on the treaty that ended the war.

8. Cite passages from the speech in which Clay refuted arguments previously introduced by his opponents. What means of refutation did he employ? Does he appear to have restated the contentions of his opponents fairly, or do you feel constrained to read the speeches in which they originally appeared?

9. Identify passages in which Clay sought to conciliate his opponents.

10. Evaluate Clay's own estimate that his arguments and conclusions were "perfectly irresistible."

11. Cite phrases, sentences, or passages that seem to you to be typical of oral (as opposed to written) style.

12. On the basis of this speech, how would you characterize Henry Clay as a man? As a politician? As a statesman? What evidence do you find in general histories and in biographies of Clay and his associates that confirms or revises the impressions you derived from reading this speech? What does this comparison of internal and external evidence teach you concerning the role of ethos in persuasion?

13. It has been said that Clay's speech probably did not directly change a single Senate vote but that it helped to influence public opinion, which in turn may have influenced the eventual vote. Do you find any evidence in the speech which might indicate Clay was appealing over the heads of the Senators to the public?

14. In his *Prologue to Conflict: The Crisis and Compromise of 1850*, Holman Hamilton provides the most detailed and most thoroughly researched account available concerning the Compromise. Study carefully the following statements drawn from his book. Then, after comparing them with the traditional treatments, account for the differences in interpretation.

"Long before [Clay's] Committee of Thirteen was formed, the Committee on Territories (which had a Democratic majority, and of which [Stephen A.] Douglas was the chairman) had considered and approved the component parts of the Omnibus. What Clay did was to connect old bills and to make the enactment of one dependent on the enactment of all. . . . At best, Clay's leadership had proved itself of dubious value in the Senate. . . . It was a serious 'error to attempt to unite . . . the various measures . . . in one bill. That course arrayed all the malcontents . . . into a formidable phalanx against the whole.' . . . [After Clay's Omnibus Compromise was defeated in the Senate, Douglas took charge and, dividing the Omnibus into separate bills, pushed each through the Senate.] It is perfectly clear that, in the House as in the Senate, Democratic leadership and Democratic followership were mainly responsible for the Compromise of 1850. . . . The dominant Senate leader, his House counterpart, most adjustment votes in both chambers, and the origin of most measures were Democratic. The Whig contribution should not be minimized, but it was supplemental."

John Caldwell Calhoun

Speech in the United States Senate, March 4, 1850, opposing the Compromise Bills

ALWAYS, John C. Calhoun (1782–1850) was a defender of the Union—but only on terms acceptable to his section. For the first third of his long career, which included service as a member of the United States House of Representatives and of the Senate and as Secretary of War, Vice President of the United States, and Secretary of State, Calhoun was an ardent nationalist of the stamp of Henry Clay. But as economic and political conditions transformed the South into a protesting minority, Calhoun reversed himself and for the remainder of his life was a sectionalist politician and political philosopher determined to find ways and means of protecting the interests of the South. He became the foremost supporter of the "State's rights" view that, inasmuch as the Federal Constitution was a "compact between sovereign states," the agent of the compact—the federal government—possessed only limited, delegated power. He also became the chief exponent of the doctrine of "nullification," or "interposition," which provided the rationalization by which a state could legally and constitutionally annul a federal law: it could simply interpose its inviolable sovereignty between the federal law and the people of the state. The hub of his political theory was that in political unions the majority must be restrained from an "unreasonable" exercise of its will upon minorities. The proper means of protecting the interests of minorities is, of course, as perplexing a problem today as it was in the time of Calhoun. Some observers believe that in the political affairs of the nation, even in the United

Nations, they see reverberations of Calhoun's concepts of "interposition," "concurrent majorities," and "political pluralism."

Traditionally Calhoun is represented as "the cast-iron man," (a phrase attached to him by the travelling Englishwoman Harriet Martineau) a stern logician. The historian John T. Morse, Jr., wrote of him: "The rigidity of his logic, the straightforwardness with which he made the journey from his premises to his conclusions, equally without mercy and without fear, took the place of brilliant oratory and personal charm." John Quincy Adams in 1818 thought him "above all sectional and factional prejudices more than any other statesman of the Union with whom I have ever acted." But by 1832–33, in opposition to tariff measures which Calhoun felt were ruinous to South Carolina, he was charging that the "constitution has gradually become a dead letter," and the federal government had degenerated into "a mere instrument of taking money away from one portion of the community, to be given to another."

Personally Calhoun was decorous, courteous, and friendly. A Northern newsman, John Dyer, thought him "so morally clean and spiritually pure . . . that it was a pleasure to have one's soul close to his soul . . . as fresh and bracing as a breeze from the prairie, the ocean, or the mountain." He was especially kind, even to the end of his life, when his health was bad, to new young Congressmen, of whatever party or political alliance, welcoming them to his rooms and advising them on how to make their influence felt.

The speech on the Compromise Bills was presented in the last month of his life, when he was so weak that he twice fainted in the streets. During the winter of 1849–50, Calhoun appeared seldom in the Senate—when he did, "looking pale and ghastly," as a newsman wrote. Nevertheless, rumors spread around Washington that the great Southerner meant to reply to Clay.

Too weak to hold a pen, Calhoun dictated his speech and arranged to present it on March 4. The Senate chamber and galleries were crowded, as they had been for the speech by Clay. Calhoun entered late and the crowd parted to make way for him as he slowly faltered into the chamber, leaning on the arm of a friend. For several minutes he remained in his seat, all eyes fixed on him, as he gathered sufficient strength to rise. Finally he stood, his mass of white hair crowning a face already grey with premonitory pallor, thanked the Senate for its courtesy in reserving time for his speech, then handed the manuscript to Senator James Mason of Virginia, who read it for him.

Afterwards, Calhoun was assisted back to his Washington boardinghouse, where, too excited to rest, he wrote to a friend: "My speech . . . was read today. . . . My friends think it among my most successful. . . . I have made up the issue between North and South. If we flinch, we are gone; but if we stand fast . . . we shall triumph, either by compelling the North to yield to our terms or declaring our Independence of them."

Twenty-seven days later Calhoun was dead. At the close of the funeral services, held in the Senate chamber, Senator Thomas Hart Benton of Missouri, one of Calhoun's bitterest critics, said: "He is not dead, sir; he is not dead. There may be no vitality in his body. But there's plenty in his doctrines."

The text of this speech is from *Works of John C. Calhoun,* ed. Richard K. Crallé, New York: Appleton, 1888, Vol. VI.

COMPROMISE SPEECH OF 1850

I have, Senators, believed from the first that the agitation of the subject of slavery would, if not prevented by some timely and effective measure, end in disunion. Entertaining this opinion, I have, on all proper occasions, endeavored to call the attention of both the two great parties which divide the country to adopt some measure to prevent so great a disaster, but without success. The agitation has been permitted to proceed, with almost no attempt to resist it, until it has reached a point when it can no longer be disguised or denied that the Union is in danger. You have thus had forced upon you the greatest and gravest question that can ever come under your consideration—*How can the Union be preserved?*

To give a satisfactory answer to this mighty question, it is indispensable to have an accurate and thorough knowledge of the nature and the character of the cause by which the Union is endangered. Without such knowledge it is impossible to pronounce, with any certainty, by what measure it can be saved; just as it would be impossible for a physician to pronounce, in the case of some dangerous disease, with any certainty, by what remedy the patient could be saved, without similar knowledge of the nature and character of the cause which produced it. The first question, then, presented for consideration, in the investigation I propose to make, in order to obtain such knowledge, is—What is it that has endangered the Union?

To this question there can be but one answer,—that the immediate cause is the almost universal discontent which pervades all the States composing the Southern section of the Union. This widely-extended discontent is not of recent origin. It commenced with the agitation of the slavery question, and has been increasing ever since. The next question, going one step further back, is—What has caused this widely diffused and almost universal discontent?

It is a great mistake to suppose, as is by some, that it originated with demagogues, who excited the discontent with the intention of aiding their personal advancement, or with the disappointed ambition of certain politicians, who resorted to it as the means of retrieving their fortunes. On the contrary, all the great political influences of the section were arrayed against excitement, and exerted to the utmost to keep the people quiet. The great mass of the people of the South were divided, as in the other section, into Whigs and Democrats. The leaders and the presses of both parties in the South were very solicitous to prevent excitement and to preserve quiet; because it was seen that the effects of the former would necessarily tend to weaken, if not destroy, the political ties which united them with their respective parties in the other section. Those who know the strength of party ties will readily appreciate the immense force which this cause exerted against agitation, and in favor of preserving quiet. But, great as it was, it was not sufficient to prevent the wide-spread discontent which now pervades the section. No; some cause, far deeper and more powerful than the one supposed, must exist, to account for discontent so wide and deep. The question then recurs—What is the cause of this discontent? It will be found in the belief of the people of the Southern States, as prevalent as the discontent itself, that they cannot remain, as things now are, consistently with honor and safety, in the Union. The next question to be considered is—What has caused this belief?

One of the causes is, undoubtedly, to be traced to the long-continued agitation of the slave question on the part of the North, and the many aggressions which they have made on the rights of the South during the time. I will not enumerate them at present, as it will be done hereafter in its proper place.

There is another lying back of it—with which this is intimately connected—that may be regarded as the great and primary cause. This is to be found in the fact that the equilibrium between the two sections, in the Government as it stood when the constitution was ratified and the Government put in action, has been destroyed. At that time there was nearly a perfect equilibrium between the two, which afforded ample means to each to protect itself against the aggression of the other; but, as it now stands, one section has the exclusive power of controlling the Government, which leaves the other without any adequate means of protecting itself against its encroachment and oppression. To place this subject distinctly before you, I have, Senators, prepared a brief statistical statement, showing the relative weight of the two sections in the Government under the first census of 1790 and the last census of 1840.

According to the former, the population of the United States, including Vermont, Kentucky, and Tennessee, which then were in their incipient condition of becoming States, but were not actually admitted, amounted to 3,929,827. Of this number the Northern States had 1,997,899, and the Southern 1,952,072, making a difference of only 45,827 in favor of the former States. The number of States, including Vermont, Kentucky, and Tennessee, were sixteen; of which eight, including Vermont, belonged to the Northern section, and eight, including Kentucky and Tennessee, to the Southern—making an equal division of the States between the two sections under the first census. There was a small preponderance in the House of Representatives, and in the electoral college, in favor of the Northern, owing to the fact that, according to the provisions of the Constitution, in estimating federal numbers five slaves count but three; but it was too small to affect sensibly the perfect equilibrium which, with that exception, existed at the time. Such was the equality of the two sections when the States composing them agreed to enter into a Federal Union. Since then the equilibrium between them has been greatly disturbed.

According to the last census the aggregate population of the United States amounted to 17,063,357, of which the Northern section contained 9,728,920, and the Southern 7,334,437, making a difference, in round numbers, of 2,400,000. The number of States had increased from sixteen to twenty-six, making an addition of ten States. In the mean time the position of Delaware had become doubtful as to which section she properly belonged. Considering her as neutral, the Northern States will have thirteen and the Southern States twelve, making a difference in the Senate of two Senators in favor of the former. According to the apportionment under the census of 1840, there were two hundred and twenty-three members of the House of Representatives, of which the Northern States had one hundred and thirty-five, and the Southern states (considering Delaware as neutral) eighty-seven, making a difference in favor of the former in the House of Representatives of forty-eight. The difference in the Senate of two members, added to this, gives to the North, in the electoral college, a majority of fifty. Since the census of 1840, four States have been added to the Union—Iowa, Wisconsin, Florida, and Texas. They leave the difference in the Senate as it stood when the census was taken; but add two to the side of the North in the House, making the present majority in the House in its favor fifty, and in the electoral college fifty-two.

The result of the whole is to give the Northern section a predominance in every department of the Government, and thereby concentrate in it the two elements which constitute the Federal Government,—majority of States, and a majority of their population, estimated in federal numbers. Whatever section concentrates the two in itself possesses the control of the entire Government.

But we are just at the close of the sixth decade, and the commencement of the seventh. The census is to be taken this year, which must add greatly to the decided preponderance of the North in the House of Representatives and in the electoral college. The prospect is, also, that a great increase will be added to its present preponderance in the Senate, during the period of the decade, by the addition of new States. Two territories, Oregon and Minnesota, are already in progress, and strenuous efforts are making to bring in three additional States from the territory recently conquered from Mexico; which, if successful, will add three other States in a short time to the Northern section, making five States; and increasing the present number of its States from fifteen to twenty, and of its Senators from thirty to forty. On the contrary, there is not a single territory in progress in the Southern section, and no certainty that any additional State will be added to it during the decade. The prospect then is, that the two sections in the Senate, should the efforts now made to exclude the South from the newly acquired territories succeed, will stand, before the end of the decade, twenty Northern States to fourteen Southern (considering Delaware as neutral), and forty Northern Senators to twenty-eight Southern. This great increase of Senators, added to the great increase of members of the House of Representatives and the electoral college on the part of the North, which must take place under the next decade, will effectually and irretrievably destroy the equilibrium which existed when the Government commenced.

Had this destruction been the operation of time, without the interference of Government, the South would have had no reason to complain; but such was not the fact. It was caused by the legislation of this Government, which was appointed, as the common agent of all, and charged with the protection of the interests and security of all. The legislation by which it has been effected, may be classed under three heads. The first is, that series of acts by which the South has been excluded from the common territory belonging to all the States as members of the Federal Union—which have had the effect of extending vastly the portion allotted to the Northern section, and restricting within narrow limits the portion left the South. The next consists in adopting a system of revenue and disbursements, by which an undue proportion of the burden of taxation has been imposed upon the South, and an undue proportion of its proceeds appropriated to the North; and the last is a system of political measures, by which the original character of the Government has been radically changed. I propose to bestow upon each of these, in the order they stand, a few remarks, with the view of showing that it is owing to the action of this Government, that the equilibrium between the two sections has been destroyed, and the whole powers of the system centered in a sectional majority.

The first of the series of acts by which the South was deprived of its due share of the territories, originated with the confederacy which preceded the existence of this Government. It is to be found in the provision of the ordinance of 1787. Its effect was to exclude the South entirely from that vast and fertile region which lies between the Ohio and the Mississippi rivers, now embracing five States and one territory. The next of the series is the Missouri compromise, which excluded the South from that large portion of Louisiana which lies north of 36° 30′, excepting what is included in the State of Missouri. The last of the series excluded the South from the whole of the Oregon Territory. All these, in the slang of the day, were what are called slave territories, and not free soil; that is, territories belonging to slaveholding powers and open to the emigration of masters with their slaves. By these several acts, the South was excluded from 1,238,025 square miles—an extent of country considerably exceeding the entire valley of the Mississippi. To the South was left the portion of the Territory of Louisiana lying south of 36° 30′, and the portion north of it included in the State of Missouri, with the portion lying south of 36° 30′, including the States of Louisiana and Arkansas, and the territory lying west of the latter, and south of 36° 30′, called the Indian country. These, with the Territory of Florida, now the State, make, in the whole, 283,503 square miles. To this must be added the territory acquired with Texas. If the whole should be added to the Southern section, it would make an increase of 325,520, which would make the whole left to the South, 609,023. But a large part of Texas is still in contest between the two sections, which leaves it uncertain what will be the real extent of the portion of territory that may be left to the South.

I have not included the territory recently acquired by the treaty with Mexico. The North is making the most strenuous efforts to appropriate the whole to herself, by excluding the South from every foot of it. If she should succeed, it will add to that from which the South has already been excluded, 526,078 square miles, and would increase the whole which the North has appropriated to herself, to 1,764,023, not including the portion that she may succeed in excluding us from in Texas. To sum up the whole, the United States, since they declared their independence, have acquired 2,373,046 square miles of territory, from which the North will have excluded the South, if she should succeed in monopolizing the newly acquired territories, about three-fourths of the whole, leaving to the South but about one-fourth.

Such is the first and great cause that has destroyed the equilibrium between the two sections in the Government.

The next is the system of revenue and disbursements which has been adopted by the Government. It is well known that the Government has derived its revenue mainly from duties on imports. I shall not undertake to show that such duties must necessarily fall mainly on the exporting States, and that the South, as the great exporting portion of the Union, has in reality paid vastly more than her due proportion of the revenue; because I deem it unnecessary, as the subject has on so many occasions been fully discussed. Nor shall I, for the same reason, undertake to show that a far greater portion of the revenue has been disbursed at the North, than its due share; and that the joint effect of these causes has been, to transfer a vast amount from South to North, which, under an equal system of revenue and disbursements, would not have been lost to her. If to this be added, that many of the duties were imposed, not for revenue, but for protection,–that is, intended to put money, not in the treasury, but directly into the pocket of the manufacturers,–some conception may be formed of the immense amount which, in the long course of sixty years, has been transferred from South to North. There are no data by which it can be estimated with any certainty; but it is safe to say, that it amounts to hundreds of millions of dollars. Under the most moderate estimate, it would be sufficient to add greatly to the wealth of the North, and thus greatly increase her population by attracting emigration from all quarters to that section.

This, combined with the great primary cause, amply explains why the North has acquired a preponderance in every department of the Government by its disproportionate increase of population and States. The former, as has been shown, has increased, in fifty years, 2,400,000 over that of the South. This increase of population, during so long a period, is satisfactorily accounted for, by the number of emigrants, and the increase of their descendants, which have been attracted to the Northern section from Europe and the South, in consequence of the advantages derived from the causes assigned. If they had not existed–if the South had retained all the capital which has been extracted from her by the fiscal action of the Government; and, if it had not been excluded by the ordinance of 1787 and the Missouri compromise, from the region lying between the Ohio and the Mississippi rivers, and between the Mississippi and the Rocky Mountains north of 36° 30′–it scarcely admits of a doubt, that it would have divided the emigration with the North, and by retaining her own people, would have at least equalled the North in population under the census of 1840, and probably under that about to be taken. She would also, if she had retained her equal rights in those territories, have maintained an equality in the number of States with the North, and have preserved the equilibrium between the two sections that existed at the commencement of the Government. The loss, then, of the equilibrium is to be attributed to the action of this Government.

But while these measures were destroying the equilibrium between the two sections, the action of the Government was leading to a radical change in its character, by concentrating all the power of the system in itself. The occasion will not permit me to trace the measures by which this great change has been consummated. If it did, it would not be difficult to show that the process commenced at an early period of the Government; and that it proceeded, almost without interruption, step by step, until it absorbed virtually its entire powers; but without going through the whole process to establish the fact, it may be done satisfactorily by a very short statement.

That the Government claims, and practically maintains the right to decide in the last resort, as to the extent of its powers, will scarcely be denied by any one coversant with the political history of the country. That it also claims the right to resort to force to maintain whatever power it claims, against all opposition, is equally certain. Indeed it is apparent, from what we daily hear, that this has become the prevailing and fixed opinion of a great majority of the community. Now, I ask, what limitation can possibly be placed upon the powers of a government claiming and exercising such rights? And, if none can be, how can the separate governments of the States maintain and protect the powers reserved to them by the Constitution—or the people of the several States maintain those which are reserved to them, and among others, the sovereign powers by which they ordained and established, not only their separate State Constitutions and Governments, but also the Constitution and Government of the United States? But, if they have no constitutional means of maintaining them against the right claimed by this Government, it necessarily follows, that they hold them at its pleasure and discretion, and that all the powers of the system are in reality concentrated in it. It also follows, that the character of the Government has been changed in consequence, from a federal republic, as it originally came from the hands of its framers, into a great national consolidated democracy. It has indeed, at present, all the characteristics of the latter, and not one of the former, although it still retains its outward form.

The result of the whole of these causes combined is—that the North has acquired a decided ascendancy over every department of this Government, and through it a control over all the powers of the system. A single section governed by the will of the numerical majority, has now, in fact, the control of the Government and the entire powers of the system. What was once a constitutional federal republic, is now converted, in reality, into one as absolute as that of the Autocrat of Russia, and as despotic in its tendency as any absolute government that ever existed.

As, then, the North has the absolute control over the Government, it is manifest, that on all questions between it and the South, where there is a diversity of interests, the interest of the latter will be sacrificed to the former, however oppressive the effects may be; as the South possesses no means by which it can resist, through the action of the Government. But if there was no question of vital importance to the South, in reference to which there was a diversity of views between the two sections, this state of things might be endured, without the hazard of destruction to the South. But such is not the fact. There is a question of vital importance to the Southern section, in reference to which the views and feelings of the two sections are as opposite and hostile as they can possibly be.

I refer to the relation between the two races in the Southern section, which constitutes a vital portion of her social organization. Every portion of the North entertains views and feelings more or less hostile to it. Those most opposed and hostile, regard it as a sin, and consider themselves under the most sacred obligation to use every effort to destroy it. Indeed, to the extent that they conceive they have power, they regard themselves as implicated in the sin, and responsible for not suppressing it by the use of all and every means. Those less opposed and hostile, regard it as a crime—an offence against humanity, as they call it; and, although not so fanatical, feel themselves bound to use all efforts to effect the same object; while those who are least opposed and hostile, regard it as a blot and a stain on the character of what they call the Nation, and feel themselves accordingly bound to give it no countenance or support. On the contrary, the Southern section regards the relation as one which cannot be destroyed without subjecting the two races to the greatest calamity, and the section to poverty, desolation, and wretchedness; and accordingly they feel bound, by every consideration of interest and safety, to defend it.

This hostile feeling on the part of the North towards the social organization of the South long lay dormant, but it only required some cause to act on those who felt most intensely that they were responsible for its continuance, to call it into action. The increasing power of this Government, and of the control of the Northern section over all its departments, furnished the cause. It was this which made an impression on the minds of many, that there was little or no restraint to prevent the Government from doing whatever it might choose to do. This was sufficient of itself to put the most fanatical portion of the North in action, for the purpose of destroying the existing relation between the two races in the South.

The first organized movement towards it commenced in 1835. Then, for the first time, societies were organized, presses established, lecturers sent forth to excite the people of the North, and incendiary publications scattered over the whole South, through the mail. The South was thoroughly aroused. Meetings were held everywhere, and resolutions adopted, calling upon the North to apply a remedy to arrest the threatened evil, and pledging themselves to adopt measures for their own protection, if it was not arrested. At the meeting of Congress, petitions poured in from the North, calling upon Congress to abolish slavery in the District of Columbia, and to prohibit what they called the internal slave trade between the States—announcing at the same time, that their ultimate object was to abolish slavery, not only in the District, but in the States and throughout the Union. At this period, the number engaged in the agitation was small, and possessed little or no personal influence.

Neither party in Congress had, at that time, any sympathy with them or their cause. The members of each party presented their petitions with great reluctance. Nevertheless, small and contemptible as the party then was, both of the great parties of the North dreaded them. They felt, that though small, they were organized in reference to a subject which had a great and a commanding influence over the Northern mind. Each party, on that account, feared to oppose their petitions, lest the opposite party should take advantage of the one who might do so, by favoring them. The effect was, that both united in insisting that the petitions should be received, and that Congress should take jurisdiction over the subject. To justify their course, they took the extraordinary ground, that Congress was bound to receive petitions on every subject, however objectionable they might be, and whether they had, or had not, jurisdiction over the subject. These views prevailed in the House of Representatives, and partially in the Senate; and thus the party succeeded in their first movements, in gaining what they proposed—a position in Congress, from which agitation could be extended over the whole Union. This was the commencement of the agitation, which has ever since continued, and which, as is now acknowledged, has endangered the Union itself.

As for myself, I believed at that early period, if the party who got up the petitions should succeed in getting Congress to take jurisdiction, that agitation would follow, and that it would in the end, if not arrested, destroy the Union. I then so expressed myself in debate, and called upon both parties to take grounds against assuming jurisdiction; but in vain. Had my voice been heeded, and had Congress refused to take jurisdiction, by the united votes of all parties, the agitation which followed would have been prevented, and the fanatical zeal that gives impulse to the agitation, and which has brought us to our present perilous condition, would have become extinguished, from the want of fuel to feed the flame. That was the time for the North to have shown her devotion to the Union; but, unfortunately, both of the great parties of that section were so intent on obtaining or retaining party ascendancy, that all other considerations were overlooked or forgotten.

What has since followed are but natural consequences. With the success of their first movement, this small fanatical party began to acquire strength; and with that, to become an object of courtship to both the great parties. The necessary consequence was, a further increase of power, and a gradual tainting of the opinions of both of the other parties with their doctrines, until the infection has extended over both; and the great mass of the population of the North, who, whatever may be their opinion of the original abolition party, which still preserves its distinctive organization, hardly ever fail, when it comes to acting, to co-operate in carrying out their measures. With the increase of their influence, they extended the sphere of their action. In a short time after the commencement of their first movement, they had acquired sufficient influence to induce the legislatures of most of the Northern States to pass acts, which in effect abrogated the clause of the Constitution that provides for the delivery up of fugitive slaves. Not long after, petitions followed to abolish slavery in forts, magazines, and dockyards, and all other places where Congress had exclusive power of legislation. This was followed by petitions and resolutions of legislatures of the Northern States, and popular meetings, to exclude the Southern States from all territories acquired, or to be acquired, and to prevent the admission of any State hereafter into the Union, which, by its Constitution, does not prohibit slavery. And Congress is invoked to do all this, expressly with the view to the final abolition of slavery in the States. That has been avowed to be the ultimate object from the beginning of the agitation until the present time; and yet the great body of both parties of the North, with the full knowledge of the fact, although disavowing the abolitionists, have co-operated with them in almost all their measures.

Such is a brief history of the agitation, as far as it has yet advanced. Now I ask, Senators, what is there to prevent its further progress, until it fulfills the ultimate end proposed, unless some decisive measure should be adopted to prevent it? Has any one of the causes, which has added to its increase from its original small and contemptible beginning until it has attained its present magnitude, diminished in force? Is the original cause of the movement—that slavery is a sin, and ought to be suppressed—weaker now than at the commencement? Or is the abolition party less numerous or influential, or have they less influence with, or control over the two great parties of the North in elections? Or has the South greater means of influencing or controlling the movements of this Government now, than it had when the agitation commenced? To all these questions but one answer can be given: No—no—no. The very reverse is true.

Instead of being weaker, all the elements in favor of agitation are stronger now than they were in 1835, when it first commenced, while all the elements of influence on the part of the South are weaker. Unless something decisive is done, I again ask, what is to stop this agitation, before the great and final object at which it aims—the abolition of slavery in the States—is consummated? Is it, then, not certain, that if something is not done to arrest it, the South will be forced to choose between abolition and secession? Indeed, as events are now moving, it will not require the South to secede, in order to dissolve the Union. Agitation will of itself effect it, of which its past history furnishes abundant proof—as I shall next proceed to show.

It is a great mistake to suppose that disunion can be effected by a single blow. The cords which bound these States together in one common Union, are far too numerous and powerful for that. Disunion must be the work of time. It is only through a long process, and successively, that the cords can be snapped, until the whole fabric falls asunder. Already the agitation of the slavery question has snapped some of the most important, and has greatly weakened all the others, as I shall proceed to show.

The cords that bind the States together are not only many, but various in character. Some are spiritual or ecclesiastical; some political; others social. Some appertain to the benefit conferred by the Union, and others to the feeling of duty and obligation.

The strongest of those of a spiritual and ecclesiastical nature, consisted in the unity of the great religious denominations, all of which originally embraced the whole Union. All these denominations, with the exception, perhaps, of the Catholics, were organized very much upon the principle of our political institutions. Beginning with smaller meetings, corresponding with the political divisions of the country, their organization terminated in one great central assemblage, corresponding very much with the character of Congress. At these meetings the principal clergymen and lay members of the respective denominations, from all parts of the Union, met to transact business relating to their common concerns. It was not confined to what appertained to the doctrines and discipline of the respective denominations, but extended to plans for disseminating the Bible—establishing missions, distributing tracts—and of establishing presses for the publication of tracts, newspapers, and periodicals, with a view of diffusing religious information—and for the support of their respective doctrines and creeds. All this combined contributed greatly to strengthen the bonds of the Union. The ties which held each denomination together formed a strong cord to hold the whole Union together; but, powerful as they were, they have not been able to resist the explosive effect of slavery agitation.

The first of these cords which snapped, under its explosive force, was that of the powerful Methodist Episcopal Church. The numerous and strong ties which held it together, are all broken, and its unity gone. They now form separate churches; and, instead of that feeling of attachment and devotion to the interests of the whole church which was formerly felt, they are now arrayed into two hostile bodies, engaged in litigation about what was formerly their common property.

The next cord that snapped was that of the Baptists—one of the largest and most respectable of the denominations. That of the Presbyterian is not entirely snapped, but some of its strands have given way. That of the Episcopal Church is the only one of the four great Protestant denominations which remains unbroken and entire.

The strongest cord, of a political character, consists of the many and powerful ties that have held together the two great parties which have, with some modifications, existed from the beginning of the Government. They both extended to every portion of the Union, and strongly contributed to hold all its parts together. But this powerful cord has fared no better than the spiritual. It resisted, for a long time, the explosive tendency of the agitation, but has finally snapped under its force—if not entirely, in a great measure. Nor is there one of the remaining cords which has not been greatly weakened. To this extent the Union has already been destroyed by agitation, in the only way it can be, by sundering and weakening the cords which bind it together.

If the agitation goes on, the same force, acting with increased intensity, as has been shown, will finally snap every cord, when nothing will be left to hold the States together except force. But, surely, that can, with no propriety of language, be called a Union, when the only means by which the weaker is held connected with the stronger portion is force. It may, indeed, keep them connected; but the connection will partake much more of the character of subjugation, on the part of the weaker to the stronger, than the union of free, independent, and sovereign States, in one confederation, as they stood in the early stages of the Government, and which only is worthy of the sacred name of Union.

Having now, Senators, explained what it is that endangers the Union, and traced it to its cause, and explained its nature and character, the question again recurs—How can the Union be saved? To this I answer, there is but one way by which it can be—and that is—by adopting such measures as will satisfy the States belonging to the Southern section, that they can remain in the Union consistently with their honor and their safety. There is, again, only one way by which this can be effected, and that is—by removing the causes by which this belief has been produced. Do *this*, and discontent will cease—harmony and kind feelings between the sections be restored—and every apprehension of danger to the Union removed. The question, then, is—How can this be done? But, before I undertake to answer this question, I propose to show by what the Union cannot be saved.

It cannot, then, be saved by eulogies on the Union, however splendid or numerous. The cry of "Union, Union–the glorious Union!" can no more prevent disunion than the cry of "Health, health–glorious health!" on the part of the physician, can save a patient lying dangerously ill. So long as the Union, instead of being regarded as a protector, is regarded in the opposite character, by not much less than a majority of the States, it will be in vain to attempt to conciliate them by pronouncing eulogies on it.

Besides this cry of Union comes commonly from those whom we cannot believe to be sincere. It usually comes from our assailants. But we cannot believe them to be sincere; for, if they loved the Union, they would necessarily be devoted to the Constitution. It made the Union,–and to destroy the Constitution would be to destroy the Union. But the only reliable and certain evidence of devotion to the Constitution is, to abstain, on the one hand, from violating it, and to repel, on the other, all attempts to violate it. It is only by faithfully performing these high duties that the Constitution can be preserved, and with it the Union.

But how stands the profession of devotion to the Union by our assailants, when brought to this test? Have they abstained from violating the Constitution? Let the many acts passed by the Northern States to set aside and annul the clause of the Constitution providing for the delivery up of fugitive slaves answer. I cite this, not that it is the only instance (for there are many others), but because the violation in this particular is too notorious and palpable to be denied. Again: have they stood forth faithfully to repel violations of the Constitution? Let their course in reference to the agitation of the slavery question, which was commenced and has been carried on for fifteen years, avowedly for the purpose of abolishing slavery in the States–an object all acknowledge to be unconstitutional–answer. Let them show a single instance, during this long period, in which they have denounced the agitators in their attempts to effect what is admitted to be unconstitutional, yet a single measure which they have brought forward for that purpose. How can we, with all these facts before us, believe that they are sincere in their profession of devotion to the Union, or avoid believing their profession is but intended to increase the vigor of their assaults and to weaken the force of our resistance?

Nor can we regard the profession of devotion to the Union, on the part of those who are not our assailants, as sincere, when they pronounce eulogies upon the Union, evidently with the intent of charging us with disunion, without uttering one word of denunciation against our assailants. If friends of the Union, their course should be to unite with us in repelling these assaults, and denouncing the authors as enemies of the

Union. Why they avoid this, and pursue the course they do, it is for them to explain.

Nor can the Union be saved by invoking the name of the illustrious Southerner whose mortal remains repose on the western bank of the Potomac. He was one of us—a slaveholder and a planter. We have studied his history, and find nothing in it to justify submission to wrong. On the contrary, his great fame rests on the solid foundation, that, while he was careful to avoid doing wrong to others, he was prompt and decided in repelling wrong. I trust that, in this respect, we profited by his example.

Nor can we find any thing in his history to deter us from seceding from the Union, should it fail to fulfill the objects for which it was instituted, by being permanently and hopelessly converted into the means of oppressing instead of protecting us. On the contrary, we find much in his example to encourage us, should we be forced to the extremity of deciding between submission and disunion.

There existed then, as well as now, a union—that between the parent country and her then colonies. It was a union that had much to endear it to the people of the colonies. Under its protecting and superintending care, the colonies were planted and grew up and prospered, through a long course of years, until they became populous and wealthy. Its benefits were not limited to them. Their extensive agricultural and other productions, gave birth to a flourishing commerce, which richly rewarded the parent country for the trouble and expense of establishing and protecting them. Washington was born and grew up to manhood under that union. He acquired his early distinction in its service, and there is every reason to believe that he was devotedly attached to it. But his devotion was a rational one. He was attached to it, not as an end, but as a means to an end. When it failed to fulfill its end, and, instead of affording protection, was converted into the means of oppressing the colonies, he did not hesitate to draw his sword, and head the great movement by which that union was for ever severed, and the independence of these States established. This was the great and crowning glory of his life, which has spread his fame over the whole globe, and will transmit it to the latest posterity.

Nor can the plan proposed by the distinguished Senator from Kentucky, nor that of the administration save the Union. I shall pass by, without remark, the plan proposed by the Senator, and proceed directly to the consideration of that of the administration. I however assure the distinguished and able Senator, that, in taking this course, no disrespect whatever is intended to him or his plan. I have adopted it, because so many Senators of distinguished abilities, who were present when he delivered his speech, and explained his plan, and who were fully capable to do justice to the side they support, have replied to him.

The plan of the administration cannot save the Union, because it can have no effect whatever, towards satisfying the States comprising the southern section of the Union, that they can, consistently with safety and honor, remain in the Union. It is, in fact, but a modification of the Wilmot Proviso. It proposes to effect the same object,—to exclude the South from all territory acquired by the Mexican treaty. It is well known that the South is united against the Wilmot Proviso, and has committed itself by solemn resolutions, to resist, should it be adopted. Its opposition *is not to the name*, but that which it *proposes to effect*. That, the Southern States hold to be unconstitutional, unjust, inconsistent with their equality as members of the common Union, and calculated to destroy irretrievably the equilibrium between the two sections. These objections equally apply to what, for brevity, I will call the Executive Proviso. There is no difference between it and the Wilmot, except in the mode of effecting the object; and in that respect, I must say, that the latter is much the least objectionable. It goes to its object openly, boldly, and distinctly. It claims for Congress unlimited power over the territories, and proposes to assert it over the territories acquired from Mexico, by a positive prohibition of slavery. Not so the Executive Provisio. It takes an indirect course, and in order to elude the Wilmot Proviso, and thereby avoid encountering the united and determined resistance of the South, it denies, by implication, the authority of Congress to legislate for the territories, and claims the right as belonging exclusively to the inhabitants of the territories. But to effect the object of excluding the South, it takes care, in the mean time, to let in emigrants freely from the Northern States and all other quarters, except from the South, which it takes special care to exclude by holding up to them the danger of having their slaves liberated under the Mexican laws. The necessary consequence is to exclude the South from the territory, just as effectually as would the Wilmot Proviso. The only difference in this respect is, that what one proposes to effect directly and openly, the other proposes to effect indirectly and covertly.

But the Executive Proviso is more objectionable than the Wilmot, in another and more important particular. The latter, to effect its object, inflicts a dangerous wound upon the Constitution, by depriving the Southern States, as joint partners and owners of the territories, of their rights in them; but it inflicts no greater wound than is absolutely necessary to effect its object. The former, on the contrary, while it inflicts the same wound, inflicts others equally great, and, if possible, greater, as I shall next proceed to explain.

In claiming the right for the inhabitants, instead of Congress, to legislate for the territories, the Executive Proviso, assumes that the sovereignty over the territories is vested in the former: or to express it in the language used in a resolution offered by one of the Senators from

Texas (General Houston, now absent), they have "the same inherent right of self-government as the people in the States." The assumption is utterly unfounded, unconstitutional, without example, and contrary to the entire practice of the Government, from its commencement to the present time, as I shall proceed to show.

The recent movement of individuals in California to form a constitution and a State government, and to appoint Senators and Representatives, is the first fruit of this monstrous assumption. If the individuals who made this movement had gone into California as adventurers, and if, as such, they had conquered the territory and established their independence, the sovereignty of the country would have been vested in them, as a separate and independent community. In that case, they would have had the right to form a constitution, and to establish a government for themselves; and if, afterwards, they thought proper to apply to Congress for admission into the Union as a sovereign and independent State, all this would have been regular, and according to established principles. But such is not the case. It was the United States who conquered California and finally acquired it by treaty. The sovereignty, of course, is vested in them, and not in the individuals who have attempted to form a constitution and a State without their consent. All this is clear, beyond controversy unless it can be shown that they have since lost or been divested of their sovereignty.

Nor is it less clear, that the power of legislating over the acquired territory is vested in Congress, and not, as is assumed, in the inhabitants of the territories. None can deny that the Government of the United States has the power to acquire territories, either by war or treaty; but if the power to acquire exists, it belongs to Congress to carry it into execution. On this point there can be no doubt, for the Constitution expressly provides, that Congress shall have power "to make all laws which shall be necessary and proper to carry into execution the foregoing powers" (those vested in Congress), "and all other powers vested by this Constitution in *the Government* of the United States, or in *any department* or *officer* thereof." It matters not, then, where the power is vested; for, if vested at all in the Government of the United States, or any of its departments, or officers, the power of carrying it into execution is clearly vested in Congress. But this important provision, while it gives to Congress the power of legislating over territories, imposes important limitations on its exercise, by restricting Congress to passing laws necessary and proper for carrying the power into execution. The prohibition extends, not only to all laws not suitable or appropriate to the object of the power, but also to all that are unjust, unequal, or unfair,—for all such laws would be unnecessary and improper, and, therefore, unconstitutional.

Having now established, beyond controversy, that the sovereignty over the territories is vested in the United States,—that is, in the several

States composing the Union,—and that the power of legislating over them is expressly vested in Congress, it follows, that the individuals in California who have undertaken to form a constitution and a State, and to exercise the power of legislating without the consent of Congress, have usurped the sovereignty of the State and the authority of Congress, and have acted in open defiance of both. In other words, what they have done is revolutionary and rebellious in its character, anarchical in its tendency, and calculated to lead to the most dangerous consequences. Had they acted from premeditation and design, it would have been, in fact, actual rebellion; but such is not the case. The blame lies much less upon them than upon those who have induced them to take a course so unconstitutional and dangerous. They have been led into it by language held here, and the course pursued by the Executive branch of the Government.

I have not seen the answer of the Executive to the calls made by the two Houses of Congress for information as to the course which it took, or the part which it acted, in reference to what was done in California. I understand the answers have not yet been printed. But there is enough known to justify the assertion, that those who profess to represent and act under the authority of the Executive, have advised, aided, and encouraged the movement, which terminated in forming, what they call a constitution and a State. General Riley, who professed to act as civil Governor, called the convention—determined on the number, and distribution of the delegates—appointed the time and place of its meeting—was present during the session—and gave its proceedings his approbation and sanction. If he acted without authority, he ought to have been tried, or at least reprimanded, and his course disavowed. Neither having been done, the presumption is, that his course has been approved. This, of itself, is sufficient to identify the Executive with his acts, and to make it responsible for them. I touch not the question, whether General Riley was appointed, or received the instructions under which he professed to act from the present Executive, or its predecessor. If from the former, it would implicate the preceding, as well as the present administration. If not, the responsibility rests exclusively on the present.

It is manifest from this statement, that the Executive Department has undertaken to perform acts preparatory to the meeting of the individuals to form their so-called constitution and government, which appertain exclusively to Congress. Indeed, they are identical, in many respects, with the provisions adopted by Congress, when it gives permission to a territory to form a constitution and government, in order to be admitted as a State into the Union.

Having now shown that the assumption upon which the Executive, and the individuals in California, acted throughout this whole affair, is unfounded, unconstitutional, and dangerous; it remains to make a few remarks, in order to show that what has been done, is contrary to the entire practice of the Government, from the commencement to the present time.

From its commencement until the time that Michigan was admitted, the practice was uniform. Territorial governments were first organized by Congress. The Government of the United States appointed the governors, judges, secretaries, marshals, and other officers; and the inhabitants of the territory were represented by legislative bodies, whose acts were subject to the revision of Congress. This state of things continued until the government of a territory applied to Congress to permit its inhabitants to form a constitution and government, preparatory to admission into the Union. The act preliminary to giving permission was, to ascertain whether the inhabitants were sufficiently numerous to authorize them to be formed into a State. This was done by taking a census. That being done, and the number proving sufficient, permission was granted. The act granting it, fixed all the preliminaries—the time and place of holding the convention; the qualification of the voters; establishment of its boundaries, and all other measures necessary to be settled previous to admission. The act giving permission necessarily withdraws the sovereignty of the United States, and leaves the inhabitants of the incipient State as free to form their constitution and government as were the original States of the Union after they had declared their independence. At this stage, the inhabitants of the territory became, for the first time, a people, in legal and constitutional language. Prior to this, they were, by the old acts of Congress, called inhabitants, and not people. All this is perfectly consistent with the sovereignty of the United States, with the powers of Congress, and with the right of a people to self-government.

Michigan was the first case in which there was any departure from the uniform rule of acting. Hers was a very slight departure from established usage. The ordinance of 1787 secured to her the right of becoming a State, when she should have 60,000 inhabitants. Owing to some neglect, Congress delayed taking the census. In the mean time her population increased, until it clearly exceeded more than twice the number which entitled her to admission. At this stage, she formed a constitution and government, without a census being taken by the United States, and Congress waived the omission, as there was no doubt she had more than a sufficient number to entitle her to admission. She was not admitted at the first session she applied, owing to some difficulty respecting the boundary between her and Ohio. The great irregularity, as to her admission, took place at the next session—but on a point which can have no possible connection with the case of California.

The irregularities in all other cases that have since occurred, are of a similar nature. In all, there existed territorial governments established by Congress, with officers appointed by the United States. In all, the territorial government took the lead in calling conventions, and fixing the preliminaries preparatory to the formation of a constitution and admission into the Union. They all recognized the sovereignty of the United States, and the authority of Congress over the territories; and wherever there was any departure from established usage, it was done on the presumed consent of Congress, and not in defiance of its authority, or the sovereignty of the United States over the territories. In this respect California stands alone, without usage or a single example to cover her case.

It belongs now, Senators, to you to decide what part you will act in reference to this unprecedented transaction. The Executive has laid the paper purporting to be the Constitution of California before you, and asks you to admit her into the Union as a State; and the question is, will you or will you not admit her? It is a grave question, and there rests upon you a heavy responsibility. Much, very much, will depend upon your decision. If you admit her, you indorse and give your sanction to all that has been done. Are you prepared to do so? Are you prepared to surrender your power of legislation for the territories—a power expressly vested in Congress by the Constitution, as has been fully established? Can you, consistently with your oath to support the Constitution, surrender the power? Are you prepared to admit that the inhabitants of the territories possess the sovereignty over them, and that any number, more or less, may claim any extent of territory they please; may form a constitution and government, and erect it into a State, without asking your permission? Are you prepared to surrender the sovereignty of the United States over whatever territory may be hereafter acquired to the first adventurers who may rush into it? Are you prepared to surrender virtually to the Executive Department all the powers which you have heretofore exercised over the territories? If not, how can you, consistently with your duty and your oaths to support the Constitution, give your assent to the admission of California as a State, under a pretended constitution and government? Again, can you believe that the project of a constitution which they have adopted has the least validity? Can you believe that there is such a State in reality as the State of California? No; there is no such State. It has no legal or constitutional existence. It has no validity, and can have none, without your sanction. How, then, can you admit it as a *State*, when, according to the provision of the Constitution, your power is limited to admitting new States. To be admitted, it must be a State,—and an existing State, independent of your sanction, before you can admit it. When you give your permission to the inhabitants of a territory to form a constitution and a State, the constitution and State they form, derive their authority from the people, and not from you. The State, before it is admitted is actually a State, and does not become so by the *act of admission*, as would be the case with California, should you admit her contrary to the constitutional provisions and established usage heretofore.

The Senators on the other side of the Chamber must permit me to make a few remarks in this connection particularly applicable to them,—with the exception of a few Senators from the South, sitting on the other side of the Chamber.—When the Oregon question was before this body, not two years since, you took (if I mistake not) universally the ground, that Congress had the sole and absolute power of legislating for the territories. How, then, can you now, after the short interval which has elapsed, abandon the ground which you took, and thereby virtually admit that the power of legislating, instead of being in Congress, is in the inhabitants of the territories? How can you justify and sanction by your votes the acts of the Executive, which are in direct derogation of what you then contended for? But to approach still nearer to the present time, how can you, after condemning, little more than a year since, the grounds taken by the party which you defeated at the last election, wheel round and support by your votes the grounds which, as explained recently on this floor by the candidate of the party in the last election, are identical with those on which the Executive has acted in reference to California? What are we to understand by all this? Must we conclude that there is no sincerity, no faith in the acts and declarations of public men, and that all is a mere acting or hollow profession? Or are we to conclude that the exclusion of the South from the territory acquired from Mexico is an object of so paramount a character in your estimation, that right, justice, constitution and consistency must all yield, when they stand in the way of our exclusion?

But, it may be asked, what is to be done with California, should she not be admitted? I answer, remand her back to the territorial condition, as was done in the case of Tennessee, in the early stage of the Government. Congress, in her case, had established a territorial government in the usual form, with a governor, judges, and other officers, appointed by the United States. She was entitled, under the deed of cession, to be admitted into the Union as a State as soon as she had sixty thousand inhabitants. The territorial government, believing it had that number, took a census, by which it appeared it exceeded it. She then formed a constitution, and applied for admission. Congress refused to admit her, on the ground that the census should be taken by the United States, and that Congress had not determined whether the territory should be formed into one or two States, as it was authorized to do under the cession. She returned quietly to her territorial condition. An act was passed to take a census by the United States, containing a provision that the territory should form one State. All afterwards was regularly conducted, and the territory admitted as a State in due form. The irregularities in the case of California are immeasurably greater, and offer much stronger reasons for pursuing the same course. But, it may be said, California may not submit. That is not probable; but if she should not, when she refuses, it will then be time for us to decide what is to be done.

Having now shown what cannot save the Union, I return to the question with which I commenced, How can the Union be saved? There is but one way by which it can with any certainty; and that is, by a full and final settlement, on the principle of justice, of all the questions at issue between the two sections. The South asks for justice, simple justice, and less she ought not to take. She has no compromise to offer, but the Constitution; and no concession or surrender to make. She has already surrendered so much that she has little left to surrender. Such a settlement would go to the root of the evil, and remove all cause of discontent, by satisfying the South, she could remain honorably and safely in the Union, and thereby restore the harmony and fraternal feelings between the sections, which existed anterior to the Missouri agitation. Nothing else can, with any certainty, finally and for ever settle the questions at issue, terminate agitation, and save the Union.

But can this be done? Yes, easily; not by the weaker party, for it can of itself do nothing—not even protect itself—but by the stronger. The North has only to will it to accomplish it—to do justice by conceding to the South an equal right in the acquired territory, and to do her duty by causing the stipulations relative to fugitive slaves to be faithfully fulfilled—to cease the agitation of the slave question, and to provide for the insertion of a provision in the constitution, by an amendment, which will restore to the South, in substance, the power she possessed of protecting herself, before the equilibrium between the sections was destroyed by the action of this Government. There will be no difficulty in devising such a provision—one that will protect the South, and which, at the same time, will improve and strengthen the Government, instead of impairing and weakening it.

But will the North agree to this? It is for her to answer the question. But, I will say, she cannot refuse, if she has half the love of the Union which she professes to have, or without justly exposing herself to the charge that her love of power and aggrandizement is far greater than her love of the Union. At all events, the responsibility of saving the Union rests on the North, and not on the South. The South cannot save it by any act of hers, and the North may save it without any sacrifice whatever, unless to do justice, and to perform her duties under the Constitution, should be regarded by her as a sacrifice.

It is time, Senators, that there should be an open and manly avowal on all sides, as to what is intended to be done. If the question is not now settled, it is uncertain whether it ever can hereafter be; and we, as the representatives of the States of this Union, regarded as governments, should come to a distinct understanding as to our respective views, in order to ascertain whether the great questions at issue can be settled or not. If you, who represent the stronger portion, cannot agree to settle them on the broad principle of justice and duty, say so; and let the States we both represent agree to separate and part in peace. If you are unwilling we should part in peace, tell us so, and we shall know what to do, when you reduce the question to submission or resistance. If you remain silent, you will compel us to infer by your acts what you intend. In that case, California will become the test question. If you admit her, under all the difficulties that oppose her admission, you compel us to infer that you intend to exclude us from the whole of the acquired territories, with the intention of destroying, irretrievably, the equilibrium between the two sections. We would be blind not to perceive in that case, that your real objects are power and aggrandizement, and infatuated not to act accordingly.

I have now, Senators, done my duty in expressing my opinions fully, freely, and candidly, on this solemn occasion. In doing so, I have been governed by the motives which have governed me in all the stages of the agitation of the slavery question since its commencement. I have exerted myself, during the whole period, to arrest it, with the intention of saving the Union, if it could be done; and if it could not, to save the section where it has pleased Providence to cast my lot, and which I sincerely believe has justice and the Constitution on its side. Having faithfully done my duty to the best of my ability, both to the Union and my section, throughout this agitation, I shall have the consolation, let what will come, that I am free from all responsibility.

Exercises

1. What is the proposition advocated by Calhoun? What major arguments did he employ to support it?

2. To what cause did he trace the rise of the spirit of secessionism?

3. Summarize Calhoun's view of the effects of partisanship. Does he appear to state two contrary views in this speech? How does his reasoning on this subject compare with Clay's?

4. How did Calhoun depict the causes of the sectional conflict? How did his interpretation differ from Clay's? Why do you think Calhoun avoided direct refutation of Clay's speech?

5. For an interpretation which differs from Calhoun's view of the "equilibrium of power" which he thought was intended by the Founding Fathers, read Abraham Lincoln's "Cooper Union Address." Which speaker, Calhoun or Lincoln, seems the more persuasive on this point? How did their persuasive methods differ?

6. Why, in contrast to the conciliatory approach used by Clay, did Calhoun emphasize his opinion that "the views and feelings of the two sections are as opposite and hostile as they can possibly be"?

7. On the basis of this speech, what impression do you have of Calhoun's personality? Do you agree with biographers John M. Wiltze, Margaret L. Coit, and R. M. T. Hunter that Calhoun was kindly, generous, just, and deeply devoted not only to the South but to the Union? How were his style and his reasoning affected by the argumentative position he chose to maintain?

8. Is there a basic difference—in ethos, in persuasive strategy, in argumentative method—between Clay's appeal to the Senators "to listen to their own reason, their own judgment, their own good sense," and Calhoun's assertion that "I have now, Senators, done my duty in expressing my opinions fully, freely, and candidly, on this solemn occasion . . . let what will come, I am free from all responsibility"? How is this difference illustrated throughout the two speeches?

9. It has been suggested by historians that instead of winning support Calhoun's speech may have hurt his cause. Can you find internal evidence in this speech which might support this point of view? What could Calhoun have done differently to have better supported the cause he advocated?

10. Outline this speech. Do you find that the text is easily partitioned into an analysis of the "problem" and a statement of the "remedy"? If so, which portion constitutes the longer part of the speech? Which is better documented? Which was probably more persuasive to the listeners? Why do you suppose that Calhoun chose to present his views in this manner?

11. Read other works of Calhoun's, such as the following: *South Carolina Exposition and Protest* of 1828; *Fort Hill Address* of 1831; *Fort Hill Letter* of August 28, 1832; and the posthumously published *Disquisition on Government* and *Discourse on the Constitution and Government of the United States*. Do his written works lend themselves as easily to outlining as does his speech on the Compromise of 1850? Compare his oral and written style, noting both similarities and differences. Do the same argumentative development and the psychological orientation appear in both the written works and in the 1850 speech? In the above-mentioned works, does Calhoun seem to demonstrate mental growth? Increasing rigidity? Increasing, or decreasing, emotionalism? Growing optimism, or negativism? Increasing concern for human rights and moral principles, or a lessening concern? Explain.

Henry David Thoreau

"Slavery in Massachusetts," delivered at the anti-slavery meeting at Framingham, Massachusetts, July 4, 1854

HENRY David Thoreau (1817–1862) is well-known as the author of *Walden* and scarcely remembered as a public speaker. Like Thomas Jefferson, Thoreau spoke seldom in public. Nevertheless, he placed high value on skill in oral discourse; and he did feel a heavy sense of personal responsibility to try to influence public opinion on crucial issues—whether by pen or tongue.

Generally Thoreau is remembered as a solitary dweller at Walden Pond, whose main converse was with woodchucks, and who denounced sociability as a counterpart to the urge felt by pigs to huddle together to keep warm. As a conversationalist he considered himself to be a "stuttering, blundering clodhopper." Moncure Daniel Conway, who knew him well, said that "He was not talkative, but his occasional monologues were extraordinary." In his *Journal* Thoreau confessed: "I would fain communicate the wealth of my life to men. . . . I know no riches I would keep back. I have no private good, unless it be my peculiar ability to serve the public." He was sufficiently interested in the Concord Lyceum to serve as its secretary (much as he disliked organizational work), and he lectured two or three times a year to Lyceum audiences.

If he did not speak often, the reason primarily was that he felt keenly the difficulty, in such a public situation, of being intimately frank and sensitively revealing of his own feelings and emotions. "I am disappointed to find that most that I am and value myself for is lost, or worse than lost, on my audience," he wrote in his *Journal.*

And on the same theme, commenting on the presumed need for audience adaptation, he noted: "If you wish to know how I think, you must endeavor to put yourself in my place. If you wish me to speak as if I were you, that is another matter."

Thoreau was a small man: short, thin, frail, with awkwardly long arms, large feet, and a huge beak of a nose that loomed out from under his flaxen hair. He neither possessed nor sought to develop any special arts of popular appeal or of platform manner. But he did possess a mind that was alert to the values and the methods of communication. He thought naturally in rhetorical terms. His goal in speaking was to change the thought and behavior of those who heard or read his speech. And this task of persuasion he undertook with considerable skill.

In the early summer of 1854 Thoreau made a special effort to seek out an audience to which he could express the anger he felt for the arrest and return to slavery of a Negro named Anthony Burns, as well as his disgust at the complacency with which the citizenry of Massachusetts accepted the operations of the Fugitive Slave Law. July 4 in New England was traditionally a day on which people gathered to hear speeches celebrating the heroism of their revolutionary ancestors. Through his Lyceum connections, Thoreau was invited to make the address for that day at Framingham. With the stoical independence which was so characteristic of him, Thoreau chose to ignore wholly the conventional significance of the holiday and to use the occasion fully for his own purpose.

The text of his lecture is taken from Henry David Thoreau, A *Yankee in Canada*, Boston: Ticknor and Fields, 1866, pp. 97–117.

SLAVERY IN MASSACHUSETTS

I lately attended a meeting of the citizens of Concord, expecting, as one among many, to speak on the subject of slavery in Massachusetts; but I was surprised and disappointed to find that what had called my townsmen together was the destiny of Nebraska, and not of Massachusetts, and that what I had to say would be entirely out of order. I had thought that the house was on fire, and not the prairie; but though several of the citizens of Massachusetts are now in prison for attempting to rescue a slave from her own clutches, not one of the speakers at that meeting expressed regret for it, not one even referred to it. It was only the disposition of some wild lands a thousand miles off, which appeared to concern them. The inhabitants of Concord are not prepared to stand by one of their own bridges, but talk only of taking up a position on the highlands beyond the Yellowstone River. Our Buttricks and Davises and Hosmers are retreating thither, and I fear that they will leave no Lexington Common between them and the enemy. There is not one slave in Nebraska; there are perhaps a million slaves in Massachusetts.

They who have been bred in the school of politics fail now and always to face the facts. Their measures are half measures and make-shifts merely. They put off the day of settlement indefinitely, and meanwhile the debt accumulates. Though the Fugitive Slave Law had not been the subject of discussion on that occasion, it was at length faintly resolved by my townsmen, at an adjourned meeting, as I learn, that the compromise compact of 1820 having been repudiated by one of the parties, "Therefore, . . . the Fugitive Slave Law of 1850 must be repealed." But this is not the reason why an iniquitous law should be repealed. The fact which the politician faces is merely, that there is less honor among thieves than was supposed, and not the fact that they are thieves.

As I had no opportunity to express my thoughts at that meeting, will you allow me to do so here?

Again it happens that the Boston Court-House is full of armed men, holding prisoner and trying a MAN, to find out if he is not really a SLAVE. Does any one think that justice or God awaits Mr. Loring's decision? For him to sit there deciding still, when this question is already decided from eternity to eternity, and the unlettered slave himself, and the multitude around have long since heard and assented to the decision, is simply to make himself ridiculous. We may be tempted to ask from whom he received his commission, and who he is that received it; what novel statutes he obeys, and what precedents are to him of authority. Such an arbiter's very existence is an impertinence. We do not ask him to make up his mind, but to make up his pack.

I listen to hear the voice of a Governor, Commander-in-Chief of the forces of Massachusetts. I hear only the creaking of crickets and the hum of insects which now fill the summer air. The Governor's exploit is to review the troops on muster days. I have seen him on horseback, with his hat off, listening to a chaplain's prayer. It chances that that is all I have ever seen of a Governor. I think that I could manage to get along without one. If *he* is not of the least use to prevent my being kidnapped, pray of what important use is he likely to be to me? When freedom is most endangered, he dwells in the deepest obscurity. A distinguished clergyman told me that he chose the profession of a clergyman, because it afforded the most leisure for literary pursuits. I would recommend to him the profession of a governor.

Three years ago, also, when the Simms tragedy was acted, I said to myself, there is such an officer, if not such a man, as the Governor of Massachusetts,—what has he been about the last fortnight? Has he had as much as he could do to keep on the fence during this moral earthquake? It seemed to me that no keener satire could have been aimed at, no more cutting insult have been offered to that man, than just what happened,—the absence of all inquiry after him in that crisis. The worst and the most I chance to know of him is, that he did not improve that opportunity to make himself known, and worthily known. He could at least have *resigned* himself into fame. It appeared to be forgotten that there was such a man or such an office. Yet no doubt he was endeavoring to fill the gubernatorial chair all the while. He was no Governor of mine. He did not govern me.

But at last, in the present case, the Governor was heard from. After he and the United States government had perfectly succeeded in robbing a poor innocent black man of his liberty for life, and, as far as they could, of his Creator's likeness in his breast, he made a speech to his accomplices, at a congratulatory supper!

I have read a recent law of this State, making it penal for any officer of the "Commonwealth" to "detain or aid in the . . . detention," anywhere within its limits, "of any person, for the reason that he is claimed as a fugitive slave." Also, it was a matter of notoriety that a writ of replevin to take the fugitive out of the custody of the United States Marshal could not be served, for want of sufficient force to aid the officer.

I had thought that the Governor was, in some sense, the executive officer of the State; that it was his business, as a Governor, to see that the laws of the State were executed; while, as a man, he took care that he did not, by so doing, break the laws of humanity; but when there is any special important use for him, he is useless, or worse than useless, and permits the laws of the State to go unexecuted. Perhaps I do not know what are the duties of a Governor; but if to be a Governor requires to subject one's self to so much ignominy without remedy, if it is to put a restraint upon my manhood, I shall take care never to be Governor of Massachusetts. I have not read far in the statutes of this Commonwealth. It is not profitable reading. They do not always say what is true; and they do not always mean what they say. What I am concerned to know is, that that man's influence and authority were on the side of the slaveholder, and not of the slave,—of the guilty, and not of the innocent,—of injustice, and not of justice. I never saw him of whom I speak; indeed, I did not know that he was Governor until this event occurred. I heard of him and Anthony Burns at the same time, and thus, undoubtedly, most will hear of him. So far am I from being governed by him. I do not mean that it was anything to his discredit that I had not heard of him, only that I heard what I did. The worst I shall say of him is, that he proved no better than the majority of his constituents would be likely to prove. In my opinion, he was not equal to the occasion.

The whole military force of the State is at the service of a Mr. Suttle, a slaveholder from Virginia, to enable him to catch a man whom he calls his property; but not a soldier is offered to save a citizen of Massachusetts from being kidnapped! Is this what all these soldiers, all this *training*, has been for these seventy-nine years past? Have they been trained merely to rob Mexico and carry back fugitive slaves to their masters?

These very nights, I heard the sound of a drum in our streets. There were men *training* still; and for what? I could with an effort pardon the cockerels of Concord for crowing still, for they, perchance, had not been beaten that morning; but I could not excuse this rub-a-dub of the "trainers." The slave was carried back by exactly such as these; i.e. by the soldier, of whom the best you can say in this connection is, that he is a fool made conspicuous by a painted coat.

Three years ago, also, just a week after the authorities of Boston assembled to carry back a perfectly innocent man, and one whom they knew to be innocent, into slavery, the inhabitants of Concord caused the bells to be rung and the cannons to be fired, to celebrate their liberty,—and the courage and love of liberty of their ancestors who fought at the bridge. As if *those* three millions had fought for the right to be free themselves, but to hold in slavery three millions others. Now-a-days, men wear a fool's-cap, and call it a liberty-cap. I do not know but there are some, who, if they were tied to a whipping-post, and could but get one hand free, would use it to ring the bells and fire the cannons to celebrate *their* liberty. So some of my townsmen took the liberty to ring and fire. That was the extent of their freedom; and when the sound of the bells died away, their liberty died away also; when the powder was all expended, their liberty went off with the smoke.

The joke could be no broader, if the inmates of the prisons were to subscribe for all the powder to be used in such salutes, and hire the jailers to do the firing and ringing for them, while they enjoyed it through the grating.

This is what I thought about my neighbors.

Every humane and intelligent inhabitant of Concord, when he or she heard those bells and those cannons, thought not with pride of the events of the 19th of April, 1775, but with shame of the events of the 12th of April, 1851. But now we have half buried that old shame under a new one.

Massachusetts sat waiting Mr. Loring's decision, as if it could in any way affect her own criminality. Her crime, the most conspicuous and fatal crime of all, was permitting him to be the umpire in such a case. It was really the trial of Massachusetts. Every moment that she hesitated to set this man free, every moment that she now hesitates to atone for her crime, she is convicted. The Commissioner on her case is God; not Edward G. God, but simple God.

I wish my countrymen to consider, that whatever the human law may be, neither an individual nor a nation can ever commit the least act of injustice against the obscurest individual, without having to pay the penalty for it. A government which deliberately enacts injustice, and persists in it, will at length even become the laughing stock of the world.

Much has been said about American slavery, but I think that we do not even yet realize what slavery is. If I were seriously to propose to Congress to make mankind into sausages, I have no doubt that most of the members would smile at my proposition, and if any believed me to be in earnest, they would think that I proposed something much worse than Congress had ever done. But if any of them will tell me that to make a man into a sausage would be much worse,—would be any worse,—than to make him into a slave,—than it was to enact the Fugitive Slave Law,—I will accuse him of foolishness, of intellectual incapacity, of making a distinction without a difference. The one is just as sensible a proposition as the other.

I hear a good deal said about trampling this law under foot. Why, one need not go out of his way to do that. This law rises not to the level of the head or the reason; its natural habitat is in the dirt. It was born and bred, and has its life, only in the dust and mire, on a level with the feet; and he who walks with freedom, and does not with Hindoo mercy avoid treading on every venomous reptile, will inevitably tread on it, and so trample it under foot,—and Webster, its maker, with it, like the dirt-bug and its ball.

Recent events will be valuable as a criticism on the administration of justice in our midst, or, rather, as showing what are the true resources of justice in any community. It has come to this, that the friends of liberty, the friends of the slave, have shuddered when they have understood that his fate was left to the legal tribunals of the country to be decided. Free men have no faith that justice will be awarded in such a case. The judge may decide this way or that; it is a kind of accident, at best. It is evident that he is not a competent authority in so important a case. It is no time, then, to be judging according to his precedents, but to establish a precedent for the future. I would much rather trust to the sentiment of the people. In their vote, you would get something of some value, at least, however small; but in the other case, only the trammelled judgment of an individual, of no significance, be it which way it might.

It is, to some extent, fatal to the courts, when the people are compelled to go behind them. I do not wish to believe that the courts were made for fair weather, and for very civil cases merely; but think of leaving it to any court in the land to decide whether more than three millions of people, in this case, a sixth part of a nation, have a right to be freemen or not? But it has been left to the courts of *justice*, so called,–to the Supreme Court of the land,–and, as you all know, recognizing no authority but the Constitution, it has decided that the three millions are, and shall continue to be slaves. Such judges as these are merely the inspectors of a pick-lock and murderer's tools, to tell him whether they are in working order or not, and there they think that their responsibility ends. There was a prior case on the docket, which they, as judges appointed by God, had no right to skip; which having been justly settled, they would have been saved from this humiliation. It was the case of the murderer himself.

The law will never make men free; it is men who have got to make the law free. They are the lovers of law and order, who observe the law when the government breaks it.

Among human beings, the judge whose words seal the fate of a man furthest into eternity is not he who merely pronounces the verdict of the law, but he, whoever he may be, who, from a love of truth, and unprejudiced by any custom or enactment of men, utters a true opinion or *sentence* concerning him. He it is that *sentences* him. Whoever can discern truth has received his commission from a higher source than the chiefest justice in the world, who can discern only law. He finds himself constituted judge of the judge. Strange that it should be necessary to state such simple truths!

I am more and more convinced that, with reference to any public question, it is more important to know what the country thinks of it, than what the city thinks. The city does not *think* much. On any moral question, I would rather have the opinion of Boxboro than of Boston and New York put together. When the former speaks, I feel as if somebody *had* spoken, as if *humanity* was yet, and a reasonable being had asserted its rights,–as if some unprejudiced men among the country's hills had at length turned their attention to the subject, and by a few sensible words redeemed the reputation of the race. When, in some obscure country town, the farmers come together to a special town-meeting, to express their opinion on some subject which is vexing the land, that, I think, is the true Congress, and the most respectable one that is ever assembled in the United States.

It is evident that there are, in this Commonwealth at least, two parties, becoming more and more distinct,–the party of the city, and the party of the country. I know that the country is mean enough, but I am glad to believe that there is a slight difference in her favor. But as yet, she has few, if any organs, through which to express herself. The editorials which she reads, like the news, come from the seaboard. Let us, the inhabitants of the country, cultivate self-respect. Let us not send to the city for aught more essential than our broadcloths and groceries; or, if we read the opinions of the city, let us entertain opinions of our own.

Among measures to be adopted, I would suggest to make as earnest and vigorous an assault on the press as has already been made, and with effect, on the church. The church has much improved within a few years; but the press is almost, without exception, corrupt. I believe that, in this country, the press exerts a greater and a more pernicious influence than the church did in its worst period. We are not a religious people, but we are a nation of politicians. We do not care for the Bible, but we do care for the newspaper. At any meeting of politicians,—like that at Concord the other evening, for instance,—how impertinent it would be to quote from the Bible! how pertinent to quote from a newspaper or from the Constitution! The newspaper is a Bible which we read every morning and every afternoon, standing and sitting, riding and walking. It is a Bible which every man carries in his pocket, which lies on every table and counter, and which the mail, and thousands of missionaries, are continually dispersing. It is, in short, the only book which America has printed, and which America reads. So wide is its influence. The editor is a preacher whom you voluntarily support. Your tax is commonly one cent daily, and it costs nothing for pew hire. But how many of these preachers preach the truth? I repeat the testimony of many an intelligent foreigner, as well as my own convictions, when I say, that probably no country was ever ruled by so mean a class of tyrants as, with a few noble exceptions, are the editors of the periodical press in *this* country. And as they live and rule only by their servility, and appealing to the worse, and not the better, nature of man, the people who read them are in the condition of the dog that returns to his vomit.

The *Liberator* and the *Commonwealth* were the only papers in Boston, as far as I know, which made themselves heard in condemnation of the cowardice and meanness of the authorities of that city, as exhibited in '51. The other journals, almost without exception, by their manner of referring to and speaking of the Fugitive Slave Law, and the carrying back of the slave Simms, insulted the common sense of the country, at least. And, for the most part, they did this, one would say, because they thought so to secure the approbation of their patrons, not being aware that a sounder sentiment prevailed to any extent in the heart of the Commonweath. I am told that some of them have improved of late; but they are still eminently time-serving. Such is the character they have won.

But, thank fortune, this preacher can be even more easily reached by the weapons of the reformer than could the recreant priest. The free men of New England have only to refrain from purchasing and reading these sheets, have only to withhold their cents, to kill a score of them at once. One whom I respect told me that he purchased Mitchell's *Citizen* in the cars, and then threw it out the window. But would not his contempt have been more fatally expressed if he had not bought it?

Are they Americans? are they New-Englanders? are they inhabitants of Lexington and Concord and Framingham, who read and support the Boston *Post, Mail, Journal, Advertiser, Courier,* and *Times?* Are these the Flags of our Union? I am not a newspaper reader, and may omit to name the worst.

Could slavery suggest a more complete servility than some of these journals exhibit? Is there any dust which their conduct does not lick, and make fouler still with its slime? I do not know whether the Boston *Herald* is still in existence, but I remember to have seen it about the streets when Simms was carried off. Did it not act its part well,—serve its master faithfully? How could it have gone lower on its belly? How can a man stoop lower than he is low? do more than put his extremities in the place of the head he has? than make his head his lower extremity? When I have taken up this paper with my cuffs turned up, I have heard the gurgling of the sewer through every column. I have felt that I was handling a paper picked out of the public gutters, a leaf from the gospel of the gambling-house, the groggery, and the brothel, harmonizing with the gospel of the Merchants' Exchange.

The majority of the men of the North, and of the South and East and West, are not men of principle. If they vote, they do not send men to Congress on errands of humanity; but while their brothers and sisters are being scourged and hung for loving liberty, while—I might here insert all that slavery implies and is,—it is the mismanagement of wood and iron and stone and gold which concerns them. Do what you will, O Government, with my wife and children, my mother and brother, my father and sister, I will obey your commands to the letter. It will indeed grieve me if you hurt them, if you deliver them to overseers to be hunted by hounds or to be whipped to death; but, nevertheless, I will peaceably pursue my chosen calling on this fair earth, until perchance, one day, when I have put on mourning for them dead, I shall have persuaded you to relent. Such is the attitude, such are the words of Massachusetts.

Rather than do thus, I need not say what match I would touch, what system endeavor to blow up; but as I love my life, I would side with the light, and let the dark earth roll from under me, calling my mother and my brother to follow.

I would remind my countrymen, that they are to be men first, and

Americans only at a late and convenient hour. No matter how valuable law may be to protect your property, even to keep soul and body together, if it do not keep you and humanity together.

I am sorry to say, that I doubt if there is a judge in Massachusetts who is prepared to resign his office, and get his living innocently, whenever it is required of him to pass sentence under a law which is merely contrary to the law of God. I am compelled to see that they put themselves, or rather, are by character, in this respect, exactly on a level with the marine who discharges his musket in any direction he is ordered to. They are just as much tools, and as little men. Certainly, they are not the more to be respected, because their master enslaves their understandings and consciences, instead of their bodies.

The judges and lawyers,—simply as such, I mean,—and all men of expediency, try this case by a very low and incompetent standard. They consider, not whether the Fugitive Slave Law is right, but whether it is what they call *constitutional.* Is virtue constitutional, or vice? Is equity constitutional, or iniquity? In important moral and vital questions, like this, it is just as impertinent to ask whether a law is constitutional or not, as to ask whether it is profitable or not. They persist in being the servants of the worst of men, and not the servants of humanity. The question is, not whether you or your grandfather, seventy years ago, did not enter into an agreement to serve the Devil, and that service is not accordingly now due; but whether you will not now, for once and at last, serve God,—in spite of your own past recreancy, or that of your ancestor,—by obeying that eternal and only just CONSTITUTION, which He, and not any Jefferson or Adams, has written in your being.

The amount of it is, if the majority vote the Devil to be God, the minority will live and behave accordingly,—and obey the successful candidate, trusting that, some time or other, by some Speaker's casting-vote, perhaps, they may reinstate God. This is the highest principle I can get out or invent for my neighbors. These men act as if they believed that they could safely slide down a hill a little way—or a good way—and would surely come to a place, by and by, where they could begin to slide up again. This is expediency, or choosing that course which offers the slightest obstacles to the feet, that is, a down-hill one. But there is no such thing as accomplishing a righteous reform by the use of "expediency." There is no such thing as sliding up hill. In morals, the only sliders are backsliders.

Thus we steadily worship Mammon, both school and state and church, and on the seventh day curse God with a tintamar from one end of the Union to the other.

Will mankind never learn that policy is not morality,—that it never secures any moral right, but considers merely what is expedient? chooses the available candidate,—who is invariably the Devil,—and what right have his constituents to be surprised, because the Devil does not behave like an angel of light? What is wanted is men, not of policy, but of probity,—who recognize a higher law than the Constitution, or the decision of the majority. The fate of the country does not depend on how you vote at the polls,—the worst man is as strong as the best at that game; it does not depend on what kind of paper you drop into the ballot-box once a year, but on what kind of man you drop from your chamber into the street every morning.

What should concern Massachusetts is not the Nebraska Bill, nor the Fugitive Slave Bill, but her own slaveholding and servility. Let the State dissolve her union with the slaveholder. She may wriggle and hesitate, and ask leave to read the Constitution once more; but she can find no respectable law or precedent which sanctions the continuance of such a Union for an instant.

Let each inhabitant of the State dissolve his union with her, as long as she delays to do her duty.

The events of the past month teach me to distrust Fame. I see that she does not finely discriminate, but coarsely hurrahs. She considers not the simple heroism of an action, but only as it is connected with its apparent consequences. She praises till she is hoarse the easy exploit of the Boston tea party, but will be comparatively silent about the braver and more disinterestedly heroic attack on the Boston Court-House, simply because it was unsuccessful!

Covered with disgrace, the State has sat down coolly to try for their lives and liberties the men who attempted to do its duty for it. And this is called *justice!* They who have shown that they can behave particularly well may perchance be put under bonds for *their good behavior*. They whom truth requires at present to plead guilty are, of all the inhabitants of the State, pre-eminently innocent. While the Governor, and the Mayor, and countless officers of the Commonwealth are at large, the champions of liberty are imprisoned.

Only they are guiltless, who commit the crime of contempt of such a court. It behooves every man to see that his influence is on the side of justice, and let the courts make their own characters. My sympathies in this case are wholly with the accused, and wholly against their accusers and judges. Justice is sweet and musical; but injustice is harsh and discordant. The judge still sits grinding at his organ, but it yields no music, and we hear only the sound of the handle. He believes that all the music resides in the handle, and the crowd toss him their coppers the same as before.

Do you suppose that that Massachusetts which is now doing these things,—which hesitates to crown these men, some of whose lawyers, and even judges, perchance, may be driven to take refuge in some poor quibble, that they may not wholly outrage their instinctive sense of justice,—do you suppose that she is anything but base and servile? that she is the champion of liberty?

Show me a free state, and a court truly of justice, and I will fight for them, if need be; but show me Massachusetts, and I refuse her my allegiance, and express contempt for her courts.

The effect of a good government is to make life more valuable,—of a bad one, to make it less valuable. We can afford that railroad, and all merely material stock, should lose some of its value, for that only compels us to live more simply and economically; but suppose that the value of life itself should be diminished! How can we make a less demand on man and nature, how live more economically in respect to virtue and all noble qualities, than we do? I have lived for the last month,—and I think that every man in Massachusetts capable of the sentiment of patriotism must have had a similar experience,—with the sense of having suffered a vast and indefinite loss. I did not know at first what ailed me. At last it occurred to me that what I had lost was a country. I had never respected the government near to which I lived, but I had foolishly thought that I might manage to live here, minding my private affairs, and forget it. For my part, my old and worthiest pursuits have lost I cannot say how much of their attraction, and I feel that my investment in life here is worth many per cent less since Massachusetts last deliberately sent back an innocent man, Anthony Burns, to slavery. I dwelt before, perhaps, in the illusion that my life passed somewhere only *between* heaven and hell, but now I cannot persuade myself that I do not dwell *wholly within* hell. The site of that political organization called Massachusetts is to me morally covered with volcanic scoriae and cinders, such as Milton describes in the infernal regions. If there is any hell more unprincipled than our rulers, and we, the ruled, I feel curious to see it. Life itself being worth less, all things with it, which minister to it, are worth less. Suppose you have a small library, with pictures to adorn the walls,—a garden laid out around,—and contemplate scientific and literary pursuits, and discover all at once that your villa, with all its contents, is located in hell, and that the justice of the peace has a cloven foot and a forked tail,—do not these things suddenly lose their value in your eyes?

I feel that, to some extent, the State has fatally interfered with my lawful business. It has not only interrupted me in my passage through Court Street on errands of trade, but it has interrupted me and every man on his onward and upward path, on which he had trusted soon to leave Court Street far behind. What right had it to remind me of Court Street? I have found that hollow which even I had relied on for solid.

I am surprised to see men going about their business as if nothing had happened. I say to myself, "Unfortunates! they have not heard the news." I am surprised that the man whom I just met on horseback should be so earnest to overtake his newly bought cows running away,—since all property is insecure, and if they do not run away again, they may be taken away from him when he gets them. Fool! does he not know that his seed-corn is worth less this year,—that all beneficent harvests fail as you approach the empire of hell? No prudent man will build a stone house under these circumstances, or engage in any peaceful enterprise which it requires a long time to accomplish. Art is as long as ever, but life is more interrupted and less available for a man's proper pursuits. It is not an era of repose. We have used up all our inherited freedom. If we would save our lives, we must fight for them.

I walk toward one of our ponds; but what signifies the beauty of nature when men are base? We walk to lakes to see our serenity reflected in them; when we are not serene, we go not to them. Who can be serene in a country where both the rulers and the ruled are without principle? The remembrance of my country spoils my walk. My thoughts are murder to the State, and involuntarily go plotting against her.

But it chanced the other day that I scented a white water-lily, and a season I had waited for had arrived. It is the emblem of purity. It bursts up so pure and fair to the eye, and so sweet to the scent, as if to show us what purity and sweetness reside in, and can be extracted from, the slime and muck of earth. I think I have plucked the first one that has opened for a mile. What confirmation of our hopes is in the fragrance of this flower! I shall not so soon despair of the world for it, notwithstanding slavery, and the cowardice and want of principle of Northern men. It suggests what kind of laws have prevailed longest and widest, and still prevail, and that the time may come when man's deeds will smell as sweet. Such is the odor which the plant emits. If Nature can compound this fragrance still annually, I shall believe her still young and full of vigor, integrity and genius unimpaired, and that there is virtue even in man, too, who is fitted to perceive and love it. It reminds me that Nature has been partner to no Missouri Compromise. I scent no compromise in the fragrance of the water-lily. It is not a *Nymphæa* DOUGLASSII. In it, the sweet, and pure, and innocent are wholly sundered from the obscene and baleful. I do not scent in this the time-serving irresolution of a Massachusetts Governor, nor of a Boston Mayor. So behave that the odor of your actions may enhance the general sweetness of the atmosphere, that when we behold or scent a flower, we may not be reminded how inconsistent your deeds are with it; for all odor is but one form of advertisement of a moral quality, and if fair actions had not been performed, the lily would not smell sweet. The foul slime stands for the sloth and vice of man, the decay of humanity; the fragrant flower that springs from it, for the purity and courage which are immortal.

Slavery and servility have produced no sweet-scented flower annually, to charm the senses of men, for they have no real life: they are merely a decaying and a death, offensive to all healthy nostrils. We do not complain that they *live*, but that they do not *get buried*. Let the living bury them; even they are good for manure.

Exercises

1. After Thoreau's death, Ralph Waldo Emerson, who knew him well and admired him highly, reluctantly concluded that Thoreau limited his potential effectiveness by being too much of a "no-sayer." Cite evidence from this speech to indicate whether Thoreau's approach to the slavery issue is primarily negative or constructively affirmative.

2. The primary persuasive strategy employed by Thoreau in this speech is irony. Identify passages in the speech which are ironic. What is irony, and how would you describe its functions? Compare Thoreau's irony with that of Swift in his essay, "A Modest Proposal." Can you think of reasons why irony may be less effective in public speaking than in essay writing (as it surely is rarer)?

3. Does Thoreau come close to offending good taste when he says that newspapers have become our Bible? Does he offend you? What point is he trying to make in this passage? Why do you think he phrases his point in the form of an extended metaphor?

4. In view of Thoreau's expressed feeling against adapting to an audience, what do you find in this speech that seems to be adaptive? Do you find elements that seem to indicate he deliberately avoids such adaptation? Does Thoreau miss a persuasive opportunity in not referring explicitly to the significance of the July 4th date? What indirect use does Thoreau make of the historic date?

5. What audience is Thoreau seeking to influence? Is his irony directed against his listeners, or at others? Is his attitude persuasively effective for the hearers (and readers) whom he seeks to influence?

6. In Thoreau's speech, the style is unusually compressed and suggestive, rather than explicit and direct—as is illustrated by his charge that citizens will only be "Americans at a late and convenient hour." Find other examples of this stylistic quality. Do you think this kind of style is as effective with listeners as with readers? Why, or why not?

7. Why do you suppose Thoreau concluded his rather savage speech with an extended reference to water lilies? Does his use of the scientific name for lilies add to, or detract from, the effectiveness of his illustration?

8. Assemble all the analogies, metaphors, and comparisons you find in this speech. Are they essential to Thoreau's method of irony? Do they add significantly to the suggestive power of his persuasion? Would the speech seem more bitter if it were less metaphorical? Is this an indication that sometimes it is wise for a speaker to blunt the full strength of his emotions?

9. Compare the abolitionist arguments suggested (rather than itemized) in this speech with those similarly hinted at in Wendell Phillips' "Toussaint L'Ouverture." Judging from these two speeches, what values do you see in the persuasive uses of indirection, suggestion, and understatement—as opposed to emphasis and rhetorical exaggeration?

10. In his discussion of newspapers, Thoreau contradicts himself in saying that without exception newspapers are corrupt and in adding later that there are a few "noble exceptions." Do you find any other contradictions in the speech? How well does Thoreau's argument support itself—by logical inevitability; by internal consistency; by appeal to fact? To what extent does he seek agreement by stylistic cleverness? By appeal to emotion? By appeal to prejudice? By exaggeration of fact?

11. What is Thoreau's view of the nature of law? What are his arguments in favor of anarchy? What would be the result if everyone insisted on obeying his own sense of what is right rather than the legislative statutes? Should the police power be used to enforce legality—or justice? Whose judgment on such a question should be the final court of appeal?

Stephen A. Douglas

Campaign Speech for United States Senate, delivered in Chicago, July 9, 1858

ONLY slightly over five feet tall, yet full in the chest and broad of shoulder, Stephen A. Douglas (1813–1861) was universally known as the Little Giant. In the raw, semi-frontier country of Illinois, where a man was judged by his physical prowess and his courage, he was recognized as a man's man. A skinny, sickly youth of twenty when he first arrived in Illinois, as an emigré from Vermont, he rapidly developed both health and a colorful, exciting political personality. Attaching himself to the Democratic Party, he proved brilliantly successful in a series of appointive and elective offices. He was, in turn, district attorney, member of the state legislature, Register of the Land Office, Secretary of State for Illinois, judge of the Illinois Supreme Court, United States Representative for two terms, and United States Senator from 1847 until his death in 1861, at the age of forty-eight. In Holman Hamilton's estimation, by the fall of 1850, he had transcended "all of the old masters" in the Senate, including Clay and Webster, and "was a personage of the first magnitude." During the crucial decade of the 1850's, he was a dominant political figure and was the finest debater in the Senate, easily eclipsing such speakers as William Seward, Charles Sumner, and Jefferson Davis. Beyond serious argument, Douglas was the strongest leader of the Democratic Party between Andrew Jackson and Woodrow Wilson, his only rivals being Grover Cleveland, who lacked his dynamic appeal, and William Jennings Bryan, who lacked his ability to coalesce support from the entire political spectrum, including business leaders, farmers, and workers. Throughout his career, according to Gerald M. Capers, "his outstanding attribute—the one which constituted most of his own success and that of his party—was the oratorical power and skill in debate which brought him his initial fame. From his schooldays until the Presidential campaign of 1860, a year before his death, the Little Giant influenced his fellow men chiefly through the spoken word."

The irony of his life and speaking career is that his name should be so despoiled by the recorders of our past. Following the Civil War, Herman E. Von Holst and James Fort Rhodes applied the devil theory of historiography to Douglas. Pinning the pattern of villain to Douglas' motives and actions, they cut his career to fit the pattern. Not until the writings of Frank H. Hodder after the turn of the century, did historians question the suitability of the pattern. Recent research by such noted historians as Roy F. Nichols, Gerald M. Capers, Holman Hamilton, and Richard Current has clearly exonerated Douglas of political immorality and, just as clearly, established his transcendence in the Senate. For example, the devil interpretation formerly caused historians to credit Clay and Webster for the Compromise of 1850, which temporarily tranquilized sectional passions. We now know, as a result of Hamilton's detailed study of the Compromise, that Clay's leadership and Webster's speaking were not the determining factors. As Richard Current writes, "Douglas himself, more than any other one man or two men, engineered the final passage of the compromise bills" of 1850. "The roles of Clay and Webster were afterward so much exaggerated as to become almost mythological." Perhaps the major reason for the distortion of Douglas' service to the country is that he opposed Abraham Lincoln for the United States Senate in 1858 and for the Presidency in 1860. An unnecessary accompaniment of our apotheosizing of Lincoln has been the denigration of Douglas.

One of the best means of comparing the positions of Douglas and Lincoln is to study their speeches in Chicago on July 9 and 10, 1858, at the beginning of the Senatorial campaign. Their more famed joint debates of later that fall are basically extensions of these speeches, marred to some extent by appeals to local biases and by the use of debaters' tricks.

About the middle of June, 1858, Abraham Lincoln accepted the nomination to the United States Senate in the electrifying "A House Divided" speech to the Republican Party convention in Springfield, Illinois. Printed in newspapers throughout the Middle West and

East, the speech was carried to millions of readers, including Senator Douglas in Washington. Realizing that Lincoln was a dangerous opponent, Douglas returned to the state to fight for his political life. Met at the state line by a special train carrying five hundred demonstrators and a brass band, his homecoming to Chicago was the most tumultuous scene in the city's history. When Douglas stepped to the balcony of the Tremont House, a crowd of thirty thousand had packed within hearing distance. After the bands, the fireworks, and the deafening cheers had subsided, Douglas' baritone voice boomed his appreciation of the unprecedented welcome, and the most momentous Senatorial campaign in history was under way.

The text of the speech is from the Chicago *Times*, July 11, 1858, and is reproduced in Paul M. Angle, *Created Equal: The Complete Lincoln-Douglas Debates of 1858*, Chicago: University of Chicago Press, 1958.

CAMPAIGN SPEECH FOR UNITED STATES SENATE

Mr. Chairman and fellow-citizens: I can find no language which can adequately express my profound gratitude for the magnificent welcome which you have extended to me on this occasion. This vast sea of human faces indicates how deep an interest is felt by our people in the great questions which agitate the public mind, and which underlie the foundations of our free institutions. A reception like this, so great in numbers that no human voice can be heard to its countless thousands—so enthusiastic that no one individual can be the object of such enthusiasm—clearly shows that there is some great principle which sinks deep in the heart of the masses, and involves the rights and liberties of a whole people, that has brought you together with a unanimity and a cordiality never before excelled, if, indeed, equalled on any occasion. I have not the vanity to believe that it is any personal compliment to me.

It is an expression of your devotion to that great principle of self-government, to which my life for many years past has been, and in the future will be devoted. If there is any one principle dearer and more sacred than all others in free governments, it is that which asserts the exclusive right of a free people to form and adopt their own fundamental law, and to manage and regulate their own internal affairs and domestic institutions.

When I found an effort being made during the recent session of Congress to force a constitution upon the people of Kansas against their will, and to force that state into the Union with a constitution which her people had rejected by more than 10,000, I felt bound as a man of honor and a representative of Illinois, bound by every consideration of duty, of fidelity, and of patriotism, to resist to the utmost of my power the consummation of that fraud. With others I did resist it, and resisted it successfully until the attempt was abandoned. We forced them to refer that constitution back to the people of Kansas, to be accepted or rejected as they shall decide at an election, which is fixed for the first Monday of August next. It is true that the mode of reference, and the form of the submission was not such as I could sanction with my vote, for the reason that it discriminated between free states and slave states; providing that if Kansas consented to come in under the Lecompton constitution it should be received with a population of 35,000; but that if she demanded another constitution, more consistent with the sentiments of her people and their feelings, that it should not be received into the Union until she has 93,420 inhabitants. I did not consider that mode of submission fair, for the reason that any election is a mockery which is not free—that any election is a fraud upon the right of the people which holds out inducements for affirmative votes, and threatens penalties for negative votes. But whilst I was not satisfied with the mode of submission, whilst I resisted it to the last, demanding a fair, a just, a free mode of submission, still, when the law passed placing it within the power of the people of Kansas at that election to reject the Lecompton constitution, and then make another in harmony with their principles and their opinions, I did not believe that either the penalties on the one hand, or the inducements on the other, would force that people to accept a constitution to which they are irreconcilably opposed. All I can say is, that if their votes can be controlled by such considerations, all the sympathy which has been expended upon them has been misplaced, and all the efforts that have been made in defence of their right to self-government have been made in an unworthy cause.

Hence, my friends, I regard the Lecompton battle as having been fought and the victory won, because the arrogant demand for the admission of Kansas under the Lecompton constitution unconditionally, whether her people wanted it or not, has been abandoned, and the principle which recognizes the right of the people to decide for themselves has been submitted to its place.

Fellow-citizens: While I devoted my best energies—all my energies, mental and physical—to the vindication of the great principle, and whilst the result has been such as will enable the people of Kansas to come into the Union, with such a constitution as they desire, yet the credit of this great moral victory is to be divided among a large number of men of various and different political creeds. I was rejoiced when I found in this great contest the Republican party coming up manfully and sustaining the principle that the people of each territory, when coming into the Union, have the right to decide for themselves whether slavery shall or shall not exist within their limits. I have seen the time when that principle was controverted. I have seen the time when all parties did not recognize the right of a people to have slavery or freedom, to tolerate or prohibit slavery, as they deemed best; but claimed that power for Congress of the United States, regardless of the wishes of the people to be affected by it, and when I found upon the Crittenden-Montgomery Bill the Republicans and Americans of the North, and I may say, too, some glorious Americans and Old Line Whigs from the South, like Crittenden and his patriotic associates, joined with a portion of the Democracy to carry out and vindicate the right of the people to decide whether slavery should or should not exist within the limits of Kansas, I was rejoiced within my secret soul, for I saw an indication that the American people, when they come to understand the principle, would give it their cordial support.

The Crittenden-Montgomery Bill was as fair and as perfect an exposition of the doctrine of popular sovereignty as could be carried out by any bill that man ever devised. It proposed to refer the Lecompton constitution back to the people of Kansas, and give them the right to accept or reject it as they pleased at a fair election, held in pursuance of law, and in the event of their rejecting it and forming another in its stead, to permit them to come into the Union on an equal footing with the original states. It was fair and just in all of its provisions! I gave it my cordial support, and was rejoiced when I found that it passed the House of Representatives, and at one time I entertained high hope that it would pass the Senate.

I regard the great principle of popular sovereignty as having been vindicated and made triumphant in this land as a permanent rule of public policy in the organization of territories and the admission of new states. Illinois took her position upon this principle many years ago. You all recollect that in 1850, after the passage of the compromise measures of that year, when I returned to my home there was great dissatisfaction expressed at my course in supporting those measures. I appeared before the people of Chicago at a mass meeting, and vindicated each and every one of those measures; and by reference to my speech on that occasion, which was printed and circulated broad-cast throughout the state at the time, you will find that I then and there said that those measures were all founded upon the great principle that every people ought to possess the right to form and regulate their own domestic institutions in their own way, and that that right being possessed by the people of the states, I saw no reason why the same principle should not be extended to all of the territories of the United States. A general election was held in this state a few months afterwards, for members of the legislature, pending which, all these question were thoroughly canvassed and discussed, and the nominees of the different parties instructed in regard to the wishes of their constituents upon them. When that election was over, and the legislature assembled, they proceeded to consider the merits of those compromise measures and the principles upon which they were predicated. And what was the result of their action? They passed resolutions, first repealing the Wilmot proviso instructions, and in lieu thereof adopted another resolution, in which they declared the great principle which asserts the right of the people to make their own form of government and establish their own institutions. That resolution is as follows:

> *Resolved.* That our liberty and independence are based upon the right of the people to form for themselves such a government as they may choose; that this great principle, the birthright of freemen, the gift of Heaven, secured to us by the blood of our ancestors, ought to be extended to future generations, and no limitation ought to be applied to this power in the organization of any territory of the U.S. of either territorial government or state constitution, provided the government so established shall be Republican, and in conformity with the Constitution of the United States.

That resolution, declaring the great principle of self-government as applicable to the territories and new states, passed the House of Representatives of this state by a vote of sixty-one in the affirmative, to only four in the negative. Thus you find that an expression of public opinion, enlightened, educated, intelligent public opinion on this question by the Representatives of Illinois, in 1851, approaches nearer to unanimity than has ever been obtained on any controverted question. That resolution was entered on the journal of the legislature of the state of Illinois, and it has remained there from that day to this, a standing instruction to her Senators and a request to her Representatives in Congress, to carry out that principle in all future cases.—Illinois therefore stands pre-eminent as the state which stepped forward early and established a platform applicable to this slavery question, concurred in alike by Whigs and Democrats, in which it was declared to be the wish of our people that thereafter the people of the territories should be left perfectly free to form and regulate their domestic institutions in their own way, and that no limitation should be placed upon that right in any form.

Hence what was my duty, in 1854, when it became necessary to bring forward a bill for the organization of the territories of Kansas and Nebraska? Was it not my duty, in obedience to the Illinois platform, to your standing instructions to your Senators, adopted with almost entire unanimity, to incorporate in that bill the great principle of self-government, declaring that it was "the true intent and meaning of the act not to legislate slavery into any state or territory, or to exclude it therefrom, but to leave the people thereof perfectly free to form and regulate their domestic institutions in their own way, subject only to the Constitution of the United States?" I did incorporate that principle in the Kansas-Nebraska Bill, and perhaps I did as much as any living man in the enactment of that bill, thus establishing the doctrine in the public policy of the country. I then defended that principle against assaults from one section of the Union. During this last winter it became my duty to vindicate it against assaults from the other section of the Union. I vindicated it boldly and fearlessly, as the people of Chicago can bear witness, when it was assailed by Freesoilers; and during this winter I vindicated and defended it as boldly and as fearlessly when it was attempted to be violated by the almost united South. I pledged myself to you on every stump in Illinois in 1854, I pledged myself to the people of other states, North and South—whenever I spoke—and in the United States Senate and elsewhere, in every forum in which I could reach the public mind or the public ear, I gave the pledge that I, so far as the power should be in my hands, would vindicate the principle of the right of the people to form their own institutions, to establish free states or slave states as they chose, and that that principle should never be violated either by fraud, by violence, by circumvention, or by any other means, if it was in my power to prevent it. I now submit to you my fellow-citizens, whether I have not redeemed that pledge in good faith! Yes, my friends, I have redeemed it in good faith, and it is a matter of heartfelt gratification to me to see these assembled thousands here to-night bearing their testimony to the fidelity with which I have advocated that principle and redeemed my pledges in connection with it.

I will be entirely frank with you. My object was to secure the right of the people of each state and of each territory, North or South, to decide the question for themselves, to have slavery or not, just as they chose; and my opposition to the Lecompton constitution was not predicated upon the ground that it was a pro-slavery constitution, nor would my action have been different had it been a free-soil constitution. My speech against the Lecompton fraud was made on the 9th of December, while the vote on the slavery clause in that constitution was not taken until the 21st of the same month, nearly two weeks after. I made my speech against the Lecompton monstrosity solely on the ground that it was a violation of the fundamental principles of free government; on the ground that it was not the act and deed of the people of Kansas; that it did not embody their will; that they were averse to it; and hence I denied the right of Congress to force it upon them, either as a free state or a slave state. I deny the right of Congress to force a slave-holding state upon an unwilling people.

I deny their right to force a free state upon an unwilling people. I deny their right to force a good thing upon a people who are unwilling to receive it. The great principle is the right of every community to judge and decide for itself, whether a thing is right or wrong, whether it would be good or evil for them to adopt it; and the right of free action, the right of free thought, the right of free judgment upon the question is dearer to every true American than any other under a free government. My objection to the Lecompton contrivance was that it undertook to put a constitution on the people of Kansas against their will, in opposition to their wishes, and thus violated the great principle upon which all our institutions rest. It is no answer to this argument to say that slavery is an evil and hence should not be tolerated. You must allow the people to decide for themselves whether it is a good or an evil. You allow them to decide for themselves whether they desire a Maine liquor law or not; you allow them to decide for themselves what kind of common schools they will have; what system of banking they will adopt, or whether they will adopt any at all; you allow them to decide for themselves the relations between husband and wife, parent and child, the guardian and ward; in fact, you allow them to decide for themselves all other questions, and why not upon this question? Whenever you put a limitation upon the right of any people to decide what laws they want, you have destroyed the fundamental principle of self-government.

In connection with this subject, perhaps, it will not be improper for me on this occasion to allude to the position of those who have chosen to arraign my conduct on this same subject. I have observed from the public prints that but a few days ago the Republican party of the state of Illinois assembled in convention at Springfield, and not only laid down their platform, but nominated a candidate for the United States Senate as my successor. I take great pleasure in saying that I have known, personally and intimately, for about a quarter of a century, the worthy gentleman who has been nominated for my place, and I will say that I regard him as a kind, amiable, and intelligent gentleman, a good citizen and an honorable opponent; and whatever issue I may have with him will be of principle, and not involving personalities.—Mr. Lincoln made a speech before that Republican Convention which unanimously nominated him for the Senate—a speech evidently well prepared and carefully written—in which he states the basis upon which he proposes to carry on the campaign during this summer. In it he lays down two distinct propositions which I shall notice, and upon which I shall take a direct and bold issue with him.

His first and main proposition I will give in his own language, scripture quotations and all, (laughter) I give his exact language—" 'A house divided against itself cannot stand.' I believe this government cannot endure, permanently, half *slave* and half *free*. I do not expect the Union to be *dissolved*. I do not expect the house to *fall*; but I do expect it to cease to be divided. It will become *all* one thing or *all* the other."

In other words, Mr. Lincoln asserts as a fundamental principle of this government, that there must be uniformity in the local laws and domestic institutions of each and all the states of the Union; and he therefore invites all the non-slaveholding states to band together, organize as one body, and make war upon slavery in Kentucky, upon slavery in Virginia, upon the Carolinas, upon slavery in all of the slave-holding states in this Union, and to persevere in that war until it shall be exterminated. He then notifies the slaveholding states to stand together as a unit and make an aggressive war upon the free states of this Union with a view of establishing slavery in them all; of forcing it upon Illinois, of forcing it upon New York, upon New England, and upon every other free state, and that they shall keep up the warfare until it has been formally established in them all. In other words, Mr. Lincoln advocates boldly and clearly a war of sections, a war of the North against the South, of the free states against the slave states—a war of extermination—to be continued relentlessly until the one or the other shall be subdued and all the states shall either become free or become slave.

Now, my friends, I must say to you frankly, that I take bold, unqualified issue with him upon that principle. I assert that it is neither desirable nor possible that there should be uniformity in the local institutions and domestic regulations of the different states of this Union. The framers of our government never contemplated uniformity in its internal concerns. The fathers of the Revolution, and the sages who made the Constitution well understood that the laws and domestic institutions which would suit the granite hills of New Hampshire would be totally unfit for the rice plantations of South Carolina; they well understood that the laws which would suit the agricultural districts of Pennsylvania and New York would be totally unfit for the large mining regions of the Pacific, or the lumber regions of Maine. They well understood that the great varieties of soil, of production and of interests, in a republic as large as this, required different local and domestic regulations in each locality, adapted to the wants and interests of each separate state, and for that reason it was provided in the federal Constitution that the thirteen original states should remain sovereign and supreme within their own limits in regard to all that was local, and internal, and domestic, while the federal government should have certain specified powers which were general and national, and could be exercised only by the federal authority.

The framers of the Constitution well understood that each locality, having separate and distinct interests, required separate and distinct laws, domestic institutions, and police regulations adapted to its own wants and its own condition; and they acted on the presumption, also, that these laws and institutions would be as diversified and as dissimilar as the states would be numerous, and that no two would be precisely alike, because the interests of the two would [not] be precisely the same. Hence, I assert, that the great fundamental principle which underlies our complex system of state and federal governments, contemplated diversity and dissimilarity in the local institutions and domestic affairs of each and every state then in the Union, or thereafter to be admitted into the confederacy. I therefore conceive that my friend, Mr. Lincoln, has totally misapprehended the great principles upon which our government rests. Uniformity in local and domestic affairs would be destructive of state rights, of state sovereignty, of personal liberty and personal freedom. Uniformity is the parent of despotism the world over, not only in politics, but in religion. Wherever the doctrine of uniformity is proclaimed, that all the states must be free or all slave, that all labor must be white or all black, that all the citizens of the different states must have the same privileges or be governed by the same regulations, you have destroyed the greatest safeguard which our institutions have thrown around the rights of the citizen.

How could this uniformity be accomplished, if it was desirable and possible? There is but one mode in which it could be obtained, and that must be by abolishing the state legislatures, blotting out state sovereignty, merging the rights and sovereignty of the states in one consolidated empire, and vesting Congress with the plenary power to make all the police regulations, domestic and local laws, uniform throughout the limits of the Republic. When you shall have done this you will have uniformity. Then the states will all be slave or all be free; then Negroes will vote everywhere or nowhere; then you will have a Maine liquor law in every state or none; then you will have uniformity in all things local and domestic by the authority of the federal government. But when you attain that uniformity, you will have converted these thirty-two sovereign, independent states, into one consolidated empire, with the uniformity of despotism reigning triumphant throughout the length and breadth of the land.

From this view of the case, my friends, I am driven irresistibly to the conclusion that diversity, dissimilarity, variety in all our local and domestic institutions, is the great safeguard of our liberties; and that the framers of our institutions were wise, sagacious, and patriotic when they made this government a confederation of sovereign states with a legislature for each, and conferred upon each legislature the power to make all local and domestic institutions to suit the people it represented, without interference from any other state or from the general Congress of the Union. If we expect to maintain our liberties we must preserve the rights and sovereignty of the states, we must maintain and carry out that great principle of self-government incorporated in the compromise measures of 1850: endorsed by the Illinois legislature in 1851; emphatically embodied and carried out in the Kansas-Nebraska Bill, and vindicated this year by the refusal to bring Kansas into the Union with a constitution distasteful to her people.

The other proposition discussed by Mr. Lincoln in his speech consists in a crusade against the Supreme Court of the United States on account of the Dred Scott decision. On this question, also, I desire to say to you unequivocally, that I take direct and distinct issue with him. I have no warfare to make on the Supreme Court of the United States, either on account of that or any other decision which they have pronounced from that bench. The Constitution of the United States has provided that the powers of government (and the constitution of each state has the same provision) shall be divided into three departments, executive, legislative, and judicial. The right and the province of expounding the Constitution, and construing the law, is vested in the judiciary established by the Constitution.–As a lawyer, I feel at liberty to appear before the Court and controvert any principle of law while the question is pending before the tribunal; but when the decision is made, my private opinion, your opinion, all other opinions must yield to the majesty of that authoritative adjudication. I wish you to bear in mind that this involves a great principle, upon which our rights, our liberty and our property all depend. What security have you for your property, for your reputation, and for your personal rights, if the courts are not upheld, and their decisions respected when once firmly rendered by the highest tribunal known to the Constitution? I do not choose, therefore, to go into any argument with Mr. Lincoln in reviewing the various decisions which the Supreme Court has made, either upon the Dred Scott case, or any other. I have no idea of appealing from the decision of the Supreme Court upon a constitutional question to the decisions of a tumultuous town meeting. I am aware that once an eminent lawyer of this city, now no more, said that the state of Illinois had the most perfect judicial system in the world, subject to but one exception, which could be cured by a slight amendment, and that amendment was to so change the law as to allow an appeal from the decisions of the Supreme Court of Illinois, on all constitutional questions, to Justice of the Peace.

My friend, Mr. Lincoln, who sits behind me, reminds me that that proposition was made when I was Judge of the Supreme Court. Be that as it may, I do not think that fact adds any greater weight or authority to the suggestion. It matters not with me who was on the bench, whether Mr. Lincoln or myself, whether a Lockwood or a Smith, a Taney or a Marshall; the decision of the highest tribunal known to the Constitution of the country must be final till it has been reversed by an equally high authority. Hence, I am opposed to this doctrine of Mr. Lincoln, by which he proposes to take an appeal from the decision of the Supreme Court of the United States, upon this high constitutional question to a Republican caucus sitting in the country. Yes, or any other caucus or town meeting, whether it be Republican, American, or Democratic. I respect the decisions of that august tribunal; I shall always bow in deference to them. I am a law-abiding man. I will sustain the Constitution of my country as our fathers have made it. I will yield obedience to the laws, whether I like them or not, as I find them on the statute book. I will sustain the judicial tribunals and constituted authorities in all matters within the pale of their jurisdiction as defined by the Constitution.

But I am equally free to say that the reason assigned by Mr. Lincoln for resisting the decision of the Supreme Court in the Dred Scott case does not in itself meet my approbation. He objects to it because that decision declared that a Negro descended from African parents who were brought here and sold as slaves is not, and cannot be a citizen of the United States. He says it is wrong, because it deprives the Negro of the benefits of that clause of the Constitution which says that citizens of one state shall enjoy all the privileges and immunities of citizens of the several states; in other words, he thinks it wrong because it deprives the Negro of the privileges, immunities, and rights of citizenship, which pertain, according to that decision, only to the white man. I am free to say to you that in my opinion this government of ours is founded on the white basis. It was made by the white man, for the benefit of the white man, to be administered by white men, in such manner as they should determine. It is also true that a Negro, an Indian, or any other man of an inferior race to a white man, should be permitted to enjoy, and humanity requires that he should have all the rights, privileges and immunities which he is capable of exercising consistent with the safety of society. I would give him every right and every privilege which his capacity would enable him to enjoy, consistent with the good of the society in which he lived. But you may ask me what are these rights and these privileges. My answer is that each state must decide for itself the nature and extent of these rights. Illinois has decided for herself. We have decided that the Negro shall not be a slave, and we have at the same time decided that he shall not vote, or serve on juries, or enjoy political privileges. I am content with that system of policy which we have adopted for ourselves. I deny the right of any other State to complain of our policy in that respect, or to interfere with it, or to attempt to change it. On the other hand, the state of Maine has decided that in that state a Negro man may vote on an equality with the white man. The sovereign power of Maine had the right to prescribe that rule for herself. Illinois has no right to complain of Maine for conferring the right of Negro suffrage, nor has Maine any right to interfere with, or complain of Illinois because she has denied Negro suffrage.

The state of New York has decided by her constitution that a Negro may vote, provided that he own $250 worth of property, but not otherwise. The rich Negro can vote, but the poor one cannot. Although that distinction does not commend itself to my judgment, yet I assert that the sovereign power of New York had a right to prescribe that form of the elective franchise. Kentucky, Virginia, and other states have provided that Negroes, or a certain class of them in those states, shall be slaves, having neither civil or political rights. Without endorsing the wisdom of that decision, I assert that Virginia has the same power by virtue of her sovereignty to protect slavery within her limits, as Illinois has to banish it forever from our own borders. I assert the right of each state to decide for itself on all these questions and I do not subscribe to the doctrine of my friend, Mr. Lincoln, that uniformity is either desirable or possible. I do not acknowledge that the states must all be free or must all be slave.

I do not acknowledge that the Negro must have civil and political rights everywhere or nowhere. I do not acknowledge that the Chinese must have the same rights in California that we would confer upon him here. I do not acknowledge that the cooley imported into this country must necessarily be put upon an equality with the white race. I do not acknowledge any of these doctrines of uniformity in the local and domestic regulations in the different states.

Thus you see, my fellow-citizens, that the issues between Mr. Lincoln and myself, as respective candidates for the U.S. Senate, as made up, are direct, unequivocal, and irreconcilable. He goes for uniformity in our domestic institutions, for a war of sections, until one or the other shall be subdued. I go for the great principle of the Kansas-Nebraska Bill, the right of the people to decide for themselves.

On the other point, Mr. Lincoln goes for a warfare upon the Supreme Court of the United States, because of their judicial decision in the Dred Scott case. I yield obedience to the decisions of that Court—to the final determination of the highest judicial tribunal known to our Constitution. He objects to the Dred Scott decision because it does not put the Negro in the possession of the rights of citizenship on an equality with the white man. I am opposed to Negro equality. I repeat that this nation is a white people—a people composed of European descendants—a people that have established this government for themselves and their posterity, and I am in favor of preserving not only the purity of the blood, but the purity of the government from any mixture or amalgamation with inferior races. I have seen the effects of this mixture of superior and inferior races—this amalgamation of white men and Indians and Negroes;

we have seen it in Mexico, in Central America, in South America, and in all the Spanish-American states, and its result has been degeneration, demoralization, and degradation below the capacity for self-government.

I am opposed to taking any step that recognizes the Negro man or the Indian as the equal of the white man. I am opposed to giving him a voice in the administration of the government. I would extend to the Negro, and the Indian, and to all dependent races every right, every privilege, and every immunity consistent with the safety and welfare of the white races; but equality they never should have, either political or social, or in any other respect whatever.

My friends, you see that the issues are distinctly drawn. I stand by the same platform that I have so often proclaimed to you and to the people of Illinois heretofore. I stand by the Democratic organization, yield obedience to its usages, and support its regular nominations. I endorse and approve the Cincinnati platform, and I adhere to and intend to carry out as part of that platform, the great principle of self-government, which recognizes the right of the people in each state and territory to decide for themselves their domestic institutions. In other words, if the Lecompton issue shall arise again, you have only to turn back and see where you have found me during the last six months, and then rest assured that you will find me in the same position, battling for the same principle, and vindicating it from assault from whatever quarter it may come, so long as I have the power to do it.

Fellow-citizens, you now have before you the outlines of the propositions which I intend to discuss before the people of Illinois during the pending campaign. I have spoken without preparation and in a very desultory manner, and may have omitted some points which I desired to discuss, and may have been less explicit on others than I could have wished. I have made up my mind to appeal to the people against the combination which has been made against me. The Republican leaders have formed an alliance, an unholy, unnatural alliance with a portion of the unscrupulous federal officeholders. I intend to fight that allied army wherever I meet them. I know they deny the alliance while avowing the common purpose, but yet these men who are trying to divide the Democratic party for the purpose of electing a Republican Senator in my place, are just as much the agents, the tools, the supporters of Mr. Lincoln as if they were avowed Republicans, and expect their reward for their services when the Republicans come into power. I shall deal with these allied forces just as the Russians dealt with the allies at Sebastopol. The Russians when they fired a broadside at the common enemy did not stop to inquire whether it hit a Frenchman, an Englishman or a Turk, nor will I stop to inquire, nor shall I hesitate, whether my blows hit the Republican leaders or their allies, who are holding the federal offices and yet acting in concert with the Republicans to defeat the Democratic party and its nominees. I do not include all of the federal office holders in this remark. Such of them as are Democrats and show their Democracy by remaining inside of the Democratic organization and supporting its nominees, I recognize as Democrats, but those who, having been defeated inside of the organization, go outside and attempt to divide and destroy the party in concert with the Republican leaders, have ceased to be Democrats, and belong to the allied army whose avowed object is to elect the Republican ticket by dividing and destroying the Democratic party.

My friends, I have exhausted myself, and I certainly have fatigued you, in the long and desultory remarks which I have made. It is now two nights since I have been in bed, and I think I have a right to a little sleep. I will, however, have an opportunity of meeting you face to face, and addressing you on more than one occasion before the November election. In conclusion, I must again say to you, justice to my own feelings demands it, that my gratitude for the welcome you have extended to me on this occasion knows no bounds, and can be described by no language which I can command. I see that I am literally at home when among my constituents. This welcome has amply repaid me for every effort that I have made in the public service during nearly twenty-five years that I have held office at your hands. It not only compensates me for the past, but it furnishes an inducement and incentive for future effort which no man, no matter how patriotic, can feel who has not witnessed the magnificent reception you have extended to me to-night on my return.

Exercises

1. What are the basic functions of Douglas' Introduction? How successful are his repeated attempts to link his listeners to his principal thesis? Do you consider the length of the Introduction appropriate? What transitions, if any, does Douglas use as a bridge between his opening comments and the Body of the speech? What changes, if any, would you have him make in the Introduction?

2. Does Douglas provide enough background information for you to follow easily his defense concerning the Lecompton constitution? Do you think he supplied enough background explanation for his hearers? Was his opening of this argument subtle? Bald? Implicative? Didactic? Explain.

3. From your knowledge of the principles of argumentation, was Douglas wise to divide the Body of the speech into two main parts: a defense of popular sovereignty and his previous record in support of that principle; and an attack upon his opponent, Abraham Lincoln?

Is the basic purpose of such a procedure to enhance one's own personal proof and to injure that of one's opponent? Explain.

4. Outline Douglas' development of each of the main heads of the Body. As well as you can, estimate the logical and psychological effectiveness of each major substantiating argument or item of evidence. To what degree do you believe each one constitutes an appeal to logic? To emotion? To rationalization? To established beliefs, biases, and culture patterns of the hearers? To reverence for forefathers? How well-suited would these appeals be to an audience of 1908? of 1958? Of the present? Explain.

5. How does Douglas connect the two main divisions of the Body? Do you consider the transition to be sufficiently smooth? Subtle? Clear? Helpful in furthering persuasion?

6. Douglas praises Lincoln before attempting to refute his policies. Is this a good or poor persuasive strategy? Explain. How does Douglas focus attention on the concepts that he intends to refute? Is this procedure clear? Persuasive? How would you characterize the mode and manner of Douglas' refutation? Dignified? Courteous? Bombastic? Scornful? Belligerent? Explain. Do you believe that Douglas magnified, or minimized, the differences between his position and that of Lincoln's? From the standpoint of persuasion, is this result good or bad? Does debate usually seem to "widen" or to "bridge" the gamut between the opposing speakers? Explain your answer.

7. How would you characterize the style of this speech? Direct? Elevated? Plain? Argumentative? Personalized? Colloquial? Abstract? Other? Explain. Compare Douglas' style with that of other speeches reported elsewhere in this book, especially the speeches by Lincoln, Emerson, Jefferson, Bryan, and Wilson. Does Douglas' style seem modern, or old-fashioned? How well-adapted do you believe it was to the needs of the speaking situation? To what extent does he make use of personal pronouns? Short sentences? Direct and rhetorical questions? Irony? Humor?

8. From the following quotation, what conclusions can you draw concerning the nature of racial attitudes existing at this time in Illinois? "Illinois has decided for herself. We have decided that the Negro shall not be a slave, and we have at the same time decided that he shall not vote, or serve on juries, or enjoy political privileges." Do you have difficulty in putting yourself in the position of the listeners? After reading the speech, do you feel that you understand better the position of the Negro in the North before the Civil War? Explain.

9. How effective do you believe Douglas' Conclusion to be? Is he wise to say that he had spoken without preparation and without sleep for two nights? To what extent does he summarize his arguments? Does he attempt a final identification with the hearers? How does he attempt to promote the proper mood?

10. Compare Douglas' view of "the supremacy of the law" with that expressed in Thoreau's "Slavery in Massachusetts" speech. How does Lincoln's position on this matter differ from that of Douglas and Thoreau? Summarize the arguments made by each of these three speakers in support of his stand. How does each try to make his views persuasively appealing?

Abraham Lincoln

Campaign Speech for United States Senate, delivered in Chicago, July 10, 1858

Of all the great men of our past, the one with whom Americans can most easily achieve an affectionate identification is Abraham Lincoln (1809–1865). Reared in exceedingly humble and straitened circumstances, he developed qualities of industry, courage, and perseverance that made him America's greatest success story. After Lincoln's example, any boy could grow up to become President! Schooled in adversity, he developed gentleness of spirit, clarity of mind, refreshing earthiness of humor, steadfastness of moral conviction, and an abiding faith in the ultimate goodness of man and in the rightness of divine judgment. Matured by personal disappointment and grueling responsibility, he developed a nobility of expression unmatched by any other American statesman, even Wilson or Jefferson. In "deathless overtones," his words still stir men's spirits to the cords of freedom and justice. More than any other speeches of our past, Lincoln's addresses as President may be read and reread with continuing satisfaction—for their ultimate goals, for their strategic policies, for their grandeur of style, for their humane love of mankind, for their sad awareness of the shortcomings of man, and for their hopeful appeal to the best in man's nature.

Before Lincoln attained greatness as a statesman and orator in the White House, he was one of the most successful lawyers in Illinois and a sometimes politician. Following his single term in the United States House of Representatives, he returned to Illinois in

1849, out of favor because of his forceful denunciations of the Mexican War. He remained inactive in politics until five years later, when Senator Stephen A. Douglas pushed through Congress the Kansas-Nebraska bill, which explicitly repealed the principle of the Missouri Compromise and territorial restrictions on slavery. Believing that popular sovereignty gave encouragement to slavery expansion, Lincoln took to the public platform. After the adjournment of Congress in 1854, when Douglas returned for a speaking tour of Illinois, Lincoln followed him about the state giving speeches of rebuttal. The most famous of their several direct debates occurred at Peoria where Lincoln achieved widespread attention for his indictment of slavery as immoral. During the next four years, Lincoln assiduously built his political alliances and developed his platform skills until he dominated the Republican Party in Illinois as thoroughly as did William Seward and Thurlow Weed in New York. At the close of the Illinois Republican State Convention, on June 16, 1858, following his nomination for United States Senator, Lincoln delivered a carefully prepared speech which was designed to startle all thoughtful persons, by asserting that a house divided against itself could not stand, and to put Douglas on the defensive, by charging that the Little Giant was part of a deliberate conspiracy to extend slavery. In Washington, when he learned of Lincoln's nomination, Douglas exclaimed, "I shall have my hands full. He is the strong man of his party—full of wit, facts, dates—and the best stump speaker, with his droll ways and dry jokes, in the West."

Hurriedly returning to Illinois, Douglas opened his campaign in a rousing speech, July 9, from the balcony of Tremont House. (See Douglas' speech printed on pp. 135–147.) The next night, Lincoln spoke to a Chicago crowd which he believed to be as large as that of Douglas and "five times as enthusiastic." Although later that fall the two men crisscrossed the state, giving more than one hundred and fifty speeches and meeting seven times in direct debates, probably the best representations of their divergent views are these speeches at the outset of the campaign. History tells us that Douglas won the election by a slim margin but that the campaign focused great publicity upon the views of both men, seriously impairing Douglas' acceptability to Southerners and introducing Lincoln to the nation as a worthy possibility for President.

The text of the speech is from the Chicago *Daily Democrat*, July 13, 1858, and is reprinted in Paul M. Angle, *Created Equal:*

The Complete Lincoln-Douglas Debates of 1858, Chicago: University of Chicago Press, 1958.

CAMPAIGN SPEECH FOR UNITED STATES SENATE

My Fellow Citizens: On yesterday evening, upon the occasion of the reception given to Senator Douglas, I was furnished with a seat very convenient for hearing him, and was otherwise very courteously treated by him and his friends, and for which I thank him and them. During the course of his remarks my name was mentioned in such a way, as I suppose renders it at least not improper that I should make some sort of reply to him. I shall not attempt to follow him in the precise order in which he addressed the assembled multitude upon that occasion, though I shall perhaps do so in the main.

There was one question to which he asked the attention of the crowd, which I deem of somewhat less importance—at least of propriety for me to dwell upon—than the others, which he brought in near the close of his speech, and which I think would not be entirely proper for me to omit attending to, and yet if I were not to give some attention to it now, I should probably forget it altogether. [Applause.] While I am upon this subject, allow me to say that I do not intend to indulge in that inconvenient mode sometimes adopted in public speaking, of reading from documents; but I shall depart from that rule so far as to read a little scrap from his speech, which notices this first topic of which I shall speak—that is, provided I can find it in the paper. (Examines the *Press and Tribune* of this morning. [A voice—"Get out your specs."]).

> I have made up my mind to appeal to the people against the combination that has been made against me!—the Republican leaders have formed an alliance, an unholy and unnatural alliance, with a portion of unscrupulous federal office-holders. I intend to fight that allied army wherever I meet them. I know they deny the alliance, but yet these men who are trying to divide the Democratic party for the purpose of electing a Republican Senator in my place, are just as much the agents and tools of the supporters of Mr. Lincoln. Hence I shall deal with this allied army just as the Russians dealt with the allies at Sebastopol—that is, the Russians did not stop to inquire, when they fired a broadside, whether it hit an Englishman, a Frenchman, or a Turk. Nor will I stop to inquire, nor shall I hesitate, whether my blows shall hit these Republican leaders or their allies who are holding the federal offices and yet acting in concert with them.

Well now, gentlemen, is not that very alarming? [Laughter.] Just to think of it! right at the outset of this canvass, I, a poor, kind, amiable, intelligent, [Laughter.] gentleman, [Laughter and renewed cheers.] I am to be slain in this way. Why, my friend, the Judge, is not only, as it turns out, not a dead lion, nor even a living one—he is the rugged Russian Bear! [Roars of laughter and loud applause.]

But if they will have it—for he says that we deny it—that there is any such alliance, as he says there is—and I don't propose hanging very much upon this question of veracity—but if he will have it that there is such an alliance—that the administration men and we are allied, and we stand in the attitude of English, French and Turk, he occupying the position of the Russian, in that case, I beg that he will indulge us while we barely suggest to him, that these allies took Sebastopol. [Long and tremendous applause.]

Gentlemen, only a few more words as to this alliance. For my part, I have to say, that whether there be such an alliance, depends, so far as I know, upon what may be a right definition of the term *alliance*. If for the Republican party to see the other great party to which they are opposed divided among themselves, and not try to stop the division and rather be glad of it—if that is an alliance I confess I am in; but if it is meant to be said that the Republicans had formed an alliance going beyond that, by which there is contribution of money or sacrifice of principle on the one side or the other, so far as the Republican party is concerned, if there be any such thing, I protest that I neither know anything of it, nor do I believe it. I will however say—as I think this branch of the argument is lugged in—I would before I leave it, state, for the benefit of those concerned, that one of those same Buchanan men did once tell me of an argument that he made for his opposition to Judge Douglas. He said that a friend of our Senator Douglas had been talking to him, and had among other things said to him: "Why, you don't want to beat Douglas?" "Yes," said he, "I do want to beat him, and I will tell you why. I believe his original Nebraska Bill was right in the abstract, but it was wrong in the time that it was brought forward. It was wrong in the application to a territory in regard to which the question had been settled; it was brought forward at a time when nobody asked him; it was tendered to the South when the South had not asked for it, but when they could not well refuse it; and for this same reason he forced that question upon our party: it has sunk the best men all over the nation, everywhere; and now when our President, struggling with the difficulties of this man's getting up, has reached the very hardest point to turn in the case, he deserts him, and I am for putting him where he will trouble us no more." [Applause.]

Now, gentlemen, that is not my argument—that is not my argument at all. I have only been stating to you the argument of a Buchanan man. You will judge if there is any force in it. [Applause.]

Popular sovereignty! everlasting popular sovereignty! [Laughter and continued cheers.] Let us for a moment inquire into this vast matter of popular sovereignty. What is popular sovereignty? We recollect that at an early period in the history of this struggle, there was another name for this same thing—*Squatter Sovereignty*. It was not exactly popular sovereignty but squatter sovereignty. What do those terms mean? What do those terms mean when used now? And vast credit is taken by our friend, the Judge, in regard to his support of it, when he declares the last years of his life have been, and all the future years of his life shall be, devoted to this matter of popular sovereignty. What is it? Why, it is the sovereignty of the people! What was squatter sovereignty? I suppose if it had any significance at all it was the right of the people to govern themselves, to be sovereign of their own affairs while they were squatted down in a country not their own, while they had squatted on a territory that did not belong to them, in the sense that a state belongs to the people who inhabit it—when it belonged to the nation—such right to govern themselves was called "Squatter Sovereignty."

Now I wish you to mark. What has become of that squatter sovereignty? What has become of it? Can you get anybody to tell you now that the people of a territory have any authority to govern themselves, in regard to this mooted question of slavery, before they form a state constitution? No such thing at all, although there is a general running fire, and although there has been a hurrah made in every speech on that side, assuming that policy had given the people of a territory the right to govern themselves upon this question; yet the point is dodged. To-day it has been decided—no more than a year ago it was decided by the Supreme Court of the United States, and is insisted upon to-day, that the people of a territory have no right to exclude slavery from a territory, that if any one man chooses to take slaves into a territory, all the rest of the people have no right to keep them out. This being so, and this decision being made one of the points that the Judge approved, and one in the approval of which he says he means to keep me down—put me down I should not say, for I have never been up. He says he is in favor of it, and sticks to it, and expects to win his battle on that decision, which says that there is no such thing as squatter sovereignty; but that any one man may take slaves into a territory, and all the other men in the territory may be opposed to it, and yet by reason of the Constitution they cannot prohibit it. When that is so, how much is left of this vast matter of squatter sovereignty I should like to know? [—A voice—"It has all gone."]

When we get back, we get to the point of the right of the people to make a constitution. Kansas was settled, for example, in 1854. It was a territory yet, without having formed a constitution, in a very regular way, for three years. All this time Negro slavery could be taken in by any few individuals, and by that decision of the Supreme Court, which the Judge approves, all the rest of the people cannot keep it out; but when they come to make a constitution they may say they will not have slavery. But it is there; they are obliged to tolerate it in some way, and all experience shows that it will be so—for they will not take the Negro slaves and absolutely deprive the owners of them. All experience shows this to be so. All that space of time that runs from the beginning of the settlement of the territory until there is sufficiency of people to make a state constitution—all that portion of time popular sovereignty is given up. The seal is absolutely put down upon it by the court decision, and Judge Douglas puts his own upon the top of that, yet he is appealing to the people to give him vast credit for his devotion to popular sovereignty. [Applause.]

Again, when we get to the question of the right of the people to form a state constitution as they please, to form it with slavery or without slavery—if that is anything new, I confess I don't know it. Has there ever been a time when anybody said that any other than the people of a territory itself should form a constitution? What is now in it, that Judge Douglas should have fought several years of his life, and pledged himself to fight all the remaining years of his life for? Can Judge Douglas find anybody on earth that said that anybody else should form a constitution for a people?

[A VOICE, "Yes."] Well, I should like you to name him; I should like to know who he was. [SAME VOICE—"John Calhoun."]

MR. LINCOLN—No, sir, I never heard of even John Calhoun saying such a thing. He insisted on the same principle as Judge Douglas; but his mode of applying it in fact, was wrong. It is enough for my purpose to ask this crowd, when ever a Republican said anything against it? They never said anything against it, but they have constantly spoken for it; and whosoever will undertake to examine the platform, and the speeches of responsible men of the party, and of irresponsible men, too, if you please, will be unable to find one word from anybody in the Republican ranks, opposed to that popular sovereignty which Judge Douglas thinks that he has invented. [Applause.] I suppose that Judge Douglas will claim in a little while, that he is the inventor of the idea that the people should govern themselves: [Cheers and laughter.]; that nobody ever thought of such a thing until he brought it forward. We do remember, that in that old Declaration of Independence, it is said that "We hold these truths to be self-evident that all men are created equal; that they are endowed by their Creator with certain inalienable rights; that among these are life, liberty, and the pursuit of happiness; that to secure these rights, governments are instituted among men, deriving their just powers from the consent of the governed." There is the origin of popular sovereignty. [Loud applause.] Who, then, shall come in at this day and claim that he invented it? [Laughter and applause.]

The Lecompton constitution connects itself with this question, for it is in this matter of the Lecompton constitution that our friend Judge Douglas claims such vast credit. I agree that in opposing the Lecompton constitution so far as I can perceive, he was right. ["Good," "good."] I do not deny that at all; and gentlemen, you will readily see why I could not deny it, even if I wanted to. But I do not wish to; for all the Republicans in the nation opposed it, and they would have opposed it just as much without Judge Douglas' aid, as with it. They had all taken ground against it long before he did. Why, the reason that he urges against that constitution, I urged against him a year before. I have the printed speech in my hand. The argument that he makes, why that constitution should not be adopted, that the people were not fairly represented nor allowed to vote, I pointed out in a speech a year ago, which I hold in my hand now, that no fair chance was to be given to the people. ["Read it," "read it."] I shall not waste your time by trying to read it. ["Read it," "read it."] Gentlemen, reading from speeches is a very tedious business, particularly for an old man that has to put on spectacles, and the more so if the man be so tall that he has to bend over to the light. [Laughter.]

A little more, now, as to this matter of popular sovereignty and the Lecompton constitution. The Lecompton constitution, as the Judge tells us, was defeated. The defeat of it was a good thing or it was not. He thinks the defeat of it was a good thing, and so do I, and we agree in that. Who defeated it?

A VOICE—Judge Douglas.

MR. LINCOLN—Yes, he furnished himself, and if you suppose he controlled the other Democrats that went with him, he furnished *three* votes, while the Republicans furnished *twenty*. [Applause.]

That is what he did to defeat it. In the House of Representatives he and his friends furnished some twenty votes, and the Republicans furnished *ninety odd*. [Loud applause.] Now who was it that did the work?

A VOICE—Douglas.

MR. LINCOLN—Why, yes, Douglas did it! To be sure he did.

Let us, however, put that proposition another way. The Republicans could not have done it without Judge Douglas. Could he have done it without them? [Applause.] Which could have come the nearest to doing it without the other? [Renewed applause. "That's it," "that's it"; "good," "good."]

A VOICE—Who killed the bill?

ANOTHER VOICE—Douglas.

MR. LINCOLN—Ground was taken against it by the Republicans long before Douglas did it. The proportion of opposition to that measure is about five to one.

A VOICE—Why don't they come out on it?

MR. LINCOLN—You don't know what you are talking about, my friend. I am quite willing to answer any gentleman in the crowd who asks an *intelligent* question. [Great applause.]

Now, who in all this country has ever found any of our friends of Judge Douglas' way of thinking, and who have acted upon this main question, that has ever thought of uttering a word in behalf of Judge Trumbull? [A voice—"we have."] I defy you to show a printed resolution passed in a Democratic meeting—I take it upon myself to defy any man to show a printed resolution of a Democratic meeting, large or small, in favor of Judge Trumbull, or any of the five to one Republicans who beat that bill. Every thing must be for the Democrats! They did every thing, and the five to one that really did the thing, they snub over, and they do not seem to remember that they have an existence upon the face of the earth. [Applause.]

Gentlemen: I fear that I shall become tedious. ["Go on, go on."] I leave this branch of the subject to take hold of another. I take up that part of Judge Douglas' speech in which he respectfully attended to me. [Laughter.]

Judge Douglas made two points upon my recent speech at Springfield. He says they are to be the issues of this campaign. The first one of these points he bases upon the language in a speech which I delivered at Springfield, which I believe I can quote correctly from memory. I said there that "we are now far into the fifth year since a policy was instituted for the avowed object and with the confident promise of putting an end to slavery agitation; under the operation of that policy, that agitation had not only not ceased, but has constantly augmented."—[A voice—"That's the very language."] "I believe it will not cease until a crisis shall have been reached and passed. A house divided against itself cannot stand. I believe this government cannot endure permanently half slave and half free." [Applause.] "I do not expect the Union to be dissolved,"—I am quoting from my speech—"I do not expect the house to fall, but I do expect it will cease to be divided. It will become all one thing or the other. Either the opponents of slavery will arrest the spread of it, and place it where the public mind shall rest in the belief that it is in the course of ultimate extinction, or its advocates will push it forward until it shall become alike lawful in all the states, North as well as South." ["Good, good."]

That is the paragraph. In this paragraph which I have quoted in your hearing, and to which I ask the attention of all, Judge Douglas thinks he discovers great political heresy. I want your attention particularly to what he has inferred from it. He says I am in favor of making all the states of this Union uniform in all their internal regulations; that in all their domestic concerns I am in favor of making them entirely uniform. He draws this inference from the language I have quoted to you. He says that I am in favor of making war by the North upon the South for the extinction of slavery; that I am also in favor of inviting (as he expresses it) the South to a war upon the North, for the purpose of nationalizing slavery. Now, it is singular enough, if you will carefully read that passage over, that I did not say that I was in favor of anything in it. I only said what I expected would take place. I made a prediction only—it may have been a foolish one perhaps. I did not even say that I desired that slavery should be put in course of ultimate extinction. I do say so now, however, [Great applause.] so there need be no longer any difficulty about that. It may be written down in the great speech. [Applause and laughter.]

Gentlemen, Judge Douglas informed you that this speech of mine was probably carefully prepared. I admit that it was. I am not master of language; I have not a fine education; I am not capable of entering into a disquisition upon dialectics, as I believe you call it; but I do not believe the language I employed bears any such construction as Judge Douglas put upon it. But I don't care about a quibble in regard to words. I know what I meant, and I will not leave this crowd in doubt, if I can explain it to them, what I really meant in the use of that paragraph.

I am not, in the first place, unaware that this government has endured eighty-two years, half slave and half free. I know that. I am tolerably well acquainted with the history of the country, and I know that it has endured eighty-two years, half slave and half free. I *believe*—and that is what I meant to allude to there—I *believe* it has endured because, during all that time, until the introduction of the Nebraska Bill, the public mind did rest, all the time, in the belief that slavery was in course of ultimate extinction. ["Good!" "Good!" and applause.] That was what gave us the rest that we had through that period of eighty-two years; at least, so I believe. I have always hated slavery, I think as much as any Abolitionist. [Applause.] I have been an Old Line Whig. I have always hated it, but I have always been quiet about it until this new era of the introduction of the Nebraska Bill began. I always believed that everybody was against it, and that it was in course of ultimate extinction. Browning thought so; the great mass of the nation have rested in the belief that slavery was in course of ultimate extinction. They had reason so to believe.

The adoption of the Constitution and its attendant history led the people to believe so; and that such was the belief of the framers of the Constitution itself. Why did those old men, about the time of the adoption of the Constitution, decree that slavery should not go into the new territory, where it had not already gone? Why declare that within twenty years the African slave trade, by which slaves are supplied, might be cut off by Congress? Why were all these acts? I might enumerate more of these acts—but enough. What were they but a clear indication that the framers of the Constitution intended and expected the ultimate extinction of that institution? [Cheers.] And now, when I say, as I said in my speech that Judge Douglas has quoted from, when I say that I think the opponents of slavery will resist the farther spread of it, and place it where the public mind shall rest with the belief that it is in course of ultimate extinction, I only mean to say, that they will place it where the founders of this government originally placed it.

I have said a hundred times, and I have now no inclination to take it back, that I believe there is no right, and ought to be no inclination in the people of the free states to enter into the slave states, and interfere with the question of slavery at all. I have said that always. Judge Douglas has heard me say it—if not quite a hundred times, at least as good as a hundred times; and when it is said that I am in favor of intefering with slavery where it exists, I know it is unwarranted by anything I have ever *intended*, and, as I believe, by anything I have ever *said*. If, by any means, I have ever used language which could fairly be construed (as, however, I believe I never have), I now correct it.

[Here the shouts of the Seventh Ward delegation announced that they were coming in procession. They were received with enthusiastic cheers.]

So much, then, for the inference that Judge Douglas draws, that I am in favor of setting the sections at war with one another. I know that I never meant any such thing, and I believe that no fair mind can infer any such thing from anything I have ever said. ["Good," "good."]

Now in relation to his inference that I am in favor of a general consolidation of all the local institutions of the various states. I will attend to that for a little while, and try to inquire, if I can, how on earth it could be that any man could draw such an inference from anything I said. I have said, very many times, in Judge Douglas' hearing, that no man believed more than I in the principle of self-government; that it lies at the bottom of all my ideas of just government, from beginning to end. I have denied that his use of that term applies properly. But for the thing itself, I deny that any man has ever gone ahead of me in his devotion to the principle, whatever he may have done in efficiency in advocating it. I think that I have said it in your hearing—that I believe each individual is naturally entitled to do as he pleases with himself and the fruit of his labor, so far as it in no wise interferes with any other man's rights–[Applause.]–that each community, as a state, has a right to do exactly as it pleases with all the concerns within that state that interfere with the rights of no other state, and that the general government, upon principle, has no right to interfere with anything other than that general class of things that does concern the whole. I have said that at all times. I have said, as illustrations, that I do not believe in the right of Illinois to interfere with the cranberry laws of Indiana, the oyster laws of Virginia, or the liquor laws of Maine. I have said these things over and over again, and I repeat them here as my sentiments.

How is it, then, that Judge Douglas infers, because I hope to see slavery put where the public mind shall rest in the belief that it is in the course of ultimate extinction, that I am in favor of Illinois going over and interfering with the cranberry laws of Indiana? What can authorize him to draw any such inference? I suppose there might be one thing that at least enabled *him* to draw such an inference that would not be true with me or with many others, that is, because he looks upon all this matter of slavery as an exceedingly little thing–this matter of keeping one-sixth of the population of the whole nation in a state of oppression and tyranny unequalled in the world. He looks upon it as being an exceedingly little thing–only equal to the question of the cranberry laws of Indiana–as something having no moral question in it–as something on a par with the question of whether a man shall pasture his land with cattle, or plant it with tobacco–so little and so small a thing, that he concludes, if I could desire that anything should be done to bring about the ultimate extinction of that little thing, I must be in favor of bringing about an amalgamation of all the other little things in the Union. Now, it so happens–and there, I presume, is the foundation of this mistake–that the Judge thinks thus; and it so happens that there is a vast portion of the American people that do *not* look upon that matter as being this very little thing. They look upon it as a vast moral evil; they can prove it is such by the writings of those who gave us the blessings of liberty which we enjoy, and that they so looked upon it, and not as an evil merely confining itself to the states where it is situated; and while we agree that, by the Constitution we assented to, in the states where it exists we have no right to interfere with it because it is in the Constitution and we are by both duty and inclination to stick by that Constitution in all its letter and spirit from beginning to end. [Great applause.]

So much then as to my disposition–my wish–to have all the state legislatures blotted out, and to have one general consolidated government, and a uniformity of domestic regulations in all the states, by which I suppose it is meant if we raise corn here, we must make sugar cane grow here too, and we must make those which grow North, grow in the South. All this I suppose he understands I am in favor of doing. Now, so much for all this nonsense—for I must call it so. The Judge can have no issue with me on a question of establishing uniformity in the domestic regulations of the states.

A little now on the other point—the Dred Scott decision. Another one of the issues he says that is to be made with me, is upon his devotion to the Dred Scott decision, and my opposition to it.

I have expressed heretofore, and I now repeat, my opposition to the Dred Scott decision, but I should be allowed to state the nature of that opposition, and I ask your indulgence while I do so. What is fairly implied by the term Judge Douglas has used, "resistance to the decision"? I do not resist it. If I wanted to take Dred Scott from his master, I would be interfering with property, and that terrible difficulty that Judge Douglas speaks of, of interfering with property, would arise. But I am doing no such thing as that, but all that I am doing is refusing to obey it as a political rule. If I were in Congress, and a vote should come up on a question whether slavery should be prohibited in a new territory, in spite of that Dred Scott decision, I would vote that it should. [Applause; "good for you"; "we hope to see it"; "that's right."]

MR. LINCOLN—That is what I would do. ["You will have a chance soon."] Judge Douglas said last night, that before the decision he might advance his opinion, and it might be contrary to the decision when it was made; but after it was made he would abide by it until it was reversed. Just so! We let this property abide by the decision, but we will try to reverse that decision. [Loud applause—cries of "good."] We will try to put it where Judge Douglas would not object, for he says he will obey it until it is reversed. Somebody has to reverse that decision, since it is made, and we mean to reverse it, and we mean to do it peaceably.

What are the uses of decisions of courts? They have two uses. As rules of property they have two uses. First—they decide upon the question before the court. They decide in this case that Dred Scott is a slave. Nobody resists that. Not only that, but they say to everybody else, that persons standing just as Dred Scott stands is as he is. That is, they say that when a question comes up upon another person it will be so decided again, unless the court decides in another way, [Cheers—cries of "good."] unless the court overrules its decision. [Renewed applause.] Well, we mean to do what we can to have the court decide the other way. That is one thing we mean to try to do.

The sacredness that Judge Douglas throws around this decision, is a degree of sacredness that has never been before thrown around any other decision. I have never heard of such a thing. Why, decisions apparently contrary to that decision, or that good lawyers thought were contrary to that decision, have been made by that very court before. It is the first of its kind; it is an astonisher in legal history. [Laughter.] It is a new wonder of the world. [Laughter and applause.] It is based upon falsehood in the main as to the facts—allegations of facts upon which it stands are not facts at all in many instances, and no decision made on any question—the first instance of a decision made under so many unfavorable circumstances—thus placed has ever been held by the profession as law, and it has always needed confirmation before the lawyers regarded it as settled law. But Judge Douglas will have it that all hands must take this extraordinary decision, made under these extraordinary circumstances, and give their vote in Congress in accordance with it, yield to it and obey it in every possible sense. Circumstances alter cases. Do not gentlemen here remember the case of that same Supreme Court, some twenty-five or thirty years ago, deciding that a national bank was constitutional? I ask, if somebody does not remember that a national bank was declared to be constitutional? ["Yes," "yes."] Such is the truth, whether it be remembered or not. The bank charter ran out, and a re-charter was granted by Congress. That re-charter was laid before General Jackson. It was urged upon him, when he denied the constitutionality of the bank, that the Supreme Court had decided that it was constitutional; and that General Jackson then said that the Supreme Court had no right to lay down a rule to govern a co-ordinate branch of the government, the members of which had sworn to support the Constitution—that each member had sworn to support that Constitution as he understood it. I will venture here to say, that I have heard Judge Douglas say that he approved of General Jackson for that act. What has now become of all his tirade about "resistance to the Supreme Court?" ["Gone up," "Gone to the Theatre."]

My fellow citizens, getting back a little, for I pass from these points, when Judge Douglas makes his threat of annihilation upon the "alliance." He is cautious to say that that warfare of his is to fall upon the leaders of the Republican party. Almost every word he utters and every distinction he makes, has its significance. He means for the Republicans that do not count themselves as leaders, to be his friends; he makes no fuss over them; it is the leaders that he is making war upon. He wants it understood that the mass of the Republican party are really his friends. It is only the leaders that are doing something, that are intolerant, and that require extermination at his hands. As this is clearly and unquestionably the light in which he presents that matter, I want to ask your attention, addressing myself to the Republicans here, that I may ask you some questions, as to where you, as the Republican party, would be placed if you sustained Judge Douglas in his present position by a re-election? I do not claim, gentlemen, to be unselfish, I do not pretend that I would not like to go to the United States Senate, [Laughter.] I make no such hypocritical pretense, but I do say to you that in this mighty issue, it is nothing to you—nothing to the mass of the people of the nation, whether or not Judge Douglas or myself shall ever be heard of after this night, it may be a trifle to either of us, but in connection with this mighty question, upon which hang the destinies of the nation, perhaps, it is absolutely nothing; but where will you be placed if you re-endorse Judge Douglas? Don't you know how apt he is—how exceedingly anxious he is at all times to seize upon anything and everything to persuade you that something *he* has done *you* did yourselves? Why, he tried to persuade you last night that our Illinois legislature instructed him to introduce the Nebraska Bill. There was nobody in that legislature ever thought of such a thing; and when he first introduced the bill, he never thought of it; but still he fights furiously for the proposition, and that he did it because there was a standing instruction to our Senators to be always introducing Nebraska bills. [Laughter and applause.] He tells you he is for the Cincinnati platform, he tells you he is for the Dred Scott decision. He tells you, not in his speech last night, but substantially in a former speech, that he cares not if slavery is voted up or down—he tells you the struggle on Lecompton is past—it may come up again or not, and if it does he stands where he stood when in spite of him and his opposition you built up the Republican party. If you endorse him you tell him you do not care whether slavery be voted up or down, and he will close, or try to close your mouths with his declaration repeated by the day, the week, the month and the year. Is that what you mean? (Cries of "no," one voice "yes.") Yes, I have no doubt you who have always been for him if you mean that. No doubt of that [A voice "hit him again."] soberly I have said, and I repeat it I think in the position in which Judge Douglas stood in opposing the Lecompton constitution he was right, he does not know that it will return, but if it does we may know where to find him, and if it does not we may know where to look for him and that is on the Cincinnati platform. Now I could ask the Republican party after all the hard names that Judge Douglas has called them by—all his repeated charges of their inclination to marry with and hug Negroes—all his declarations of Black Republicanism—by the way we are improving, the black has got rubbed off—but with all that, if he be endorsed by Republican votes where do you stand? Plainly you stand ready saddled, bridled and harnessed and waiting to be driven over to the slavery extension camp of the nation [A voice "we will hang ourselves first."]—just ready to be driven over tied together in a lot—to be driven over, every man with a rope around his neck, that halter being held by Judge Douglas. That is the question. If Republican men have been in earnest in what they have done, I think they had better not do it, but I think that the Republican party is made up of those who, as far as they can peaceably, will oppose the extension of slavery, and who will hope for its ultimate extinction. If they believe it is wrong in grasping up the new lands of the continent, and keeping them from the settlement of free white laborers, who want the land to bring up their families upon; if they are in earnest, although they may make a mistake, they will grow restless, and the time will come when they will come back again and re-organize, if not by the same name, at least upon the same principles as their party now has. It is better, then, to save the work while it is begun. You have done the labor; maintain it—keep it. If men choose to serve you, go with them; but as you have made up your organization upon principle, stand by it; for, as surely as God reigns over you, and has inspired your mind, and given you a sense of propriety, and continues to give you hope, so surely you will still cling to these ideas, and you will at last come back again after your wanderings, merely to do your work over again. [Loud applause.]

We were often—more than once at least—in the course of Judge Douglas' speech last night, reminded that this government was made for white men—that he believed it was made for white men. Well, that is putting it into a shape in which no one wants to deny it, but the Judge then goes into his passion for drawing inferences that are not warranted. I protest, now and forever, against that counterfeit logic which presumes that because I do not want a Negro woman for a slave, I do necessarily want her for a wife. [Laughter and cheers.] My understanding is that I need not have her for either, but as God made us separate, we can leave one another alone and do one another much good thereby. There are white men enough to marry all the white women, and enough black men to marry all the black women, and in God's name let them be so married. The Judge regales us with the terrible enormities that take place by the mixture of the races; that the inferior race bears the superior down. Why, Judge, if we do not let them get together in the territories they won't mix there. [Immense applause.]

A VOICE—"Three cheers for Lincoln." [The cheers were given with a hearty good will.]

MR. LINCOLN—I should say at least that that is a self-evident truth. Now, it happens that we meet together once every year, sometime about the 4th of July, for some reason or other. These 4th of July gatherings I suppose have their uses. If you will indulge me, I will state what I suppose to be some of them.

We are now a mighty nation, we are thirty—or about thirty millions of people, and we own and inhabit about one-fifteenth part of the dry land of the whole earth. We run our memory back over the pages of history for about eighty-two years and we discover that we were then a very small people in point of numbers, vastly inferior to what we are now, with a vastly less extent of country,—with vastly less of everything we deem desirable among men,—we look upon the change as exceedingly advantageous to us and to our posterity, and we fix upon something that happened away back, as in some way or other being connected with this rise of prosperity. We find a race of men living in that day whom we claim as our fathers and grandfathers; they were iron men, they fought for the principle that they were contending for; and we understood that by what they then did it has followed that the degree of prosperity that we now enjoy has come to us. We hold this annual celebration to remind ourselves of all the good done in this process of time, of how it was done and who did it, and how we are historically connected with it; and we go from these meetings in better humor with ourselves—we feel more attached the one to the other, and more firmly bound to the country we inhabit. In every way we are better men in the age, and race, and country in which we live for these celebrations. But after we have done all this we have not yet reached the whole. There is something else connected with it. We have besides these men—descended by blood from our ancestors—among us perhaps half our people who are not descendants at all of these men, they are men who have come from Europe—German, Irish, French and Scandinavian—men that have come from Europe themselves, or whose ancestors have come hither and settled here, finding themselves our equals in all things. If they look back through this history to trace their connection with those days by blood, they find they have none, they cannot carry themselves back into that glorious epoch and make themselves feel that they are part of us, but when they look through that old Declaration of Independence they find that those old men say that "We hold these truths to be self-evident, that all men are created equal," and then they feel that that moral sentiment taught in that day evidences their relation to those men, that it is the father of all moral principle in them, and that they have a right to claim it as though they were blood of the blood, and flesh of the flesh of the men who wrote that Declaration, [Loud and long continued applause.] and so they are. This is the electric cord in that Declaration that links the hearts of patriotic and liberty-loving men together, that will link those patriotic hearts as long as the love of freedom exists in the minds of men throughout the world. [Applause.]

Now, sirs, for the purpose of squaring things with this idea of "don't care if slavery is voted up or voted down," for sustaining the Dred Scott decision [A voice—"Hit him again"], for holding that the Declaration of Independence did not mean anything at all, we have Judge Douglas giving his exposition of what the Declaration of Independence means, and we have him saying that the people of America are equal to the people of England. According to his construction, you Germans are not connected with it. Now I ask you in all soberness, if all these things, if indulged in, if ratified, if confirmed and endorsed, if taught to our children, and repeated to them, do not tend to rub out the sentiment of liberty in the country, and to transform this government into a government of some other form. Those arguments that are made, that the inferior race are to be treated with as much allowance as they are capable of enjoying; that as much is to be done for them as their condition will allow. What are these arguments? They are the arguments that kings have made for enslaving the people in all ages of the world. You will find that all the arguments in favor of king-craft were of this class; they always bestrode the necks of the people, not that they wanted to do it, but because the people were better off for being ridden. That is their argument, and this argument of the Judge is the same old serpent that says you work and I eat, you toil and I will enjoy the fruits of it. Turn it whatever way you will—whether it come from the mouth of a king, or excuse for enslaving the people of his country, or from the mouth of men of one race as a reason for enslaving the men of another race, it is all the same old serpent, and I hold if that course of argumentation that is made for the purpose of convincing the public mind that we should not care about this, should be granted, it does not stop with the negro. I should like to know if taking this old Declaration of Independence, which declares that all men are equal upon principle and making exceptions to it where will it stop. If one man says it does not mean a negro, why not another say it does not mean some other man? If that Declaration is not the truth, let us get the statute book, in which we find it and tear it out! Who is so bold as to do it! [Voices—"me" "no one," &c.] If it is not true let us tear it out! [cries of "no, no,"] let us stick to it them, [cheers] let us stand firmly by it then. [Applause.]

It may be argued that there are certain conditions that make necessities and impose them upon us, and to the extent that a necessity is imposed upon a man he must submit to it. I think that was the condition in which we found ourselves when we established this government. We had slavery among us, we could not get our constitution unless we permitted them to remain in slavery, we could not secure the good we did secure if we grasped for more, and having by necessity submitted to that much, it does not destroy the principle that is the charter of our liberties. Let that charter stand as our standard.

My friend has said to me that I am a poor hand to quote Scripture. I will try it again, however. It is said in one of the admonitions of the Lord, "As your Father in Heaven is perfect, be ye also perfect." The Savior, I suppose, did not expect that any human creature could be perfect as the Father in Heaven; but He said, "As your Father in Heaven is perfect, be ye also perfect." He set that up as a standard, and he who did most towards reaching that standard, attained the highest degree of moral perfection. So I say in relation to the principle that all men are created equal, let it be as nearly reached as we can. If we cannot give freedom to every creature, let us do nothing that will impose slavery upon any other creature. [Applause.] Let us then turn this government back into the channel in which the framers of the Constitution originally placed it. Let us stand firmly by each other. If we do not so we are turning in the contrary direction, that our friend Judge Douglas proposes—not intentionally—as working in the traces tend to make this one universal slave nation. [A voice—"that is so."] He is one that runs in that direction, and as such I resist him.

My friends, I have detained you about as long as I desired to do, and I have only to say, let us discard all this quibbling about this man and the other man—this race and that race and the other race being inferior, and therefore they must be placed in an inferior position—discarding our standard that we have left us. Let us discard all these things, and unite as one people throughout this land, until we shall once more stand up declaring that all men are created equal.

My friends, I could not, without launching off upon some new topic, which would detain you too long, continue to-night. [Cries of "go on."] I thank you for this most extensive audience that you have furnished me to-night. I leave you, hoping that the lamp of liberty will burn in your bosoms until there shall no longer be a doubt that all men are created free and equal.

Exercises

1. What are the distinctive characteristics of Lincoln's Introduction? How do you account for its brevity and for Lincoln's failure to refer either to the audience or to the speaking occasion? Compare this Introduction with those of other speeches in this volume.

2. How effective are Lincoln's attempts to ridicule Douglas and Douglas' positions? How important is his use of humor in such efforts?

3. One of Lincoln's most effective forensic devices is turning the tables. From the speech, select several examples of Lincoln's employing Douglas' own language as a means of refuting the Little Giant. To what extent does Lincoln depend upon sarcasm and wit in these endeavors?

4. What persuasive gain do you believe Lincoln hoped to achieve by the following personal reference? "Gentlemen, Judge Douglas informed you that this speech of mine was probably carefully pre-

pared. I admit that it was. I am not master of language; I have not a fine education; I am not capable of entering into a disquisition upon dialectics, as I believe you call it; but I do not believe the language I employed bears any such construction as Judge Douglas put upon it."

5. Would you characterize Lincoln's style as being more informal, or more direct, than that of Douglas? Compare Lincoln's informality and directness in this speech with the style used in the speeches by Patrick Henry and Theodore Roosevelt given elsewhere in this volume; with the style of Lincoln's Gettysburg Address and his First and Second Inaugurals. If you find any significant differences, how do you account for them?

6. From your background reading explain why President Buchanan, although a Democrat was using all of the power and prestige of the Presidency to defeat Douglas. Find examples in this speech of Lincoln's efforts to exploit the division among the Democrats. How effective are these efforts? Does his drollery highlight or weaken the effect?

7. In the speech of Douglas, on July 9, and that of Lincoln, on July 10, which speaker treats his opponent with greater courtesy? Which seems to represent his opponent's views with greater fidelity? Which resorts more to debaters' tricks to carry his arguments? Which presents his arguments with greater clarity and specificity? Which speech is more entertaining?

8. How skillful in general is Lincoln's handling of interruptions? For one of the interruptions, explain how Lincoln attempts to use it to further persuasion.

9. How sound is Lincoln's argument that the founding fathers "intended and expected the ultimate extinction" of slavery? In what famous speech did Lincoln develop this contention at considerable length and with much success?

10. If you had been a Republican in Chicago in 1858, would you have been pleased, or displeased, with Lincoln's defense of his "house divided" statement? Explain.

11. In his efforts to persuade those Republicans who favored Douglas, Lincoln compared them to dumb beasts "ready saddled, bridled and harnessed . . . every man with a rope around his neck." How effective do you suppose this analogy was in 1858? If used by a present-day politician?

12. In his indictment of slavery, Lincoln employs Biblical quotations, as well as references to the Declaration of Independence and

the Constitution. Inasmuch as pro-slavery speakers for many years had been using the same sources in defense of their cause, how persuasive do you suppose these allusions were? Does Lincoln seem to say in abolitionist Chicago that he believes in the equality of the races? Later in the campaign he emphatically denies such a belief. If the two positions seem to be contradictory, how do you account for the differences?

13. Is Lincoln's Conclusion a recapitulation of the entire speech or merely a rounding off of the last major point of the Body? Is it intended to emphasize a particular mood or idea which Lincoln considers to be the essential difference between himself and Douglas?

Wendell Phillips 

"Toussaint L'Ouverture,"
given many times to lyceum audiences, beginning in 1860

ORATOR, lawyer, popular lecturer, and reformer, Wendell Phillips (1811–1884) was perhaps the most successfully abrasive agitator in American history. Born into the Boston Brahmin caste, Phillips was graduated from Harvard College in 1831 and Harvard law school in 1834 and was admitted to the Massachusetts Bar. Brought to an intense conversion experience through the preaching of Lyman Beecher, about 1826, his deeply religious nature was grossly offended by witnessing the mobbing of William Lloyd Garrison in Boston in 1835. Gaining instant fame because of his fiery speech at Faneuil Hall, 1837, protesting the murder of abolitionist Elton P. Lovejoy, he soon became the leading platform speaker for the anti-slavery movement. During the years prior to Fort Sumter, he went to the fanatical extremes of cursing the U.S. Constitution, advocating disunion, and urging others to refuse to vote or hold office under a government which was in fact "a covenant with death and agreement with hell." Referring to Abraham Lincoln as the "slave-hound of Illinois," Phillips maintained a running criticism of the conduct of the war by the President and the cabinet. With the slaves freed, he agitated for their integration into the mainstream of American life and spoke widely in support of woman suffrage, rights of labor, fair treatment for Indians, abolishment of capital punishment, money and banking reforms, better educational opportunities, and temperance.

In addition to his prominence as a speaker for reform, Phillips was noted as a eulogist and one of the most popular lecturers of his day. Among his better known eulogies were those on Charles Sumner, Daniel O'Connell, and William Lloyd Garrison. Among his more famous lectures were "Surrender of Sins," "Street Life in Europe," and "The Lost Arts," which was delivered first in 1838 and repeated perhaps more than two thousand times.

Passionately devoted to justice, as he conceived it, he considered that the ends justified the means. Intolerant of divergent opinions, and unperceptive of the complexities of societal change, he tended to be careless in his use of facts and abusive of the reputations of others. Although fond of quoting Garrison's statement, "Brother, I have need to be on fire, for I have mountains of ice around me to melt," Phillips was moderate and restrained in delivery. Even violent invectives were uttered with quiet assurance. Brilliantly effective in repartee with hostile auditors, he ever retained the dignified, physically restrained manner of a gentleman. A master of impromptu speaking, he maintained the simple directness of "animated conversation," even when giving memorized speeches. His speaking could be refreshing as well as vituperative; but even in his noncontroversial lectures his speaking had a sharpness of wit and a crusading abrasiveness that rasped into wakefulness the thinking and the conscience of his hearers.

One of Phillips' more interesting lectures is his eulogy of Toussaint L'Ouverture, given many times to lyceum audiences—the first time perhaps in 1860. Although Phillips' account is overdrawn, placing L'Ouverture above Washington, Cromwell, Brutus, Hampden and, indeed, above all other figures in history, his eloquent tribute establishes the liberator of Haiti as a gallant soldier and noble soul, treacherously betrayed by white men. Phillips' purpose is persuasively developed, largely by narration and assertion: to confound detractors who doubt the Negroes' courage, character, and capability for improvement.

The text comes from Wendell Phillips, *Speeches, Lectures, and Letters*, Boston: Lee and Shepard, 1892.

TOUSSAINT L'OUVERTURE

Ladies and Gentlemen: I have been requested to offer you a sketch made some years since, of one of the most remarkable men of the last generation,—the great St. Domingo chief, Toussaint L'Ouverture, an unmixed Negro, with no drop of white blood in his veins. My sketch is at once a biography and an argument,—a biography, of course very brief, of a Negro soldier and statesman, which I offer you as an argument in behalf of the race from which he sprung. I am about to compare and weigh races; indeed, I am engaged tonight in what you will think the absurd effort to convince you that the Negro race, instead of being that object of pity or contempt which we usually consider it, is entitled, judged by the facts of history, to a place close by the side of the Saxon. Now races love to be judged in two ways,—by the great men they produce, and by the average merit of the mass of the race. We Saxons are proud of Bacon, Shakespeare, Hampden, Washington, Franklin, the stars we have lent to the galaxy of history; and then we turn with equal pride to the average merit of Saxon blood, since it streamed from its German home. So, again, there are three tests by which races love to be tried. The first, the basis of all, is courage,—the element which says, here and to-day, "This continent is mine, from the Lakes to the Gulf: let him beware who seeks to divide it!" [Cheers.] And the second is the recognition that force is doubled by purpose; liberty regulated by law is the secret of Saxon progress. And the third element is persistency, endurance; first a purpose, then death or success. Of these three elements is made that Saxon pluck which has placed our race in the van of modern civilization.

In the hour you lend me to-night, I attempt the Quixotic effort to convince you that the Negro blood, instead of standing at the bottom of the list, is entitled, if judged either by its great men or its masses, either by its courage, its purpose, or its endurance, to a place as near ours as any other blood known in history. And, for the purpose of my argument, I take an island, St. Domingo, about the size of South Carolina, the third spot in America upon which Columbus placed his foot. Charmed by the magnificence of its scenery and fertility of its soil, he gave it the fondest of all names, Hispaniola, Little Spain. His successor, more pious, rebaptized it from St. Dominic, St. Domingo; and when the blacks, in 1803, drove our white blood from its surface, they drove our names with us, and began the year 1804 under the old name, Hayti, the land of mountains. It was originally tenanted by filibusters, French and Spanish, of the early commercial epochs, the pirates of that day as of ours. The Spanish took the eastern two thirds, the French the western third of the island, and they gradually settled into colonies. The French, to whom my story belongs, became the pet colony of the mother land. Guarded by peculiar privileges, enriched by the scions of wealthy houses, aided by the unmatched fertility of the soil, it soon was the richest gem in the Bourbon crown; and at the period to which I call your attention, about the era of our Constitution, 1789, its wealth was almost incredible. The effeminacy of the white race rivalled that of the Sybarite of antiquity, while the splendor of their private life outshone Versailles, and their luxury found no mate but in the mad prodigality of the Caesars. At this time the island held about thirty thousand whites, twenty or thirty thousand mulattoes, and five hundred thousand slaves. The slave-trade was active. About twenty-five thousand slaves were imported annually; and this only sufficed to fill the gap which the murderous culture of sugar annually produced. The mulattoes, as with us, were children of the slaveholders, but, unlike us, the French slaveholder never forgot his child by a bondwoman. He gave him everything but his name,—wealth, rich plantations, gangs of slaves; sent him to Paris for his education, summoned the best culture of France for the instruction of his daughters, so that in 1790 the mulatto race held one third of the real estate and one quarter of the personal estate of the island. But though educated and rich, he bowed under the same yoke as with us. Subjected to special taxes, he could hold no public office, and, if convicted of any crime, was punished with double severity. His son might not sit on the same seat at school with a white boy; he might not enter a church where a white man was worshipping; if he reached a town on horseback, he must dismount and lead his horse by the bridle; and when he died, even his dust could not rest in the same soil with a white body. Such was the white race and the mulatto,—the thin film of a civilization beneath which surged the dark mass of five hundred thousand slaves.

It was over such a population,—the white man melted in sensuality; the mulatto feeling all the more keenly his degradation from the very wealth and culture he enjoyed; the slave, sullen and indifferent, heeding not the quarrels or the changes of the upper air,—it was over this population that there burst, in 1789, the thunder-storm of the French Revolution. The first words which reached the island were the motto of the Jacobin Club,—"Liberty, Equality." The white man heard them aghast. He had read of the streets of Paris running blood. The slave heard them with indifference; it was a quarrel in the upper air, between other races, which did not concern him. The mulatto heard them with a welcome which no dread of other classes could quell. Hastily gathered into conventions, they sent to Paris a committee of the whole body, laid at the feet of the National Convention the free gift of six millions of francs, pledged one fifth of their annual rental toward the payment of the national debt, and only asked in return that this yoke of civil and social contempt should be lifted from their shoulders.

You may easily imagine the temper in which Mirabeau and Lafayette welcomed this munificent gift of the free mulattoes of the West Indies, and in which the petition for equal civil rights was received by a body which had just resolved that all men were equal. The Convention hastened to express its gratitude, and issued a decree which commences thus: "All freeborn French citizens are equal before the law." Ogé was selected—the friend of Lafayette, a lieutenant-colonel in the Dutch service, the son of a wealthy mulatto woman, educated in Paris, the comrade of all the leading French Republicans—to carry the decree and the message of French Democracy to the island. He landed. The decree of the National Convention was laid on the table of the General Assembly of the island. One old planter seized it, tore it in fragments, and trampled it under his feet, swearing by all the saints in the calendar that the island might sink before they would share their rights with bastards. They took an old mulatto, worth a million, who had simply asked for his rights under that decree, and hung him. A white lawyer of seventy, who drafted the petition, they hung at his side. They took Ogé, broke him on the wheel, ordered him to be drawn and quartered, and one quarter of his body to be hung up in each of the four principal cities of the island; and then they adjourned.

You can conceive better than I can describe the mood in which Mirabeau and Danton received the news that their decree had been torn in pieces and trampled under foot by the petty legislature of an island colony, and their comrade drawn and quartered by the orders of its Governor. Robespierre rushed to the tribune and shouted, "Perish the colonies rather than sacrifice one iota of our principles!" The Convention reaffirmed their decree, and sent it out a second time to be executed.

But it was not then as now, when steam has married the continents. It took months to communicate; and while this news of the death of Ogé and the defiance of the National Convention was going to France, and the answer returning, great events had taken place in the island itself. The Spanish or the eastern section, perceiving these divisions, invaded the towns of the western, and conquered many of its cities. One half of the slaveholders were Republicans, in love with the new constellation which had just gone up in our Northern sky, seeking to be admitted a State in this Republic, plotting for annexation. The other half were loyalists, anxious, deserted as they supposed themselves by the Bourbons, to make alliance with George III. They sent to Jamaica, and entreated its Governor to assist them in their intrigue. At first, he lent them only a few hundred soldiers. Some time later, General Howe and Admiral Parker were sent with several thousand men, and finally, the English government entering more seriously into the plot, General Maitland landed with four thousand Englishmen on the north side of the island, and gained many successes. The mulattoes were in the mountains, awaiting events. They distrusted the government, which a few years before they had assisted to put down an insurrection of the whites, and which had forfeited its promise to grant them civil privileges. Deserted by both sections, Blanchelande, the Governor, had left the capital, and fled for refuge to a neighboring city.

In this state of affairs, the second decree reached the island. The whites forgot their quarrel, sought out Blanchelande, and obliged him to promise that he never would publish the decree. Affrighted, the Governor consented to that course, and they left him. He then began to reflect that in reality he was deposed, that the Bourbons had lost the sceptre of the island. He remembered his successful appeal to the mulattoes, five years before, to put down an insurrection. Deserted now by the whites and by the mulattoes, only one force was left him in the island,—that was the blacks: they had always remembered with gratitude the *code noir*, black code, of Louis XIV., the first interference of any power in their behalf. To the blacks Blanchelande appealed. He sent a deputation to the slaves. He was aided by the agents of Count d'Artois, afterward Charles X., who was seeking to do in St. Domingo what Charles II. did in Virginia (whence its name of Old Dominion), institute a reaction against the rebellion at home. The two joined forces, and sent first to Toussaint. Nature made him a Metternich, a diplomatist. He probably wished to avail himself of this offer, foreseeing advantage to his race, but to avail himself of it so cautiously as to provide against failure, risking as little as possible till the intentions of the other party had been tested, and so managing as to be able to go on or withdraw as the best interest of his race demanded. He had practised well the Greek rule, "Know thyself," and thoroughly studied his own part. Later in life, when criticising his great mulatto rival, Rigaud, he showed how well he knew himself. "I know Rigaud," he said; "he drops the bridle when he gallops, he shows his arm when he strikes. For me, I gallop also, but know where to stop: when I strike I am felt, not seen. Rigaud works only by blood and massacre. I know how to put the people in movement: but when I appear, all must be calm."

He said, therefore, to the envoys, "Where are your credentials?" "We have none." "I will have nothing to do with you." They then sought François and Biassou, two other slaves of strong passions, considerable intellect, and great influence over their fellow-slaves, and said, "Arm, assist the government, put down the English on the one hand, and the Spanish on the other"; and on the 21st of August, 1791, fifteen thousand blacks, led by François and Biassou, supplied with arms from the arsenal of the government, appeared in the midst of the colony. It is believed that Toussaint, unwilling himself to head the movement, was still desirous that it should go forward, trusting, as proved the case, that it would result in benefit to his race. He is supposed to have advised François in his course,—saving himself for a more momentous hour.

This is what Edward Everett calls the Insurrection of St. Domingo. It bore for its motto on one side of its banner, "Long live the King"; and on the other, "We claim the Old Laws." Singular mottoes for a rebellion! In fact, it was the *posse comitatus*; it was the only French army on the island; it was the only force that had a right to bear arms; and what it undertook, it achieved. It put Blanchelande in his seat; it put the island beneath his rule. When it was done, the blacks said to the Governor they had created, "Now, grant us one day in seven; give us one day's labor; we will buy another, and with the two buy a third,"—the favorite method of emancipation at that time. Like the Blanchelande of five years before, he refused. He said, "Disarm! Disperse!" and the blacks answered, "The right hand that has saved you, the right hand that has saved the island for the Bourbons, may perchance clutch some of our own rights"; and they stood still. [Cheering.] This is the first insurrection, if any such there were in St. Domingo,—the first determined purpose on the part of the Negro, having saved the government, to save himself.

Now let me stop a moment to remind you of one thing. I am about to open to you a chapter of bloody history,—no doubt of it. Who set the example? Who dug up from its grave of a hundred years the hideous punishment of the wheel, and broke Ogé, every bone, a living man? Who flared in the face of indignant and astonished Europe the forgotten barbarity of quartering the yet palpitating body? Our race. And if the black man learned the lesson but too well, it does not lie in our lips to complain. During this whole struggle, the record is,—written, mark you, by the white man,—the whole picture from the pencil of the white race,—that for one life the Negro took in battle, in hot and bloody fight, the white race took, in the cool malignity of revenge, three to answer for it. Notice, also, that up to this moment the slave had taken no part in the struggle, except at the bidding of the government; and even then, not for himself, but only to sustain the laws.

At this moment, then, the island stands thus: The Spaniard is on the east triumphant; the Englishman is on the northwest intrenched; the mulattoes are in the mountains waiting; the blacks are in the valleys victorious; one half the French slaveholding element is republican, the other half royalist; the white race against the mulatto and the black; the black against both; the Frenchman against the English and Spaniard; the Spaniard against both. It is a war of races and a war of nations. At such a moment Toussaint L'Ouverture appeared.

He had been born a slave on a plantation in the north of the island,—an unmixed Negro,—his father stolen from Africa. If anything, therefore, that I say of him to-night moves your admiration, remember, the black race claims it all,—we have no part nor lot in it. He was fifty years old at this time. An old Negro had taught him to read. His favorite books were Epictetus, Raynal, Military Memoirs, Plutarch. In the woods, he learned some of the qualities of herbs, and was village doctor. On the estate, the highest place he ever reached was that of coachman. At fifty, he joined the army as physician. Before he went, he placed his master and mistress on shipboard, freighted the vessel with a cargo of sugar and coffee, and sent them to Baltimore, and never afterward did he forget to send them, year by year, ample means of support. And I might add, that, of all the leading negro generals, each one saved the man under whose roof he was born, and protected the family. [Cheering.]

Let me add another thing. If I stood here to-night to tell the story of Napoleon, I should take it from the lips of Frenchmen, who find no language rich enough to paint the great captain of the nineteenth century. Were I here to tell you the story of Washington, I should take it from your hearts,–you, who think no marble white enough on which to carve the name of the Father of his Country. [Applause.] I am about to tell you the story of a Negro who has left hardly one written line. I am to glean it from the reluctant testimony of Britons, Frenchmen, Spaniards,–men who despised him as a Negro and a slave, and hated him because he had beaten them in many a battle. All the materials for his biography are from the lips of his enemies.

The second story told of him is this. About the time he reached the camp, the army had been subjected to two insults. First, their commissioners, summoned to meet the French Committee, were ignominiously and insultingly dismissed; and when, afterward, François, their general, was summoned to a second conference, and went to it on horseback, accompanied by two officers, a young lieutenant, who had known him as a slave, angered at seeing him in the uniform of an officer, raised his riding-whip and struck him over the shoulders. If he had been the savage which the Negro is painted to us, he had only to breathe the insult to his twenty-five thousand soldiers, and they would have trodden out the Frenchmen in blood. But the indignant chief rode back in silence to his tent, and it was twenty-four hours before his troops heard of this insult to their general. Then the word went forth, "Death to every white man!" They had fifteen hundred prisoners. Ranged in front of the camp, they were about to be shot. Toussaint, who had a vein of religious fanaticism, like most great leaders,–like Mohammed, like Napoleon, like Cromwell, like John Brown [Cheers.],–he could preach as well as fight,–mounting a hillock, and getting the ear of the crowd, exclaimed: "Brothers, this blood will not wipe out the insult to our chief; only the blood in yonder French camp can wipe it out. To shed that is courage; to shed this is cowardice and cruelty beside";–and he saved fifteen hundred lives. [Applause.]

I cannot stop to give in detail every one of his efforts. This was in 1793. Leap with me over seven years; come to 1800; what has he achieved? He has driven the Spaniard back into his own cities, conquered him there, and put the French banner over every Spanish town; and for the first time, and almost the last, the island obeys one law. He has put the mulatto under his feet. He has attacked Maitland, defeated him in pitched battles, and permitted him to retreat to Jamaica; and when the French army rose upon Laveaux, their general, and put him in chains, Toussaint defeated them, took Laveaux out of prison, and put him at the head of his own troops. The grateful French in return named him General-in-Chief. *Cet homme fait l'ouverture partout*, said one,—"This man makes an opening everywhere,"—hence his soldiers named him L'Ouverture, *the opening*.

This was the work of seven years. Let us pause a moment, and find something to measure him by. You remember Macaulay says, comparing Cromwell with Napoleon, that Cromwell showed the greater military genius, if we consider that he never saw an army till he was forty; while Napoleon was educated from a boy in the best military schools in Europe. Cromwell manufactured his own army; Napoleon at the age of twenty-seven was placed at the head of the best troops Europe ever saw. They were both successful; but, says Macaulay, with such disadvantages, the Englishman showed the greater genius. Whether you allow the inference or not, you will at least grant that it is a fair mode of measurement. Apply it to Toussaint. Cromwell never saw an army till he was forty; this man never saw a soldier till he was fifty. Cromwell manufactured his own army—out of what? Englishmen,—the best blood in Europe. Out of the middle class of Englishmen,—the best blood of the island. And with it he conquered what? Englishmen,—their equals. This man manufactured his army out of what? Out of what you call the despicable race of Negroes, debased, demoralized by two hundred years of slavery, one hundred thousand of them imported into the island within four years, unable to speak a dialect intelligible even to each other. Yet out of this mixed, and, as you say, despicable mass, he forged a thunderbolt and hurled it at what? At the proudest blood in Europe, the Spaniard, and sent him home conquered [Cheers.]; at the most warlike blood in Europe, the French, and put them under his feet; at the pluckiest blood in Europe, the English, and they skulked home to Jamaica. [Applause.] Now if Cromwell was a general, at least this man was a soldier. I know it was a small territory; it was not as large as the continent; but it was as large as that Attica, which, with Athens for a capital, has filled the earth with its fame for two thousand years. We measure genius by quality, not by quantity.

Further,—Cromwell was only a soldier; his fame stops there. Not one line in the statute-book of Britain can be traced to Cromwell; not one step in the social life of England finds its motive power in his brain. The state he founded went down with him to his grave. But this man no sooner put his hand on the helm of state, than the ship steadied with an upright keel, and he began to evince a statesmanship as marvellous as his military genius. History says that the most statesmanlike act of Napoleon was his proclamation of 1802, at the peace of Amiens, when, believing that the indelible loyalty of a native-born heart is always a sufficient basis on which to found an empire, he said: "Frenchmen, come home. I pardon the crimes of the last twelve years; I blot out its parties; I found my throne on the hearts of all Frenchmen,"–and twelve years of unclouded success showed how wisely he judged. That was in 1802. In 1800 this Negro made a proclamation; it runs thus: "Sons of St. Domingo, come home. We never meant to take your houses or your lands. The Negro only asked that liberty which God gave him. Your houses wait for you; your lands are ready; come and cultivate them";– and from Madrid and Paris, from Baltimore and New Orleans, the emigrant planters crowded home to enjoy their estates, under the pledged word that was never broken of a victorious slave. [Cheers.]

Again, Carlyle has said, "The natural king is one who melts all wills into his own." At this moment he turned to his armies,–poor, ill-clad, and half-starved,–and said to them: Go back and work on these estates you have conquered; for an empire can be founded only on order and industry, and you can learn these virtues only there. And they went. The French Admiral, who witnessed the scene, said that in a week his army melted back into peasants.

It was 1800. The world waited fifty years before, in 1846, Robert Peel dared to venture, as a matter of practical statesmanship, the theory of free trade. Adam Smith theorized, the French statesmen dreamed, but no man at the head of affairs had ever dared to risk it as a practical measure. Europe waited till 1846 before the most practical intellect in the world, the English, adopted the great economic formula of unfettered trade. But in 1800 this black, with the instinct of statesmanship, said to the committee who were drafting for him a Constitution: "Put at the head of the chapter of commerce that the ports of St. Domingo are open to the trade of the world." [Cheers.] With lofty indifference to race, superior to all envy or prejudice, Toussaint had formed this committee of eight white proprietors and one mulatto,–not a soldier nor a Negro on the list, although Haytian history proves that, with the exception of Rigaud, the rarest genius has always been shown by pure Negroes.

Again, it was 1800, at a time when England was poisoned on every page of her statue-book with religious intolerance, when a man could not enter the House of Commons without taking an Episcopal communion, when every State in the Union, except Rhode Island, was full of the intensest religious bigotry. This man was a Negro. You say that is a superstitious blood. He was uneducated. You say that makes a man narrow-minded. He was a Catholic. Many say that is but another name for intolerance. And yet–Negro, Catholic, slave–he took his place by the side of Roger Williams, and said to his committee: "Make it the first line of my Constitution that I know no difference between religious beliefs." [Applause.]

Now, blue-eyed Saxon, proud of your race, go back with me to the commencement of the century, and select what statesman you please. Let him be either American or European; let him have a brain the result of six generations of culture; let him have the ripest training of university routine; let him add to it the better education of practical life; crown his temples with the silver of seventy years; and show me the man of Saxon lineage for whom his most sanguine admirer will wreathe a laurel rich as embittered foes have placed on the brow of this Negro,—rare military skill, profound knowledge of human nature, content to blot out all party distinctions, and trust a state to the blood of its sons,—anticipating Sir Robert Peel fifty years, and taking his station by the side of Roger Williams before any Englishman or American had won the right;—and yet this is the record which the history of rival states makes up for this inspired black of St. Domingo. [Cheers.]

It was 1801. The Frenchmen who lingered on the island described its prosperity and order as almost incredible. You might trust a child with a bag of gold to go from Samana to Port-au-Prince without risk. Peace was in every household; the valleys laughed with fertility; culture climbed the mountains; the commerce of the world was represented in its harbors. At this time Europe concluded the Peace of Amiens, and Napoleon took his seat on the throne of France. He glanced his eyes across the Atlantic, and, with a single stroke of his pen, reduced Cayenne and Martinique back into chains. He then said to his Council, "What shall I do with St. Domingo?" The slaveholders said, "Give it to us." Napoleon turned to the Abbé Gregoire, "What is your opinion?" "I think those men would change their opinions, if they changed their skins." Colonel Vincent, who had been private secretary to Toussaint, wrote a letter to Napoleon, in which he said: "Sire, leave it alone; it is the happiest spot in your dominions; God raised this man to govern; races melt under his hand. He has saved you this island; for I know of my own knowledge that, when the Republic could not have lifted a finger to prevent it, George III. offered him any title and any revenue if he would hold the island under the British crown. He refused, and saved it for France." Napoleon turned away from his Council, and is said to have remarked, "I have sixty thousand idle troops; I must find them something to do." He meant to say, "I am about to seize the crown; I dare not do it in the faces of sixty thousand republican soldiers: I must give them work at a distance to do." The gossip of Paris gives another reason for his expedition against St. Domingo. It is said that the Satirists of Paris had christened Toussaint, the Black Napoleon; and Bonaparte hated his black shadow. Toussaint had unfortunately once addressed him a letter, "The first of the blacks to the first of the whites." He did not like the comparison. You would think it too slight a motive. But let me remind you of the present Napoleon, that when the epigrammatists of Paris christened his wasteful and tasteless expense at Versailles, *Soulouquerie*, from the name of Soulouque, the Black Emperor, he deigned to issue a specific order forbidding the use of the word. The Napoleon blood is very sensitive. So Napoleon resolved to crush Toussaint from one motive or another, from the prompting of ambition, or dislike of this resemblance,—which was very close. If either imitated the other, it must have been the white, since the Negro preceded him several years. They were very much alike, and they were very French,—French even in vanity, common to both. You remember Bonaparte's vainglorious words to his soldiers at the Pyramids: "Forty centuries look down upon us." In the same mood, Toussaint said to the French captain who urged him to go to France in his frigate, "Sir, your ship is not large enough to carry me." Napoleon, you know, could never bear the military uniform. He hated the restraint of his rank; he loved to put on the gray coat of the Little Corporal, and wander in the camp. Toussaint also never could bear a uniform. He wore a plain coat, and often the yellow Madras handkerchief of the slaves. A French lieutenant once called him a maggot in a yellow handkerchief. Toussaint took him prisoner next day, and sent him home to his mother. Like Napoleon, he could fast many days; could dictate to three secretaries at once; could wear out four or five horses. Like Napoleon, no man ever divined his purpose or penetrated his plan. He was only a Negro, and so, in him, they called it hypocrisy. In Bonaparte we style it diplomacy. For instance, three attempts made to assassinate him all failed, from not firing at the right spot. If they thought he was in the north in a carriage, he would be in the south on horseback; if they thought he was in the city in a house, he would be in the field in a tent. They once riddled his carriage with bullets; he was on horseback on the other side. The seven Frenchmen who did it were arrested. They expected to be shot. The next day was some saint's day; he ordered them to be placed before the high altar, and, when the priest reached the prayer for forgiveness, came down from his high seat, repeated it with him, and permitted them to go unpunished. [Cheers.] He had that wit common to all great commanders, which makes its way in a camp. His soldiers getting disheartened, he filled a large vase with powder, and, scattering six grains of rice in it, shook them up, and said: "See, there is the white, there is the black; what are you afraid of?" So when people came to him in great numbers for office, as it is reported they do sometimes even in Washington, he learned the first words of a Catholic prayer in Latin, and, repeating it, would say, "Do you understand that?" "No, sir." "What! want an office, and not know Latin? Go home and learn it!"

Then, again, like Napoleon,—like genius always,—he had confidence in his power to rule men. You remember when Bonaparte returned from Elba, and Louis XVIII. sent an army against him, Bonaparte descended from his carriage, opened his coat, offering his breast to their muskets, and saying, "Frenchmen, it is the Emperor!" and they ranged themselves behind him, *his* soldiers, shouting, "*Vive l'Empereur!*" That was in 1815. Twelve years before, Toussaint, finding that four of his regiments had deserted and gone to Leclerc, drew his sword, flung it on the grass, went across the field to them, folded his arms, and said, "Children, can you point a bayonet at me?" The blacks fell on their knees, praying his pardon. His bitterest enemies watched him, and none of them charged him with love of money, sensuality, or cruel use of power. The only instance in which his sternest critic has charged him with severity is this. During a tumult, a few white proprietors who had returned, trusting his proclamation, were killed. His nephew, General Moise, was accused of indecision in quelling the riot. He assembled a court-martial, and, on its verdict, ordered his own nephew to be shot, sternly Roman in thus keeping his promise of protection to the whites. Above the lust of gold, pure in private life, generous in the use of his power, it was against such a man that Napoleon sent his army, giving to General Leclerc, the husband of his beautiful sister Pauline, thirty thousand of his best troops, with orders to reintroduce slavery. Among these soldiers came all of Toussaint's old mulatto rivals and foes.

Holland lent sixty ships. England promised by special message to be neutral; and you know neutrality means sneering at freedom, and sending arms to tyrants. [Loud and long-continued applause.] England promised neutrality, and the black looked out on the whole civilized world marshalled against him. America, full of slaves, of course was hostile. Only the Yankee sold him poor muskets at a very high price. [Laughter.] Mounting his horse, and riding to the eastern end of the island, Samana, he looked out on a sight such as no native had ever seen before. Sixty ships of the line, crowded by the best soldiers of Europe, rounded the point. They were soldiers who had never yet met an equal, whose tread, like Cæsar's, had shaken Europe,—soldiers who had scaled the Pyramids, and planted the French banners on the walls of Rome. He looked a moment, counted the flotilla, let the reins fall on the neck of his horse, and, turning to Christophe, exclaimed: "All France is come to Hayti; they can only come to make us slaves; and we are lost!" He then recognized the only mistake of his life,—his confidence in Bonaparte, which had led him to disband his army.

Returning to the hills, he issued the only proclamation which bears his name and breathes vengeance: "My children, France comes to make us slaves. God gave us liberty; France has no right to take it away. Burn the cities, destroy the harvests, tear up the roads with cannon, poison the wells, show the white man the hell he comes to make";–and he was obeyed. [Applause.] When the great William of Orange saw Louis XIV. cover Holland with troops, he said, "Break down the dikes, give Holland back to ocean"; and Europe said, "Sublime!" When Alexander saw the armies of France descend upon Russia, he said, "Burn Moscow, starve back the invaders"; and Europe said, "Sublime!" This black saw all Europe marshalled to crush him, and gave to his people the same heroic example of defiance.

It is true, the scene grows bloodier as we proceed. But, remember, the white man fitly accompanied his infamous attempt to *reduce freemen to slavery* with every bloody and cruel device that bitter and shameless hate could invent. Aristocracy is always cruel. The black man met the attempt, as every such attempt should be met, with war to the hilt. In his first struggle to gain his freedom, he had been generous and merciful, saved lives and pardoned enemies, as the people in every age and clime have always done when rising against aristocrats. Now, to save his liberty, the Negro exhausted every means, seized every weapon, and turned back the hateful invaders with a vengeance as terrible as their own, though even now he refused to be cruel.

Leclerc sent word to Christophe that he was about to land at Cape City. Christophe said, "Toussaint is governor of the island. I will send to him for permission. If without it a French soldier sets foot on shore, I will burn the town, and fight over its ashes."

Leclerc landed. Christophe took two thousand *white* men, women, and children, and carried them to the mountains in safety, then with his own hands set fire to the splendid palace which French architects had just finished for him, and in forty hours the place was in ashes. The battle was fought in its streets, and the French driven back to their boats. [Cheers.] Wherever they went, they were met with fire and sword. Once, resisting an attack, the blacks, Frenchmen born, shouted the Marseilles Hymn, and the French soldiers stood still; they could not fight the Marseillaise. And it was not till their officers sabred them on that they advanced, and then they were beaten. Beaten in the field, the French then took to lies. They issued proclamations, saying, "We do not come to make you slaves; this man Toussaint tells you lies. Join us, and you shall have the rights you claim." They cheated every one of his officers, except Christophe and Dessalines, and his own brother Pierre, and finally these also deserted him, and he was left alone. He then sent word to Leclerc, "I will submit. I could continue the struggle for years,–could prevent a single Frenchman from safely quitting your camp. But I hate bloodshed. I have fought only for the liberty of my race. Guarantee that, I will submit and come in." He took the oath to be a faithful citizen; and on the same crucifix

Leclerc swore that he should be faithfully protected, and that the island should be free. As the French general glanced along the line of his splendidly equipped troops, and saw, opposite, Toussaint's ragged, ill-armed followers, he said to him, "L'Ouverture, had you continued the war, where could you have got arms?" "I would have taken yours," was the Spartan reply. [Cheers.] He went down to his house in peace; it was summer. Leclerc remembered that the fever months were coming, when his army would be in hospitals, and when one motion of that royal hand would sweep his troops into the sea. He was too dangerous to be left at large. So they summoned him to attend a council; and here is the only charge made against him,—the only charge. They say he was fool enough to go. Grant it; what was the record? The white man lies shrewdly to cheat the Negro. Knight-errantry was truth. The foulest insult you can offer a man since the Crusades is, You lie. Of Toussaint, Hermona, the Spanish general, who knew him well, said, "He was the purest soul God ever put into a body." Of him history bears witness, "He never broke his word." Maitland was travelling in the depths of the woods to meet Toussaint, when he was met by a messenger, and told that he was betrayed. He went on, and met Toussaint, who showed him two letters,—one from the French general, offering him any rank if he would put Maitland in his power, and the other his reply. It was, "Sir, I have promised the Englishman that he shall go back." [Cheers.] Let it stand, therefore, that the negro, truthful as a knight of old, was cheated by his lying foe. Which race has reason to be proud of such a record?

But he was not cheated. He was under espionage. Suppose he had refused: the government would have doubted him,—would have found some cause to arrest him. He probably reasoned thus: "If I go willingly, I shall be treated accordingly"; and he went. The moment he entered the room, the officers drew their swords, and told him he was prisoner; and one young lieutenant who was present says, "He was not at all surprised, but seemed very sad." They put him on shipboard, and weighed anchor for France. As the island faded from his sight, he turned to the captain, and said, "You think you have rooted up the tree of liberty, but I am only a branch; I have planted the tree so deep that all France can never root it up." [Cheers.] Arrived in Paris, he was flung into jail, and Napoleon sent his secretary, Caffarelli, to him, supposing he had buried large treasures. He listened awhile, then replied, "Young man, it is true I have lost treasures, but they are not such as you come to seek." He was then sent to the Castle of St. Joux, to a dungeon twelve feet by twenty, built wholly of stone, with a narrow window, high up on the side, looking out on the snows of Switzerland. In winter, ice covers the floor; in summer, it is damp and wet. In this living tomb the child of the sunny tropic was left to die. From this dungeon he wrote two letters to Napoleon. One of them ran thus:—

> "Sire, I am a French citizen. I never broke a law. By the grace of God, I have saved for you the best island of your realm. Sire, of your mercy grant me justice."

Napoleon never answered the letters. The commandant allowed him five francs a day for food and fuel. Napoleon heard of it, and reduced the sum to three. The luxurious usurper, who complained that the English government was stingy because it allowed him only six thousand dollars a month, stooped from his throne to cut down a dollar to a half, and still Toussaint did not die quick enough.

This dungeon was a tomb. The story is told that, in Josephine's time, a young French marquis was placed there, and the girl to whom he was betrothed went to the Empress and prayed for his release. Said Josephine to her, "Have a model of it made, and bring it to me." Josephine placed it near Napolean. He said, "Take it away,—it is horrible!" She put it on his footstool, and he kicked it from him. She held it to him the third time, and said, "Sire, in this horrible dungeon you have put a man to die." "Take him out," said Napoleon, and the girl saved her lover. In this tomb Toussaint was buried, but he did not die fast enough. Finally, the commandant was told to go into Switzerland, to carry the keys of the dungeon with him, and to stay four days; when he returned, Toussaint was found starved to death. That imperial assassin was taken twelve years after to his prison at St. Helena, planned for a tomb, as he had planned that of Toussaint, and there he whined away his dying hours in pitiful complaints of curtains and titles, of dishes and rides. God grant that when some future Plutarch shall weigh the great men of our epoch, the whites against the blacks, he do not put that whining child at St. Helena into one scale, and into the other the negro meeting death like a Roman, without a murmur, in the solitude of his icy dungeon!

From the moment he was betrayed, the Negroes began to doubt the French, and rushed to arms. Soon every Negro but Maurepas deserted the French. Leclerc summoned Maurepas to his side. He came, loyally bringing with him five hundred soldiers. Leclerc spiked his epaulettes to his shoulders, shot him, and flung him into the sea. He took his five hundred soldiers on shore, shot them on the edge of a pit, and tumbled them in. Dessalines from the mountain saw it, and, selecting five hundred French officers from his prisons, hung them on separate trees in sight of Leclerc's camp; and born, as I was, not far from Bunker Hill, I have yet found no reason to think he did wrong. [Cheers.] They murdered Pierre

Toussaint's wife at his own door, and after such treatment that it was mercy when they killed her. The maddened husband, who had but a year before saved the lives of twelve hundred white men, carried his next thousand prisoners and sacrificed them on her grave.

The French exhausted every form of torture. The Negroes were bound together and thrown into the sea; any one who floated was shot,—others sunk with cannonballs tied to their feet; some smothered with sulphur fumes,—others strangled, scourged to death, gibbeted; sixteen of Toussaint's officers were chained to rocks in desert islands,—others in marshes, and left to be devoured by poisonous reptiles and insects. Rochambeau sent to Cuba for bloodhounds. When they arrived, the young girls went down to the wharf, decked the hounds with ribbons and flowers, kissed their necks, and, seated in the amphitheatre, the women clapped their hands to see a Negro thrown to these dogs, previously starved to rage. But the Negroes besieged this very city so closely that these same girls, in their misery, ate the very hounds they had welcomed.

Then flashed forth that defying courage and sublime endurance which show how alike all races are when tried in the same furnace. The Roman wife, whose husband faltered when Nero ordered him to kill himself, seized the dagger, and, mortally wounding her own body, cried, "Poetus, it is not hard to die." The world records it with proud tears. Just in the same spirit, when a Negro colonel was ordered to execution, and trembled, his wife seized his sword, and, giving herself a death-wound, said, "Husband, death is sweet when liberty is gone."

The war went on. Napoleon sent over thirty thousand more soldiers. But disaster still followed his efforts. What the sword did not devour, the fever ate up. Leclerc died. Pauline carried his body back to France. Napoleon met her at Bordeaux, saying, "Sister, I gave you an army,—you bring me back ashes." Rochambeau—the Rochambeau of our history—left in command of eight thousand troops, sent word to Dessalines: "When I take you, I will not shoot you like a soldier, or hang you like a white man; I will whip you to death like a slave." Dessalines chased him from battle-field to battle-field, from fort to fort, and finally shut him up in Samana. Heating cannon-balls to destroy his fleet, Dessalines learned that Rochambeau had begged of the British admiral to cover his troops with the English flag, and the generous Negro suffered the boaster to embark undisturbed.

Some doubt the courage of the Negro. Go to Hayti, and stand on those fifty thousand graves of the best soldiers France ever had, and ask them what they think of the Negro's sword. And if that does not satisfy you, go to France, to the splendid mausoleum of the Counts of Rochambeau, and to the eight thousand graves of Frenchmen who skulked home under the English flag, and ask them. And if that does not satisfy you, come home, and if it had been October, 1859, you might have come by way of quaking Virginia, and asked her what she thought of Negro courage.

You may also remember this,—that we Saxons were slaves about four hundred years, sold with the land, and our fathers never raised a finger to end that slavery. They waited till Christianity and civilization, till commerce and the discovery of America, melted away their chains. Spartacus in Italy led the slaves of Rome against the Empress of the world. She murdered him, and crucified them. There never was a slave rebellion successful but once, and that was in St. Domingo. Every race has been, some time or other, in chains. But there never was a race that, weakened and degraded by such chattel slavery, unaided, tore off its own fetters, forged them into swords, and won its liberty on the battle-field, but one, and that was the black race of St. Domingo. God grant that the wise vigor of our government may avert that necessity from our land,—may raise into peaceful liberty the four million committed to our care, and show under democratic institutions a statesmanship as far-sighted as that of England, as brave as the Negro of Hayti!

So much for the courage of the Negro. Now look at his endurance. In 1805 he said to the white men, "This island is ours; not a white foot shall touch it." Side by side with him stood the South American republics, planted by the best blood of the countrymen of Lope de Vega and Cervantes. They topple over so often that you could no more daguerrotype their crumbling fragments than you could the waves of the ocean. And yet, at their side, the Negro has kept his island sacredly to himself. It is said that at first, with rare patriotism, the Haytien government ordered the destruction of all the sugar plantations remaining, and discouraged its culture, deeming that the temptation which lured the French back again to attempt their enslavement. Burn over New York to-night, fill up her canals, sink every ship, destroy her railroads, blot out every remnant of education from her sons, let her be ignorant and penniless, with nothing but her hands to begin the world again,—how much could she do in sixty years? And Europe, too, would lend you money, but she will not lend Hayti a dollar. Hayti, from the ruins of her colonial dependence, is become a civilized state, the seventh nation in the catalogue of commerce with this country, inferior in morals and education to none of the West Indian isles. Foreign merchants trust her courts as willingly as they do our own. Thus far, she has foiled the ambition of Spain, the greed of England, and the malicious statesmanship of Calhoun. Toussaint made her what she is. In this work there was grouped around him a score of men, mostly of pure Negro blood, who ably seconded his efforts. They were able in war and skilful in civil affairs, but not, like him, remarkable for that rare mingling of high qualities which alone makes true greatness, and insures a man leadership among those otherwise almost his equals. Toussaint was indisputably their chief. Courage, purpose, endurance,—these are the tests. He did plant a state so deep that all the world has not been able to root it up.

I would call him Napoleon, but Napoleon made his way to empire over broken oaths and through a sea of blood. This man never broke his word. "NO RETALIATION" was his great motto and the rule of his life; and the last words uttered to his son in France were these: "My boy, you will one day go back to St. Domingo; forget that France murdered your father." I would call him Cromwell, but Cromwell was only a soldier, and the state he founded went down with him into his grave. I would call him Washington, but the great Virginian held slaves. This man risked his empire rather than permit the slave-trade in the humblest village of his dominions.

You think me a fanatic to-night, for you read history, not with your eyes, but with your prejudices. But fifty years hence, when Truth gets a hearing, the Muse of History will put Phocion for the Greek, and Brutus for the Roman, Hampden for England, Fayette for France, choose Washington as the bright, consummate flower of our earlier civilization, and John Brown the ripe fruit of our noonday [Thunders of applause.], then, dipping her pen in the sunlight, will write in the clear blue, above them all, the name of the soldier, the statesman, the martyr, TOUSSAINT L'OUVERTURE. [Long-continued applause.]

Exercises

1. In his opening, does Phillips make any attempt to establish common ground with those who may oppose his thinking? Does he use the "Yes" technique? How would you characterize his approach? Bald? Direct? Oblique? Suggestive? Explain. In stating the point of his speech and listing the criteria by which he expects to substantiate his point, Phillips is employing which kind of argumentative proposition: Proposition of Fact or Value, or Proposition of Policy? How suitable are the criteria in terms of the logical compass of the subject? In terms of the psychological aspects of persuasion? How does Phillips narrow the base of his speech? Is this skillfully done? Explain.

2. What is the underlying method of reasoning employed in this speech: deduction or induction? To what extent does Phillips universalize from the specifics presented? How persuasive do you consider these applications?

3. In your judgment, which of the two sets of criteria mentioned in the Introduction receives greater attention in the speech? In the

first set of criteria, which criterion is given more attention? Which less attention? Why? In the second set of criteria, which measurement is given greater prominence? Which the lesser prominence? Why?

4. Aside from this speech, would you say that, generally speaking, the microcosm argument—the claim that a single entity is the epitome of an entire class, as L'Ouverture was the "epitome" of the Negro race—is adequate "proof" either from an intellectual or psychological viewpoint? Why or why not?

5. In this speech do you believe that Phillips effects complete lasting agreement? Something less than total accord, but still a significant gain? Do you believe that Phillips deliberately uses exaggeration for effect anywhere in the speech? Explain. Speakers sometimes use exaggeration to give listeners a stronger push along the continuum of persuasion than could be accomplished by the use of more moderate claims which may actually be closer to the speaker's true beliefs. Thus, a President may ask for considerably larger foreign aid appropriations than he expects, or perhaps even wants, to receive. In terms of platform persuasion, how effective do you believe is such use of overstatement? Explain, using examples of current or recent speakers.

6. How effective and how ethical do you consider Phillips' method of inserting value judgments at psychologically appropriate places in what purports to be a relatively objective factual narration? In such situations, is the persuasive intent of the speaker to cause the auditor to relax his intellectual and attitudinal defenses in the process of being carried along by the narrational currents; then, when the listener's guard is down, to drive home a controversial judgment with rapier assertiveness? Accept or reject this analysis of persuasive intent and apply your views to this speech, to other speeches you have heard or read.

7. How helpful do you consider Phillips' use of signposts, such as the following? "I cannot stop to give in detail every one of his efforts. This was in 1793. Leap with me over seven years; come to 1800; what has he achieved? . . . This was the work of seven years. Let us pause a moment, and find something to measure him by. . . ." Find other examples of signposts in the form of transitions, internal summaries, alerts to important ideas about to be expressed, terse reminders of time or place in the narration, and so on.

8. Compare the style of this speech with that of Emerson's "The American Scholar," reported earlier in this volume. Which more closely approximates conversational style? Which is more vivid and

impressive? Which is more intellectually demanding of the listeners? Which offers greater appeal to significant basic wants? Which makes greater use of personal pronouns? Restatement? Complex sentence structure? Balanced sentences? Epigrammatic expressions? In your answers keep in mind the intent and the reputation of the speaker, the nature of the means of persuasion available to the speaker, and the probable character of the audiences.

9. What does the editorial comment "thunders of applause" tell us about the audience's status of persuasion, when Phillips equates John Brown with George Washington? How would a modern audience respond to such an assertion? What is your reaction to Phillips' claim that L'Ouverture was superior to Washington and, in fact, was the greatest man in world history?

10. How effective would this speech be if delivered today? Explain some of the relevant differences in beliefs and attitudes which exist between audiences of today and those which heard Phillips' speech on L'Ouverture. In what ways would today's audiences be easier to reach with this speech? In what ways more difficult? What was the status of race equality in 1860 and in the ensuing decades when Phillips was active? In those days could a listener sympathize with Phillips' point, without fearing that such agreement would "commit" him or "cost him something"? Today has the Negro so clearly established his equality of intelligence and character that such a speech as this is "old hat"? If Phillips were to give this speech today, what changes in structure, development, or style would you advise him to make? Be specific in terms of the kinds of audiences you envisage.

Henry Ward Beecher

"The Success of American Democracy," sermon in Plymouth Congregational Church, Brooklyn, New York, April 13, 1862, the anniversary Sunday of the attack on Fort Sumter

HENRY Ward Beecher (1813–1887), generally considered the greatest member of a great family, was one of the most eloquent and influential of all the preachers in American history. Well worthy of study for their speaking are his father Lyman Beecher and his brother Edward. A sister, Catherine, won fame as an educational reformer. Another sister, Harriet Beecher Stowe, wrote *Uncle Tom's Cabin.* Henry Ward Beecher won his reputation principally in the pulpit of his Plymouth Church in Brooklyn and on the Chautauqua and commercial lecture platforms. Theologians credit him with having exerted great influence in changing the Christian view of God from that of a stern law-giver to that of a loving father, and with having mitigated the awful fear of hellfire. The agnostic Robert Green Ingersoll testified, "I think Mr. Beecher has liberalized the English-speaking people of the world."

Yet as a child Beecher was not considered especially bright by his family and teachers. His articulation was so muffled and cluttered that an aunt said of him: "When Henry is sent to me with a message, I always make him say it three times. The first time I have no manner of an idea, than if he spoke Choctaw; the second, I catch now and then a word; by the third time I begin to understand." It was a speech-teacher, John Lovell, who helped to arouse his ambition and to awaken him to a sense of his potential abilities—by being interested in what he had to say, and by helping him to say it effectively. Years later, in London, Beecher told an audience how much public speaking meant to him: "I fed on the privilege of making men hear things, because I was a public speaker. I gloried in my gifts, not because they brought praise, for they brought the other thing continually; but men would come and would hear, and I rejoiced in it."

When Beecher was invited to Brooklyn, and was able to plan his own new church, he abandoned the traditional pulpit and asked the architect to build a platform that extended well out into the congregation; for, he said: "I want the audience to surround me, so that they will come up on every side, and behind me, so that I shall be in the centre of the crowd, and have the people surge all about me." Gradually Beecher's sermons became less orthodox, more pragmatic. He welcomed Darwin's theory of evolution "with joy." When he was criticized for his growing tendency to discuss political, social, and economic problems, he retorted: "The moment a man so conducts his profession that it touches the question of right and wrong, he comes into my sphere."

So greatly did his reputation grow that the Yale Divinity School invited him to inaugurate a series of annual lectures (which still persists) on the goals and methods of preaching. In the first of these lectures, January 31, 1872, Beecher declared: "There is no trade that requires so long an apprenticeship as preaching." He dated his own success from the Sunday he first realized he should start his sermon with what his congregation already knew and accepted and should develop it by "analyzing the people I was preaching to." By these means he became not only the most influential preacher of his time but also one of the most popular public lecturers. Instructing the divinity students in how to preach well, he told them: "Your office is to do the chief part of the thinking and to arrange the truth, while their part is to experience the motive-power, and take the incitement toward a better life."

During the early part of the Civil War, before the Emancipation Proclamation, President Lincoln was under constant attack by most of the abolitionists; and the Northerners were often discouraged by what was considered inept leadership in the war and by the success of the Southern armies. In the sermon which we present, Beecher deliberately undertook to try to instill in his listeners (and in the North generally, for his sermons were published and were widely read) a refreshened spirit of pride and of optimism.

The text of this sermon is taken from Henry Ward Beecher, *Patriotic Addresses,* ed. John H. Howard, New York: J. B. Ford, 1872.

THE SUCCESS OF AMERICAN DEMOCRACY

"So the king of the South shall come into his kingdom, and shall return into his own land. But his sons shall be stirred up, and shall assemble a multitude of great forces: and one shall certainly come, and overflow, and pass through: then shall he return, and be stirred up even to his fortress. And the king of the South shall be moved with choler, and shall come forth and fight with him, even with the king of the North: and he shall set forth a great multitude; but the multitude shall be given into his hand. And when he hath taken away the multitude, his heart shall be lifted up; and he shall cast down many ten thousands; but he shall not be strengthened by it. For the king of the North shall return, and shall set forth a multitude greater than the former, and shall certainly come after certain years with a great army and with much riches. And in those times there shall many stand up against the king of the South; also the robbers of thy people shall exalt themselves to establish the vision: but they shall fall. So the king of the North shall come, and cast up a mount, and take the most fenced cities: and the arms of the South shall not withstand, neither his chosen people, neither shall there be any strength to withstand. But he that cometh against him shall do according to his own will, and none shall stand before him; and he shall stand in the glorious land, which by his hand shall be consumed. He shall also set his face to enter with the strength of his whole kingdom. And equality"—or conditions of equality—*"shall be with him; thus shall he do."—Dan. xi. 9–17.*

I do not use these words in any close historical sense. They are a very poetic and glowing description of a conflict in which, with a singular fitness to our times, both the terms North and South, and the events which were predicted, are strikingly suggestive. And although a sharp exegesis might destroy some parts of the seeming analogy, I shall consider them as a splendid poetic imagery. As such, I think you will agree with me that it is a remarkable passage, and it not only describes the past with great accuracy, but throws a blazing light upon the times that are to come. We are in the midst of times the most exciting; times that demand faith; times in which the teachings and prophecies of Scripture come with peculiar emphasis.

You will remember the scenes of one year ago. It was just such a bright and beautiful day as this has been. The air was full of news. These great cities boiled like caldrons. The people had learned that the guns had opened upon Fort Sumter. Treason was consummated! Our hearts yearned toward the brave garrison. We hoped that the leaders and their companions in arms would sustain the stronghold. Our hearts felt the cold breath of horror, when at last it was known that the flag of the Union had been assaulted. The forts that had belched their fire upon that flag had been built underneath its protection. They had carried it for years upon their flag-staff. The very guns that were flaming upon it had been founded and forged under its flowing folds. The men that aimed them had been born and reared under its protection. That flag had been the honored ensign of our people in their memorable struggle for independence. It had seen the British arms laid down before it. It had been honored in every land. Our men-of-war had borne it, without disgrace, to every part of the world. Nor was there a port upon the globe where men chose or dared to insult that national emblem. That inglorious wickedness was reserved to our own people! It was by American hands that it was dishonored, slit with balls, and trailed in the dust!

That a crime so unnatural and monstrous was then going on, makes the anniversary of this day memorable above all Sabbaths of our history. It was an infernal insurrection against liberty, good government, and civilization, on the most sacred day of the week! We shall not soon experience a like excitement again. Although but a year ago, it seems ten years. And, in ordinary history, ten years are not so full of matter as has been this single year. It is full of events visible, but yet more full of those things that do not come under corporeal observation.

Such has been the intensity of public feeling, that it has seemed as if nothing was doing. We have chidden those in authority, and felt that due speed had not been made. But within one twelvemonth a gigantic army has been raised and drilled; all its equipments created; all the material of war produced and collected together. The cannon that now reverberate across the continent, a twelvemonth ago were sleeping ore in the mountains. The clothing of thousands was fleece upon the backs of sheep. As we look back, we can scarcely believe our own senses, that so much has been done; although, at every single hour of it, it seemed as if little was being done,—for all the speed and all the power of this great government were not so fast and eager as our thoughts and desires were.

A navy has sprung forth, almost at a word; and, stranger still, by the skill of our inventors and naval constructors, a new era has been inaugurated in naval warfare. It is probable that forts and ships have come to the end of one dispensation, and that the old is to give place hereafter to the new.

The history of this year is the history of the common people of America. It is memorable on account of the light that it throws upon them. We are fond of talking of *American ideas*. There are such things as American ideas, distinctive, peculiar, national. Not that they were first discovered here, or that they are only entertained here; but because more than anywhere else they lie at the root of the institutions, and are working out the laws and the policies of this people.

The root idea is this: that man is the most sacred trust of God to the world; that his value is derived from his moral relations from his divinity. Looked at in his relations to God and the eternal world, every man is so valuable that you cannot make distinction between one and another. If you measure a man by the skill that he can exhibit, and the fruit of it, there is great distinction between one and another. Men are not each worth the same thing to society. All men cannot think with a like value, nor work with a like product. And if you measure man as a producing creature—that is, in his secular relations—men are not alike valuable. But when you measure men on their spiritual side, and in their affectional relations to God and the eternal world, the lowest man is so immeasurable in value that you cannot make any practical difference between one man and another. Although, doubtless, some are vastly above others, the lowest and least goes beyond your power of conceiving, and your power of measuring. This is the root idea, which, if not recognized, is yet operative. It is the fundamental principle of our American scheme, that is, Man is above nature. Man, by virtue of his original endowment and affiliation to the Eternal Father, is superior to every other created thing. There is nothing to be compared with man. All governments are from him and for him, and not over him and upon him. All institutions are not his masters, but his servants. All days, all ordinances, all usages, come to minister to the chief and the king, God's son, man, of whom God only is master. Therefore he is to be thoroughly enlarged, thoroughly empowered by development, and then thoroughly trusted. This is the American idea,—for we stand in contrast with the world in holding and teaching it; that men, having been once thoroughly educated, are to be absolutely trusted.

The education of the common people follows, then, as a necessity. They are to be fitted to govern. Since all things are from them and for them, they must be educated to their function, to their destiny. No pains are spared, we know, in Europe, to educate princes and nobles who are to govern. No expense is counted too great, in Europe, to prepare the governing classes for their function. America has her governing class, too; and that governing class is the whole people. It is a slower work, because it is so much larger. It is never carried so high, because there is so much more of it. It is easy to lift up a crowned class. It is not easy to lift up society from the very foundation. That is the work of centuries. And therefore, though we have not an education so deep nor so high as it is in some other places, we have it broader than it is anywhere else in the world; and we have learned that for ordinary affairs intelligence among the common people is better than treasures of knowledge among particular classes of the people. School books do more for the country than encyclopædias.

And so there comes up the American conception of a common people as an order of nobility, or as standing in the same place to us that orders of nobility stand to other peoples. Not that, after our educated men and men of genius are counted out, we call all that remain the common people. The whole community, top and bottom and intermediate, the strong and the weak, the rich and the poor, the leaders and the followers, constitute with us the commonwealth; in which laws spring from the people, administration conforms to their wishes, and they are made the final judges of every interest of the State.

In America there is not one single element of civilization that is not made to depend, in the end, upon public opinion. Art, law, administration, policy, reformations of morals, religious teaching, all derive, in our form of society, the most potent influence from the common people. For although the common people are educated in preconceived notions of religion, the great intuitions and instincts of the heart of man rise up afterwards, and in their turn influence back. So there is action and reaction.

It is this very thing that has led men that are educated, in Europe, to doubt the stability of our nation. Owing to a strange ignorance on their part, our glory has seemed to them our shame, and our strength has seemed to them our weakness, and our invincibility has seemed to them our disaster and defeat. This impression of Europeans has been expressed in England in language that has surprised us, and that one day will surprise them. We know more of it in England because the English language is our mother tongue, and we are more concerned to know what England thinks of us than any other nation.

But it is impossible that nations educated into sympathy with strong governments, and with the side of those that govern, should sympathize with the governed. In this country the sympathy goes with the governed, and not with the governing, as much as in the other countries it goes with the governing, and not with the governed. And abroad they are measuring by a false rule, and by a homebred and one-sided sympathy.

It is impossible for men who have not seen it to understand that there is no society possible that will bear such expansion and contraction, such strains and burdens, as a society made up of free educated common people, with democratic institutions. It has been supposed that such a society was the most unsafe, and the least capable of control of any. But whether tested by external pressure, or, as now, by the most wondrous internal evils, an educated democratic people are the strongest government that can be made on the face of the earth. In no other form of society is it so safe to set discussion at large. Nowhere else is there such safety in the midst of apparent conflagration. Nowhere else is there such entire rule, when there seems to be such entire anarchy. A foreigner would think, pending a presidential election, that the end of the world had come. The people roar and dash like an ocean. "No government," he would say, "was ever strong enough to hold such wild and tumultuous enthusiasm, and zeal, and rage." True. There is not a *government* strong enough to hold them. Nothing but *self*-government will do it: that will. Educate men to take care of themselves, individually and in masses, and then let the winds blow; then let the storms fall; then let excitements burn, and men will learn to move freely upon each other, as do drops of water in the ocean. Our experience from generation to generation has shown that, though we may have fantastic excitements; though the whole land may seem to have swung from its moorings on a sea of the wildest agitation, we have only to let the silent-dropping paper go into the box, and that is the end of the commotion. To-day, the flames mount to heaven; and on every side you hear the most extravagant prophecies and the fiercest objurgations; and both sides know that, if they do not succeed, the end of the world will have come. But to-morrow the vote is declared, and each side go home laughing, to take hold of the plough and the spade; and they are satisfied that the nation is safe after all.

And we have come to ridicule the idea of danger from excitements. Where else was there ever a nation that could bear to have every question, no matter how fiery or how fierce, let loose to go up and down, over hill and through valley, without police or government restraint upon the absolute liberty of the common people? Where else was ever a government that could bear to allow entire free discussion? We grow strong under it. Voting is the cure of evil with us. Liberty, that is dangerous abroad, is our very safety. And since our whole future depends upon our rightly understanding this matter,—the liberty of the common people, and the glory of the common people,—and since this government of our educated common people is to be the death of slavery, and to spread over this continent an order of things for which in past experience there is no parallel, and for which men's ideas are not prepared,—we do well to take heed of this memorable year of the common people. For histories will register this year of 1861–62 as the year of the common people of America.

I. One year ago there fell a storm upon the great heart of the common people, which swayed it as the ocean is swayed. It has not calmed itself yet. It was that shot at the American flag that touched the national heart. No one knew before what a depth of feeling was there. We did not know how our people had clustered about that banner all their ideas of honor and patriotism and glory. We did not know how the past and future met and stood together upon that flag in the imagination of every American. In an hour all this was disclosed. And what was the manifestation of that hour? All things that separated the common people of America were at once forgotten. There rose up, with appalling majesty, the multitude of the common people. The schemes of treachery, the political webs that had been framed, went down in a moment; and the voice of the common people it was that called the government to be energetic, to take courage, and to rescue the land.

But I would not have you suppose that the common people gave forth merely an unreasoning zeal,—a furious burst of patriotic emotion. The common people of the North had, and they still have, a clear, comprehensive, and true idea of American nationality, such as we looked for in vain in many of the leaders of past times. They had taken in the right view of national unity. They had a right view of the trust of territory held in common by all, for all, on this continent. They felt, more than any others, that Divine Providence had given to this people, not a northern part, not a middle ridge, not a southern section, but an undivided continent. They held it, not for pride, not for national vanity, not to be cut and split into warring sections, but as a sacred trust, held for sublimest ends of human happiness, in human liberty. And the instincts and intuitions of the common people it was that made this, not a struggle for sectional precedency, but a struggle for the maintenance of the great national trust, and for the establishment of American ideas over the whole American continent. And our government felt that they could lean back on the brave heart of the great intelligent people.

While, then, men of our own blood are ignorant and blind; while even to this hour the ablest statesmen in the British Parliament are declaring, though in a friendly spirit in most respects, that it were better that an amicable settlement and separation should take place, and that they should live apart who cannot live peaceably together, our common people are greater than parliaments or than ministers; and they see, and feel, and know, that God has rolled upon them a duty, not of present peace, but of future stability, national grandeur, and continental liberty. This is the doctrine of the common people, and it will stand.

For that idea our common people are giving their sons, their blood, and their treasure, and they will continue to the uttermost to give them.

For this sake see what a common people can do. One of the most difficult things for any people to do, for any reason, is to lay aside their animosities and malignant feelings. But this great common people have laid aside every animosity, every party feeling, and all political disagreements; and for one year they have maintained an honest unity. I am more proud of the substantial unity that has been wrought out in the North, than of any battle that has been fought. It is the noblest evidence of the strength of our form of government.

The common people have given without stint their sons, their substance, and their ingenuity: and they are not weary of giving. They have consented patiently to the interruption of their industries, and to all the burdens which taxes bring. Taxes touch men in a very tender place; for human nature resides very strongly in the particular neighborhood where taxes anchor. And if anything takes hold of men and brings them to their bearings, it is the imposition of burdens that are felt in the pocket. I sometimes think that men can carry burdens on their hearts more easily than on their exchequer. But they have taken both the burdens of taxation and bereavements, they have given both blood and money; and they are willing to bear the load as long as it is necessary to secure this continent to liberty.

They have demanded of this Administration which they themselves ordained, that it should not spare them. The only thing that the people have ever been disposed to blame the government for has been that it has not moved fast enough; that it has not done enough. "Take more; call for more; do more!" is the demand of the people upon the government.

They have accepted the most unwonted and dangerous violations of the fundamental usages of this land with implicit submission. They are a proud people, jealous of their rights; a proud people, the flash of whose eye is like blood when they are wronged in their fundamental rights; and yet, the precious writ of *habeas corpus* has been suspended, and they have consented. They have been restricted in their intercourse to a degree altogether unprecedented, and they have judged it expedient to submit.

They have submitted to the limitation of speech and discussion,—a thing most foreign to American ideas. The arrest of men without legal process or accusation, and their imprisonment and long duress without trial,—these are new in our times and in this land. And yet, under all these interruptions of our most grave and important principles and rights, the people have been calm; they have trusted their government; and they have been willing to wait.

These are dangerous things, even in extremity; but for their sakes who control the affairs of this nation, and that they might have the most unlimited power to crush the rebellion, and establish liberty, the common people, with magnanimous generosity, have yielded up these imperishable rights.

When the whole national heart beat with gratification at the arrest of men who had been at the root of this grand treachery, mark, I beseech of you, the bearing of the common people of America. If there was one thing about which they were expected to rage like wolves, it was this. Nothing in external circumstances could be more irritating and aggravating than those exhibitions of foreign feeling which came to our knowledge. I know that the diplomatic language of the two governments was very smooth and unexceptionable; and I am informed that the tone of many of the local papers of England was kind; but all the English papers that I saw, with one or two exceptions, were of such a spirit that I will characterize them only by saying that good breeding was not common where the editors of them lived. If there was one single missile more offensive than another, it was eagerly sought out. Tried on the side of revenge; tried on the side of national animosities; tried by foreign impertinence and unkindness; tried at home in the midst of treachery, in the midst of war, in the midst of troubles and burdens, and in the midst of an interrupted commerce,—mark the heroic conduct of this great American people.

Government pronounced its judgment against the feelings and expectations of the common people. Slidell and Mason were to be given up. There was silence instantly, and thoughtfulness, throughout this land. Then came acquiescence, full, cheerful, uncomplaining. I have yet to see a single paper that seriously, after the appearance of the letter of the Secretary of State, made one complaint or ill-natured remark. Such a thing was never before seen in the history of the world. Mason and Slidell might have been taken from Washington to Boston Harbor under the care of a single officer, without molestation from the common people of America. These are the common people that they are pleased to call the mob of America; but not among the crowned heads and privileged classes, not among any other people on the earth, is there such stability, such order, such self-restraint, such dignity, and such sublime nobility, as there is among the educated common people of America. God bless them! Under the terrible inflictions of battle, under griefs innumerable, in the midst of desolations that go to the very heart of families, there is the same noble, patient, uncomplaining cheerfulness and devotion to this great cause.

II. The history of this year has silently developed many convictions based upon great truths. It has, in the first place, revolutionized the whole opinion of men as to the relative military power of the Free States and Slave States of America. It was an almost undisputed judgment, that the habits of the South bred prowess; that they were chivalric; that their educated men were better officers than ours; and that their common people, in the hour of battle, would be better soldiers than the laboring classes of the North. It never was our faith, it never was our belief, but that the laboring and educated common people were just as much better for military development, when the time came, as for ordinary industrial purposes. Events have justified our impressions in this regard.

Let us look, for a moment, at the line of battle. Passing by the earlier conflicts prematurely brought on, in which the advantage was, without good conduct on either side, in favor of Southern men, what is the general conclusion from that line of conflicts that subsequently followed each other almost without interruption, from Hilton Head, Beaufort, Roanoke, New-Berne, Fort Henry, Fort Donelson, Somerset, Nashville, Island Number Ten, Pittsburg Landing?

Without further particularizing, what have been the general results of this series of conflicts? The rebels are swept out of the upper and eastern parts of Virginia. They have lost one portion of North Carolina. Their seaboard is almost taken from them. They have been driven from Kentucky and Missouri, and in Tennessee they are close pressed on Memphis itself. They are on the eve, apparently, of losing the great metropolis of the Southwest. And has there been one single field in which Northern endurance and courage have not been made to appear eminent over Southern? In the battle of Pittsburg Landing what a disparity there was in generalship between the North and the South! That battle was won by the soldiers. The Southwestern men had every advantage in military skill, and on our side the only advantage was that we had men who would not be beaten. Our soldiers had little help of generalship. It was hands, and not brains, that conquered there.

This matter, then, will, from this time forth, stand on different ground. It is not for the sake of vaingloryying that I make these allusions. If it were not that I have a moral end in view, I should think them unseasonable; but we shall never have peace until we have respect, we shall never have respect so long as a boasting Southern effete population think that they can overmaster Northern sturdy yeomen. When they know what Northern muscle and blows mean, they will respect them; and when they respect them, we shall be able to live in harmony with them: and not till then.

But there are many other things that have been evolved in the history of the year. There have been convictions wrought in the minds of the thinking common people that will not be easily worn out. There is coming to be a general conviction, that men brought up under the influence of slavery are contaminated to the very root, and they cannot make good citizens of a republic. The radical nature of slavery is such as to destroy the possibility of good citizenship in the masses of men. Exceptions there are, because even in the Slave States there are large neighborhoods where slavery does not exist, and where many men are superior to their circumstances. But the average tendency of slave influences is to narrow men; to make them selfish; to unfit them for public spirit; to destroy that large patriotism from which comes the feeling of nationality.

I think there is a widening conviction, that slavery and its laws, and liberty and its institutions, cannot exist under one government. And I think that, if it were not for the impediment of supposed constitutional restrictions there would be an almost universal disposition to sweep, as with a deluge, this gigantic evil out of our land. The feeling of the people in this matter is unmistakable. The recommendation of the President of these United States, which has been corroborated by the resolution of Congress, is one of the most memorable events of our history. The fact that a policy of emancipation has been recommended by the Chief Magistrate, and indorsed by Congress, cannot be overestimated in importance. Old John Quincy Adams lifted his head in the grave, methinks, when that resolution was carried,—he that was almost condemned for treason because he dared to introduce in Congress a subject that looked towards emancipation. Last Friday—a day not henceforth to be counted inauspicious—was passed the memorable bill giving liberty to the slave in the District of Columbia. One might almost say, if the President had signed it, "Lord, now let thy servant depart in peace, according to thy word; for mine eyes have seen thy salvation." It is worth living for a lifetime to see the capital of our government redeemed from the stigma and shame of being a slave mart. I cannot doubt that the President of the United States will sign that bill. It shall not shake my confidence in him, but it certainly will not change my judgment that it should be signed, if he does not sign it. It would have been better if it had been signed the moment that it was received; but we have found out by experience that though Abraham Lincoln is sure, he is slow; and that though he is slow, he is sure!

I think that it is beginning to be seen that the North, for its own sake, must exert every proper constitutional influence, and every moral influence, to cleanse the South from the contamination of slavery. What gambling-houses and drinking-saloons are to the young men of a neighborhood, taking hold of their animal passions, and corrupting them where human nature is most temptable, undermining their character, and wasting their stamina, the Southern marts are to our common people. The animal parts of our nature come naturally into sympathy with the South. The Southern institution is an academy of corruption to the animal feelings of the whole people, and it will continue to be throwing back into our system elements of inflammation and trouble as long as it exists. I dread such a settlement of this controversy as will follow whenever all malignant passions and political machinations shall have swept the bad men of the North and of the South together again for future legislation.

We have begun, also, to suspect another thing, which we shall learn more and more thoroughly; and that is, that hereafter, in this nation, the North must prevail. For the North is the nation, and the South is but the fringe. The heart is here; the trunk is here; the brain is here. The most exquisite compliment ever paid to New England was in the secret scheme and machination of the leaders of the rebellion, which it was supposed would be successful. They meant to threaten secession and war, and arouse a party in the North that would unite with them, and then reconstruct in such a way as to leave New England out, and take all the rest of the nation in. Had they succeeded, they would have been in the condition of a man that should go to bed whole at night, and wake up in the morning without his head! For the brain of this nation is New England. There is not a part that does not derive its stimulus and supply from that fountain of laws and ideas. Well may they wish to exclude from their corrupt constitution and laws that part of this nation which has been the throne of God. Well may they desire to separate themselves from that portion of our country which has been the source of all that is godlike in American history. But I do not think that they will cut off our head. And hereafter I think it will be felt more and more that the North is the nation: not New England, but the whole North from ocean to ocean,—all that is comprised in the Northern loyal Free States. It is the foundation of industry; it is the school of intelligence; it is the home of civilized institutions; it is the repository of those principles which are the foundation of our political fabric; and if we hope to save the government and our peculiar ideas, it is the North that must save them, and not the South. We may just as well say it as to disguise it. Whatever may be wise or unwise, expedient or inexpedient, in times of party management, I do not hesitate to say, and I repeat it again and again, that the North is this nation, and that the North must govern it: not against the Constitution, but by the Constitution; not against law, but through law; not for selfishness, but for the well-being of the whole; not to aggrandize itself, but to enrich every State in the Union, from the North to the South, and from the East to the West. The South are prodigal sons; they are wasters; they are destroyers. The North has conservative forces; and now that she has come to govern, she will be derelict, she will forfeit every claim to respect, and she will bring the judgment of God on her head, if she hesitates to take the government, and maintain it till she has carried the principles of the American people of this continent triumphantly through.

Since, then, her ascendency means liberty, the thrift of the common people, and the progress of civilization, the North owes it to the nation itself not to yield up that ascendency. One side or the other must prevail. Let it be that side that carries forward to the future the precious legacies of the past. There go two principles looking to the future. One is represented by our flag, and all its starry folds. Liberty; democratic equality; Christianity; God, the only king; right, the only barrier and restraint; and then, God and right being respected, liberty to all, from top to bottom, and the more liberty the stronger and safer,—that is the Northern conception. And that is the precious seed that shall pierce to State after State, rolling westward her empire. What has the North done? Look at Michigan; look at Ohio; look at Indiana; look at Illinois; look at Wisconsin; look at Iowa. These are the fruits of Northern ideas. And where is the South? Look at Missouri; look at Texas. See what States she rears. And which of these shall be the seed-planter of the future? Which shall carry the victorious banner? Shall the South carry her bastard bunting, bearing the pestiferous seed of slavery, degradation, and national rottenness? or shall the North, advancing her banner, carry with her stars and stripes all that they symbolize,—God's glory in man's liberty? I think—and I thank God for it—that the great heart of this people is beginning to accept this destiny, and that it is becoming the pride of their future.

There is but one other thing that I will say, for I do not wish to weary you with too long a discussion of that which is dear to my own heart as life itself. While there have been many incidental ills and evils occasioned by the present conflict, it has had one good effect in amalgamating this heterogeneous people. Since we have received millions from foreign lands, there have been some political jealousies toward those belonging to other nations. I think you have seen the end of that most un-American Native-Americanism. There is not one nation that has not contributed its quota to fight the battles of liberty. The blood of the Yankee has mingled with the blood of the Irishman. Right beside our Curtis was the noble Sigel. Right by the side of the wounded American lay the wounded German. Two tongues met when they spoke the common words, Land, Liberty, God, and Freedom. And now there is no foreign blood among us. They are ours. They have earned their birth here. Their nativity is as if our mothers bore them and nursed them. America has received all her foreign population, now, with a more glorious adoption, and they are our kindred. God be thanked for this substantial benefit. War, with all its horrors, is not without its incidental advantages.

Is the year, then, that is just past, to have a parallel and sequence in the year that is come? What is to be the future? What are our prospects and hopes? I am not a prophet. I cannot lift the veil from what is before us. I can only express my own judgment. Perhaps you think I am sanguine. I think I am not sanguine, though I am hopeful. And yet I have no other thought than that victory awaits us at every step. We are able to bear our share of defeat. If the blessing of liberty is too great to be purchased at so cheap a price, let God tell us the price, and we are ready to pay it. We have more sons to give. We can live lower, and on less. Our patience is scarcely drawn upon. The sources of our prosperity are hardly touched. And I think I may say for you, and the great American common people, "We will give every dollar that we are worth, every child that we have, and our own selves; we will bring all that we are, and all that we have, and offer them up freely; but this country shall be one, and undivided. We will have one Constitution, and one liberty, and that universal." The Atlantic shall sound it, and the Pacific shall echo it back, deep answering to deep, and it shall reverberate from the Lakes on the North to the unfrozen Gulf on the South,—"One nation; one Constitution; one starry banner!" Hear it, England!—one country, and indivisible. Hear it, Europe!—one people, and inseparable. One God; one hope; one baptism; one Constitution; one government; one nation; one country; one people,—cost what it may, we will have it!

Exercises

1. In his seventh lecture to the Yale divinity students, Beecher said that "an illustration is a window in an argument, and lets in light"; and he added, "Illustrations are as natural to me as breathing." Examine this sermon in terms of its pictorial qualities. Identify Beecher's analogies, metaphors, similes, and other vivid figures of speech. Evaluate their effectiveness in view of Edmund Burke's reminder, in his "Essay on the Sublime and the Beautiful," that illustrations should direct attention *to* rather than divert interest *from* the point the speaker wishes to make. Do Beecher's pictorial images pinpoint or expand the meaning he wants his listeners to acquire? Do they help make his points memorable? Do they conceal shallowness in his thinking or do they illuminate its depths?
2. Why, in Beecher's opinion, may some ideas be called "American"? In his judgment, what is the basic American idea? Do you agree? How does he substantiate his view?
3. Restate in your own words why to some European critics of that time "our glory has seemed to them our shame."
4. What was the "Mason and Slidell" incident? Why did Beecher refer to it without explaining it? What conclusion did he draw from it?
5. Outline this sermon, noting its theme, its purpose, the Introduction and the Conclusion, and the two main ideas, with their subordinate points. What function is served by the rather lengthy Biblical text?
6. In what terms did Beecher evaluate Lincoln? How does this accord with the Lincoln enshrined in history?

7. Compare and contrast Beecher's contention that New England is the "brain" of the Union with Emerson's challenge to individual intelligence in "The American Scholar." How does each speaker substantiate his contention? Which is more convincing? Why?

8. Compare this speech with Beecher's address on "The Raising of the Union Flag over Fort Sumter," on April 14, 1865—which appears also in *Patriotic Addresses*, pp. 676–697. In what significant respect did Beecher's views change between 1862 and 1865? Why? What unifying consistency binds the two speeches together?

9. Compare Beecher's concluding paragraph with the sentiments expressed by Winston Churchill in his war speeches in 1940, calling upon the British people to so stand that in the long view of history men should say of them, "This was their finest hour."

10. Analyze this speech to illustrate what you mean by "style." Contrast "good" and "bad" style. Evaluate Beecher's style in terms of Aristotle's insistence upon clarity and George Campbell's emphasis upon the value of liveliness. In what respects, if any, does Beecher's style seem better suited to oral than to written discourse?

11. Judging from this speech, what kind of man do you think Beecher was? Is this view supported by your reading of others of his speeches? By his biography? By accounts of historians? What does Beecher's career illustrate concerning the importance of ethos?

William Jennings Bryan 

"The Cross of Gold,"
given at the Democratic Party Convention in Chicago, July 8, 1896

As the Democratic Party candidate for President in 1896, William Jennings Bryan (1860–1925) led the last aggressive protest of agrarian provincialism against capitalist industrialism. During the previous three decades the main thrust of the nation had been in industry and finance. The agrarian America of pre-Civil War years had been transformed into a world power of vast industrial potential. In the process, a dangerously uneven distribution of the new wealth had provoked ugly resentment among the farmers and, to a less overt extent, among the great masses. The sufferings of the farmers in the late 1880's and the 1890's were acute, growing out of deflation, low prices, drought, inadequate credit, and poor marketing facilities. Partly because of Bryan's speaking on free silver during his two terms in the United States House of Representatives and during lecture tours about the country, great numbers of people came to believe that the main source of social and economic injustice was the gold standard. Bimetallism, they thought, would increase the supply of money in circulation, improve credit, raise prices, and end the depression. After the monetary system had been corrected, the nation could then turn to other needed reforms.

Most of the delegates elected to the Democratic convention in 1896 were silver Democrats. Seizing control of the convention machinery, they determined the choice for keynote speaker and for permanent chairman, as well as the seating of contested delegations. Their triumph was complete over the conservatives who had long dominated the Party and who had bitterly opposed the silver agitators as being tinged with red and threatening anarchy and national bankruptcy. Nevertheless, their victory seemed hollow. For two days an unending succession of tedious orators had castigated the conservative policies of the Republicans and of Cleveland's administration. None of the speeches had caught fire, and the delegates seemed bored and restive. The first excitement of the convention was stirred near the end of the second day by the announcement that a debate on the financial plank of the platform would be held at the beginning of the following session. Senators David Hill and William Vilas and former Governor William Russell of Massachusetts were to represent the sound money side, and Benjamin Tillman and Bryan were to speak for free silver. The personalities involved and the direct confrontation between the conservatives and the silverites gave the debates a dramatic appeal. At the appointed time, the hall was crowded with 20,000 persons, most of them eager to cheer for the pro-silver speakers. Tillman's speech, however, seemed inappropriately vindictive and sectional. The frustrations of the pro-silver delegates deepened as Hill, Vilas, and Russell presented persuasively the time-worn arguments for sound money and conservative policies. No convention speaker had yet caught the imagination of the listeners. None had preached the coinage of silver as the cause of Christ and of humanity. None had echoed what the silver supporters felt in their hearts and minds. Then the magnificent voice of the "Boy Orator of the Platte" filled the hall, giving voice to their thoughts, uplifting them, and overwhelming them. By a huge margin, the Convention voted for the free silver platform, and the next day nominated Bryan for President on the fifth ballot.

In the ensuing campaign, Bryan's oratory was the chief weapon of the Democrats. Whistle-stopping through the country, Bryan spoke to perhaps 5,000,000 persons, more than had ever before listened to an orator. This proved not quite enough, however, to offset the unprecedented millions of dollars spent by the Republicans, Mark Hanna's astutely managed compaign, and the army of 18,000 speakers who fanned out across the country to counteract Bryan's efforts.

Bryan was to be an important national figure for thirty more years. He ran twice more for the Presidency, served briefly as Secretary of State, helped secure the Democratic Presidential nomination for Woodrow Wilson, earned a small fortune as a Chautauqua lecturer, and, following the World War, led the fundamentalist crusade against modern science. Important though they were, these activities represented a long denouement of his career. The climax, when his speaking altered the direction of history, came in 1896, during the Democratic Convention and the Presidential campaign. At that time, his oratory awakened the conscience of the nation and prepared the way for the Progressive reforms of Theodore Roosevelt and Woodrow Wilson.

The text of the speech was taken from *Speeches of William Jennings Bryan, Revised and Arranged by Himself*, 2 Vols., Vol. I, New York: Funk and Wagnalls, 1909.

THE CROSS OF GOLD

I would be presumptuous, indeed, to present myself against the distinguished gentlemen to whom you have listened if this were a mere measuring of abilities; but this is not a contest between persons. The humblest citizen in all the land, when clad in the armor of a righteous cause, is stronger than all the hosts of error. I come to speak to you in defense of a cause as holy as the cause of liberty—the cause of humanity.

When this debate is concluded, a motion will be made to lay upon the table the resolution offered in commendation of the administration, and also the resolution offered in condemnation of the administration. We object to bringing this question down to the level of persons. The individual is but an atom; he is born, he acts, he dies; but principles are eternal; and this has been a contest over a principle.

Never before in the history of this country has there been witnessed such a contest as that through which we have just passed. Never before in the history of American politics has a great issue been fought out as this issue has been, by the voters of a great party. On the fourth of March, 1895, a few Democrats, most of them members of Congress, issued an address to the Democrats of the nation, asserting that the money question was the paramount issue of the hour; declaring that a majority of the Democratic party had the right to control the action of the party on this paramount issue; and concluding with the request that the believers in the free coinage of silver in the Democratic party should organize, take charge of, and control the policy of the Democratic party. Three months later, at Memphis, an organization was perfected, and the silver Democrats went forth openly and courageously proclaiming their belief, and declaring that, if successful, they would crystallize into a platform the declaration which they had made. Then began the conflict. With a zeal approaching the zeal which inspired the Crusaders who followed Peter the Hermit, our silver Democrats went forth from victory unto victory until they are now assembled, not to discuss, not to debate, but to enter up the judgment already rendered by the plain people of this country. In this contest brother has been arrayed against brother, father against son. The warmest ties of love, acquaintance and association have been disregarded; old leaders have been cast aside when they have refused to give expression to the sentiments of those whom they would lead, and new leaders have sprung up to give direction to this cause of truth. Thus has the contest been waged, and we have assembled here under as binding and solemn instructions as were ever imposed upon representatives of the people.

We do not come as individuals. As individuals we might have been glad to compliment the gentleman from New York [Senator Hill], but we know that the people for whom we speak would never be willing to put him in a position where he could thwart the will of the Democratic party. I say it was not a question of persons, it was a question of principle, and it is not with gladness, my friends, that we find ourselves brought into conflict with those who are now arrayed on the other side.

The gentleman who preceded me [ex-Governor Russell] spoke of the State of Massachusetts; let me assure him that not one present in all this convention entertains the least hostility to the people of the State of Massachusetts, but we stand here representing the people who are the equals, before the law, of the greatest citizens in the State of Massachusetts. When you [*turning to the gold delegates*] comes before us and tell us that we are about to disturb your business interests, we reply that you have disturbed our business interests by your course.

We say to you that you have made the definition of a business man too limited in its application. The man who is employed for wages is as much a business man as his employer, the attorney in a country town is as much a business man as the corporation counsel in a great metropolis; the merchant at the cross-roads store is as much a business man as the merchant of New York; the farmer who goes forth in the morning and toils all day—who begins in the spring and toils all summer—and who by the application of brain and muscle to the natural resources of the country creates wealth, is as much a business man as the man who goes upon the board of trade and bets upon the price of grain; the miners who go down a thousand feet into the earth, or climb two thousand feet upon the cliffs, and bring forth from their hiding places the precious metals to be poured into the channels of trade are as much business men as the few financial magnates who, in a back room, corner the money of the world. We come to speak for this broader class of business men.

Ah, my friends, we say not one word against those who live upon the

Atlantic coast, but the hardy pioneers who have braved all the dangers of the wilderness, who have made the desert to blossom as the rose—the pioneers away out there [*pointing to the West*], who rear their children near to Nature's heart, where they can mingle their voices with the voices of the birds—out there where they have erected school houses for the education of their young, churches where they praise their Creator, and cemeteries where rest the ashes of their dead—these people, we say, are as deserving of the consideration of our party as any people in this country. It is for these that we speak. We do not come as aggressors. Our war is not a war of conquest; we are fighting in the defense of our homes, our families, and posterity. We have petitioned, and our petitions have been scorned; we have entreated, and our entreaties have been disregarded; we have begged, and they have mocked when our calamity came. We beg no longer; we petition no more. We defy them.

The gentleman from Wisconsin has said that he fears a Robespierre. My friends, in this land of the free you need not fear that a tyrant will spring up from among the people. What we need is an Andrew Jackson to stand, as Jackson stood, against the encroachments of organized wealth.

They tell us that this platform was made to catch votes. We reply to them that changing conditions make new issues, that the principles on which Democracy rests are as everlasting as the hills, but that they must be applied to new conditions as they arise. Conditions have arisen, and we are here to meet those conditions. They tell us that the income tax ought not be brought in here; that it is a new idea. They criticize us for our criticism of the Supreme Court of the United States. My friends, we have not criticized; we have simply called attention to what you already know. If you want criticisms, read the dissenting opinions of the court. There you will find criticisms. They say that we passed an unconstitutional law; we deny it. The income tax law was not unconstitutional when it was passed; it was not unconstitutional when it went before the Supreme Court for the first time; it did not become unconstitutional until one of the judges changed his mind, and we cannot be expected to know when a judge will change his mind. The income tax is just. It simply intends to put the burdens of government upon the backs of the people. I am in favor of an income tax. When I find a man who is not willing to bear his share of the burdens of the government which protects him, I find a man who is unworthy to enjoy the blessings of a government like ours.

They say that we are opposing national bank currency; it is true. If you will read what Thomas Benton said, you will find he said that, in searching history, he could find but one parallel to Andrew Jackson; that was Cicero, who destroyed the conspiracy of Cataline and saved Rome. Benton said that Cicero only did for Rome what Jackson did for us when he destroyed the bank conspiracy and saved America. We say in our platform that we believe that the right to coin and issue money is a function of government. We believe it. We believe that it is a part of sovereignty, and can no more with safety be delegated to private individuals than we could afford to delegate to private individuals the power to make penal statutes or levy taxes. Mr. Jefferson, who was once regarded as good Democratic authority, seems to have differed in opinion from the gentleman who has addrest us on the part of the minority. Those who are opposed to this proposition tell us that the issue of paper money is a function of the bank, and that the Government ought to go out of the banking business. I stand with Jefferson rather than with them, and tell them, as he did, that the issue of money is a function of government, and that banks ought to go out of the governing business.

They complain about the plank which declares against life tenure in office. They have tried to strain it to mean that which it does not mean. What we oppose by that plank is the life tenure which is being built up in Washington, and which excludes from participation in official benefits the humbler members of society.

Let me call your attention to two or three important things. The gentleman from New York says that he will propose an amendment to the platform providing that the proposed change in our monetary system shall not affect contracts already made. Let me remind you that there is no intention of affecting those contracts which according to present laws are made payable in gold; but if he means to say that we cannot change our monetary system without protecting those who have loaned money before the change was made, I desire to ask him where, in law or in morals, he can find justification for not protecting the debtors when the act of 1873 was passed, if he now insists that we must protect the creditors.

He says he will also propose an amendment which will provide for the suspension of free coinage if we fail to maintain the parity within a year. We reply that when we advocate a policy which we believe will be successful, we are not compelled to raise a doubt as to our own sincerity by suggesting what we shall do if we fail. I ask him, if he would apply his logic to us, why he does not apply it to himself. He says he wants this country to try to secure an international agreement. Why does he not tell us what he is going to do if he fails to secure an international agreement? There is more reason for him to do that than there is for us to provide against the failure to maintain the parity. Our opponents have tried for twenty years to secure an international agreement, and those are waiting for it most patiently who do not want it at all.

And now, my friends, let me come to the paramount issue. If they ask us why it is that we say more on the money question than we say upon the tariff question, I reply that, if protection has slain its thousands, the gold standard has slain its tens of thousands. If they ask us why we do not embody in our platform all the things that we believe in, we reply that when we have restored the money of the Constitution all other necessary reforms will be possible; but that until this is done there is no other reform that can be accomplished.

Why is it that within three months such a change has come over the country? Three months ago, when it was confidently asserted that those who believe in the gold standard would frame our platform and nominate our candidate, even the advocates of the gold standard did not think that we could elect a President. And they had good reason for their doubt, because there is scarcely a State here today asking for the gold standard which is not in the absolute control of the Republican party. But note the change. Mr. McKinley was nominated at St. Louis upon a platform which declared for the maintenance of the gold standard until it can be changed into bimetallism by international agreement. Mr. McKinley was the most popular man among the Republicans, and three months ago everybody in the Republican party prophesied his election. How is it to-day? Why, the man who was once pleased to think that he looked like Napoleon—that man shudders to-day when he remembers that he was nominated on the anniversary of the battle of Waterloo. Not only that, but as he listens he can hear with ever-increasing distinctness the sounds of the waves as they beat upon the lonely shores of St. Helena.

Why this change? Ah, my friends, is not the reason for the change evident to any one who will look at the matter? No private character, however pure, no personal popularity, however great, can protect from the avenging wrath of an indignant people a man who will declare that he is in favor of fastening the gold standard upon this country, or who is willing to surrender the right of self-government and place the legislative control of our affairs in the hands of foreign potentates and powers.

We go forth confident that we shall win. Why? Because upon the paramount issue of this campaign there is not a spot of ground upon which the enemy will dare to challenge battle. If they tell us that the gold standard is a good thing, we shall point to their platform and tell them that their platform pledges the party to get rid of the gold standard and substitute bimetallism. If the gold standard is a good thing, why try to get rid of it? I call your attention to the fact that some of the very people who are in this convention to-day and who tell us that we ought to declare in favor of international bimetallism—thereby declaring that the gold standard is wrong and that the principle of bimetallism is better—these very people four months ago were open and avowed advocates of the gold standard, and were then telling us that we could not legislate two metals together, even with the aid of all the world. If the gold standard is a good thing, we ought to declare in favor of its retention and not in favor of abandoning it; and if the gold standard is a bad thing, why should we wait until other nations are willing to help us to let go? Here is the line of battle, and we care not upon which issue they force the fight; we are prepared to meet them on either issue or on both. If they tell us that the gold standard is the standard of civilization, we reply to them that this, the most enlightened of all the nations of the earth, has never declared for a gold standard and that both the great parties this year are declaring against it. If the gold standard is the standard of civilization, why, my friends, should we not have it? If they come to meet us on that issue we can present the history of our nation. More than that; we can tell them that they will search the pages of history in vain to find a single instance where the common people have ever declared themselves in favor of the gold standard. They can find where the holders of fixt investments have declared for a gold standard, but not where the masses have.

Mr. Carlisle said in 1878 that this was a struggle between "the idle holders of idle capital" and "the struggling masses, who produce the wealth and pay the taxes of the country"; and, my friends, the question we are to decide is: Upon which side will the Democratic party fight; upon the side of "the idle holders of idle capital" or upon the side of "the struggling masses"? That is the question which the party must answer first, and then it must be answered by each individual hereafter. The sympathies of the Democratic party, as shown by the platform, are on the side of the struggling masses who have ever been the foundation of the Democratic party. There are two ideas of government. There are those who believe that, if you will only legislate to make the well-to-do prosperous, their prosperity will leak through on those below. The Democratic idea, however, has been that if you legislate to make the masses prosperous, their prosperity will find its way up through every class which rests upon them.

You come to us and tell us that the great cities are in favor of the gold standard; we reply that the great cities rest upon our broad and fertile prairies. Burn down your cities and leave our farms, and your cities will spring up again as if by magic; but destroy our farms and the grass will grow in the streets of every city in the country.

My friends, we declare that this nation is able to legislate for its own people on every question, without waiting for the aid or consent of any other nation on earth; and upon that issue we expect to carry every State in the Union. I shall not slander the inhabitants of the fair State of Massachusetts nor the inhabitants of the State of New York by saying that, when they are confronted with the proposition, they will declare that this nation is not able to attend to its own business. It is the issue of 1776 over again. Our ancestors, when but three millions in number, had the courage to declare their political independence of every other nation; shall we, their descendants, when we have grown to seventy millions, declare that we are less independent than our forefathers? No, my friends, that will never be the verdict of our people. Therefore we care not upon what lines the battle is fought. If they say bimetallism is good, but that we cannot have it until the other nations help us, we reply that, instead of having a gold standard because England has, we will restore bimetallism, and then let England have bimetallism because the United States has it. If they dare to come out in the open field and defend the gold standard as a good thing, we will fight them to the uttermost. Having behind us the producing masses of this nation and the world, supported by the commercial interests, the laboring interests, and the toilers everywhere, we will answer their demand for a gold standard by saying to them: You shall not press down upon the brow of labor this crown of thorns, you shall not crucify mankind upon a cross of gold.

Exercises

1. Bryan's Cross of Gold speech has been criticized because it "says nothing new," "contains little solid argument," and "is highly emotionalized." In your judgment, how valid are these criticisms? Be sure to keep in mind the nature of the speaking occasion and the needs of the listeners. Bryan once wrote that "Persuasive speech is from heart to heart, not from mind to mind." What does this statement tell you about Bryan's rhetorical theories and practices?

2. One of the significant differences between Bryan's speaking and that of the other debaters at the Convention is that his words could easily be heard by the entire audience, but their words could be understood only with difficulty. Is clear and accurate enunciation as important today as formerly? Is powerful vocal projection? Explain.

3. Early in the speech, Bryan denies that silver is a sectional or class issue. Does he later appeal to sectionalism? To class animosity? If he does make such appeals, how important to the speech are they? In speaking to a highly polarized audience, do speakers frequently link their causes to lofty ideals, and then appeal to pragmatic, even selfish, motives? Would this procedure be more, or less, effective in addressing a highly favorable audience than a neutral audience? Than a hostile audience? If Bryan does not make appeals to class interests and sectionalism, would such appeals have made his speech more effective?

4. A frequently used persuasive device is to promote the transfer of emotional approval or disapproval. Thus, Bryan tries to link himself and his followers to Peter the Hermit and the Crusaders, to

Jackson, to Jefferson, to Cicero, and to Revolutionary War ancestors. Also, he attempts to associate the Republican nominee, William McKinley, with Napoleon. How successful do you think these attempts at transfer are?

5. In his efforts at persuasion, does Bryan use the "bandwagon" or "herd" technique? Does he assume the truth of his points, or does he attempt to prove their truth? Does he oversimplify? Does he appeal to prejudice? Does he reason "after the fact"? That is, does he supply reasons and evidence which will reinforce the listeners' predetermined beliefs? Or, does he provide information and logic which will enable them to think through the problem at hand? Does the following statement from Bryan help you to formulate answers to the above questions? "After an unsatisfactory opening of the debate and after our side had been pounded unmercifully by the giants of the other side, all that was necessary to success was to put into words the sentiments of a majority of the delegates to the Convention—to be the voice of a triumphant majority."

6. What is Bryan's attitude toward the opposing debaters? Is this attitude consistent, or inconsistent, with his religious nature? What are his primary methods of refutation? Compare these methods with those used by Lincoln and Douglas in speeches reported earlier in this volume.

7. A passage in this speech is reminiscent of one in Patrick Henry's "Liberty or Death" speech. Identify the passages. Which one do you prefer?

8. Evaluate Bryan's definition of a businessman. Compare his definition with that appearing in *Webster's Third New International Dictionary*. Do you consider his definition well adjusted to the audience?

9. Does Bryan's eulogy of the pioneers "who made the desert to blossom as the rose" seem a bit "hammy"? Why was it effective in the Convention? Is this sort of rhetoric heard in the political conventions of today? If so, how effective is it? If not effective, why not?

Theodore Roosevelt

"The Man with the Muck-Rake,"
delivered at the laying of the cornerstone of
the Office Building for the United States House of Representatives,
April 14, 1906

In his nearly eight years in the Presidency, Theodore Roosevelt (1858–1919) was not successful in his objectives of curbing big business or in tranquilizing the apprehensions of great segments of the people. Also, Roosevelt so dominated the reform element in the Republican Party to such an enormous extent that few liberals of stature were ready for national leadership when he retired in 1909. Furthermore, with Calvinistic faith in the divine righteousness of his cause and in the infallibility of his leadership, he led the liberal forces out of the Republican Party into a foredoomed Bull Moose Party in 1912, thereby aborting liberalism as a consequential element in the G.O.P. A capstone indictment would seem to be that of Henry Steele Commager: "Roosevelt was the instrument chosen by destiny for the implementation of a reform movement whose origins he scarcely knew, whose character he but dimly understood, whose objectives he failed to appreciate, and whose consequences he often deplored."

Despite these negative assessments, Roosevelt ranks among the great political leaders of American history. The youngest and most ebullient President, he revitalized the nation. His strident cries of alarm alerted the people to the need for vigorous action to solve the problems of the new industrial era. His sermonizing energized them to demand reforms. His promised correctives damped the smoldering radical, even revolutionary, sentiments. In the estimation of Samuel Eliot Morison, Roosevelt "was the only President since the Civil War who understood, even imperfectly, what had happened to the country in the last thirty years. . . . His place in history is that of the first of four Presidents—himself, Wilson, the other Roosevelt, and Kennedy—who worked out a coherent domestic and foreign policy to meet the realities of the twentieth century."

A borrower rather than an innovator of ideas, Roosevelt possessed a rare intuitive grasp of political strategy. He was a conservative in action who enjoyed the support of most of the business community. He was a liberal in language who won the hosannas of the reformers. He was an imperialist and moralist who stirred the fervent nationalistic and patriotic spirit of the times. He acquired a popular reputation as a trust buster, but he preached the necessity of monopolies. He exemplified arch individualism, but he advocated big government to regulate big business. He castigated Bryan as being "silly," "vicious," and a "madman," but he appropriated much of the platform of Bryan and the Populists. Realizing that the people were deeply troubled during the McKinley and Roosevelt administrations by the escalading prices, by the burgeoning trusts, by the rapid accumulation of vast fortunes, and by the siren voices of Socialists and labor leaders, Roosevelt saw that increasing numbers would come to believe in the necessity for conservative reforms. He gave direction to the national impulse for reform by selling to the people their own nascent desires for honesty in government, for regulating big business, for conserving natural resources, for carrying a big stick, and for utilizing the government to establish social justice. When asked how he achieved unprecedented support from the people, he responded: I attempted "to put into words what is in their hearts and minds but not their mouths." Although possessing the oversimplification inherent in any capsulated judgment, Roosevelt's statement explains the essence of his political success.

A correlative of his instinctive grasp of political strategy was his capacity for leadership. In his own judgment, "If I have anything at all resembling genius, it is the gift for leadership." His endless, discursive speechmaking, his ubiquity, his contagious enthusiasm, his hate for defeat, his energy and vitality, his good taste, his erudition, his warrior strain, his advocacy of the strenuous life, his voluminous and felicitous writing, his courage, his common touch, his benevolence, his homilies, his constant evangelizing—all of these facets, and many others, combined to produce a sparkling personality which was uniquely appealing to great numbers of people. As Hermann Hagedorn suggests, "He entered into men's lives, kindled fires in them, impelled them to scorn ease and safety and rejoice to do the fine, the difficult thing" and "to take a pride in their country and her welfare."

One of the more interesting examples of Roosevelt's reflection of the times is his "The Man with the Muck-Rake" speech. Claiming to fear the revolutionary cast of the writings of certain social critics, Roosevelt denounced irresponsible journalism and, in the process, preached an extended homily that included denunciations of both plutocrats and radicals.

The text of the speech is taken from Theodore Roosevelt, *Addresses and Papers,* ed. Willis Fletcher Johnson, New York: Sun Dial Press, 1908.

THE MAN WITH THE MUCK-RAKE

Over a century ago Washington laid the cornerstone of the Capitol in what was then little more than a tract of wooded wilderness here beside the Potomac. We now find it necessary to provide by great additional buildings for the business of the government. This growth in the need for the housing of the government is but a proof and example of the way in which the nation has grown and the sphere of action of the national government has grown. We now administer the affairs of a nation in which the extraordinary growth of population has been outstripped by the growth of wealth and the growth in complex interests. The material problems that face us to-day are not such as they were in Washington's time, but the underlying facts of human nature are the same now as they were then. Under altered external form we war with the same tendencies toward evil that were evident in Washington's time, and are helped by the same tendencies for good. It is about some of these that I wish to say a word to-day.

In Bunyan's "Pilgrim's Progress" you may recall the description of the Man with Muck-Rake, the man who could look no way but downward, with the muck-rake in his hand; who was offered a celestial crown for his muck-rake, but who would neither look up nor regard the crown he was offered, but continued to rake to himself the filth of the floor.

In "Pilgrim's Progress" the Man with the Muck-Rake is set forth as the example of him whose vision is fixed on carnal instead of on spiritual things. Yet he also typifies the man who in this life consistently refuses to see aught that is lofty, and fixes his eyes with solemn intentness only on that which is vile and debasing. Now, it is very necessary that we should not flinch from seeing what is vile and debasing. There is filth on the floor, and it must be scraped up with the muck-rake; and there are times and places where this service is the most needed of all the services that can be performed. But the man who never does anything else, who never thinks or speaks or writes save of his feats with the muck-rake, speedily becomes, not a help to society, not an incitement to good, but one of the most potent forces for evil.

There are in the body politic, economic and social, many and grave evils, and there is urgent necessity for the sternest war upon them. There should be relentless exposure of and attack upon every evil man, whether politician or business man, every evil practice, whether in politics, in business or in social life. I hail as a benefactor every writer or speaker, every man who, on the platform or in book, magazine or newspaper, with merciless severity makes such attack, provided always that he in his turn remembers that the attack is of use only if it is absolutely truthful. The liar is no whit better than the thief, and if his mendacity takes the form of slander he may be worse than most thieves. It puts a premium upon knavery untruthfully to attack an honest man, or even with hysterical exaggeration to assail a bad man with untruth. An epidemic of indiscriminate assault upon character does not good but very great harm. The soul of every scoundrel is gladdened whenever an honest man is assailed, or even when a scoundrel is untruthfully assailed.

Now, it is easy to twist out of shape what I have just said, easy to affect to misunderstand it, and, if it is slurred over in repetition, not difficult really to misunderstand it. Some persons are sincerely incapable of understanding that to denounce mudslinging does not mean the indorsement of whitewashing; and both the interested individuals who need whitewashing and those others who practise mudslinging like to encourage such confusion of ideas. One of the chief counts against those who make indiscriminate assault upon men in business or men in public life is that they invite a reaction which is sure to tell powerfully in favor of the unscrupulous scoundrel who really ought to be attacked, who ought to be exposed, who ought, if possible, to be put in the penitentiary. If Aristides is praised overmuch as just, people get tired of hearing it; and overcensure of the unjust finally and from similar reasons results in their favor.

Any excess is almost sure to invite a reaction, and, unfortunately, the reaction, instead of taking the form of punishment of those guilty of the excess, is very apt to take the form either of punishment of the unoffending or of giving immunity, and even strength, to offenders. The effort to make financial or political profit out of the destruction of character can only result in public calamity. Gross and reckless assaults on character—whether on the stump or in newspaper, magazine or book—create a morbid and vicious public sentiment, and at the same time act as a profound deterrent to able men of normal sensitiveness and tend to prevent them from entering the public service at any price. As an instance in point, I may mention that one serious difficulty encountered in getting the right type of men to dig the Panama Canal is the certainty that they will be exposed, both without, and, I am sorry to say, sometimes within, Congress, to utterly reckless assaults on their character and capacity.

At the risk of repetition let me say again that my plea is, not for immunity to, but for the most unsparing exposure of, the politician who betrays his trust, of the big business man who makes or spends his fortune in illegitimate or corrupt ways. There should be a resolute effort to hunt every such man out of the position he has disgraced. Expose the crime and hunt down the criminal; but remember that even in the case of crime, if it is attacked in sensational, lurid and untruthful fashion, the attack may do more damage to the public mind than the crime itself. It is because I feel that there should be no rest in the endless war against the forces of evil that I ask that the war be conducted with sanity as well as with resolution. The men with the muck-rakes are often indispensable to the well-being of society, but only if they know when to stop raking the muck, and to look upward to the celestial crown above them, to the crown of worthy endeavor. There are beautiful things above and around about them; and if they gradually grow to feel that the whole world is nothing but muck their power of usefulness is gone. If the whole picture is painted black there remains no hue whereby to single out the rascals for distinction from their fellows. Such painting finally induces a kind of moral color blindness; and people affected by it come to the conclusion that no man is really black and no man really white, but they are all gray. In other words, they neither believe in the truth of the attack nor in the honesty of the man who is attacked; they grow as suspicious of the accusation as of the offence; it becomes wellnigh hopeless to stir them either to wrath against wrongdoing or to enthusiasm for what is right; and such a mental attitude in the public gives hope to every knave, and is the despair of honest men.

To assail the great and admitted evils of our political and industrial life with such crude and sweeping generalizations as to include decent men in the general condemnation means the searing of the public conscience. There results a general attitude either of cynical belief in and indifference to public corruption or else of a distrustful inability to discriminate between the good and the bad. Either attitude is fraught with untold damage to the country as a whole. The fool who has not sense to discriminate between what is good and what is bad is wellnigh as dangerous as the man who does discriminate and yet chooses the bad. There is nothing more distressing to every good patriot, to every good American, than the hard, scoffing spirit which treats the allegation of dishonesty in a public man as a cause for laughter. Such laughter is worse than the crackling of thorns under a pot, for it denotes not merely the vacant mind, but the heart in which high emotions have been choked before they could grow to fruition.

There is any amount of good in the world, and there never was a time when loftier and more disinterested work for the betterment of mankind was being done than now. The forces that tend for evil are great and terrible, but the forces of truth and love and courage and honesty and generosity and sympathy are also stronger than ever before. It is a foolish and timid no less than a wicked thing to blink at the fact that the forces of evil are strong, but it is even worse to fail to take into account the strength of the forces that tell for good. Hysterical sensationalism is the very poorest weapon wherewith to fight for lasting righteousness. The men who with stern sobriety and truth assail the many evils of our time, whether in the public press, or in magazines, or in books, are the leaders and allies of all engaged in the work for social and political betterment. But if they give good reason for distrust of what they say, if they chill the ardor of those who demand truth as a primary virtue, they thereby betray the good cause and play into the hands of the very men against whom they are nominally at war.

In his "Ecclesiastical Polity" that fine old Elizabethan divine, Bishop Hooker, wrote:

"He that goeth about to persuade a multitude that they are not so well governed as they ought to be, shall never want attentive and favorable hearers; because they know the manifold defects whereunto every kind of regimen is subject, but the secret lets and difficulties, which in public proceedings are innumerable and inevitable, they have not ordinarily the judgment to consider."

This truth should be kept constantly in mind by every free people desiring to preserve the sanity and poise indispensable to the permanent success of self-government. Yet, on the other hand, it is vital not to permit this spirit of sanity and self-command to degenerate into mere mental stagnation. Bad though a state of hysterical excitement is, and evil though the results are which come from the violent oscillations such excitement invariably produces, yet a sodden acquiescence in evil is even worse. At this moment we are passing through a period of great unrest—social, political and industrial unrest. It is of the utmost importance for our future that this should prove to be not the unrest of mere rebelliousness against life, of mere dissatisfaction with the inevitable inequality of conditions, but the unrest of a resolute and eager ambition to secure the betterment of the individual and the nation. So far as this movement of agitation throughout the country takes the form of a fierce discontent with evil, of a determination to punish the authors of evil, whether in industry or politics, the feeling is to be heartily welcomed as a sign of healthy life.

If, on the other hand, it turns into a mere crusade of appetite against appetite, of a contest between the brutal greed of the "have-nots" and the brutal greed of the "haves," then it has no significance for good, but only for evil. If it seeks to establish a line of cleavage, not along the line which divides good men from bad, but along that other line, running at right angles thereto, which divides those who are well off from those who are less well off, then it will be fraught with immeasurable harm to the body politic.

We can no more and no less afford to condone evil in the man of capital than evil in the man of no capital. The wealthy man who exults because there is a failure of justice in the effort to bring some trust magnate to an account for his misdeeds is as bad as, and no worse than, the so-called labor leader who clamorously strives to excite a foul class feeling on behalf of some other labor leader who is implicated in murder. One attitude is as bad as the other, and no worse; in each case the accused is entitled to exact justice; and in neither case is there need of action by others which can be construed into an expression of sympathy for crime.

It is a prime necessity that if the present unrest is to result in permanent good the emotion shall be translated into action, and that the action shall be marked by honesty, sanity and self-restraint. There is mighty little good in a mere spasm of reform. The reform that counts is that which comes through steady, continuous growth; violent emotionalism leads to exhaustion.

It is important to this people to grapple with the problems connected with the amassing of enormous fortunes, and the use of those fortunes, both corporate and individual, in business. We should discriminate in the sharpest way between fortunes well won and fortunes ill won; between those gained as an incident to performing great services to the community as a whole, and those gained in evil fashion by keeping just within the limits of mere law-honesty. Of course no amount of charity in spending such fortunes in any way compensates for misconduct in making them. As a matter of personal conviction, and without pretending to discuss the details or formulate the system, I feel that we shall ultimately have to consider the adoption of some such scheme as that of a progressive tax on all fortunes, beyond a certain amount, either given in life or devised or bequeathed upon death to any individual—a tax so framed as to put it out of the power of the owner of one of these enormous fortunes to hand on more than a certain amount to any one individual; the tax, of course, to be imposed by the national and not the state government. Such taxation should, of course, be aimed merely at the inheritance or transmission in their entirety of those fortunes swollen beyond all healthy limits.

Again, the national government must in some form exercise supervision over corporations engaged in interstate business—and all large corporations are engaged in interstate business—whether by license or otherwise, so as to permit us to deal with the far-reaching evils of overcapitalization. This year we are making a beginning in the direction of serious effort to settle some of these economic problems by the railway rate legislation. Such legislation, if so framed, as I am sure it will be, as to secure definite and tangible results, will amount to something of itself; and it will amount to a great deal more in so far as it is taken as a first step in the direction of a policy of superintendence and control over corporate wealth engaged in interstate commerce, this superintendence and control not to be exercised in a spirit of malevolence toward the men who have created the wealth, but with the firm purpose both to do justice to them and to see that they in return do justice to the public at large.

The first requisite in the public servants who are to deal in this shape with corporations, whether as legislators or as executives, is honesty. This honesty can be no respecter of persons. There can be no such thing as unilateral honesty. The danger is not really from corrupt corporations; it springs from the corruption itself, whether exercised for or against corporations.

The eighth commandment reads, "Thou shalt not steal." It does not read, "Thou shalt not steal from the rich man." It does not read, "Thou shalt not steal from the poor man." It reads simply and plainly, "Thou shalt not steal." No good whatever will come from that warped and mock morality which denounces the misdeeds of men of wealth and forgets the misdeeds practised at their expense; which denounces bribery, but blinds itself to blackmail; which foams with rage if a corporation secures favors by improper methods, but merely leers with hideous mirth if the corporation is itself wronged. The only public servant who can be trusted honestly to protect the rights of the public against the misdeed of a corporation is that public man who will just as surely protect the corporation itself from wrongful aggression. If a public man is willing to yield to popular clamor and do wrong to the men of wealth or to rich corporations, it may be set down as certain that if the opportunity comes he will secretly and furtively do wrong to the public in the interest of a corporation.

But, in addition to honesty, we need sanity. No honesty will make a public man useful if that man is timid or foolish, if he is a hot-headed zealot or an impracticable visionary. As we strive for reform we find that it is not at all merely the case of a long uphill pull. On the contrary, there is almost as much of breeching work as of collar work; to depend only on traces means that there will soon be a runaway and an upset. The men of wealth who to-day are trying to prevent the regulation and control of their business in the interest of the public by the proper government authorities will not succeed, in my judgment, in checking the progress of the movement. But if they did succeed they would find that they had sown the wind and would surely reap the whirlwind, for they would ultimately provoke the violent excesses which accompany a reform coming by convulsion instead of by steady and natural growth.

On the other hand, the wild preachers of unrest and discontent, the wild agitators against the entire existing order, the men who act crookedly, whether because of sinister design or from mere puzzleheadedness, the men who preach destruction without proposing any substitute for what they intend to destroy, or who propose a substitute which would be far worse than the existing evils—all these men are the most dangerous opponents of real reform. If they get their way they will lead the people into a deeper pit than any into which they could fall under the present system. If they fail to get their way they will still do incalculable harm by provoking the kind of reaction which in its revolt against the senseless evil of their teaching would enthrone more securely than ever the very evils which their misguided followers believe they are attacking.

More important than aught else is the development of the broadest sympathy of man for man. The welfare of the wageworker, the welfare of the tiller of the soil, upon these depend the welfare of the entire country; their good is not to be sought in pulling down others; but their good must be the prime object of all our statesmanship.

Materially, we must strive to secure a broader economic opportunity for all men, so that each shall have a better chance to show the stuff of which he is made. Spiritually and ethically we must strive to bring about clean living and right thinking. We appreciate that the things of the body are important; but we appreciate also that the things of the soul are immeasurably more important. The foundation stone of national life is, and ever must be, the high individual character of the average citizen.

Exercises

1. According to George E. Mowry, "Perhaps no other single force was more responsible for the success of the progressive movement than the group of popular writers" like Ida Tarbell, Lincoln Steffens, and Upton Sinclair, who exposed the hitherto undisclosed seamy side of government, business, and society. In his private communications, in addition to the "Muck-Rake" speech, Roosevelt complained that journalists were "building up a revolutionary feeling which will most probably take the form of a political campaign." Richard Hofstadter suggests that the writers denounced by Roosevelt

"were doing far more to build up support for him among the public than they were to create a 'revolutionary feeling.'" On the basis of your background reading, would you agree with the views of Roosevelt or those of the above-mentioned historians? How do you accommodate Roosevelt's denouncing of the revolutionary strain in 1906 with his advocacy of reforms in 1910 and 1912 which were truly revolutionary for the times?

2. Rhetorical critics have tended to assume a cause-effect relationship between the "Muck-Rake" speech and the decline of sensational journalism. Can you find evidence that the wave of sensational exposés had about run its course prior to the speech and was ready to recede? If so, why did Roosevelt pick this time to speak out against the muckrakers? Why had he waited through so many months of sensationalism? The San Francisco earthquake occurred a few days after the speech was given. What influence do you suppose that this catastrophe had upon the attention given the speech? What can you learn from a study of this speech concerning the hazards of estimating the effect of a particular address?

3. One of the major differences between the approach of Roosevelt and that of Bryan and Wilson was Roosevelt's acceptance of monopolies. He did not wish to "bust" them but to convert "bad" trusts into "good" ones by government regulation. The Democrats tended to fear big business as such, and they sought to control trusts by regulation of competition. Do you find overtones of this difference of approach in the "Muck-Rake" speech? If so, why? If not, why not?

4. In the Introduction does Roosevelt proceed from the ceremonial requirements of the occasion to his theme too quickly? Too slowly? At the correct pace? Would his purpose have been better served if he had detailed some of the "tendencies toward evil" with which Washington had struggled and the means which Washington had employed to cope with them? Does the speech have a Conclusion? If so, what seems to be its purpose? Would you say that Roosevelt's final appeals are broad or narrow? Abstract or concrete? Hortatory or reflective?

5. Itemize in two parallel columns the charges which Roosevelt made against the reformist journalists and his balancing assertions that criticisms of existing evils must be welcomed and supported. Does this balanced construction give the appearance of arguing both sides at the same time? If not, why not? If so, what explanation can you give for the general tone of the speech being denunciatory?

6. Why does Roosevelt place so much dependence upon the quotations of two English writers from the seventeenth and sixteenth centuries, John Bunyan and Richard Hooker?

7. Roosevelt recognizes that his criticism of the reformers could easily be twisted and misunderstood. Can you suggest ways in which he could have done more than he did to prevent possible misunderstandings of this kind? Is his renunciation of "wild preachers of unrest and discontent" compatible with the freedom of speech and the unfettered criticism which democracy requires?

8. Outline the speech. Is there a clear progression or development of thought? Does the speech seem to turn back upon its own train again and again? Why does Roosevelt employ this method of development?

9. Compare the style of this speech with that in Roosevelt's descriptive writings, such as *Winning of the West, African Game Trails,* or *Through the Brazilian Wilderness.* Does Roosevelt speak like a writer or write like a speaker? What difference do you expect to find between oral and written discourse?

Woodrow Wilson 

"The Fourteen Points," delivered to a joint session of Congress, January 8, 1918

ON October 4, 1918, the imperial chancellor of Germany, Maximilian Wilhelm, notified President Woodrow Wilson (1856–1924): "The German government accepts the program set forth by the President of the United States in his message to Congress of January 8, 1918, and in his later pronouncements, especially his speech of September 27, as a basis for peace negotiations." Thus Wilson's "Fourteen Points" address helped to bring to a close the most destructive war the world had yet witnessed. Although the resulting treaty did not produce a "just and lasting peace," Wilson's pleas for international understanding remain unmatched for their eloquence and idealism.

The beginnings of Wilson's eloquence and idealism can be traced to his boyhood home. His rigid adherence to moral and religious principles were early instilled in him by his father, a Presbyterian minister. As early as the age of four, he was encouraged by his father to think through what he wished to say and then to express his thoughts with clarity and exactness. Long before he became an adult, felicity of expression had become a habit with him. Until the death of his father in 1903, Wilson submitted his writings to him for criticism. One of his father's admonitions that exerted a great influence upon him was, "Don't shoot at your meanings with birdshot and hit the whole countryside; shoot with a rifle at things you have to say."

Later, as a student at Princeton University and the University of Virginia, Wilson excelled in public speaking and debate. Becoming a close student of American, British, and classical orators, he practiced declaiming famous speeches and, as a sophomore contributor to the *Princetonian,* advised his classmates that, "Only as the constant companion of Demosthenes, Cicero, Burke, Fox, Canning, and Webster can we hope to become orators." After earning his Ph.D. in history and government at Johns Hopkins University, Wilson taught at Bryn Mawr, Connecticut Wesleyan, and Princeton, before being named President of Princeton in 1902. During his professorial career, Wilson's lectures and published writings were characterized by an aptness and brilliance of style that made him the most popular lecturer on campus and a nationally prominent educator. During his years as a university president, he acquired national popularity by his numerous speeches and writings on educational and political questions and, despite his crowded schedule, he maintained an active interest in collegiate debate. The Princeton professor in charge of debate later recalled that Wilson "visited us often and expressed a good many times to the students his faith in debating as a developmental force in education."

By the time Wilson entered politics as candidate for governor of New Jersey, he had developed an amazingly intimate platform manner. One of those who heard him speak at this time, a cab driver who had previously opposed his candidacy, reported: "Mr. Wilson is a man of the people. You never saw anything like it. When he speaks to you, you feel like he was going to put his finger on your nose." As Governor, and later as President of the United States, Wilson employed his skill in speaking to effect sweeping domestic reforms. After America entered the World War, Wilson's oratory was his chief means of awakening the national conscience and harnessing it to the "crusade for freedom." Placing America's intervention upon the highest moral plane, he preached the cause of justice and self-determination for all peoples, including the Central Powers. His address on the "Fourteen Points," and subsequent speeches which clarified and amplified these Points, energized the Allied people to greater efforts and weakened the resistance of the Germans.

In retrospect, it seems possible that Wilson based his appeals too restrictively upon abstract moral principles. When his idealistic utterances became obviously disparate from the materialistic performances of less worthy men, it was perhaps inevitable that the great masses forsook the dazzling preachments of individual responsibility and world citizenship and returned to their customary political apathy, isolationism, and self seeking. Nonetheless, Wilson's speaking represents the finest aspirations of the human spirit. In his address on the "Fourteen Points," America was experiencing one of her finest hours.

The text of the speech was taken from the *Congressional Record,* Vol. 56, January 8, 1918.

THE FOURTEEN POINTS

Gentlemen of the Congress: Once more, as repeatedly before, the spokesmen of the Central Empires have indicated their desire to discuss the objects of the war and the possible bases of a general peace. Parleys have been in progress at Brest-Litovsk between representatives of the Central Powers, to which the attention of all the belligerents has been invited for the purpose of ascertaining whether it may be possible to extend these parleys into a general conference with regard to terms of peace and settlement. The Russian representatives presented not only a perfectly definite statement of the principles upon which they would be willing to conclude peace but also an equally definite program of the concrete applications of those principles. The representatives of the Central Powers, on their part, presented an outline of settlement which, if much less definite, seemed susceptible of liberal interpretation until their specific program of practical terms was added. That program proposed no concessions at all either to the sovereignty of Russia or to the preferences of the populations with whose fortunes it dealt, but meant, in a word, that the Central Empires were to keep every foot of territory their armed forces had occupied,—every province, every city, every point of vantage,—as a permanent addition to their territories and their power. It is reasonable conjecture that the general principles of settlement which they at first suggested originated with the more liberal statesmen of Germany and Austria, the men who have begun to feel the force of their own peoples' thought and purpose, while the concrete terms of actual settlement came from the military leaders who have no thought but to keep what they have got. The negotiations have been broken off. The Russian representatives were sincere and in earnest. They cannot entertain such proposals of conquest and domination.

The whole incident is full of significance. It is also full of perplexity. With whom are the Russian representatives dealing? For whom are the representatives of the Central Empires speaking? Are they speaking for the majorities of their respective parliaments or for the minority parties, that military and imperialistic minority which has so far dominated their whole policy and controlled the affairs of Turkey and of the Balkan states which have felt obliged to become their associates in this war? The Russian representatives have insisted, very justly, very wisely, and in true spirit of modern democracy, that the conferences they have been holding with the Teutonic and Turkish statesmen should be held within open, not closed, doors, and all the world has been audience, as was desired. To whom have we been listening, then? To those who speak the spirit and intention of the Resolution of the German Reichstag of the ninth of July last, the spirit and intention of the liberal leaders and parties of Germany, or to those who resist and defy that spirit and intention and insist upon conquest and subjugation? Or are we listening, in fact, to both, unreconciled and in open and hopeless contradiction? These are very serious and pregnant questions. Upon the answer to them depends the peace of the world.

But, whatever the results of the parleys at Brest-Litovsk, whatever the confusions of counsel and of purpose in the utterances of the spokesmen of the Central Empires, they have again attempted to acquaint the world with their objects in the war and have again challenged their adversaries to say what their objects are and what sort of settlement they would deem just and satisfactory. There is no good reason why that challenge should not be responded to, and responded to with the utmost candor. We did not wait for it. Not once, but again and again, we have laid our whole thought and purpose before the world, not in general terms only, but each time with sufficient definition to make it clear what sort of definite terms of settlement must necessarily spring out of them. Within the last week Mr. Lloyd George has spoken with admirable candor and in admirable spirit for the people and Government of Great Britain. There is no confusion of counsel among the adversaries of the Central Powers, no uncertainty of principle, no vagueness of detail. The only secrecy of counsel, the only lack of fearless frankness, the only failure to make definite statement of the objects of the war, lies with Germany and her Allies. The issues of life and death hang upon these definitions. No statesman who has the least conception of his responsibility ought for a moment to permit himself to continue this tragical and appalling outpouring of blood and treasure unless he is sure beyond a peradventure that the objects of the vital sacrifice are part and parcel of the very life of Society and that people for whom he speaks think them right and imperative as he does.

There is, moreover, a voice calling for these definitions of principle and of purpose which is, it seems to me, more thrilling and more compelling than any of the many moving voices with which the troubled air of the world is filled. It is the voice of the Russian people. They are prostrate and all but helpless, it would seem, before the grim power of

Germany, which has hitherto known no relenting and no pity. Their power, apparently, is shattered. And yet their soul is not subservient. They will not yield either in principle or in action. Their conception of what is right, of what it is humane and honorable for them to accept, has been stated with a frankness, a largeness of view, a generosity of spirit, and a universal human sympathy which must challenge the admiration of every friend of mankind; and they have refused to compound their ideals or desert others that they themselves may be safe. They call to us to say what it is that we desire, in what, if in anything, our purpose and our spirit differ from theirs; and I believe that the people of the United States would wish me to respond, with utter simplicity and frankness. Whether their present leaders believe it or not, it is our heartfelt desire and hope that some way be opened whereby we may be privileged to assist the people of Russia to attain their utmost hope of liberty and ordered peace.

It will be our wish and purpose that the processes of peace, when they are begun, shall be absolutely open and that they shall involve and permit henceforth no secret understandings of any kind. The day of conquest and aggrandizement is gone by; so is also the day of secret covenants entered into in the interest of particular governments and likely at some unlooked-for moment to upset the peace of the world. It is this happy fact, now clear to the view of every public man whose thoughts do not still linger in an age that is dead and gone, which makes it possible for every nation whose purposes are consistent with justice and the peace of the world to avow now or at any other time the objects it has in view.

We entered this war because violations of right had occurred which touched us to the quick and made the life of our own people impossible unless they were corrected and the world secured once for all against their recurrence. What we demand in this war, therefore, is nothing peculiar to ourselves. It is that the world be made fit and safe to live in; and particularly that it be made safe for every peace-loving nation which, like our own, wishes to live its own life, determine its own institutions, be assured of justice and fair dealing by other peoples of the world as against force and selfish aggression. All the peoples of the world are in effect partners in this interest, and for our own part we see very clearly that unless justice be done to others it will not be done to us. The program of the world's peace, therefore, is our program; and that program, the only possible program as we see it, is this:

I. Open covenants of peace, openly arrived at, after which there shall be no private international understandings of any kind but diplomacy shall proceed always frankly and in the public view.

II. Absolute freedom of navigation upon the seas, outside territorial waters, alike in peace and in war, except as the seas may be closed in whole or in part by international action for the enforcement of international covenants.

III. The removal, so far as possible, of all economic barriers and the establishment of an equality of trade conditions among all the nations consenting to the peace and associating themselves for its maintenance.

IV. Adequate guarantees given and taken that national armaments will be reduced to the lowest point consistent with domestic safety.

V. A free, open-minded, and absolutely impartial adjustment of all colonial claims, based upon a strict observance of the principle that in determining all such questions of sovereignty the interests of the populations concerned must have equal weight with the equitable claims of the government whose title is to be determined.

VI. The evacuation of all Russian territory and such a settlement of all questions affecting Russia as will secure the best and freest cooperation of the other nations of the world in obtaining for her an unhampered and unembarrassed opportunity for the independent determination of her own political development and national policy and assure her of a sincere welcome into the society of free nations under institutions of her own choosing; and, more than a welcome, assistance also of every kind that she may need and may herself desire. The treatment accorded Russia by her sister nations in the months to come will be the acid test of their good will, of their comprehension of her needs as distinguished from their own interests, and of their intelligent and unselfish sympathy.

VII. Belgium, the whole world will agree, must be evacuated and restored, without any attempt to limit the sovereignty which she enjoys in common with all other free nations. No other single act will serve as this will serve to restore confidence among the nations in the laws which they have themselves set and determined for the government of their relations with one another. Without this healing act the whole structure and validity of international law is forever impaired.

VIII. All French territory should be freed and the invaded portions restored, and the wrong done to France by Prussia in 1871 in the matter of Alsace-Lorraine, which has unsettled the peace of the world for nearly fifty years, should be righted, in order that peace may once more be made secure in the interest of all.

IX. A readjustment of the frontiers of Italy should be effected along clearly recognizable lines of nationality.

X. The peoples of Austria-Hungary, whose place among the nations we wish to see safeguarded and assured, should be accorded the freest opportunity of autonomous development.

XI. Rumania, Serbia, and Montenegro should be evacuated; occupied territories restored; Serbia accorded free and secure access to the sea; and the relations of the several Balkan states to one another determined by friendly counsel along historically established lines of allegiance and nationality; and international guarantees of the political and economic independence and territorial integrity of the several Balkan states should be entered into.

XII. The Turkish portions of the present Ottoman Empire should be assured a secure sovereignty, but the other nationalities which are now under the Turkish rule should be assured an undoubted security of life and an absolutely unmolested opportunity of autonomous development, and the Dardanelles should be permanently opened as a free passage to the ships and commerce of all nations under international guarantees.

XIII. An independent Polish state should be erected which should include the territories inhabited by indisputably Polish populations, which should be assured a free and secure access to the sea, and whose political and economic independence and territorial integrity should be guaranteed by international covenant.

XIV. A general association of nations must be formed under specific covenants for the purpose of affording mutual guarantees of political independence and territorial integrity to great and small states alike.

In regard to these essential rectifications of wrong and assertions of right we feel ourselves to be intimate partners of all the governments and peoples associated together against the Imperialists. We cannot be separated in interest or divided in purpose. We stand together until the end.

For such arrangements and covenants we are willing to fight and to continue to fight until they are achieved; but only because we wish the right to prevail and desire a just and stable peace such as can be secured only by removing the chief provocations to war, which this program does remove. We have no jealousy of German greatness, and there is nothing in this program that impairs it. We grudge her no achievement or distinction of learning or of pacific enterprise such as have made her record very bright and very enviable. We do not wish to injure her or to block in any way her legitimate influence or power. We do not wish to fight her either with arms or with hostile arrangements of trade if she is willing to associate herself with us and the other peace-loving nations of the world in covenants of justice and law and fair dealing. We wish her only to accept a place of equality among the peoples of the world,—the new world in which we now live,—instead of a place of mastery.

Neither do we presume to suggest to her any alteration or modification of her institutions. But it is necessary, we must frankly say, and necessary as a preliminary to any intelligent dealings with her on our part, that we should know whom her spokesmen speak for when they speak to us, whether for the Reichstag majority or for the military party and the men whose creed is imperial domination.

We have spoken now, surely, in terms too concrete to admit of any further doubt or question. An evident principle runs through the whole program I have outlined. It is the principle of justice to all peoples and nationalities, and their right to live on equal terms of liberty and safety with one another, whether they be strong or weak. Unless this principle be made its foundation no part of the structure of international justice can stand. The people of the United States could act upon no other principle; and to the vindication of this principle they are ready to devote their lives, their honor, and everything that they possess. The moral climax of this the culminating and final war for human liberty has come, and they are ready to put their own strength, their own highest purpose, their own integrity and devotion to the test.

Exercises

1. A longtime friend of Wilson's analyzed his speechmaking in this way: "He was more a debater than an orator. His appeal was to intellect, his aim was conviction, and his ultimate purpose was to provide grounds for wise and effective conduct." On the basis of your study of the "Fourteen Points" speech, would you agree with this analysis? Does the quoted statement seem to be self contradictory? Compare the general tone of this speech with that of Bryan's "Cross of Gold" speech and Theodore Roosevelt's "The Man with the Muck-Rake" speech.

2. Wilson once wrote that the objective of speechmaking "is persuasion and conviction—the control of other minds." Would you say that this was the purpose of the Fourteen Points speech?

3. Are idealism and high moral principles primarily intellectual or emotional in character? Do they involve both emotions and intellect? Inasmuch as Wilson consistently appealed to high principles, making them the backbone of his speeches as well as his policies, were his speeches primarily appeals to the mind or to the emotions?

4. After the Armistice, Wilson was criticized as being intolerant, suspicious, and ill-tempered, and as possessing a Messianic complex. Do you find any suggestion of these alleged characteristics present in the "Fourteen Points" address?

5. Does history indicate that Wilson was right, or wrong, in making the following assertion? "There is no confusion of counsel among the adversaries of the Central Powers, no uncertainty of principle, no vagueness of detail. The only secrecy of counsel, the only lack of fearless frankness, the only failure to make definite statement of the objectives of the war, lies with Germany and her Allies." If he was wrong, should he have known the facts? If he did

not know the facts, why didn't he? If he did know the facts and they were counter to his statement, could Wilson's statement be explained as "rhetorical license"? To what extent, if any, did secret agreements among the Allies undercut the idealistic proposals of Wilson, following the Armistice?

6. Does this speech have an Introduction in the usual sense of the term? If so where does it end and the Body begin? What functions does it serve?

7. Is this speech as interesting to read as other speeches in this book? Why is this true, or not true? To what extent would the speech possess greater attention values to the actual audience in 1918?

8. In what ways does Wilson appeal to proximity and vital significance as factors of interest?

9. Why does Wilson fail to include in the "Fourteen Points" a statement of the principle of self-determinism? Is this principle inherent in several of the Points? Was this principle an unrealizable ideal at that time? Today?

10. In the speech try to find examples of the following: antithesis; repetition; restatement; personification; simile; metaphor; balanced construction; alliteration; direct question; rhetorical question; parallel construction.

11. Does the speech have a climax? If so, where does it come? Explain how the speech builds toward this peak of attention. If the speech does not have a climax, explain whether or not you believe the address would have been strengthened by such a culmination. Compare Wilson's use, or neglect, of climax with Bryan's dramatic structure of his "Cross of Gold" speech.

12. How would you characterize the style of this speech? Expository? Argumentative? Hortatory? Compare the style of the "Fourteen Points" address with that in Wilson's War Message to Congress on April 2, 1917, in his "Too Proud to Fight" speech to the Democratic Party Convention on May 11, 1915, and in his First Inaugural Address. In which does he sound most like an academic lecturer? Most like a minister? In which do you find the greatest use of "the telling phrase"? Explain your answers.

Harry Emerson Fosdick

"A Christian Conscience About War,"
Geneva, Switzerland, September 13, 1925,
in the cathedral, to audience of League of Nations delegates

HARRY Emerson Fosdick (1878–) was educated at Colgate University, Union Theological Seminary, and Columbia University. His first pastorate was the Baptist Church, Montclair, New Jersey, 1904–1915; then he preached in the Fifth Avenue Presbyterian Church, New York City, 1915–1924; for the remainder of his ministerial career he served the Riverside Church (independent Baptist), until his retirement in 1946. He was also a professor at the Union Theological Seminary, teaching homiletics (1908–1915) and practical theology (1915–1946). In 1926 he commenced broadcasting his sermons over radio and the following year NBC started carrying them nationwide on a program called National Vespers. For several years, until World War II interfered, his sermons were rebroadcast to England, Africa, New Zealand, and Australia.

In the words of an admiring Congregational minister, Edgar DeWitt Jones, Fosdick "toiled terribly" over his sermons. Every morning, for five days a week, he shut himself in his study, not even answering the telephone. His method was to think about members of his congregation until he found a problem that was real and grievous for many of them; to keep thinking until he found a solution for that problem; then to write his sermon, customarily according to a pattern that incorporated a long introduction, a fully developed first point, a moderately developed second point, a concisely stated third point, and a brief conclusion. During his preparation he read "omnivorously," for, as he said, if he were to grow in his ministry he should for every sermon topic "read every worthwhile thing that has been written in the last fifty years about it."

Although every sermon he delivered was written in full and read word for word, Fosdick sought to achieve the extemporaneous quality of "real talk." As Lionel Crocker quotes him, in "The Rhetorical Theory of Harry Emerson Fosdick," *Quarterly Journal of Speech,* 22 (April, 1936), pp. 207–213: "When a man has got hold of a real difficulty in the life and thinking of his people and is trying to meet it, he finds himself not so much dogmatically thinking for them as cooperatively thinking with them." Fosdick thought much about the techniques, especially the organization, of speaking; and he valued highly the preparation of a solidly thoughtful and informed message squarely aimed at the solution of a problem currently troubling the minds of his listeners. The exceptional clarity of his sermons was produced by lucid development, simple and direct sentence structure, careful choice of precise and familiar words, and by the uncluttered concentration upon the essence of his theme. Possibly his sermons lacked the rich pictorial quality of Phillips Brooks and the homely illustrative profusion of Henry Ward Beecher—the two earlier preachers who he felt influenced him most. There was a sparseness about the sermons of Fosdick, but this was the lean efficiency of an arrow flying straight toward its mark.

In his speech to the League of Nations delegates, Fosdick wished to impress his listeners concerning the worsening of international relations which threatened the renewal of war. France had re-occupied the German Rhineland. Germany was in deep distress economically—her currency almost valueless—and Hitler's Nazis were winning huge audiences for his preachments of hatred. In July and August of 1925, Mussolini smashed the last remnants of effective opposition to his dictatorship, including the closing of all independent newspapers in Italy. Germany was not yet a member of the League of Nations; Russia was not yet accepted as an equal by her sister nations; Japan was pressing her ruinous Twenty-five Demands upon China; the United States was withdrawn into isolationism. The Versailles Treaty had obviously failed to provide an international climate conducive to lasting peace. In addition to sensitizing his listeners to the deepening problems of international relations, Fosdick wished to persuade them that the answer to the world's problems lay in certain basic Christian truths.

The text of this sermon is taken from W. Norwood Brigance, *Classified Speech Models,* 1928, New York: Crofts, with the especial permission of the Reverend Mr. Fosdick.

A CHRISTIAN CONSCIENCE ABOUT WAR

"All they that take the sword shall perish by the sword."
(*Matthew* 26:52)

One ought to read with awe these words spoken nearly two thousand years ago and only now beginning to seem obviously true. Reliance on violence is suicidal, said Jesus. "All they that take the sword shall perish with the sword."

When the Master said that, it could not possibly have seemed to be true. Then it seemed evident that those who took the sword and knew how to use it could rule the world. Reliance on violence did not seem suicidal but necessary, salutary, and rich in its rewards. In these words of Jesus we have one of those surprising insights where, far ahead of the event, a seer perceives an obscure truth which only long afterward will emerge clear, unmistakable, imperative, so that all men must believe it.

Pythagoras in the sixth century B.C. had such a flare of insight when he guessed that the sun did not go about the earth but that the earth circled about a central fire. It was a surprising leap of intuition. No one believed it. Long centuries had to pass before Copernicus and Galileo came and people in general were convinced of what Pythagoras with his inner eye had seen. So when the Master said that the sword would destroy those who used it, that seemed incredible. War suicidal! The world did not even note this strange thing that He said, and ever since men have tried to explain it away or laugh it off as idealism too lofty for this earth. But today that insight of the Master comes to its own. Once more the seer is justified of his vision. Reliance on violence is self-defeating; war is suicidal; civilization itself cannot survive it. That fact has been written in fire across the world until not seers alone, but multitudes of plain people of every tongue, tribe, and nation under heaven are beginning to see the truth once so incredible—"If mankind does not end war, war will end mankind."

Today my plea is simple and direct. Of all the people on earth who ought to take in earnest this unforeseeable confirmation of the Master's insight, Christians come first. This question of war and its denial of the method and spirit of Jesus is peculiarly their business. Speaking from this historic Christian pulpit to Christians of many races and nations gathered here, one finds himself inevitably concerned with that matter—addressing, as it were, the conscience of Christendom about war. The destinies of humankind depend upon the arousing of that conscience. Here in Geneva you once more are setting your minds to the high task of working out the technique of international cooperation. In this sanctuary we set ourselves this morning to consider the dynamic without which all technique will fail—the conscience of Christians about war.

Doubtless we represent here many different kinds of Christianity. We belong to different Churches, hold various theories about ecclesiastical polity, subscribe to diverse creeds. But one thing does unite us all. We start with and include the Master Himself. To all of us He is the Lord and His way is the way of life. At the fountainhead of our Christianity is Jesus Christ. His life with the Father, His faith in the moral possibilities of man, His devotion to the Kingdom of Heaven on earth, His Good Samaritan, His Golden Rule, His Sermon on the Mount, His law of finding life by losing it, His insight into the self-defeating nature of violence, and His substitution of the way of love—all this is included in any special kind of Christianity we severally may profess. How, then, can any of us avoid the conviction that this colossal and ominous question of war, upon the answer to which the future of man depends, is in particular a crucial affair for Christianity? It has been said again and again that if another war befalls us and shakes civilization to its foundations, as it surely would, the Christians of the world will be to blame. Surely that is true. The continuance of war will advertise that the 576,000,000 professed Christians on earth have not had an earnest conscience about their Master's view of life; it will bear evidence that while they have called Him, "Lord, Lord," they have not been willing to do what He said.

Let us dwell, then, on some elements that ought to enter into the operation of the conscience of Christians about war.

For one thing, there is plainly the futility of war to achieve any of the purposes that Christianity is meant to serve. Indeed, there is modern war's futility to achieve any good purposes whatever. Once it was possible really to win a war. Once victors and vanquished stood in such opposite categories at a war's conclusion that there was no possibility of mistaking the prestige, prosperity, increased power and happiness of the one and the dismal annihilation of the other, but one shocking revelation of the last war was the indiscriminate ruin in which war plunged victor, vanquished, and neutrals alike, the ferocious and untamable way in which war, once let loose, tore at the garments of civilization as a whole so that, regardless of who won it, half the world found itself unclad and shivering when the storm was over.

In the history of war we have one more example of a mode of social action possibly possessing at the beginning more of good than evil, which has outgrown its good, accentuated its evil, and become at last an intolerable thing.

That was true of slavery. Men at first reduced to slavery those whom else they would have slaughtered after battle. Slavery was a substitute for massacre, profitable, doubtless, but also merciful. It was a forward step from brutal murder to enforced labor. But slavery did not retain its philanthropic good. In the end it outgrew all its benefits and became an intolerable curse. In an evolutionary world ethics and modes of social action evolve also.

So there may have been times when war could serve good ends, when armed conflict was a means of social progress. Of this war or that it may be claimed that the sword won benefactions lacking which mankind would be the poorer. At least, there is little use in arguing the contrary. For the conviction now growing strong in this generation's mind is that whatever may have been true about war in times past, modern war is futile to achieve any good or Christian thing.

To fight with the gigantic paraphernalia of modern science; to make war in our intimately inter-related and delicately balanced modern world, where our most indispensable means of existence already have become international; to fight, not with armies against armies as of old, but with entire populations massed against entire populations so that bombs rain indiscriminate destruction on whole cities and blockades mean indiscriminate starvation to millions of families; to make war now, when an average five hours of fighting, as in the last war, burns up the endowment of a great university; to fight, knowing that, agreements or no agreements to limit the weapons of war, demonic forces like gas and bacteria are certain to be used—that is obviously futile to achieve any good thing for which a Christian man might wish or pray.

The old appeals for war in the name of good cause fall coldly now on the instructed ear and cease to carry conviction to thoughtful minds. "Would you not go to war to protect the weak?" men ask. The answer seems obvious. A modern war to protect the weak—that is a grim jest. See how modern war protects the weak: 10,000,000 known dead soldiers; 3,000,000 presumed dead soldiers; 13,000,000 dead civilians; 20,000,000 wounded; 3,000,000 prisoners; 9,000,000 war orphans; 5,000,000 war widows; 10,000,000 refugees. What can we mean—modern war protecting the weak? The conviction grows clear in increasing multitudes of minds that modern war is no way to protect the weak.

A World Court would protect the weak. A League of Nations would protect the weak. An international mind, backed by a Christian conscience, that would stop the race for armaments, provide cooperative substitutes for violence, forbid the nations to resort to force, and finally outlaw war altogether—that would protect the weak. But this is clear:

war will not do it. It is the weak by millions who perish in every modern war.

As for Christianity, the dilemma which it faces in all this seems unmistakable. The war system as a recognized method of international action is one thing; Christianity with all its purposes and hopes is another; and not all the dialectic of the apologists can make the two lie down in peace together. We may have one or we may have the other, but we cannot permanently have both.

Another stake which Christianity has in this task of overpassing war and providing international substitutes for it lies in the new and ominous developments of nationalism. In our modern world nationalism, with its attendant patriotic emotions and loyalties, has increasingly taken a form which threatens to be the chief rival of Christianity. To be sure, passionate love of country is nothing modern or new. Its roots are deep in man's instincts and man's history. We here today are patriots. We intend to be patriots. We should think less of each other if we were not patriots. Love of fatherland is one of the oldest, deepest, most instinctive and most noble sentiments of man.

But within the last four hundred years nationalism has taken a new and startling form in our Western world. With the England of Elizabeth, the France of Louis XI, the Russia of Peter the Great, the development began which more and more has nationalized both the inner and the outer life of all of us. Our politics have become nationalized until the aggrandizement of one's own country in the competitive struggle with other nationalities has been the supreme aim of statesmanship. Our economic life has become nationalized; the powerful financial interests of each nation have wielded so enormous an influence over its statecraft that government, with its army and navy to back it, has frequently been a docile instrument for the furtherance of the country's economic aims. Our education has become nationalized; our children have been taught from infancy history all out of perspective, with national egoism for its organizing center and with hatred of other nations masquerading as patriotic training of the young. Even our religion has been nationalized; with state churches or without them, the center of loyalty in the religious life of the people has increasingly become the nation. Let Protestantism acknowledge its large responsibility for this in Western Christendom! In our fight for liberty we broke up the inclusive mother church into national churches; we reorganized the worship of the people around nationalistic ideals; we helped to identify religion and patriotism. And so far has that identification gone that now, when war breaks, the one God of all humanity, whom Christ came to reveal, is split up into little tribal deities, and before these pagan idols even Christians pray for the blood of their enemies.

Never before has human life, its statecraft, its economics, its education, its religion, on so large a scale been organized on a nationalistic basis, and the issue is obvious. The supreme object of devotion for multitudes is the nation. In practical action they know no higher God. They really worship Caesar. That is the limit of their loyalty. What once was said of the king is said now of the nation: it can do no wrong. And such sheer paganism is sometimes openly flaunted, at least in my country, and I presume in yours, as, "Our country! . . . may she always be in the right; but our country, right or wrong."

Nevertheless, at the same time that this nationalistic process has been going on, another movement has been gathering headway. The enlarging fellowship of human life upon this planet, which began with the clan and tribe and has moved out through ever widening circles of communication and contact, has now become explicitly and overwhelmingly international, and it never can be crowded back again. Moreover, within this unescapable internationalism of modern life, not yet adequately recognized in government, mankind has been learning one great lesson from his social experiments. In area after area he has succeeded in getting what he wanted, not by violence, but by overpassing violence and substituting cooperation. That is what social progress consists in. All social progress can be defined as carrying over one more realm of human life from the régime of force to the régime of cooperation. Wherever we have civilized any social group, the essential thing which has happened is that in that group, not force, but cooperation has become the arbiter.

That is true of the family. A household where men captured their wives, exposed their children in infancy, relied for obedience on the power of life and death over their offspring, would be recognizably uncivilized. A civilized family, with all its faults, enters into marriage by mutual consent, relies on reasonableness, not on force, for its coherence, and from the beginning welcomes children into the democracy of the household. At least we have learned that violence is no way to bring up a good family. The same path of progress we have traveled in education. Once violence ruled our schools. It was said of an old pedagogue, the Rev. James Boyer, that "it was lucky the cherubim who took him to heaven were nothing but wings and faces or he infallibly would have flogged them by the way." But now our schools at their best would be ashamed to rely on violence since reasonableness and cooperation so plainly offer, not only a more ideal, but a more effective substitute. In religion also, being civilized means traveling that road from violence to cooperation. Once force was used to compel faith. If a man wished to be a Christian he could be a Christian, but if he did not wish to be a Christian he had to be a Christian, and the centuries are sad with the horrors of religious persecution. But social progress has largely left all that behind and what compelled its supersession was not sentimentality but the insight that violence is self-defeating, that force is no way to get religion. So, too, has government been carried over from violence to cooperation. The process is lamentably incomplete, but, so far as it has gone, it has furnished the indispensable background for all the civilization we possess. Still upon our Western clothes we wear the buttons, now decorative only, on which once our fathers' swordbelts hung. How impossible it would have seemed to them that the time would ever come when the common carrying of private weapons would be unnecessary because cooperative and peaceful government had provided a substitute!

In one realm after another the Master's insight has proved true. Violence defeats itself. It is no way to achieve family life or education or religion or stable government. Those who rely on it as their mainstay and effective instrument are sure to miss what they are seeking to achieve. Always progress has consisted in carrying over human life from violence to cooperation.

And now we face the next great step, the most momentous step in human history. Can we achieve a like result with our international relationships? Can we carry them over from brutality and organized slaughter to reasonableness and cooperation? How the best thinking and praying of our time center around that hope of superseding belligerent nationalism with cooperative international substitutes for war!

Here, then, we face one of the most crucial and dramatic conflicts of loyalty that men ever dealt with. On the one side, our life has been organized as never before in history on a nationalistic basis. On the other hand, the one hope of humanity today, if it is to escape devastating ruin, lies in rising above and beyond this nationalism and organizing the world for peace. On the one side is a narrow patriotism saying, "My country against yours," on the other, a wider patriotism saying, "My country with yours for the peace of mankind." Is there any question where real Christianity must stand in that conflict? Is there any question that if she does not stand there she faces the most tragic and colossal moral failure of her history? One would like to cry so that all Christians should hear: Followers of Christ, so often straining out the gnat and swallowing the camel, tithing mint, anise, and cummin, and neglecting the weightier matters of the law, what do all the minutiae of creed and institution that distinguish us amount to in the presence of this gigantic problem in which one of the central meanings of Christ for the world is involved? A narrow belligerent nationalism is today the most explicit and thoroughgoing denial of Christianity, its thought of God and its love of man, that there is on earth.

How evident this central problem is when we try to discuss the real issues of the world today! Some still see those issues in terms of one nation against another. That is the level on which their thinking runs. America versus Japan or France versus Germany—so in a long list of nation against nation they see the world's affairs. How desperately real the problems are on that level no one needs to be told, but, after all, those are not the deepest issues. A clear conviction grows in the best thinking of today that mankind's realest conflict of interest is not between this nation and that, but between the forward-looking, progressive, open-minded people of all nations, who have caught a vision of humanity organized for peace, and the backward-looking, reactionary, militaristic people of the same nations. The deepest line of conflict does not run vertically between the nations; it runs horizontally through all the nations. The salvation of humanity from self-destruction depends on which side of that conflict wins.

What has happened thus to make a local, national patriotism, however sacred and beautiful in many of its forms, inadequate to meet our present need is clear. In unforgettable words the world has been told by a great patriot: "Patriotism is not enough." Why is it not enough? Well, patriotism once took men of little, local loyalties and expanded their outlook and allegiance. They had been citizens of a shire; patriotism made them citizens of a nation. Patriotism once called men to the widest imaginable outreach of their devotion; it broke down local provincialisms; it stretched human horizons; it demanded unaccustomed breadth of vision and unselfishness of life. To be a patriot for the nation meant a large loyalty as against the meanness and parochialism of a local mind. But the world has moved. Life has expanded and become international. Now it is possible for patriotism to fall from its high estate. Instead of calling men to wider horizons, it can keep them within narrow ones. Once the issue was patriotism versus a small parochialism; now the question may become patriotism versus a large care for humanity. Once patriotism was the great enemy of provincialism; now it can be made to mean provincialism and to sanctify the narrow mind.

This conflict of loyalties creates your difficult problems here in Geneva. You know how tenacious the adhesions of nationalism are, how difficult to entwine the thoughts and affections of men around new ideals and new methods of world peace. But this inner struggle between two loyalties goes deeper than the realm of statesmanship; it runs far down into the souls of men where the destinies of religion lie. How can a man be a follower of Jesus Christ and still be a belligerent nationalist, when once this better hope of a world organized for peace has dawned upon his view? Whatever else Christianity may believe in, it must believe in God, Father of all men; it must believe in men of every tribe, tongue, people, and nation, as God's children; it must believe in the Kingdom of God on earth. The spirit of Christianity is not narrowly nationalistic, but universally inclusive. When the world, therefore, organizes itself on the basis of belligerent nationalism the very genius of the Christian Gospel is at stake. Once more we can have our old war systems with their appalling modern developments, or we can have Christianity, but we cannot permanently have both. They worship irreconcilable gods.

I need not, and I must not, press the analysis further. Two generations ago one of our great statesmen, Charles Sumner, said, "Not that I love country less, but Humanity more, do I now and here plead the cause of a higher and truer patriotism. I cannot forget that we are men by a more sacred bond than we are citizens—that we are children of a common Father more than we are Americans." Shall not each one of us here pray for his own country, as I pray earnestly for mine, that that spirit may come into the ascendency? Christianity essentially involves it.

The first Christians saw this. "The early Christian Church," says a recent writer, "was the first peace society." Then came Christianity's growing power—the days when Christians, no longer outcast, were stronger than their adversaries, until at last the imperial household of Constantine himself accepted Christianity. Then Christianity, joined with the state, forgot its earlier attitudes, bowed to the necessities of imperial action, became sponsor for war, blesser of war, cause of war, fighter of war. Since then the Church has come down through history too often trying to carry the cross of Jesus in one hand and a dripping sword in the other, until now when Christians look out upon the consequence of it all, this abysmal disgrace of Christendom making mockery of the Gospel, the conviction rises that we would better go back to our first traditions, our early purity, and see whether those first disciples of the Lord were not nearer right than we have been.

We cannot reconcile Jesus Christ and war—that is the essence of the matter. That is the challenge which today should stir the conscience of Christendom. War is the most colossal and ruinous social sin that afflicts mankind; it is utterly and irremediably unchristian; in its total method and effect it means everything that Jesus did not mean and it means nothing that He did mean; it is a more blatant denial of every Christian doctrine about God and man than all the theoretical atheists on earth ever could devise. It would be worth while, would it not, to see the Christian Church claim as her own this greatest moral issue of our time, to see her lift once more, as in our fathers' days, a clear standard against the paganism of this present world and, refusing to hold her conscience at the beck and call of belligerent states, put the Kingdom of God above nationalism and call the world to peace? That would not be the denial of patriotism but its apotheosis.

Here today, as an American, under this high and hospitable roof, I cannot speak for my government, but both as an American, and as a

Christian I do speak for millions of my fellow citizens in wishing your great work, in which we believe, for which we pray, our absence from which we painfully regret, the eminent success which it deserves. We work in many ways for the same end—a world organized for peace. Never was an end better worth working for. The alternative is the most appalling catastrophe mankind has ever faced. Like gravitation in the physical realm, the law of the Lord in the moral realm bends for no man and no nation: "All they that take the sword shall perish with the sword."

Exercises

1. Analyze this sermon in terms of Fosdick's own description of his methods in Charles A. McGlon, "How I prepare my Sermons: A Symposium," *Quarterly Journal of Speech,* 40 (Feb., 1954), pp. 50–52; and Gilbert Stillman McVaugh, "Structural Analysis of the Sermons of Dr. Harry Emerson Fosdick," *Quarterly Journal of Speech,* 18 (Nov., 1932), pp. 531–546. Does this sermon illustrate the organizational plan described in both articles? Does it illustrate Dr. Fosdick's general plan of building a sermon around a problem that is real to his listeners? Does he try to solve their problems in ways that seem realistic to them? Defend your answer.

2. Fosdick's principal mode of proof in this sermon is the generous use of general illustrations. What is a general illustration? Identify as many as you can in this sermon. How does he relate them to his theme?

3. What is the theme of this sermon? Its purpose? What main ideas support the purpose? What does he attempt to accomplish in his Introduction; in the Conclusion?

4. Describe and give examples of the stylistic attributes of this sermon—and illustrate them with passages from it.

5. For each of the following quotations from the sermon, discuss its pertinence in terms of what has happened in world history since 1925:

   a) "The supreme object of devotion for multitudes is the nation."
   b) "The deepest line of conflict does not run vertically between the nations; it runs horizontally through all the nations."
   c) "War is the most colossal and ruinous social sin that afflicts mankind."

6. In terms of the relations of nations holding many diverse religious faiths, evaluate Fosdick's point that the destinies of mankind depend upon the arousal of the Christian conscience.

7. Evaluate the contrast used by Fosdick in his point that patriotism once served a useful purpose, now serves a harmful one. If he is right, what is the remedy? If he is wrong, wherein is his error?

8. Fosdick's quotation from Charles Sumner is from Sumner's speech, "The True Grandeur of Nations," delivered on July 4, 1845. (Sumner's speech is found in his *Addresses on War* [Boston: Ginn and Co., 1902].) Read the account of that speech in Robert T. Oliver's *History of Public Speaking in America*, pp. 261–262. Then read Sumner's speech. Compare the reasoning, the style, the persuasive appeal of Fosdick and Sumner. Evaluate the comparative merit of their proposed solutions. Can you propose a more practical solution than did either speaker? Is there a solution?

9. In the light of events in recent years, evaluate Fosdick's assertion that "within the last four hundred years nationalism has taken a new and startling form in our Western world."

10. Evaluate Fosdick's assertion that "the Church has come down through history too often trying to carry the cross of Jesus in one hand and a dripping sword in the other."

11. Both Fosdick and Sumner appealed for pacifism in a time of peace. Contrast their persuasive problem and their persuasive strategy with the problem confronted by Senator Thomas Corwin when he spoke in the United States Senate on February 11, 1847, excoriating the war with Mexico, and with the methods of persuasion employed by Corwin. (Corwin's speech is available in *Life and Speeches of Thomas Corwin*, ed. Josiah Morrow [Cincinnati: W. H. Anderson, 1896].)

12. From the speeches by Fosdick, Sumner, and Corwin, illustrate possible meanings in the famous comment by Dr. Samuel Johnson that "Patriotism is the last refuge of a scoundrel."

13. Reconsider the arguments of these three pacifistic speakers in terms of Woodrow Wilson's address to the Congress on April 2, 1917, calling for a Declaration of War against Germany.

Franklin D. Roosevelt

"The Arsenal of Democracy," given over nation-wide radio, December 29, 1940

THE key to Franklin D. Roosevelt's (1882–1945) influence is provided by his last words, written for a Jefferson Day address he would not live to present: "The only limit to our realization of tomorrow will be our doubts of today. Let us move forward with strong and active faith." Few historians allege that he was a superbly gifted administrator or a deeply profound thinker. Nor was he an idealist in the likeness of Woodrow Wilson. Nevertheless, he was a great President both in peace and in war. His genius lay in his ability to lead and to inspire. He stressed always the affirmative. He sought always the attainable. With a richness of imagination, an astute sense of political timing, a perceptive feel for apt expression, and a sure instinct for tapping the wellsprings of popular support, he was able to shape American history—and the destiny of the world.

During his first campaign for President, Roosevelt explained his conception of political leadership: "Government includes the art of formulating a policy and using the political technique to attain so much of that policy as will receive general support; persuading, leading, sacrificing, teaching always, because the greatest duty of a statesman is to educate." Far more than any President before him, Roosevelt relied upon the spoken word as a means of educating others. Radio carried his voice hundreds of times into the nation's homes. So many millions of persons listened to his fireside chats on Sunday evenings that he was forced to select another time for such broadcasts—ministers were complaining about depleted church attendance. In his speaking, Roosevelt followed a simple formula for helping the people to identify themselves with his policies. Everyone, he would explain, was engaged in the common effort; his voice was merely the expression of the hopes and desires of the people; national needs were based upon personal needs; the individual was not a cipher—no matter how poor he might be, he possessed dignity and a just share in the opportunities and benefits of society. Those who opposed Rooseveltian policies were characterized either directly or indirectly as enemies of the public welfare. Domestic and international problems were clearly and eloquently stated. The solutions frequently were deficient in logical support and fuzzy in detail, but they always seemed obtainable and were always persuasively optimistic. The depression could be conquered, the war could be won, the world could be made a better place. The projection of personal warmth, of understanding compassion, of a willingness to try new answers, of a drive to accomplish great things, and of the jaunty verve of a man in love with living gave to his speaking an uplifting thrust that was exhilarating.

Few of those who identified their aspirations with Roosevelt's policies cared that he was born to great wealth and family influence, that he had been educated at exclusive Groton and at Harvard University, or that he had never been hungry or had never experienced failure. They knew and cared that, although he could not stand without support, his spirit had triumphed radiantly over the braces on his legs. They knew that he understood them and that he cared about them. He could be trusted with their hopes and their faith. For better or for worse, he led the people out of the Great Depression and into a new world of government determinism. For results not yet assessible, he led the nation from isolation into war and, finally, to the shores of peace. Throughout his twelve epochal Presidential years, Roosevelt's spoken eloquence was his chief means of leadership.

In Roosevelt's judgment, his most important speech between 1933 and 1941 was the Arsenal of Democracy fireside chat on December 29, 1940. Re-elected in November of that year by a substantial majority, he believed that most Americans would support greater involvement in the War if the issues were made clear to them. Roosevelt's estimation of the success of this speech was supported by the mail response, which was greater than for any other speech since his First Inaugural. Early in January 1941, Roosevelt sent to Congress a program for the establishment of Lend-Lease. Its passage ended any pretensions to neutrality and ordained America's eventual entry into the War.

The text is taken from the *New York Times*, December 30, 1940, © 1940 by The New York Times Company, and reprinted by permission.

THE ARSENAL OF DEMOCRACY

My friends: This is not a fireside chat on war. It is a talk on national security; because the nub of the whole purpose of your President is to keep you now, and your children later, and your grandchildren much later, out of a last-ditch war for the preservation of American independence and all of the things that American independence means to you and to me and to ours.

Tonight, in the presence of a world crisis, my mind goes back eight years to a night in the midst of a domestic crisis. It was a time when the wheels of American industry were grinding to a full stop, when the whole banking system of our country had ceased to function.

I well remember that while I sat in my study in the White House, preparing to talk with the people of the United States, I had before my eyes the picture of all those Americans with whom I was talking. I saw the workmen in the mills, the mines, the factories; the girl behind the counter; the small shopkeeper; the farmer doing his Spring plowing; the widows and the old men wondering about their life's savings.

I tried to convey to the great mass of American people what the banking crisis meant to them in their daily lives.

Tonight I want to do the same thing, with the same people, in this new crisis which faces America.

We met the issue of 1933 with courage and realism. We face this new crisis—this new threat to the security of our nation—with the same courage and realism.

Never before since Jamestown and Plymouth Rock has our American civilization been in such danger as now.

For on September 27, 1940—this year—by an agreement signed in Berlin, three powerful nations, two in Europe and one in Asia, joined themselves together in the threat that if the United States of America interfered with or blocked the expansion program of these three nations—a program aimed at world control—they would unite in ultimate action against the United States.

The Nazi masters of Germany have made it clear that they intend not only to dominate all life and thought in their own country, but also to enslave the whole of Europe, and then to use the resources of Europe to dominate the rest of the world.

It was only three weeks ago that their leader stated this: "There are two worlds that stand opposed to each other." And then in defiant reply to his opponents he said this: "Others are correct when they say: 'With this world we cannot ever reconcile ourselves.' . . . I can beat any other power in the world." So said the leader of the Nazis.

In other words, the Axis not merely admits but the Axis proclaims that there can be no ultimate peace between their philosophy—their philosophy of government—and our philosophy of government.

In view of the nature of this undeniable threat, it can be asserted, properly and categorically, that the United States has no right or reason to encourage talk of peace until the day shall come when there is a clear intention on the part of the aggressor nations to abandon all thought of dominating or conquering the world.

At this moment the forces of the States that are leagued against all peoples who live in freedom are being held away from our shores. The Germans and the Italians are being blocked on the other side of the Atlantic by the British and by the Greeks, and by thousands of soldiers and sailors who were able to escape from subjugated countries. In Asia the Japanese are being engaged by the Chinese nation in another great defense.

In the Pacific Ocean is our fleet.

Some of our people like to believe that wars in Europe and in Asia are of no concern to us. But it is a matter of most vital concern to us that European and Asiatic war-makers should not gain control of the oceans which lead to this hemisphere.

One hundred and seventeen years ago the Monroe Doctrine was conceived by our government as a measure of defense in the face of a threat against this hemisphere by an alliance in Continental Europe. Thereafter, we stood guard in the Atlantic, with the British as neighbors. There was no treaty. There was no "unwritten agreement."

And yet there was the feeling, proven correct by history, that we as neighbors could settle any disputes in peaceful fashion. And the fact is that during the whole of this time the Western Hemisphere has remained free from aggression from Europe or from Asia.

Does any one seriously believe that we need to fear attack anywhere in the Americas while a free Britain remains our most powerful naval neighbor in the Atlantic? And does any one seriously believe, on the other hand, that we could rest easy if the Axis powers were our neighbors there?

If Great Britain goes down, the Axis powers will control the Continents of Europe, Asia, Africa, Australasia, and the high seas—and they will be in a position to bring enormous military and naval resources against this hemisphere. It is no exaggeration to say that all of us in all the Americas would be living at the point of a gun—a gun loaded with explosive bullets, economic as well as military.

We should enter upon a new and terrible era in which the whole world, our hemisphere included, would be run by threats of brute force. And to survive in such a world, we would have to convert ourselves permanently into a militaristic power on the basis of war economy.

Some of us like to believe that even if Britain falls, we are still safe, because of the broad expanse of the Atlantic and of the Pacific.

But the width of those oceans is not what it was in the days of clipper ships. At one point between Africa and Brazil the distance is less than it is from Washington to Denver, Colorado, five hours for the latest type of bomber. And at the north end of the Pacific Ocean, America and Asia almost touch each other.

Why, even today we have planes that could fly from the British Isles to New England and back again without refueling. And remember that the range of the modern bomber is ever being increased.

During the past week many people in all parts of the nation have told me what they wanted me to say tonight. Almost all of them expressed a courageous desire to hear the plain truth about the gravity of the situation. One telegram, however, expressed the attitude of the small minority who want to see no evil and hear no evil, even though they know in their hearts that evil exists. That telegram begged me not to tell again of the ease with which our American cities could be bombed by any hostile power which had gained bases in this Western Hemisphere. The gist of that telegram was: "Please, Mr. President, don't frighten us by telling us the facts."

Frankly and definitely there is danger ahead—danger against which we must prepare. But we well know that we cannot escape danger, or the fear of danger, by crawling into bed and pulling the covers over our heads.

Some nations of Europe were bound by solemn nonintervention pacts with Germany. Other nations were assured by Germany that they need never fear invasion. Nonintervention pact or not, the fact remains that they were attacked, overrun, thrown into modern slavery at an hour's notice or even without any notice at all.

As an exiled leader of one of these nations said to me the other day, "the notice was a minus quantity. It was given to my government two hours after German troops had poured into my country in a hundred places." The fate of these nations tells us what it means to live at the point of a Nazi gun.

The Nazis have justified such actions by various pious frauds. One of these frauds is the claim that they are occupying a nation for the purpose of "restoring order." Another is that they are occupying or controlling a nation on the excuse that they are "protecting it" against the aggression of somebody else.

For example, Germany has said that she was occupying Belgium to save the Belgians from the British. Would she then hesitate to say to any South American country: "We are occupying you to protect you from aggression by the United States"?

Belgium today is being used as an invasion base against Britain, now fighting for its life. And any South American country, in Nazi hands, would always constitute a jumping off place for German attack on any one of the other republics of this hemisphere.

Analyze for yourselves the future of two other places even nearer to Germany if the Nazis won. Could Ireland hold out? Would Irish freedom be permitted as an amazing pet exception in an unfree world? Or the islands of the Azores, which still fly the flag of Portugal after five centuries? You and I think of Hawaii as an outpost of defense in the Pacific. And yet the Azores are closer to our shores in the Atlantic than Hawaii is on the other side.

There are those who say that the Axis powers would never have any desire to attack the Western Hemisphere. That is the same dangerous form of wishful thinking which has destroyed the powers of resistance of so many conquered peoples. The plain facts are that the Nazis have proclaimed, time and again, that all other races are their inferiors and therefore subject to their orders. And most important of all, the vast resources and wealth of this American hemisphere constitute the most tempting loot in all of the round world.

Let us no longer blind ourselves to the undeniable fact that the evil forces which have crushed and undermined and corrupted so many others are already within our own gates. Your government knows much about them and every day is ferreting them out.

Their secret emissaries are active in our own and in neighboring countries. They seek to stir up suspicion and dissension, to cause internal strife. They try to turn capital against labor, and vice versa. They try to reawaken long slumbering racial and religious enmities which should have no place in this country. They are active in every group that promotes intolerance. They exploit for their own ends our own natural abhorrence of war.

These trouble-breeders have but one purpose. It is to divide our people, to divide them into hostile groups and to destroy our unity and shatter our will to defend ourselves.

There are also American citizens, many of them in high places, who, unwittingly in most cases, are aiding and abetting the work of these agents. I do not charge these American citizens with being foreign agents. But I do charge them with doing exactly the kind of work that the dictators want done in the United States.

These people not only believe that we can save our own skins by shutting our eyes to the fate of other nations. Some of them go much further than that. They say that we can and should become the friends and even the partners of the Axis powers. Some of them even suggest that we should imitate the methods of the dictatorships. But Americans never can and never will do that.

The experience of the past two years has proven beyond doubt that no nation can appease the Nazis. No man can tame a tiger into a kitten by stroking it. There can be no appeasement with ruthlessness. There can be no reasoning with an incendiary bomb. We know now that a nation can have peace with the Nazis only at the price of total surrender.

Even the people of Italy have been forced to become accomplices of the Nazis; but at this moment they do not know how soon they will be embraced to death by their allies.

The American appeasers ignore the warning to be found in the fate of Austria, Czechoslovakia, Poland, Norway, Belgium, the Netherlands, Denmark and France. They tell you that the Axis powers are going to win anyway; that all of this bloodshed in the world could be saved, that the United States might just as well throw its influence into the scale of a dictated peace and get the best out of it that we can.

They call it a "negotiated peace." Nonsense! Is it a negotiated peace if a gang of outlaws surrounds your community and on threat of extermination makes you pay tribute to save your own skins?

Such a dictated peace would be no peace at all. It would be only another armistice, leading to the most gigantic armament race and the most devastating trade wars in all history. And in these contests the Americas would offer the only real resistance to the Axis powers. With all their vaunted efficiency, with all their parade of pious purpose in this war, there are still in their background the concentration camp and the servants of God in chains.

The history of recent years proves that the shootings and the chains and the concentration camps are not simply the transient tools but the very altars of modern dictatorships. They may talk of a "new order" in the world, but what they have in mind is only a revival of the oldest and worst tyranny. In that there is no liberty, no religion, no hope.

The proposed "new order" is the very opposite of a United States of Europe or a United States of Asia. It is not a government based upon the consent of the governed. It is not a union of ordinary, self-respecting men and women to protect themselves and their freedom and their dignity from oppression. It is an unholy alliance of power and pelf to dominate and to enslave the human race.

The British people and their allies today are conducting an active war against this unholy alliance. Our own future security is greatly dependent on the outcome of that fight. Our ability to "keep out of war" is going to be affected by that outcome.

Thinking in terms of today and tomorrow, I make the direct statement to the American people that there is far less chance of the United States getting into war if we do all we can now to support the nations defending themselves against attack by the Axis than if we acquiesce in their defeat, submit tamely to an Axis victory, and wait our turn to be the object of attack in another war later on.

If we are to be completely honest with ourselves, we must admit that there is risk in any course we may take. But I deeply believe that the great majority of our people agree that the course that I advocate involves the least risk now and the greatest hope for world peace in the future.

The people of Europe who are defending themselves do not ask us to do their fighting. They ask us for the implements of war, the planes, the tanks, the guns, the freighters which will enable them to fight for their liberty and for our security. Emphatically we must get these weapons to them, get them to them in sufficient volume and quickly enough so that we and our children will be saved the agony and suffering of war which others have had to endure.

Let not the defeatists tell us that it is too late. It will never be earlier. Tomorrow will be later than today.

Certain facts are self-evident.

In a military sense Great Britain and the British Empire are today the spearhead of resistance to world conquest. And they are putting up a fight which will live forever in the story of human gallantry.

There is no demand for sending an American expeditionary force outside our own borders. There is no intention by any member of your government to send such a force. You can, therefore, nail, nail any talk about sending armies to Europe as deliberate untruth.

Our national policy is not directed toward war. Its sole purpose is to keep war away from our country and away from our people.

Democracy's fight against world conquest is being greatly aided, and must be more greatly aided, by the rearmament of the United States and by sending every ounce and every ton of munitions and supplies that we can possibly spare to help the defenders who are in the front lines. And it is no more unneutral for us to do that than it is for Sweden, Russia and other nations near Germany to send steel and ore and oil and other war materials into Germany every day in the week.

We are planning our own defense with the utmost urgency, and in its vast scale we must integrate the war needs of Britain and the other free nations which are resisting aggression.

This is not a matter of sentiment or of controversial personal opinion. It is a matter of realistic, practical military policy, based on the advice of our military experts who are in close touch with existing warfare. These military and naval experts and the members of the Congress and the Administration have a single-minded purpose—the defense of the United States.

This nation is making a great effort to produce everything that is necessary in this emergency—and with all possible speed. And this great effort requires great sacrifice.

I would ask no one to defend a democracy which in turn would not defend every one in the nation against want and privation. The strength of this nation shall not be diluted by the failure of the government to protect the economic well-being of its citizens.

If our capacity to produce is limited by machines, it must ever be remembered that these machines are operated by the skill and the stamina of the workers. As the government is determined to protect the rights of the workers, so the nation has a right to expect that the men who man the machines will discharge their full responsibilities to the urgent needs of defense.

The worker possesses the same human dignity and is entitled to the same security of position as the engineer or the manager or the owner. For the workers provide the human power that turns out the destroyers, and the planes and the tanks.

The nation expects our defense industries to continue operation without interruption by strikes or lockouts. It expects and insists that management and workers will reconcile their differences by voluntary or legal means, to continue to produce the supplies that are so sorely needed.

And on the economic side of our great defense program, we are, as you know, bending every effort to maintain stability of prices and with that the stability of the cost of living.

Nine days ago I announced the setting up of a more effective organization to direct our gigantic efforts to increase the production of munitions. The appropriation of vast sums of money and a well-coordinated executive direction of our defense efforts are not in themselves enough. Guns, planes, ships and many other things have to be built in the factories and the arsenals of America. They have to be produced by workers and managers and engineers with the aid of machines which in turn have to be built by hundreds of thousands of workers throughout the land.

In this great work there has been splendid cooperation between the government and industry and labor. And I am very thankful.

American industrial genius, unmatched throughout all the world in the solution of production problems, has been called upon to bring its resources and its talents into action. Manufacturers of watches, of farm implements, of linotypes and cash registers and automobiles, and sewing machines and lawn mowers and locomotives, are now making fuses and bomb packing crates and telescope mounts and shells and pistols and tanks.

But all of our present efforts are not enough. We must have more ships, more guns, more planes—more of everything. And this can be accomplished only if we discard the notion of "business as usual." This job cannot be done merely by superimposing on the existing productive facilities the added requirements of the nation for defense.

Our defense efforts must not be blocked by those who fear the future consequences of surplus plant capacity. The possible consequences of failure of our defense efforts now are much more to be feared.

And after the present needs of our defense are past, a proper handling of the country's peacetime needs will require all of the new productive capacity, if not still more.

No pessimistic policy about the future of America shall delay the immediate expansion of those industries essential to defense. We need them.

I want to make it clear that it is the purpose of the nation to build now with all possible speed every machine, every arsenal, every factory that we need to manufacture our defense material. We have the men—the skill—the wealth—and above all, the will.

I am confident that if and when production of consumer or luxury goods in certain industries requires the use of machines and raw materials that are essential for defense purposes, then such production must yield, and will gladly yield, to our primary and compelling purpose.

So I appeal to the owners of plants—to the managers—to the workers—to our own government employes—to put every ounce of effort into producing these munitions swiftly and without stint. With this appeal I give you the pledge that all of us who are officers of your government will devote ourselves to the same whole-hearted extent to the great task that lies ahead.

As planes and ships and guns and shells are produced, your government, with its defense experts, can then determine how best to use them to defend this hemisphere. The decision as to how much shall be sent abroad and how much shall remain at home must be made on the basis of our overall military necessities.

We must be the great arsenal of democracy. For us this is an emergency as serious as war itself. We must apply ourselves to our task with the same resolution, the same sense of urgency, the same spirit of patriotism and sacrifice as we would show were we at war.

We have furnished the British great material support and we will furnish far more in the future.

There will be no "bottlenecks" in our determination to aid Great Britain. No dictator, no combination of dictators, will weaken that determination by threats of how they will construe that determination.

The British have received invaluable military support from the heroic Greek Army and from the forces of all the governments in exile. Their strength is growing. It is the strength of men and women who value their freedom more highly than they value their lives.

I believe that the Axis powers are not going to win this war. I base that belief on the latest and best of information.

We have no excuse for defeatism. We have every good reason for hope—hope for peace, yes, and hope for the defense of our civilization and for the building of a better civilization in the future.

I have the profound conviction that the American people are now determined to put forth a mightier effort than they have ever yet made to increase our production of all the implements of defense, to meet the threat to our democratic faith.

As President of the United States, I call for that national effort. I call for it in the name of this nation which we love and honor and which we are privileged and proud to serve. I call upon our people with absolute confidence that our common cause will greatly succeed.

Exercises

1. Why does Roosevelt begin with a deliberately negative statement? Why does Roosevelt refer to the earlier domestic crisis? What appeals to personal proof does he make in the Introduction? Is there a clear division between the Introduction and the Body?

2. Carefully outline the entire speech. Does the organizational structure provide for suitable emphasis, coherence, and unity? Is the speech more, or less, tightly packed than other speeches in this book?

3. How does Roosevelt prepare the listeners for his refutation of critics? What are his chief means of discounting the critics? To what extent does he use deduction? Induction? Causal argument? Personal proof? Emotional proof? Does he attempt to prove by logical argument? Does he assert the truth of his position and then explain or clarify it? Does this process seem to "prove" without actually doing

so? Why was Roosevelt so emphatic in denying that American forces would be sent outside the country?

4. Adolph A. Berle, Jr., says that Roosevelt designed his radio speeches to offer "some definite appeal to every class or group of people." To what classes does Roosevelt appeal in this speech? To what lengths does he go to assure each group that its interests are receiving, and will receive, proper attention? To praise each for its current and past efforts? To urge each to greater efforts and cooperation? Do these appeals seem bald? Contrived? Natural?

5. According to Robert Sherwood, in order to "hearten the people who are doing the fighting," Roosevelt included the sentences, "I believe that the Axis powers are not going to win this war. I base that belief on the latest and best information." Sherwood learned later from Harry Hopkins that this information "was no more than Roosevelt's own private confidence that Lend-Lease . . . would make Axis victory impossible." Do you believe that this constituted a legitimate use of "rhetorical license"?

6. In the continuum between extremely simple and extremely complex style, where would you place the style of Roosevelt? Do you find any sentences in the speech that would not be clear to a somewhat dull adult? Does the simplicity of style ever "insult" your intelligence? Why does Roosevelt use so many short paragraphs? How does the average sentence length compare with that in other speeches in this collection? Using Thorndike's *Teacher's Word Book of 20,000 Words*, estimate the percent of words in this speech which are in the first 500 most commonly used words. In the first 5,000 words.

7. Roosevelt delighted in using tired, familiar figures in fresh, new ways. Explain how he achieved maximum persuasive effect by using the following figures: ". . . we cannot escape danger . . . by crawling into bed and pulling the covers over our heads." ". . . the small minority who want to see no evil and hear no evil. . . ." "No man can tame a tiger into a kitten by stroking it." Find other examples of figurative language in the speech.

8. Roosevelt and his speech writers planned each sentence for maximum oral effect. Study each sentence to estimate why he used the particular choice of words, of sentence construction, of types of imagery, and of motive appeals.

9. Does this speech contain a greater, or lesser, use of personal pronouns than the speeches in this volume by Kennedy, Wilson, Truman, and Bryan?

10. The key phrase "We must be the great arsenal of democracy" was borrowed from a newspaper editorial and suggested to the President by Harry Hopkins. Roosevelt had much help on this and all of his other speeches. How ethical is the practice of ghostwriting? To what extent is it necessary? To what degree is it used more, or less, by modern Presidents than by Lincoln, Jefferson, and Washington?

Harry S. Truman

"Acceptance Speech," delivered at the Democratic Party National Convention, July 15, 1948

No other President ever assumed such awesome responsibilities upon such abrupt notice as did Harry S. Truman (1884–). Almost universally deprecated as "the commonplace man in a grey fedora" when he entered office, Mr. Truman soon demonstrated that he was an exceptionally unaverage Chief Executive. His seven years as President were years of crises. In swift succession came the San Francisco Conference and the creation of the United Nations, the atomic destruction of Hiroshima and Nagasaki, the Truman Doctrine, the Marshall Plan, the birth of NATO, the development of the hydrogen bomb, Korea, the dismissal of General MacArthur, and Point Four. In all of these events, and many others, Mr. Truman demonstrated decisive and forceful leadership, courage, and personal and political integrity.

Mr. Truman's development of statesmanlike stature was somewhat analogous to his development as a public speaker. In an interview shortly after he left the Presidency, Mr. Truman told one of the authors of this anthology that he had had no early talent for public speaking. Everything he had learned about speechmaking he had learned "the hard way." "My first speech was a complete failure," he said. "It took a lot of appearances after that before I felt at home on the platform and could put my ideas across the way I wanted." When asked to identify the greatest influences upon his development as a speaker, Mr. Truman mentioned first his unassuageable appetite for reading. "I have always been a great reader," he recalled. "Before I was twelve I had read the Bible twice. Since then I've read it two more times. I carried home a lot of books from that little library in Independence. As a boy, I read Mark Twain, Shakespeare, George Eliot, Sir Walter Scott, and many others. I enjoyed them all. It was from my reading during this period that I acquired my love of history. I suppose few men in America today have accumulated a greater storehouse of irrelevant and inconsequential historical data than I have! Reading history is still one of my chief enjoyments. A good understanding of the history of government is a 'must' for the public servant."

The second influence upon his development as a speaker mentioned by Mr. Truman was his political experience: "I came up from the political grassroots. My early political experiences in Missouri taught me a lot about human nature. Among other things, I learned that a successful leader cannot afford to lose the common touch. To be a leader of an audience, or of a political party, for that matter, one must be accepted by that group as being one of its members. Like a successful politician, a good speaker must understand and like people before he can hope to influence them."

The third influence suggested by Mr. Truman was his opportunity to learn how to speak effectively through the practical experience of speaking to thousands of audiences. In particular he recalled his Senatorial campaign speaking: "I didn't know it at the time, of course, but my campaigns for the Senate in 1934 and 1940 were excellent preparation for the Presidential campaign in 1948. In each Senatorial campaign I toured the state of Missouri talking 'off-the-cuff' anywhere from six to sixteen times a day; at night over the radio or before a more formal gathering I would read from a typed copy. In the 1940 campaign I practiced a good many of my speeches by reading them into a recording machine. On the basis of what I heard I made adaptations in what I said and how I said it."

When asked if there was a high point in his speaking, Mr. Truman explained that as President speechmaking had been his "most effective means of reaching the American people." Then he added, "Although I delivered hundreds of speeches prior to 1948, I never gained any reputation as a speaker until the campaign of that year. My most successful speech? I believe it was my acceptance address at the Democratic National Convention. That speech was something of a personal spiritual milestone. From that time on, I never doubted that we would win."

Undoubtedly this acceptance speech was a turning point in the political fortunes of Mr. Truman and, therefore, a decisive moment in the history of the Republic. It was early in the morning of July 15, 1948, when Presidential nominee Harry S. Truman was escorted to the speaker's platform in the huge Philadelphia convention hall. He was well aware at the time that the Democratic Party was splintered, "dispirited and dejected" and that relatively few persons, even within his own party, thought he had a chance to win. "I meant to give them something to cheer about and something to campaign for," Mr. Truman later recalled in his *Memoirs*. "It took only a short sentence to bring the delegates to their feet. That was when I said, 'Senator Barkley and I will win this election and make these Republicans like it—don't you forget that.' . . . The Democrats had been waiting to hear somebody say positively that we were going to win, and the effect on them was electric." Near the end of his fighting speech, Mr. Truman sprang the "first big surprise of the campaign": he announced that he was calling a special session of Congress to give the Republicans a chance before the November election to live up to the platform of "promises" adopted by the Republican Party's National Convention. According to Mr. Truman's *Memoirs*, "This announcement . . . electrified the convention to a new pitch of confidence and enthusiasm." Mr. Truman's estimation of the effects of his speech was that "it reinvigorated the whole Party." Historians seem to be in substantive agreement, with this particular assessment.

Harry S. Truman may not have been a great man; but there was greatness in the man. He may not have been a Websterian orator; but his speaking was instrumental in winning an election and, thereby, affecting the course of the nation and, indeed, the course of the world.

The text of this speech is taken from *Vital Speeches*, August 1, 1948, and is reprinted by permission.

ACCEPTANCE SPEECH

I am sorry that the microphones are in your way, but they have to be where they are because I've got to be able to see what I'm doing, as I always am able to see what I am doing.

I can't tell you how very much I appreciate the honor which you've just conferred upon me. I shall continue to try to deserve it. I accept the nomination, and I want to thank this convention for its unanimous nomination of my good friend and colleague, Senator Barkley, of Kentucky.

He's a great man and a great public servant. Senator Barkley and I will win this election and make these Republicans like it, don't you forget that. We'll do that because they're wrong and we're right, and I'll prove it to you in just a few minutes.

This convention met to express the will and reaffirm the beliefs of the Democratic party. There have been differences of opinion. Those differences have been settled by a majority vote, as they should be, and now it's time for us to get together and beat the common enemy and it's up to you.

We'll be working together for victory and a great cause. Victory has become a habit of our party. It's been elected four times in succession and I'm convinced it will be elected a fifth time next November.

The reason is that the people know the Democratic party is the people's party and the Republican party is the party of special interests and it always has been and always will be.

The record of the Democratic party is written in the accomplishments of the last sixteen years. I don't need to repeat them. They have been very ably placed before this convention by the keynote speaker, the candidate for Vice-President, and by the permanent chairman.

Confidence and security have been brought to the American people by the Democratic party. Farm income has increased from less than $2,500,000,000 in 1933 to more than $18,000,000,000 in 1947. Never in the world were the farmers of any republic or any kingdom or any other country, as prosperous as the farmers of the United States, and if they don't do their duty by the Democratic party they're the most ungrateful people in the world.

The wages and salaries in this country have increased from $29,000,000,000 in 1933 to more than $128,000,000,000 in 1947. That's labor, and labor never had but one friend in politics, and that was the Democratic party and Franklin D. Roosevelt.

And I'll say to labor just what I've said to the farmers. They are the most ungrateful people in the world if they pass the Democratic party by this year.

The total national income has increased from less than $40,000,000,000 in 1933 to $203,000,000,000 in 1947, the greatest in all the history of the world. These benefits have been spread to all the people because it's the business of the Democratic party to see that the people get a fair share of these things.

This last Eightieth Congress proved just the opposite for the

Republicans. The record on foreign policy of the Democratic party is that the United States has been turned away permanently from isolationism, and we've converted the greatest and best of the Republicans to our viewpoint on that subject.

The United States has to accept its full responsibility for leadership in international affairs. We have been the backers and the people who organized and started the United Nations, first started under that great Democratic President Woodrow Wilson in the League of Nations. The League was sabotaged by the Republicans in 1920, and we must see that the United Nations continues a strong and going body, so we can have everlasting peace in the world.

We've removed the trade barriers in the world, which is the best asset we can have for peace. Those trade barriers must not be put back into operation again. We have started a foreign-aid program which means the recovery of Europe and China and the Far East. We instituted the program for Greece and Turkey, and I'll say to you that all these things were done in a co-operative bi-partisan manner.

The foreign-relations committees of the Senate and the House were taken into the full confidence of the President in every one of these moves.

As I've said time and time again, foreign policy should be the policy of the whole nation, and not a policy of one party or the other. Partisanship should stop at the water's edge, and I shall continue to preach that through this whole campaign.

I'd like to say a word or two now about what I think the Republican philosophy is, and I'll speak from actions and from history and from experience. The situation in 1932 was due to the policy of the Republican party control of the government of the United States.

The Republican party favors the privileged few and not the common, every-day man. Ever since its inception, that party has been under the control of special privilege, and they concretely proved it in the Eightieth Congress. They proved it by the things they did to the people and not for them. They proved it by the things they failed to do.

Now let's look at some of them, just a few. Time and time again I recommended the extension of price control before it expired on June 30, 1946. I asked for that extension in September, 1945. In November, 1945, in a message on the State of the Union in 1946. That price control legislation didn't come to my desk until June 30, 1946, on the day on which it was supposed to expire, and it was such a rotten bill that I couldn't sign it.

Then thirty days after that they sent me one that was just as bad and I had to sign it, because they quit and went home.

It was said when O. P. A. died that prices would adjust themselves, for the benefit of the country. They've adjusted themselves all right.

They've gone all the way off the chart in adjusting themselves at the expense of the consumer and for the benefit of the people who hold the goods.

I called a special session of Congress in November, 1947—Nov. 17, 1947—and I set out a ten-point program for the welfare and benefit of this country; among other things, stand-by price controls. I got nothing. The Congress has still done nothing.

Way back, four and a half years ago while I was in the Senate we passed the housing bill in the Senate known as the Wagner-Ellender-Taft bill. It was a bill to clear the slums in the big cities, and to help erect low-rent housing. That bill, as I said, passed the Senate four years ago, but it died in the House. That bill was reintroduced in the Eightieth Congress as the Taft-Ellender-Wagner bill—the name was slightly changed.

But it was practically the same bill and it passed the Senate, but was allowed to die in the House of Representatives. The Banking and Currency Committee sat on that bill, and it was finally forced out of the committee when the Rules Committee took charge, and it's still in the Rules Committee.

But desperate pleas from Philadelphia, in that convention that met here three weeks ago, didn't get that housing bill passed. They passed a bill that's called a housing bill, which isn't worth the paper it's written on.

In the field of labor, we needed moderate legislation to promote labor-management relations. But Congress instead issued the so-called Taft-Hartley act, which has disrupted labor-management relations and will cause strife and bitterness for years to come if it's not repealed, and the Democratic platform says it's got to be repealed.

I tried to strengthen the Labor Department. The Republican platform of 1944 said if they were in power they'd build up a strong Labor Department. Do you know what they've done to the Labor Department? They've simply torn it up. There's only one bureau left that's functioning and they've cut the appropriation on that so it can hardly function.

I recommended an increase in the minimum wage. What did they do? Nothing, absolutely nothing. I suggested that the schools in this country are crowded, teachers underpaid, and that there is a shortage of teachers. One of the greatest national needs is more and better schools.

I urged the Congress to provide $300,000,000 to aid the states in meeting the present educational crisis. The Congress did nothing about it. Time and again I have recommended improvements in the social security law, including extending protection to those not now covered, to increase the amount of the benefits, reduce the eligibility age of women from sixty-five to sixty years. Congress studied the matter for two years but couldn't find time to extend increased benefits, but it did find time to take social security benefits away from 750,000 people.

And they passed that over my veto.

I repeatedly asked the Congress to pass a health program. The nation suffers from lack of medical care. That situation can be remedied any time the Congress wants to act upon it. Everybody knows that I recommended to the Congress a civil-rights program. I did so because I believe it to be my duty under the Constitution. Some of the members of my own party disagreed with me violently on this matter, but they stand up and do it openly. People can tell where they stand. But the Republicans all profess to be for these measures, but the Eightieth Congress didn't act and they had enough men there to do it, and they could have had cloture, and they didn't have to have a filibuster. There were enough people in that Congress to vote for cloture.

Now everybody likes to have a little surplus. But we must reduce the national debt in times of prosperity, and when tax relief can be given without regard to those who need it most, and not go to those who need it least, as this Republican rich-man's tax bill did when they passed it over my veto, on the third try.

The first one of these tax bills they sent me was so rotten that they couldn't even stomach it themselves. They finally did send one that was somewhat improved, but it still helps the rich and sticks the knife into the back of the poor.

Now the Republicans came here a few weeks ago and they wrote up a platform. I hope you've all read that platform. They adopted a platform, and that platform had a lot of promises and statements of what the Republican party is for and what they would do if they were in power.

They promised to do in that platform a lot of things I've been asking them to do, and that they've refused to do when they had the power. The Republican platform cries about cruelly high prices. I have been trying to get them to do something about high prices ever since they met the first time.

Now listen to this one. This one is equally as bad and as cynical. The Republican platform comes out for slum clearance and low rental housing. I've been trying to get them to pass that housing bill ever since they met the first time, and it's still resting in the Rules Committee today.

The Republican platform pledges equality of educational opportunity. I've been trying to get them to do something about that ever since they came there, and that bill is at rest in the House of Representatives.

The Republican platform urges extending and increasing social security benefits. Think of that—increasing social security benefits, and yet when they had the opportunity they took 750,000 people off the social security rolls.

I wonder if they think they can fool the people of the United States with such poppycock as that?

There's a long list of these promises in that Republican platform and if it weren't so late I'd tell you about all of them.

I discussed a number of these failures of the Republican Eightieth Congress, and every one of them is important. Two of them are of major concern to every American family; the failure to do anything about high prices, and the failure to do anything about housing.

My duty as President requires that I use every means within my power to get the laws the people need on matters of such importance and urgency. I am therefore calling this Congress back into session on the 26th of July.

On the twenty-sixth day of July, which out in Missouri they call Turnip Day, I'm going to call that Congress back and I'm going to ask them to pass laws halting rising prices and to meet the housing crisis which they say they're for in their platform. At the same time I shall ask them to act on other vitally needed measures such as aid to education, which they say they're for; a national health program, civil-rights legislation, which they say they're for; an increase in the minimum wage—which I doubt very much they're for; an extension of social security coverage and increased benefits, which they say they're for; funds for projects needed in our program to provide public power and cheap electricity.

By indirection, this Eightieth Congress has tried to sabotage the power policy which the United States has pursued for fourteen years. That power lobby is just as bad as the real estate lobby, which is sitting on the housing bill. I shall ask for adequate and decent law for displaced persons in place of the anti-Semitic, anti-Catholic law which this Eightieth Congress passed.

Now my friends, if there is any reality behind that Republican platform, we ought to get some action out of the short session of the Eightieth Congress. They could do this job in fifteen days if they wanted to do it. They'll still have time to go out and run for office. They're going to try and dodge their responsibility, they're going to drag all the red herrings they can across this campaign. But I'm here to say to you that Senator Barkley and I are not going to let them get away with it.

Now what that worst Eightieth Congress does in its special session will be the test. The American people will not decide by listening to mere words or by reading a mere platform. They will decide on the record. The record as it has been written. And in the record is that stark truth that the battle lines for 1948 are the same as they were back in 1932 when the nation lay prostrate and helpless as the result of Republican misrule and inaction.

In 1932 we were attacking the citadel of special privilege and greed; we were fighting to drive the money changers from the temple. Today in 1948 we are the defenders of the stronghold of democracy and of equal opportunity. The haven of the ordinary people of this land and not of the favored classes or of the powerful few.

The battle cry is just the same now as it was in 1932 and I paraphrase the words of Franklin D. Roosevelt as he issued the challenge in accepting his nomination at Chicago: This is more than a political call to arms. Give me your help. Not to win votes alone, but to win in this new crusade and keep America secure and safe for its own people.

Now my friends, with the help of God, and the whole-hearted push which you can put behind this campaign, we can save this country from a continuation of the Eightieth Congress and from misrule from now on. I must have your help! You must get in and push and win this election. The country can't afford another Republican Congress.

Exercises

1. Teachers customarily advise speakers not to apologize when opening a speech. Do you believe that Mr. Truman's first sentence helped or hurt his effectiveness? Explain the reasons for your statement. At the outset, how does Mr. Truman foster favorable relations with his listeners? Why does he mention Senator Barkley? How does he prepare his listeners logically and psychologically for his message?

2. This speech was tremendously effective in securing the support of the immediate audience and in furthering the interests of the Democratic Party. In your judgment, does it also constitute "good literature"? Why or why not?

3. A major function of a speech of this kind is to reinforce the beliefs and feelings of the favorably predisposed audience in the hall. That Mr. Truman was extremely successful in stirring enthusiastic responses from the delegates is evidenced by the joyous and sustained ovations which repeatedly interrupted his presentation. Another function of such a speech is to influence the radio and the reading audience. What effect do you suppose the hortatory tone had upon the secondary audience? Explain your answer.

4. How successfully did Mr. Truman build his speech toward a climax? What was the climax? Do you consider that Mr. Truman's climactic proposal was an astute debater's trick or a reasonable challenge to the Republicans? Explain.

5. How would you characterize Mr. Truman's style? Formal? Plain? Complicated? Objective? Belligerent? Compressed? Generalized? "Punchy"? Other? From the speech, collect examples of strong

language, as "sticks the knife in the back," "poppycock," "citadel of special privilege and greed." Write a brief but adequately detailed analysis of Mr. Truman's style. As part of your answer, compare the style of this speech with that of Franklin D. Roosevelt's "Arsenal of Democracy" and of Stephen A. Douglas' "Campaign Speech for the United States Senate."

6. What contribution do you think that this speech, or Mr. Truman's speaking throughout the 1948 campaign, might have made to the theory or practice of public speaking? Explain your answer.

7. Prepare a detailed outline of the speech. In the outline, identify each usage of a type of supporting material. Write a 300-word analysis of Mr. Truman's use of supporting materials, estimating both their "quality" and their probable effectiveness.

8. How did Mr. Truman attempt to unite and to energize the badly fragmented Democratic Party? What is a "straw man argument"? Did Mr. Truman employ a "straw .man argument" to help prepare Democrats and the nation for the ensuing Republican campaign? Explain. How did Mr. Truman promote the identification with his cause: By the delegates? By Democrats throughout the Nation? By other voters? Explain.

9. In his attacks upon the Republican Party, to what extent, if any, did Mr. Truman direct divisive appeals to Catholics? To Jews? To persons on relief? To immigrants? To blue-collar workers? To Negroes? To liberals? To shopkeepers? To farmers? To teachers? To the elderly? A basic methodology in Mr. Truman's speech was to contrast the purposes and performances of the Republican Party with those of the Democratic Party. In doing so, did he—or did he not—stretch the differences into an unrealistic "black and white," or "God and devil" gamut? How did Mr. Truman attempt to allign the Bible and God on the side of the Democrats? What appeals, if any, did Mr. Truman make to fear? Jealousy? Love of country? Brotherhood? Suppressed hatred? Idealism? Self-interest?

10. Did Mr. Truman make effective use of restatement? What are the differences and similarities between restatement and redundancy?

11. Re-evaluate this speech (and your personal reactions to it) after reading the following articles from the *Quarterly Journal of Speech*: Jennings, Randolph, "Truman—the Winning Speaker," 34 (Dec., 1948), pp. 421ff; Cole S. Brembeck, "Truman at the Whistle Stops," 38 (Feb., 1952), pp. 42ff; and Eugene E. White and Clair R. Henderlider, "What Harry S. Truman Told Us about His Speaking," 40 (Feb., 1954), pp. 37ff.

Adlai Ewing Stevenson

"Today's Most Fateful Fact," delivered at McGill University, Montreal, Canada, on May 29, 1959, upon acceptance of the honorary degree of Doctor of Laws

SOME few American politicians have won world-wide acclaim, for their qualities of statesmanship, or for their personalities, or both. Included in this small group are Woodrow Wilson, Franklin D. Roosevelt, and John F. Kennedy—all of whom were elected to the Presidency—and Adlai Ewing Stevenson (1900–1965) who twice failed of such election. The attitude toward Stevenson of many intellectuals in America as well as abroad was stated by John Steinbeck in his foreword to a 1952 volume of Stevenson's speeches: "I was in Europe at convention time. Europe was, as nearly as we could tell, pretty solidly behind Eisenhower. So was I, as solid as possible. Then gradually the newspapers in France and England and Italy began to print remarks by a man named Stevenson, first a phrase, then a sentence, then a paragraph. When I left England very recently nearly every newspaper was printing a daily Stevenson box on the front page. Europe has switched to Stevenson. So have I." Far more than for most political figures, Stevenson's reputation was established primarily by the style and the sentiments of his speeches. The *Washington Post* declared that as early as July 26, 1952 (when Stevenson, as Governor of Illinois, made a speech welcoming the Democratic Convention to Chicago), "listening Americans knew that they had an orator on their hands."

In an age of ghost-written political speeches, Stevenson insisted on writing his own. And in the profession of politics, often marked by evasion and vagueness in the discussion of issues, Stevenson boldly declared: "Let's talk sense to the American people! Let's tell them the truth, that there are no gains without pains, that we are now on the eve of great decisions, not easy decisions, like resistance when you're attacked, but a long, patient, costly struggle which alone can assure triumph over the great enemies of man—war, poverty, and tyranny—and the assaults upon human dignity which are the most grievous consequences of each." Then he added: "Better we lose the election than mislead the people."

Stevenson did, in fact, lose two elections to the Presidency, in 1952 and 1956. He had ample opportunity to savor the advice given him in his 29th year by his father, who lay near death, that "politics is a hazardous life, full of ingratitudes"; then, weak and in pain, his father whispered to him the words "obligation," and "do what you must." To his admiring followers Stevenson seemed a man driven to public life by a sense of responsibility rather than attracted to it by ambition. In accepting the Presidential nomination in 1952, he told the delegates: "I have not sought the honor you have done me. . . . I would not seek your nomination for the Presidency because the burdens of that office stagger the imagination. Its potential for good or evil now and in the years of our lives smothers exultation and converts vanity to prayer."

Born into a family renowned for public service, Stevenson was well educated (at Princeton and at Northwestern University Law School), widely travelled, and moderately wealthy. Shy and reticent as a young adult, he was not then a good public speaker and took no active part in public affairs. The depression that commenced with the stock market collapse in 1929 aroused his social consciousness, and he responded to President Roosevelt's invitation to serve first in the Agricultural Adjustment Administration and next in the Foreign Economic Administration. In 1944 he returned to Chicago as Director of the Council on Foreign Relations, in which position he began to give frequent speeches and rapidly developed skills of the platform. When delegates from fifty nations gathered in San Francisco to sign the Charter of the United Nations, Stevenson was there as Press Secretary for the American delegation; and the next year he served as Senior Advisor to the U.S. delegates to the first General Assembly of the United Nations, in London. In 1948 he campaigned for the governorship of Illinois, making a dozen speeches a day, and won with the largest plurality in the state's history. *Time* newsmagazine declared that "a dazzling new political star had been born," and described him as "a suave, able, well-liked socialite lawyer with an anxious expression, a rueful laugh, a lemony sense of humor." The last act in his political drama (following the two unsuccessful Presidential campaigns) was his service as U.S. Ambassador to the United Nations, from 1961 until his death by heart attack on the sidewalk as he was leaving the American Embassy in London.

With his international reputation and his interest in world affairs, Stevenson had a sympathetic audience when he spoke to the Commencement audience at McGill University. Nevertheless, Canadian feelings toward the United States were aggravated by a series of disputes between the two countries and by a sharp rebuke the American Secretary of State had delivered publicly to the Canadian Prime Minister. Stevenson's persuasive problem was to penetrate the surface irritations to the bedrock of common interests shared by the neighbor nations. He also wished to highlight, both for his immediate audience and for American newspaper readers, what he conceived to be the major issue of our time.

The text of the speech is taken from Adlai E. Stevenson, *Putting First Things First: A Democratic View*, New York: Random House, copyright ©, 1960. It is used by special permission.

TODAY'S MOST FATEFUL FACT

I think Bernard Shaw once said that he never resisted temptation because he had found that the things that were bad for him did not tempt him. I wish I could say the same. But I can't. I find honorary degrees always tempting, and often bad for me: tempting because we all—even ex-politicians—hope to be mistaken for scholars, and bad because if you then make a speech the mistake is quickly exposed.

This is my predicament here today. I am honored, and you have to listen to a speech. It hardly seems fair.

I thought—as all visiting Americans do—to talk to you about the Canadian-American relations which are in one of our cyclical periods of irritation. But I have changed my mind because like most family relationships, ours are so intimate and so involved that analysis is difficult. Not long ago I found Canadian confirmation for this in some words of the editor of the Victoria *Times:*

> "All the current wrangles of the border—trade, investment, seaway tolls, Columbia River electric power, farm surpluses, and the rest—represent for us Canadians only one thing, precious beyond economic

calculation. So far we have been unable to articulate that thing clearly.
"We know what it means just the same. The whole problem of the border today—as always since the American Revolution—is that our neighbors *don't* know what it means, and won't bother to find out."

I think Mr. Hutchinson is right. We Americans mostly *don't* know and we ought to find out about our closest friend and neighbor and biggest customer. But I wonder if Canadians know as much about the United States as they should, too? Perhaps we ought to appoint a joint commission of international psychoanalysts to help us. And if they started to work today, I would like to make two or three suggestions for better understanding of the United States in Canada.

In the first place, it seems to me that Canadians, like other friends abroad, sometimes speak as if they thought the United States should always act promptly and decisively to satisfy their needs and complaints, regardless of the needs and wishes of American voters. They don't expect their own governments to behave the same way, and are fully aware that domestic political pressures limit the actions of their governments. For our government to behave as they suggest, it would have to be, in effect, a dictatorship, unresponsive to the opinion and desires of its own voters and able therefore to take prompt, decisive action abroad. But would Canada prefer that kind of a neighbor rather than the present one with all of its faults and weaknesses?

Another point I would ask our friends, and especially our neighbors, to remember is that the American system of government was designed primarily for the efficient compromise of conflicts between the states and the various sectional interests—economic, racial, religious, etc. At that time an effective scheme for composing internal differences was not only sensible but essential to the unification and survival of the sprawling infant country. The system was not designed for rapid, decisive action in the realm of foreign affairs. In those days we had few foreign affairs and wanted less. But now our internal differences are perhaps less urgent, while our external problems have become infinitely complex and acute.

Our system may be obsolete, but, as Canadians will understand, any social-political system, especially in a democracy, is subject to a constant time lag. It can adjust to new circumstances and demands only gradually and painfully. Yet in the United States we have made many adjustments in the past twenty-five years—some very far-reaching—and I think it could be argued at least that no other nation has shown greater flexibility and capacity for growth.

It remains true, however, that we are not adjusting as rapidly as we should, and *must*, in this period of bewildering and fast change in the world, and to match the swiftness, certainty and secrecy of the dictatorships. But is it unreasonable of us Americans to expect, on this score, some of the patience and understanding which you Canadians expect of us?

I would like to suggest, too, that sometimes our friends ask too much of us. Some Canadians, for instance, sound as if they would like us to solve their surplus wheat problem for them when we can't solve our own. The fact is that even if our political system were not hobbled by built-in structural and historical defects we could hardly meet the political and economic demands upon us from all sides, no matter how much we want to be helpful. We are neither that wise nor that rich. We cannot supply, for instance, the massive capital investment which has been so essential to Canada's growth and is now needed so badly by all the underdeveloped countries.

And that brings me to what I really wanted to talk about: the things we will have to do together, the things that unite us, and the great unfinished business of this generation of Canadians and Americans who share the values of Western society, of which McGill University is one of the greatest repositories.

In free nations, where no strict ideology is imposed from above, there are recurrent times of ferment and questioning. These are always times of turmoil and confusion. Old ideas are discarded, new directions sought, and sometimes in the midst of it all, it is not altogether easy to perceive the main areas of decision and the proper scope of the debate.

Little more than a century ago, such a phase of questioning and revaluation was in full swing in Britain. The first onrush of the industrial revolution had changed the face of the land. It was a world of inhuman working hours, of child labor, of poverty herded into vast insanitary cities. And all this coexisted with great wealth and comfort for a few. "Two nations," wrote the wise Disraeli, of "privilege and the people," of "wealth and poverty," live side by side. Charles Dickens gave these "two nations" life and breath in his imperishable novels. Reformers—Lord Shaftesbury, the Christian Socialists, the free churches, the dogged forerunners of the labor movement—fought the widespread idea that no reform or intervention was possible since *laissez faire* had been preordained by an all-seeing Providence. And—ominously—Engels fed the evils of infant industrialism into the incendiary imagination of Karl Marx. Some decades afterwards a similar ferment was at work in America, sparking the reforming energies of William Jennings Bryan, Theodore Roosevelt, Woodrow Wilson and many other leaders of our post-Civil War period.

What the reformers finally did was to create the conviction that no decent society could tolerate so wide a gulf between the "two nations." In a hundred different methods of analysis and reform, they sought to establish reasonable methods of dealing with the vast problems—and opportunities—unleashed by industrialism and by the wealth it created but did not equitably distribute among the creators.

I believe a comparable period of questioning and concern has opened in the West in the last decade. We face the end of the period of unquestioned Western supremacy. We face the rising claims of the vast majority of mankind. Some of the results of modernization have spread now to the whole human race, and once again the consequence of industrialism, undirected by broader aims of public policy, has been to recreate Disraeli's "two nations" in the world at large. One, a small minority of comparative wealth and privilege, lives in the main around the North Atlantic. Here in fortunate North America its per capita annual income is from $600 to $2,000. But the per capita income for two-thirds of humanity is not more than $100. In India, the greatest single democratic community in the world, the average is not much above $60 a head.

Here, then, repeated on a world scale in mid-20th century, are the riches and poverty side by side of mid-19th century England. And we would need the pen of a Dickens to paint the contrast between the comfortable dwellings of a thousand Western cities and the hovels of the miserable millions I have seen from Hong Kong to Johannesburg.

In my judgment this disparity of living standards is the most important and fateful fact in the world today. And the worst of it is that instead of getting better it is getting worse. The rich are getting richer and the poor poorer as their population grows faster than production. The precondition of any effective world policies in the West is an imaginative understanding of the implications of this race between resources and population; of this growing gap between a small wealthy white Western minority who have modernized and the vast majority of mankind who have not.

Once again I believe our situation resembles the 19th century. Then our forebears discovered that charity by individuals was not a complete answer. Government action, financed by the community as a whole, was necessary to make the basic improvements in health, housing and education without which the poorer members of society would lack the strength to raise themselves. A wider sharing in the wealth created by private industry—through better wages and working conditions—had a large part to play also.

Many anxious debates on the practicability of ever helping anyone to help himself accompanied the working out of these principles. Yet the outcome of the debate was the decision to achieve "the general welfare." And from it has arisen a society which, no doubt, has its flaws and blemishes but which in scope, opportunity—and, let us add, consuming power—has no equal in human history.

This outcome should encourage us now that we are involved in a new and much more complex version of the old debate. We must see that the problem of wealth and poverty in the world at large cannot be solved by handouts from individual states. Charity, with all its uncertainty and intermittence, is not the issue. Our task, as the wealthy members of world society, is to link our resources to a systematic, long-term program of education and basic development which will give the world's masses the opportunity to help themselves and bring them into effective social and economic partnership with the more developed communities. And nothing, I think, would be more appropriate than that the beneficiaries of the Marshall Plan of ten years ago should now join with America and Canada in a comparable effort for the less developed areas.

In this process I believe the basic test must be need and ability to absorb capital usefully, just as need, not virtue, has been the test inside Western society. India, for example, is close to the economic "take off" point of self-sustaining investment. It is well provided with trained administrative and technical staff and has in addition an expanding, enterprising, private sector. All this gives the hope that a really imaginative effort in India would be successful.

I would like to add that the problem is not one of government policy alone. Now—as in the 19th century debate—private enterprise has a pivotal part to play. It is concerned, rightly concerned, for the security of its investments and its returns in underdeveloped areas. It seeks reasonable guarantees, but I would like to see those guarantees worked out so that, in return for security, private firms working abroad give assurances of worker training, promotion to managerial responsibility, local directorships and the building up of a solid body of local investors and savers. All American companies may not have been as alert as they might be to these pre-conditions of responsible operation abroad. But attitudes are changing like the times and they are the chief means by which private industry can do more than simply contribute to economic development.

So, our new and common task is to assist in the search for internal stability, economic growth, and external security—without interventions which outrage national feelings and lead to a greater vulnerability to Communist agitation. It is a task of immense delicacy and immense urgency and on it turns, I believe, the future of the uncommitted world. We will have to think of it with the same, or a greater, sense of urgency that we think of our military defenses.

The passing of the old colonial age has been so sudden and the emergence of the new post-colonial phase so fraught with new risks and dilemmas that it is not surprising to find the Western powers uncertain and fumbling in this first decade of the new era. The changes in thought and habit which it demands on both sides of the Atlantic are vast. In the normal rhythms of history they would have demanded scores of years, even centuries, to emerge. Now they must be learned overnight. Small wonder, then, that we blunder and hesitate.

In the United States we shall have to recover from the illusion of effortless security and wealth which a fortunate 19th century, shielded by British power, has taught us to regard virtually as a natural right. We have to learn that there is no safety now in isolation, no safety in drift or self-deception, that no single "solution" or formula or declaration will rid us of the need of having a foreign policy at all.

All of us are involved. All the nations enlisted in the cause of freedom must, I fear, face years of joint responsibility, of working patiently with each other in pursuit of joint solutions, not despairing at early setbacks, not rejoicing too soon, but recognizing that world order is not made in a day or sustained with half thoughts and half measures.

Canada is uniquely endowed to set the issues in their right perspective—both on the side of the donors and of the recipients of assistance. I think it essential that our efforts should be international and multi-national. Few nations are better placed to set that ideal consistently before us. Canada has its part in every international grouping of consequence. Its role in the United Nations has been outstanding. It is a respected member of the Colombo Plan group, an elder daughter of the Commonwealth. Its links with the United States are—in spite of or perhaps because of recurrent conflicts of interest—the model of neighborliness. And its two cultures—English and French—give it special links with the European community. The channels of communication open to Canada thus branch out in every direction and the influence it has exercised through all of them has, I believe, been outstandingly generous and constructive.

All this makes me hope that, in the debate ahead, Canada will not be slow to use its influence, particularly in Washington and London where its voice is so eagerly attended to, to remind the statesmen of other wealthy and fortunate countries that good fortune is a responsibility, not a right or privilege.

But, equally, Canada has a vital word to say to the underdeveloped nations. For Canada still has vast untapped resources and needs outside capital to advance. It can underline to others the fact that capital assistance from abroad, public or private, does not destroy independence or lessen dignity or weaken in any way a nation's essential right to be itself and to speak its mind.

Equally, its membership in a commonwealth of nations drawn from every creed and color has not lessened its effectiveness. On the contrary, this association gives it contacts, understanding and sympathies not open to nations who have thrown off or never known the Commonwealth's friendly association between equal powers.

I trust, therefore, that Canada will make its contribution to the world's great debate tirelessly and generously; that the vision it has shown in so many of its post-war policies will continue to give light to all of us as we grapple with the hazards and the opportunities that lie ahead for the whole family of man.

And now, before I bid you goodbye, let me add a word to the graduating classes who are about to leave this place.

I think you are fortunate to live in this stirring time of revolution.

I know you are fortunate to have lived in this famous community of scholars.

Here at McGill your education has begun. But it has not finished—and when you leave I hope you will remember why you came, and the insights that were opened for you here in this treasury of the Western Culture.

And I hope that you will take away with you:
A remorseless respect for free inquiry;
Contempt for tyranny over the mind or person of man; and
Reverence for things you cannot see.

Exercises

1. Note the two strands in Stevenson's introduction: a bit of humor to establish rapport, and a frank avowal of the difficulties then roiling American-Canadian relations. Do you think he was wise to turn the tables, pointing out that Canadians probably misunderstand Americans as much as we misunderstand them? Was he wise to give Canadians advice on how they should reform their opinions of the United States? Why do you suppose he took this tack? How did he seek to render his advice palatable?

2. To what extent do you think his "advice to the Canadians" was aimed also as counsel to Americans? Do you find his comments on the obsolescence of our political system to be sound? Does he make any specific suggestions for reform of our system? Should he have done so? Do his observations suggest to you (or might they have suggested to his listeners) any desirable changes?

3. How did Stevenson manage his transition from the Introduction to the Body of his speech? What might have been his reason for mentioning American aid to Canada? Why did he phrase this reference casually, almost parenthetically? Should he have been more explicit? Should he have avoided this subject altogether? What use

did he later make of this reminder of American investment in Canada?

4. What is "today's most fateful fact"? Rephrase it in your own words.

5. In what respects, according to Stevenson, are the United States and Canada similar? What common tasks and goals do they share? Are these significant enough to counter the surface irritabilities in the relations of the two countries?

6. Trace the general pattern of the literal analogy which Stevenson drew between the "two nations" in 19th-century England and the "two nations" in today's world. Does his unusual use of the word "nations" suggest that human welfare actually transcends consideration of national boundaries?

7. Do you see any reason why Stevenson might have chosen to compare 20th-century problems to those of the 19th century? Should he have made the point explicitly that the earlier problems were solved, as a basis for confidence that the current problems could be solved?

8. Cite reasons why Stevenson praised Canada. In what respects did he find Canada to be peculiarly well qualified to take a leading role in dealing with the "most fateful fact" of our time?

9. What did Stevenson mean when he said India is at the "take-off" stage? Do you agree that "need" not "virtue" should be the determining factor in deciding what countries should receive aid from the United States? Would the reference to India have special pertinence for Stevenson's audience?

10. How would you characterize Stevenson's style? Note his plain-speaking, about Americans as well as about Canadians ("We are neither that wise nor that rich.") Note his frequent references to history and to literature. Find examples of parallelisms, of comparisons, and of the use of "couplets"—such as "questioning and concern," "flaws and blemishes," and "uncertainty and intermittence."

11. Note that the speech has two separate conclusions—the second one being an admonition to the graduating class. Is there any way in which the second conclusion supports the first one?

12. Do you agree with Stevenson's judgment that the "most fateful fact" today is the growing "disparity of living standards"?

13. Prepare a speech of your own in which you deal with the world problem of unequal distribution of wealth. What solution can you offer? Why was Stevenson's solution rather indefinite? Should he have been more explicit?

John F. Kennedy

Inaugural Address, given January 20, 1961

SELDOM has there been such a spontaneous outpouring of grief throughout the world as that which attended the death of John F. Kennedy (1917–1963). Future generations may find it hard to account for the universality and the depth of the sorrow. At the time of his death, President Kennedy had not yet achieved a distinguished record of legislation passed, and on various important matters he had reached an impasse with Congress. The Western Alliance was shaky. The hoped-for thawing in the Cold War had not yet developed into a warming trend. Furthermore, Kennedy's record during his six years as a member of the House of Representatives and eight years as a member of the Senate had been good, but not outstanding. Why, then, did many millions of individuals feel a personal identification with President Kennedy and experience an acute personal loss upon his passing? To a large extent what had captured their imaginations and had epitomized their aspirations was an amorphous something called by numerous observers "the Kennedy style."

"The Kennedy style" was the man. The man was the orator. The style, the man, the orator were unique. One analyst has written that Kennedy "gave us an exhilarating vision of political dignity." Another has called him a "bright, vivid personality" whose "every act and appearance appealed to our pride and gave us fresh confidence in ourselves and our country." Numerous others have pointed out that the grace, elegance, and urbanity of President and Mrs. Kennedy brightened society and improved its taste and its respect for things of the mind and spirit.

The most obvious aspect of "the Kennedy style" was his articulateness: the economy, brilliance, and eruditeness of his language; the nimbleness, felicity, and rapier wit of his impromptu communication, as in the TV Presidential press conferences and in the 1960 TV debates with Richard Nixon, which Kennedy and most observers believed won the election for him. "The Kennedy style" reflected his interest in writing. His undergraduate thesis at Harvard University, *Why England Slept,* became a best seller, and his *Profiles in Courage,* written during his convalescence from a spinal operation, earned him a Pulitzer Prize. "The Kennedy style" reflected his appreciation of the beautiful in nature and in man's works. A month before his death, he told an audience at Amherst College: "I look forward to an America which will reward achievement in the arts as we reward achievement in business or statecraft . . . which will not be afraid of grace and beauty . . . which commands respect . . . not only for its strength, but for its civilization as well."

"The Kennedy style" reflected his temperance, caution, and courage. A genuine war hero, he spoke of man's "walking a narrow ledge." "Peace and freedom do not come cheap," he told a University of North Carolina audience, "and we are destined, all of us here today, to live out most if not all of our lives in uncertainty and challenge and peril." "The Kennedy style" reflected his love of action. As he told a 1960 election-eve crowd in the Boston Garden, "I ran for the Presidency of the United States because it is the center of action and, in a free society, the chief responsibility of the President is to set before the American people the unfinished business of our country."

"The Kennedy style" reflected his sense of history and his deep and intimate knowledge of the workings of government. This gave him a personal detachment which lifted his speaking and actions above the pompous, the petty, and the mundane. "The Kennedy style" reflected his respect for learning, the learned, and the power of reason. John Kenneth Galbraith suggests that his "belief in human intelligence gave a glow to his style." Perhaps more than any President since Jefferson, he was a man of the Renaissance. Rejecting the banal and the pat, he was committed to intelligence and reason. In a speech which he had prepared for presentation in Dallas, he wrote, "In a world of complex and continuing problems, in a world full of frustrations and irritations, America's leadership must be guided by the lights of learning and reason or else those who confuse rhetoric with reality and the plausible with the possible will gain the popular ascendancy with their seemingly swift and simple solutions to every world problem." Possessing incredible powers of mental self-discipline and a driving energy, he amazed others with his immediate grasp of details concerning all problems relating to his office.

Finally, and perhaps most important, "the Kennedy style" reflected his devotion to ideals and to spiritual faith. In the speech which he did not live to deliver in Dallas, he had planned to close with these words: "We in this country, in this generation, are—by destiny rather than choice—the watchmen on the walls of world freedom. We ask, therefore, that we may be worthy of our power and responsibility—that we may exercise our strength with wisdom and restraint—and that we may achieve in our time and for all time the ancient vision of peace on earth, goodwill toward men. That must always be our goal—and the righteousness of our cause must always underlie our strength. For as was written long ago: 'Except the Lord keep the city, the watchman waketh but in vain.' "

The amorphous something called "the Kennedy style," the man, the orator are exemplified in John F. Kennedy's Inaugural Address. One of the shortest of such speeches, it is also one of the most eloquent. Because of impending crises in the Congo, Laos, Cuba, and elsewhere, the message dealt exclusively with foreign affairs.

The text of the speech comes from *Inaugural Addresses of the Presidents of the United States*, Washington, D.C.: United States Government Printing Office, 1961.

INAUGURAL ADDRESS

Mr. Chief Justice, President Eisenhower, Vice President Nixon, President Truman, reverend clergy, fellow citizens, we observe today not a victory of party, but a celebration of freedom—symbolizing an end, as well as a beginning—signifying renewal, as well as change. For I have sworn before you and Almighty God the same solemn oath our forebears prescribed nearly a century and three-quarters ago.

The world is very different now. For man holds in his mortal hands the power to abolish all forms of human poverty and all forms of human life. And yet the same revolutionary beliefs for which our forebears fought are still at issue around the globe—the belief that the rights of man come not from the generosity of the state, but from the hand of God.

We dare not forget today that we are the heirs of that first revolution. Let the word go forth from this time and place, to friend and foe alike, that the torch has been passed to a new generation of Americans—born in this century, tempered by war, disciplined by a hard and bitter peace, proud of our ancient heritage—and unwilling to witness or permit the slow undoing of those human rights to which this nation has always been committed, and to which we are committed today at home and around the world.

Let every nation know, whether it wishes us well or ill, that we shall pay any price, bear any burden, meet any hardship, support any friend, oppose any foe, in order to assure the survival and the success of liberty.

This much we pledge—and more.

To those old allies whose cultural and spiritual origins we share, we pledge the loyalty of faithful friends. United, there is little we cannot do in a host of cooperative ventures. Divided, there is little we can do—for we dare not meet a powerful challenge at odds and split asunder.

To those new states whom we welcome to the ranks of the free, we pledge our words that one form of colonial control shall not have passed away merely to be replaced by a far greater iron tyranny. We shall not always expect to find them supporting our view. But we shall always hope to find them strongly supporting their own freedom—and to remember that, in the past, those who foolishly sought power by riding the back of the tiger ended up inside.

To those peoples in the huts and villages across the globe struggling to break the bonds of mass misery, we pledge our best efforts to help them help themselves, for whatever period is required—not because the Communists may be doing it, not because we seek their votes, but because it is right. If a free society cannot help the many who are poor, it cannot save the few who are rich.

To our sister republics south of our border, we offer a special pledge—to convert our good words into good deeds, in a new alliance for progress, to assist free men and free governments in casting off the chains of poverty. But this peaceful revolution of hope cannot become the prey of hostile powers. Let all our neighbors know that we shall join with them to oppose aggression or subversion anywhere in the Americas. And let every other power know that this hemisphere intends to remain the master of its own house.

To that world assembly of sovereign states, the United Nations, our last best hope in an age where the instruments of war have far outpaced the instruments of peace, we renew our pledge of support—to prevent it from becoming merely a forum for invective—to strengthen its shield of the new and the weak—and to enlarge the area in which its writ may run.

Finally, to those nations who would make themselves our adversary, we offer not a pledge but a request: that both sides begin anew the quest for peace, before the dark powers of destruction unleashed by science engulf all humanity in planned or accidental self-destruction.

We dare not tempt them with weakness. For only when our arms are sufficient beyond doubt can we be certain beyond doubt that they will never be employed.

But neither can two great and powerful groups of nations take comfort from our present course—both sides overburdened by the cost of modern weapons, both rightly alarmed by the steady spread of the deadly atom, yet both racing to alter that uncertain balance of terror that stays the hand of mankind's final war.

So let us begin anew—remembering on both sides that civility is not a sign of weakness, and sincerity is always subject to proof. Let us never negotiate out of fear. But let us never fear to negotiate.

Let both sides explore what problems unite us instead of laboring those problems which divide us.

Let both sides, for the first time, formulate serious and precise proposals for the inspection and control of arms—and bring the absolute power to destroy other nations under the absolute control of all nations.

Let both sides seek to invoke the wonders of science instead of its terrors. Together let us explore the stars, conquer the deserts, eradicate disease, tap the ocean depths, and encourage the arts and commerce.

Let both sides unite to heed in all corners of the earth the command of Isaiah—to "undo the heavy burdens and to let the oppressed go free."

And if a beachhead of cooperation may push back the jungle of suspicion, let both sides join in creating a new endeavor, not a new balance of power, but a new world of law, where the strong are just and the weak secure and the peace preserved.

All this will not be finished in the first hundred days. Nor will it be finished in the first thousand days, nor in the life of this Administration, nor even perhaps in our lifetime on this planet. But let us begin.

In your hands, my fellow citizens, more than in mine, will rest the final success or failure of our course. Since this country was founded, each generation of Americans has been summoned to give testimony to its national loyalty. The graves of young Americans who answered the call to service are found around the globe.

Now the trumpet summons us again—not as a call to bear arms, though arms we need; not as a call to battle, though embattled we are; but a call to bear the burden of a long twilight struggle, year in, and year out, "rejoicing in hope, patient in tribulation"—a struggle against the common enemies of man: tyranny, poverty, disease, and war itself.

Can we forge against these enemies a grand and global alliance, north and south, east and west, that can assure a more fruitful life for all mankind? Will you join in that historic effort?

In the long history of the world, only a few generations have been granted the role of defending freedom in its hour of maximum danger. I do not shrink from this responsibility—I welcome it. I do not believe that any of us would exchange places with any other people or any other generation. The energy, the faith, the devotion which we bring to this endeavor will light our country and all who serve it—and the glow from that fire can truly light the world.

And so, my fellow Americans, ask not what your country can do for you: Ask what you can do for your country.

My fellow citizens of the world: Ask not what America will do for you, but what together we can do for the freedom of man.

Finally, whether you are citizens of America or citizens of the world, ask of us the same high standards of strength and sacrifice which we ask of you. With a good conscience our only sure reward, with history the final judge of our deeds, let us go forth to lead the land we love, asking His blessing and His help, but knowing that here on earth God's work must truly be our own.

Exercises

1. Unlike the hostility which had characterized the change in power in 1953, the Inauguration of 1961 was conducted in an atmosphere of extreme cordiality. How does this comport with the personalities of the two chief participants, Dwight D. Eisenhower and John F. Kennedy? Do reflections of this spirit of good feeling seem to appear in the speech?

2. During the ceremonies prior to President Kennedy's address, several possibly distracting incidents occurred. In the course of Richard Cardinal Cushing's invocation, special security men were needed to cope with a foot heater that was sending streams of smoke around the speaker. Somewhat later, the wind and sun glare disturbed Robert Frost's attempts to read a poem which he had composed as a special preface to his reciting of "The Gift Outright." After awkward attempts to shield the reading copy from the sun, and after rejecting Vice President Lyndon B. Johnson's efforts to help, the old poet recited from memory "The Gift Outright." A few minutes later, Mr. Johnson stumbled in repeating the oath of office, altering one of the lines noticeably. To what extent, if any, do you think these disturbances might have marred the dignity of the occasion and made Kennedy's job more difficult? Might these incidents have improved the receptivity of the audience at the capitol?

Of the TV audience? Can you think of any rhetorical reasons why Kennedy slipped out of his overcoat before he took the oath of office and made his speech?

3. What reasons can you advance for the unusual brevity of the address?

4. Outline the speech, including the Introduction and Conclusion. What method does Kennedy employ in the Introduction to emphasize the New Frontier spirit of his administration. Why does he link his Inauguration with the past? How does he do this? What kinds of appeals appear in both the Introduction and Conclusion? Does the Conclusion have summarizing qualities? What evidence can you cite to prove that the Conclusion contains the emotional and stylistic climax of the speech?

5. After making an inclusive general statement of national purpose, Kennedy offers pledges to different groups of persons. Why does he address these particular groups? Is there any significance in the order of listing?

6. When he comes to "those nations who would make themselves our adversary," Kennedy says, "we offer not a pledge but a request." Is there special significance in this phrasing? What elements of common bond does he offer the enemy? How does he achieve a sense of urgency? Why does he use a Biblical quotation in addressing Communists? Does he offer any specific proposals of accommodation? Why does he begin this section with the request, "that both sides begin anew the quest for peace," and close it with the exhortation, "But let us begin."?

7. Compare the tone and content of this speech with that of the First Inaugural addresses by Jefferson, Franklin D. Roosevelt, and Wilson.

8. Compare this speech with the "Arsenal of Democracy" speech in the usage of figurative language, repetition, parallel sentence structure, rhythm, and antithesis.

9. How does Kennedy appeal to the pride of Americans? To tradition? How does he attempt to energize his listeners? To dramatize his own vigorous acceptance of responsibility? Does he call for a crusade without labeling it as such? If so, why does he not identify it as a crusade? Why does he stress self-sacrifice, devotion to excellence, and willingness to exert maximum effort? Why does he combine appeals to religious faith and to self-reliance? Compare the idealism in this speech with that in Wilson's "Fourteen Points" speech. Of the two speeches, which seems to be based more on hard-headed realism?

Martin Luther King, Jr.

"I Have a Dream . . . ," delivered at the Lincoln Monument, Washington, D.C., on August 28, 1963

On August 28, 1963, the centenary of the Emancipation Proclamation, an audience of more than 200,000 massed in front of the Lincoln Memorial. Together with a nation-wide radio and television audience, they heard Martin Luther King, Jr. (1929–   ) deliver the featured address which climaxed the "March on Washington"—an unprecedented mass protest dramatizing the movement for civil rights for American Negroes. The Detroit labor leader Walter Reuther called the March and the speech by the Reverend Mr. King "the beginning of a great moral crusade to arouse Americans to the unfinished work of American democracy."

The day had been anticipated in many quarters with great apprehension. Ever since 1956, and especially during the summers of 1961, 1962, and 1963, there had been outbreaks of violence and growing tension in the struggle over school desegregation, voting registration, and the demands by Negroes for access to public accommodations and for better jobs. Many feared that the massing of militant civil rightists in the hot and humid weather of Washington might lead to violence. President John F. Kennedy suggested that because of the legislative action which was being taken to speed desegregation, the March should be called off. The results were far different from some expectations. Order prevailed; following King's speech, the crowd dispersed and returned home. The promise of the Negro leaders that there would be no violence was fulfilled.

Martin Luther King, Jr. (baptized "Michael") was born into a family that was well educated and successful. His father was a Baptist minister, as had been his maternal grandfather. His mother, prior to her marriage, had been a school teacher. Growing up in Atlanta, Georgia, Michael was shocked, at the age of six, when his closest friend, the son of a white grocer, was forbidden by his parents to play anymore with him. His mother explained to him about segregation and urged him to be proud of the heritage of his race. His father renamed both himself and his son Martin Luther King, and admonished him to lead a life of courage and of faith worthy of the great Protestant.

It was not until King's junior year at Morehouse College, in Atlanta, that he decided to enter the ministry. After graduation he attended the predominantly white Crozer Theological Seminary, at Chester, Pennsylvania, from which he graduated as the outstanding member of the senior class. The award for this honor was a Fellowship adequate to finance his studies for the doctorate. King selected Boston College for his graduate studies and received his Ph.D. in philosophy in 1955. From Boston he went to Montgomery, Alabama, as Minister of the Dexter Avenue Baptist Church.

As President of the Montgomery Improvement Association, in 1956 King organized a year-long boycott of the Montgomery transit system, which continued until a federal court order ended segregated seating on the city buses. The success of the Montgomery protest movement launched a nation-wide series of civil rights demonstrations. Citing the teachings and practice of Mahatma Gandhi, King advocated protest without violence. Nevertheless, his home was bombed on January 30, 1956, and on December 23 of that year a shotgun blast was fired into his front door. Arrested and jailed for his leadership of the boycott, King wrote the eloquent "Letter from the Montgomery Jail."

In 1961–62, as President of the Southern Christian Leadership Conference, King led anti-segregation demonstrations in Albany, Georgia, resulting in his arrest on December 16, 1961, and July 10, 1962. Both times he was released when his fines were paid without his consent. On July 27, he was again arrested, and this time he served a brief jail sentence. The following September he was assaulted by a member of the American Nazi party while speaking at a meeting in Shreveport, Louisiana.

Despite the occasional violence with which his movement was resisted, King continued to advocate passive resistance in the spirit of brotherhood. In an NBC-TV interview he said: "As soon as we pass out of this shock period I believe that whites and Negroes will work together without bitterness." In *Newsweek*, he was quoted as saying: "This is a protest of passive resistance depending upon moral and spiritual forces. We will return good for evil. Christ showed us the way and Mahatma Gandhi showed us it could work." That Spring, King and his wife were invited to be state guests of Ghana and of India. In October, 1964, a year after the March on Washington, he was awarded the Nobel Peace Prize, the twelfth American to be so honored.

The available evidence indicates that there was a lack of close coordination among the Negro leaders who planned the March on Washington. Apparently no decision was made concerning the speaking program until a few hours before the March was to begin. Dr. King accordingly did not prepare his speech until the night preceding the March. He wrote it in longhand, completing the draft at about four in the morning.

The text of the speech is taken from a tape recording made by Professors Carroll C. Arnold, Douglas Ehninger, and John C. Gerber, and printed in their *The Speaker's Resource Book*, Chicago: Scott, Foresman & Company, 1966. It is used with their permission and that of Reverend Martin Luther King, Jr.

"I HAVE A DREAM . . . ,"

I am happy to join with you today in what will go down in history as the greatest demonstration for freedom in the history of our nation.

Five score years ago, a great American, in whose symbolic shadow we stand today, signed the Emancipation Proclamation. This momentous decree came as a great beacon light of hope to millions of Negro slaves who had been seared in the flames of withering injustice. It came as a joyous daybreak to end the long night of their captivity.

But one hundred years later, the Negro is still not free. One hundred years later, the life of the Negro is still sadly crippled by the manacles of segregation and the chains of discrimination. One hundred years later, the Negro lives on a lonely island of poverty in the midst of a vast ocean of material prosperity. One hundred years later, the Negro is still languished in the corners of American society and finds himself an exile in his own land. So we have come here today to dramatize a shameful condition.

In a sense we have come to our nation's Capitol to cash a check.

When the architects of our republic wrote the magnificent words of the Constitution and the Declaration of Independence, they were signing a promissory note to which every American was to fall heir. This note was a promise that all men would be guaranteed the unalienable rights of life, liberty, and the pursuit of happiness.

It is obvious today that America has defaulted on this promissory note insofar as her citizens of color are concerned. Instead of honoring this sacred obligation, America has given the Negro people a bad check; a check which has come back marked "insufficient funds." But we refuse to believe that the bank of justice is bankrupt. We refuse to believe that there are insufficient funds in the great vaults of opportunity of this nation. So we have come to cash this check—a check that will give us upon demand the riches of freedom and the security of justice. We have also come to this hallowed spot to remind America of the fierce urgency of *now*. This is no time to engage in the luxury of cooling off or to take the tranquilizing drug of gradualism. *Now* is the time to make real the promises of Democracy. *Now* is the time to rise from the dark and desolate valley of segregation to the sunlit path of racial justice. *Now* is the time to open the doors of opportunity to all of God's children. *Now* is the time to lift our nation from the quicksands of racial injustice to the solid rock of brotherhood. *Now* is the time to make justice a reality for all of God's children.

It would be fatal for the nation to overlook the urgency of the moment. This sweltering summer of the Negro's legitimate discontent will not pass until there is an invigorating autumn of freedom and equality. 1963 is not an end, but a beginning. Those who hope that the Negro needed to blow off steam and will now be content will have a rude awakening if the nation returns to business as usual. There will be neither rest nor tranquillity in America until the Negro is granted his citizenship rights. The whirlwinds of revolt will continue to shake the foundations of our nation until the bright day of justice emerges.

But there is something that I must say to my people who stand on the warm threshold which leads into the palace of justice. In the process of gaining our rightful place we must not be guilty of wrongful deeds. Let us not seek to satisfy our thirst for freedom by drinking from the cup of bitterness and hatred. We must forever conduct our struggle on the high plane of dignity and discipline. We must not allow our creative protest to degenerate into physical violence. Again and again we must rise to the majestic heights of meeting physical force with soul force. The marvelous new militancy which has engulfed the Negro community must not lead us to a distrust of all white people, for many of our white brothers, as evidenced by their presence here today, have come to realize that their destiny is tied up with our destiny. And they have come to realize that their freedom is inextricably bound to our freedom. We cannot walk alone.

And as we walk, we must make the pledge that we shall always march ahead. We cannot turn back. There are those who ask the devotees of civil rights, "When will you be satisfied?" We can never be satisfied as long as the Negro is the victim of the unspeakable horrors of police brutality. We can never be satisfied as long as our bodies, heavy with the fatigue of travel, cannot gain lodging in the motels of the highways and the hotels of the cities. We cannot be satisfied as long as the Negro's basic mobility is from a smaller ghetto to a larger one. We can never be satisfied as long as our children are stripped of their selfhood and robbed of their dignity by signs stating "For Whites Only." We cannot be satisfied as long as a Negro in Mississippi cannot vote and a Negro in New York believes he has nothing for which to vote. No, no, we are not satisfied, and we will not be satisfied until justice rolls down like waters and righteousness like a mighty stream.

I am not unmindful that some of you have come here out of great trials and tribulations. Some of you have come fresh from narrow jail cells. Some of you have come from areas where your quest for freedom left you battered by the storms of persecution and staggered by the winds of police brutality. You have been the veterans of creative suffering. Continue to work with the faith that unearned suffering is redemptive.

Go back to Mississippi, go back to Alabama, go back to South Carolina, go back to Georgia, go back to Louisiana, go back to the slums and ghettos of our northern cities, knowing that somehow this situation can and will be changed. Let us not wallow in the valley of despair.

I say to you today, my friends, even though we face the difficulties of today and tomorrow, I still have a dream. It is a dream deeply rooted in the American dream.

I have a dream that one day this nation will rise up and live out the true meaning of its creed: "We hold these truths to be self-evident; that all men are created equal."

I have a dream that one day on the red hills of Georgia the sons of former slaves and the sons of former slaveowners will be able to sit down together at the table of brotherhood.

I have a dream that one day even the state of Mississippi, a state sweltering with the heat of injustice, sweltering with the heat of oppression, will be transformed into an oasis of freedom and justice.

I have a dream that my four little children will one day live in a nation where they will not be judged by the color of their skin but by the content of their character.

I have a dream today.

I have a dream that one day, down in Alabama, with its vicious racists, with its Governor having his lips dripping with the words of interposition and nullification, one day right there in Alabama little black boys and little black girls will be able to join hands with little white boys and white girls as sisters and brothers.

I have a dream today.

I have a dream that one day every valley shall be exalted, every hill and mountain shall be made low, the rough places will be made plane, and the crooked places will be made straight, and the glory of the Lord shall be revealed, and all flesh shall see it together.

This is our hope. This is the faith with which I return to the South. With this faith we will be able to hew out of the mountain of despair a stone of hope. With this faith we will be able to transform the jangling discords of our nation into a beautiful symphony of brotherhood. With this faith we will be able to work together, to pray together, to struggle together, to go to jail together, to stand up for freedom together, knowing that we will be free one day.

This will be the day when all of God's children will be able to sing with new meaning

> My country, 'tis of thee,
> Sweet land of liberty,
> Of thee I sing:
> Land where my fathers died,
> Land of the pilgrims' pride,
> From every mountain-side
> Let freedom ring.

And if America is to be a great nation this must become true. So let freedom ring from the prodigious hilltops of New Hampshire. Let freedom ring from the mighty mountains of New York. Let freedom ring from the heightening Alleghenies of Pennsylvania!

Let freedom ring from the snowcapped Rockies of Colorado!

Let freedom ring from the curvacious slopes of California!

But not only that; let freedom ring from Stone Mountain of Georgia!

Let freedom ring from Lookout Mountain of Tennessee!

Let freedom ring from every hill and molehill of Mississippi. From every mountainside, let freedom ring. And when this happens—when we let freedom ring, when we let it ring from every village and every hamlet, from every state and every city, we will be able to speed up that day when all of God's children, black men and white men, Jews and Gentiles, Protestants and Catholics, will be able to join hands and sing in the words of the old Negro spiritual, "Free at last! free at last! thank God almighty, we are free at last!"

Exercises

1. Why do you think that King early in the speech used the phrase, "Five score years ago . . ."? Does "the sweltering summer of the Negro's legitimate discontent" remind you of the often-quoted opening line of Shakespeare's "King Richard III": "Now is the winter of our discontent"? What is meant by a "literary allusion"? Does King use such allusions effectively? Is it an advantage or a disadvantage for the speaker to suggest an allusion by a paraphrase? Would it be better for the speaker to make a specific reference to the source being used? Are there other literary or historical allusions in this speech?

2. Note the contrast between the colloquial passages, such as, "We have come to our nation's Capitol to cash a check," and the ritualistic quality in the repetition of the phrases, "I have a dream," and "Let freedom ring." What parallelisms do you find in the speech? Is the mixture of the colloquial and ritualistic kinds of style effective or jarring?

3. Do you find effective the extensive figurative analogy of the "promissory note"—which quickly became "a bad check" and then a presumably "good check"? Are scrambled analogies always to be condemned? Read the passage on "mixed metaphors" in H. W. Fowler, A *Dictionary of Modern English Usage* (New York: Oxford University Press, 1950, pp. 350–352) in which Fowler condemns such "scrambling" as "tasteless word selection." Do you agree with Fowler? Do you consider this passage in King's speech a stylistic flaw? Or is it effective in clarifying the point and making it vivid?

4. In the sentence, "Again and again we must rise to the majestic heights of meeting physical force with soul force," the term *soul force* is borrowed from Mahatma Gandhi. Did you recognize this source in your own reading of the speech? Now that you know the source, does this add effectiveness to King's statement? Should he have pointed out the resemblance between the March on Washington and Gandhi's Salt March to the Sea, organized in 1930?

5. In the speech are phrases usually considered *trite,* such as "trials and tribulations," "valley of despair," "to blow off steam," etc. Find still other examples. Do you think these expressions reflect the haste with which the speech was written, or do they have a persuasive function? Could you improve such phrases by rewriting them?

6. What does King mean by "the tranquilizing drug of gradualism"? Would the idea have been more impressive if he had amplified his description?

7. Do you find that aspects of the style were particularly well suited for the large audience, which had marched together all day and which had joined in the singing of songs and the shouting of slogans?

8. Does the style seem particularly well suited to its large radio and television audience? In what respects might King's two different audiences be affected favorably by different kinds of style? Do you find evidence that King was trying to reach both audiences? Explain.

9. What is the purpose of the speech? Is the purpose explicitly stated? Phrase the purpose in your own words.

10. By what main arguments was the purpose supported?

11. Does King attempt to placate, or to convince, those who do not believe that Negroes are treated unjustly and that this injustice must end?

12. Do you feel that King described accurately the position of the Negro in America? Does he exaggerate the Negro's plight? Minimize it?

Pope Paul VI

"Address at the United Nations," delivered to the U.N. General Assembly, October 4, 1965

DURING the four-and-a-half-year reign of Pope John XXIII, the Roman Catholic Church began its most thorough program of *aggiornamento* (catching up with today) in more than four centuries. Under his successor, Pope Paul VI (1897–), the Church continued its internal dialogue over a wide spectrum of church-world questions, ranging from birth control to psychoanalysis for monks. With great interest Americans followed the news releases which detailed the debates at the Vatican Ecumenical Council between the progressives—who wished to move the Church rapidly into accommodation with the modern world, and the conservatives—who wished less change, or perhaps no change at all. Only a month prior to the Pope's announced visit to New York, many Americans were gladdened by a lop-sided vote of Vatican II, endorsing the principle of religious liberty. Nevertheless, to many Americans who were gravely concerned with the changes the Church made, or failed to make, in its relations with the non-Catholic community, the posture of Pope Paul VI seemed disappointingly unclear. Furthermore, to some Americans not only was his liberalism suspect, but his personality and manner seemed to contrast with that of the highly popular Pope John.

As the pontiff's plane touched down at the John F. Kennedy International Airport on the morning of October 4, 1965, perhaps some of the millions of TV viewers were preoccupied with thoughts concerning the Pope's enigmatic attitudes toward "liberalization" of the Church. If so, a few minutes later such thoughts were probably whisked from their minds. A small man in white robes and a crimson cape with gold embroidery was then standing on a small red-carpeted platform. As a stiff wind flapped his cape, he read a "greetings to you, America": "The first Pope to set foot upon your land blesses you with all his heart. He renews, as it were, the gesture of your discoverer, Christopher Columbus, when he planted the cross of Christ in this blessed soil."

From this moment until his departure late that night, His Holiness scored an unprecedented personal triumph. In addition to the TV viewers, more than five million persons joined with the Pope in creating the greatest spectacle in the city's history and one of the memorable moments of western civilization. Throughout a jammed schedule the Pope charmed the nation as it watched his triumphal tour of midtown Manhattan, his speech at the United Nations, his celebration of the mass at Yankee Stadium, his visit to the New York World's Fair, and his departure.

Perhaps the journalist Loudon Wainwright caught the essence of the day: "Somehow the theatricality of his visit to America illuminated the genuine character of the man. His calm poise . . . his personal dignity transcended the drama. Everything he did seemed precisely right to me." Also, Wainwright may have epitomized the rhetorical essence of the Pope's address at the United Nations, the official reason for his visit, when he wrote: "If one had only read them in the newspaper, the Pope's words would not have been the least surprising. In fact, taken by themselves, they were exactly those words a pope might be expected to deliver. . . . Yet, as Paul spoke them, the words somehow became much more. The element that changed them was the way the Pope spoke. His words were transformed by his astounding conviction—in the face of man's relentless history of depravity and war—that the peace he called for was possible. . . . His sincerity was unmistakable, and that, I think, is sufficient to move most men, to stir them with both hope and fear. . . . His message not only afforded a triumph of humanity over its own suicidal thrust, it placed on every man the burden of trying to accomplish it."

By means of Early Bird satellite, much of Europe watched live on television the Pope's mission to the United Nations. According to press reports, the public reaction was generally warm in western Europe, enthusiastic in largely Catholic Latin America and tepid in

Iron Curtain countries. According to the *Washington Post*, the speech "was generally praised in the world press . . . for its direct appeal for peace, but there was little optimism that the Pope's words would influence the world political situation." At the United Nations, observers agreed that the Pontiff's visit bolstered the prestige of the U.N., and Soviet Foreign Minister Andrei Gromyko was quoted as saying that the Pope's speech was "one of the most important statements ever made before the United Nations."

If assessing the ultimate effect of this speech is an impossibility, perhaps the estimate of Emmet John Hughes may at least illuminate the nature of the speaker: "He did the nearly impossible: He spoke and moved and blessed like a messenger on a 2,000-year journey. If John [Pope John XXIII] gave the world a sense of humanity, beyond forgetting, Paul has evoked a quality surely no less fitting to his place among men: a sense of sanctity. In the presence of John, the millions of many faiths felt the spiritual chill in their lives lifted: he appeared to give off the warming glow of a log fire. For matching millions, the sight of Paul in New York tended to inspire an image no less magnetic: the pure and powerful magic of a candle flame. For he has seemed almost to prove that it may not be too late, in the bloodied lives of the nations of men, for yet one more ceremony of innocence."

The text of this speech comes from the *Washington Post*, October 5, 1965.

ADDRESS AT THE UNITED NATIONS

As we commence our address to this unique world audience, we wish to thank your Secretary General, U Thant, for the invitation which he extended to us to visit the United Nations, on the occasion of the twentieth anniversary of the foundation of this world institution for peace and for collaboration between the peoples of the entire earth.

Our thanks also to the President of the General Assembly, Mr. Amitore Fanfani, who used such kind language in our regard from the very day of his election.

We thank all of you here present for your kind welcome, and we present to each one of you our deferential and sincere salutation. In friendship you have invited us and admitted us to this meeting; and it is as a friend that we are here today.

We express to you our cordial personal homage, and we bring you that of the entire second Vatican Ecumenical Council now meeting in Rome, and represented here by the eminent Cardinals who accompany us for this purpose.

In their name and in our own, to each and every one of you, honor and greeting!

This encounter, as you all understand, marks a simple and at the same time a great moment. It is simple because you have before you a humble man; your brother; and among you all, representatives of sovereign states, the least invested, if you wish to think of him thus, with a minuscule, as it were symbolic, temporal sovereignty, only as much as is necessary to be free to exercise his spiritual mission, and to assure all those who deal with him that he is independent of every other sovereignty of this world.

But he, who now addresses you, has no temporal power, nor any ambition to compete with you. In fact, we have nothing to ask for, no question to raise; we have only a desire to express and a permission to request; namely, that of serving you insofar as we can, with disinterest, with humility and love.

This is our first declaration. As you can see, it is so simple as to seem insignificant to this assembly, which always treats of most important and most difficult matters.

We said also, however, and all here today feel it, that this moment is also a great one. Great for us, great for you.

For us: you know well who we are. Whatever may be the opinion you have of the Pontiff of Rome, you know our mission.

We are the bearer of a message for all mankind. And this we are, not only in our own personal name and in the name of the great Catholic family; but also in that of those Christian brethren who share the same sentiments which we express here, particularly of those who so kindly charged us explicitly to be their spokesman here.

Like a messenger who, after a long journey, finally succeeds in delivering the letter which has been entrusted to him, so we appreciate the good fortune of this moment, however brief, which fulfills a desire nourished in the heart for nearly 20 centuries.

For, as you will remember, we are very ancient; we here represent a long history; we here celebrate the epilogue of a wearying pilgrimage in search of a conversation with the entire world, ever since the command was given to us: Go and bring the good news to all peoples.

Now, you here represent all peoples, allow us to tell you that we have a message, a happy message, to deliver to each one of you and to all.

I. We might call our message a ratification, a solemn moral ratification of this lofty institution. This message comes from our historical experience.

As "an expert in humanity," we bring to this organization the suffrage of our recent predecessors, that of the entire Catholic episcopate and our own, convinced as we are that this organization represents the obligatory path of modern civilization and of world peace.

In saying this, we feel we are making our own the voice of the dead and of the living; of the dead who fell in the terrible wars of the past; of the living who survived those wars, bearing in their hearts a condemnation of those who would try to renew wars; and also of those living who rise up fresh and confident, the youth of the present generation, who legitimately dream of a better human race.

And we also make our own the voice of the poor, the disinherited, the suffering, of those who hunger and thirst for justice, for the dignity of life, for freedom, for well-being and progress. The peoples of the earth turn to the United Nations as the last hope of concord and peace; we presume to present here, with their tribute of honor and of hope, our own tribute also. That is why this moment is great for you, also.

II. We feel that you are already aware of this. Hearken now to the continuation of our message. It becomes a message of good wishes for the future. The edifice which you have constructed must never fall; it must be perfected, and made equal to the needs which world history will present.

You mark a stage in the development of mankind from which retreat must never be admitted but from which it is necessary that advance be made.

To the pluralism of states, which can no longer ignore one another, you offer an extremely simple and fruitful formula of coexistence.

First of all, you recognize and distinguish the ones and the others. You do not confer existence upon states; but you qualify each single nation as fit to sit in the orderly congress of peoples.

That is, you grant recognition, of the highest ethical and juridical value, to each single sovereign national community, guaranteeing it an honored international citizenship.

This in itself is a great service to the cause of humanity, namely to define clearly and to honor the national subjects of the world community, and to classify them in a juridical condition, worthy thereby of being recognized and respected by all, and from which there may derive an orderly and stable system of international life.

You give sanction to the great principle that the relations between peoples should be regulated by reason, by justice, by law, by negotiation; not by force, nor by violence, not by war, not by fear or by deceit.

Thus it must be. Allow us to congratulate you for having had the wisdom to open this hall to the younger peoples, to those states which have recently attained independence and national freedom. Their presence is the proof of the universality and magnanimity which inspire the principles of this institution.

Thus it must be. This is our praise and our good wish; and, as you can see, we do not attribute these as from outside; we derive them from inside, from the very genius of your institution.

III. Your charter goes further than this, and our message advances with it. You exist and operate to unite the nations, to bind states together.

Let us use this second formula: to bring the ones together with the others.

You are an association. You are a bridge between peoples. You are a network of relations between states. We would almost say that your chief characteristic is a reflection, as it were, in the temporal field, of what our Catholic Church aspires to be in the spiritual field; unique and universal.

In the ideological construction of mankind, there is on the natural level nothing superior to this. Your vocation is to make brothers not only of some but of all peoples, a difficult undertaking, indeed; but this it is, your most noble undertaking. Is there anyone who does not see the necessity of coming thus progressively to the establishment of a world authority, able to act efficaciously on the juridical and political levels?

Once more we reiterate our good wish: Advance always! We will go further, and say: strive to bring back among you any who have separated themselves, and study the right method of uniting to your pact of brotherhood, in honor and loyalty, those who do not yet share in it.

Act so that those still outside will desire and merit the confidence of all; and then be generous in granting such confidence. You have the good fortune and the honor of sitting in this assembly of peaceful community; hear us as we say: ensure that the reciprocal trust which here unites you, and enables you to do good and great things, may never be undermined or betrayed.

IV. The inherent logic of this wish, which might be considered to pertain to the very structure of your organization, leads us to complete it with other formulas. Thus, let no one, inasmuch as he is a member of your union, be superior to the others: never one above the other.

This is the formula of equality. We are well aware that it must be completed by the evaluation of other factors besides simple membership in this institution; but equality, too, belongs to its constitution.

You are not equal, but here you make yourselves equal.

For several among you, this may be an act of high virtue; allow us to say this to you, as the representative of a religion which accomplishes salvation through the humility of its divine founder. Men cannot be brothers if they are not humble.

It is pride, no matter how legitimate it may seem to be, which provokes tension and struggles for prestige, for predominance, colonialism, egoism; that is, pride disrupts brotherhood.

V. And now our message reaches its highest point, which is, at first, a negative point.

You are expecting us to utter this sentence, and we are well aware of its gravity and solemnity:

Not the ones against the others, never again, never more!

It was principally for this purpose that the organization of the United Nations arose: against war, in favor of peace!

Listen to the lucid words of the great departed John Kennedy, who proclaimed, four years ago: "Mankind must put an end to war, or war will put an end to mankind."

Many words are not needed to proclaim this loftiest aim of your institution. It suffices to remember that the blood of millions of men, that numberless and unheard of sufferings, useless slaughter and frightful ruin, are the sanction of the pact which unites you, with an oath which must change the future history of the world:

No more war, war never again! Peace, it is peace which must guide the destinies of peoples and of all mankind.

Gratitude to you, glory to you, who for 20 years have labored for peace. Gratitude and glory to you for the conflicts which you have prevented or have brought to an end. The results of your efforts in recent days in favor of peace, even if not yet proved decisive, are such as to deserve that we, presuming to interpret the sentiments of the world, express to you both praise and thanks.

Gentlemen, you have performed and you continue to perform a great work: the education of mankind in the ways of peace. The U.N. is the great school where that education is imparted. And we are today in the Assembly Hall of that school.

Everyone taking his place here becomes a pupil and also a teacher in the art of building peace. When you leave this hall, the world looks upon you as the architects and constructors of peace.

Peace, as you know, is not built up only by means of politics, by the balance of forces and of interests. It is constructed with the mind, with ideas, with works of peace.

You labor in this great construction. But you are still at the beginnings.

Will the world ever succeed in changing that selfish and bellicose mentality which, up to now, has been interwoven into so much of its history?

It is hard to foresee; but it is easy to affirm that it is toward that new history—peaceful, truly human, history, as promised by God to men of good will, that we must resolutely march; the roads thereto are already well marked out for you; and the first is that of disarmament.

If you wish to be brothers, let the arms fall from your hands. One cannot love while holding offensive arms.

Those armaments, especially those terrible arms which modern science has given you, long before they produce victims and ruins, nourish bad feelings, create nightmares, distrust and somber resolutions; they demand enormous expenditures; they obstruct projects of union and useful collaboration; they falsify the psychology of peoples.

As long as man remains that weak, changeable and even wicked being that he often shows himself to be, defensive arms will, unfortunately, be necessary.

You, however, in your courage and valiance, are studying the ways of guaranteeing the security of international life, without having recourse to arms.

This is a most noble aim, this the peoples expect of you, this must be obtained.

Let unanimous trust in this institution grow, let its authority increase; and this aim, we believe, will be secured.

Gratitude will be expressed to you by all peoples, relieved as they will then be from the crushing expenses of armaments, and freed from the nightmare of an ever imminent war.

We rejoice in the knowledge that many of you have considered favorably our invitation, addressed to all states in the cause of peace from Bombay, last December, to divert to the benefit of the developing countries at least a part of the savings, which could be realized by reducing armaments.

We here renew that invitation, trusting in your sentiments of humanity and generosity.

VI. In so doing, we become aware that we are echoing another principle which is structural to the United Nations, which is its positive and affirmative high point; namely, that you work here not only to avert conflicts between states, but also to make them capable of working the ones for the others.

You are not satisfied with facilitating mere coexistence between nations; you take a much greater step forward, one deserving of our praise and our support—you organize the brotherly collaboration of peoples.

In this way a system of solidarity is set up, and its lofty civilized aims win the orderly and unanimous support of all the family of peoples for the common good and for the good of each individual.

This aspect of the organization of the United Nations is the most beautiful; it is its most truly human visage; it is the ideal of which mankind dreams on its pilgrimage through time; it is the world's greatest hope; it is, we presume to say, the reflection of the loving and transcendent design of God for the progress of the human family on earth—a reflection in which we see the message of the gospel which is heavenly become earthly.

Indeed, it seems to us that here we hear the echo of the voice of our predecessors, and particularly of that of Pope John XXIII, whose message of "Pacem in Terris" was so honorably and significantly received among you.

You proclaim here the fundamental rights and duties of man, his dignity, his freedom—and above all his religious freedom. We feel that you thus interpret the highest sphere of human wisdom and, we might add, its sacred character. For you deal here above all with human life; and the life of man is sacred; no one may dare offend it. Respect for life, even with regard to the great problem of birth, must find here in your assembly its highest affirmation and its most reasoned defense.

You must strive to multiply bread so that it suffices for the tables of mankind, and not rather favor an artificial control of birth, which would be irrational, in order to diminish the number of guests at the banquet of life.

It does not suffice, however, to feed the hungry, it is necessary also to assure to each man a life conformed to his dignity. This too you strive to perform. We may consider this the fulfillment before our very eyes, and by your efforts of that prophetical announcement so applicable to your institution: "They will melt down their swords into plowshares, their spears into pruning forks."

Are you not using the prodigious energies of the earth and the magnificent inventions of science, no longer as instruments of death but as tools of life for humanity's new era?

We know how intense and ever more efficacious are the efforts of the United Nations and its dependent world agencies to assist those governments who need help to hasten their economic and social progress.

We know how ardently you labor to overcome illiteracy and to spread good culture throughout the world; to give men adequate modern medical assistance; to employ in man's service the marvelous resources of science, of technique and of organization—all of this is magnificent, and merits the praise and support of all, including our own.

We ourself wish to give the good example, even though the smallness of our means is inadequate to the practical and quantitative needs. We intend to intensify the development of our charitable institutions to combat world hunger and fulfill world needs. It is thus, and in no other way, that peace can be built up.

VII. One more word, gentlemen, our final word: this edifice which you are constructing does not rest upon merely material and earthly foundations, for thus it would be a house built upon sand; and above all, it is based on our own consciences.

The hour has struck for our "conversion," for personal transformation, for interior renewal. We must get used to thinking of man in a new way; and in a new way also of men's life in common; with a new manner, too, of conceiving the paths of history and the destiny of the world, according to the words of Saint Paul: "You must be clothed in the new self, which is created in God's image, justified and sanctified through the truth" (Ephesians IV, 23).

The hour has struck for a halt, a moment of recollection, of reflection, almost of prayer; a moment to think anew of our common origin, our history, our common destiny.

Today as never before, in our era so marked by human progress, there is need for an appeal to the moral conscience of man. For the danger comes not from progress nor from science; indeed, if properly utilized, these could rather resolve many of the grave problems which assail mankind.

No, the real danger comes from man himself, wielding ever more powerful arms, which can be employed equally well for destruction or for the loftiest conquests.

In a word, then, the edifice of modern civilization must be built upon spiritual principles which alone can not only support it but even illuminate and animate it.

We believe, as you know, that these indispensable principles of superior wisdom must be founded upon faith in God, that unknown God of whom Saint Paul spoke to the Athenians in the Areopagus: unknown to them, although without realizing it, they sought Him and He was close to them, as happens also to many men of our times.

To us, in any case, and to all those who accept the ineffable revelation which Christ has given us of Him, He is the living God, the Father of all men.

Exercises

1. Inasmuch as the Pope speaks understandable English, what might have been the reasons why he read this speech in French? Do you think that the process of translation which, of course, ran concurrently with the Pontiff's delivery, reduced the ideational impact of his speech? The psychological impact?

2. The Introduction of this address was possibly somewhat longer than that of the speeches of most visitors to the United Nations.

What reasons can you suggest for this extended length? What did the Pope try to accomplish in the opening? How did he achieve these purposes?

3. In this speech, how did the Pope reinforce his ethos?

4. Outline the entire speech, including the Introduction and Conclusion. Why do you suppose His Holiness structured the Body around seven main heads? Is the standard textbook advice against using more than five main points in the Body invalidated by this successful speech? By President Franklin D. Roosevelt's frequent usage of more than five main points in his speeches?

5. Pope Paul evidenced extremely high regard for the objectives, the past services, and the future endeavors of the United Nations. In one place he characterized the organization as "the last hope of concord and peace." What effect do you think this sentiment might have had upon world opinion? Upon general public opinion in the United States? Upon conservatives generally in the United States? Upon the right-wing elements in the U.S. Catholic community?

6. How did the Pope link the Catholic Church with the United Nations? How did he associate himself and his speech with Saint Paul? With President John F. Kennedy? Explain possible reasons for these analogies.

7. Drawing upon your knowledge of style, especially as acquired through the study of earlier speeches in this volume, write an analysis of the style of this speech. As part of your answer, contrast the style and general tone of this address with that of Harry S. Truman's "Acceptance Speech" and Woodrow Wilson's "The Fourteen Points."

8. Does the speech seem to have a Conclusion? Or, does the last principle of the Pope's "message, a happy message, to deliver to each one of you and to all" serve the functions of a Conclusion? Does this ending represent the high point of the speech? Does the speech seem to build toward a climax? Explain.

9. One sentence from the speech received especially wide attention and was variously interpreted: "You must strive to multiply bread so that it suffices for the tables of mankind, and not rather favor an artificial control of birth, which would be irrational, in order to diminish the number of guests at the banquet of life." Some observers were quoted as believing this expression to be unsuited to the occasion, or to presage a later full expression of His Holiness' conservative views, or to be merely a "generality" for the "solace of conservative theologians" in his Church. By means of collateral

reading, attempt to establish the meaning probably intended by the Pope.

10. The NBC reporter attached to the Vatican, Edward R. Levine, stated before the Pope's visit that "neither the Pope nor any one else at the Vatican" expected the speech to advance appreciably the cause of world peace. The Pope's purpose in making the visit, according to Mr. Levine, was to enhance the prestige of the Papacy—not, of course, for purposes of self-aggrandizement, but to shore up the Pope's capacity in the Vatican Ecumenical Council to influence the direction and amount of change in the Church's relations with the world. In the hindsight provided by history, does Mr. Levine's assessment seem reasonable? On the basis of outside reading, explain your reactions to Mr. Levine's statements.

11. By means of as wide reading as your time permits, re-create the spectacle of the Pope's day in New York City. Do the same for the Reverend George Whitefield's triumphal tour of New England during the Great Awakening. What elements of similarity do you discover between, on the one hand, the Pope's visit to New York and his speech at the U.N. and, on the other, Whitefield's visit to New England and his sermon "Abraham's Offering Up His Son Isaac"? What major differences?